Popular Government and the Supreme Court

Securing the Public Good and Private Rights

Lane V. Sunderland

University Press of Kansas

Coventry University

Published by the University Press of Kansas (Lawrence, Kansas
66049), which was organized by the Kansas Board of Regents and is
operated and funded by Emporia State University, Fort Hays State
University, Kansas State University, Pittsburg State University,
the University of Kansas, and Wichita State University

Library of Congress Cataloging-in-Publication Data

Sunderland, Lane V.
Popular government and the Supreme Court : securing the public
good and private rights / Lane V. Sunderland.
p. cm.
Includes bibliographical references (p.   ) and index.
ISBN 0-7006-0743-9 (alk. paper)
1. United States—Constitutional law—Philosophy. 2. United
States. Supreme Court. 3. Civil rights—United States.
4. Judicial power—United States. 5. Natural law. I. Title.
KF4550.S83 1995
342.73—dc20
[347.302]   95-31164

British Library Cataloguing in Publication Data is available.

Printed in the United States of America

10 9 8 7 6 5 4 3 2 1

For my family

CONTENTS

ACKNOWLEDGMENTS

I am grateful to the Earhart Foundation for its sustained and generous support of my research efforts, which resulted in this book. The Fellowship Division of the National Endowment for the Humanities, the Faculty Research Program of Knox College, and the Midwest Occasional Fellowship Program also provided support for my work. The atmosphere at Knox College encourages scholarship as an adjunct to teaching and nurtures intellectual freedom. I am also indebted to the late Chief Justice Warren E. Burger, who, in numerous conversations about the Constitution, deepened my understanding of the role of the Supreme Court in American government. Chief Justice William H. Rehnquist and Judge John C. Godbold provided an environment that encouraged me to continue my scholarship during the time I served as a Supreme Court Judicial Fellow. I am also grateful to His Grace, the Duke of Devonshire, to Peter Day, and to Michael Pearman, who graciously allowed me access to the papers and manuscripts of Thomas Hobbes at Chatsworth House.

I am fortunate to have had the benefit of great teachers and supportive professional colleagues. I am particularly grateful to Professor Harry V. Jaffa, the late Martin Diamond, Professor Henry J. Abraham, Professor Peter M. Schotten, and Professor Richard G. Stevens. Professor Stevens read the manuscript and made helpful suggestions to improve it. Professor Schotten read drafts of the manuscript and made numerous valuable suggestions. Professor Joe Williams made useful comments on an early draft of Part I. Professors Robert Lowry Clinton and Ronald Kahn and an anonymous reader made careful and helpful suggestions that improved the book. Michael Briggs of the University Press of Kansas provided guidance and encouragement throughout the writing of this book. Melissa Arney provided able editorial help. I gratefully acknowledge permission to reprint revised portions of articles previously published by the *Political Science Reviewer, Public Interest Law Review, Wake Forest Law Review,* and *Benchmark.*

I am fortunate to have had scores of students at Knox College who have helped with my scholarship in direct or indirect ways, among whom are Robert C. Long, Randall Rademaker, Laurie Hane, Scott Szala, Julie Rademaker, Jeff Hockett, Patricia Matthews, Alyson Gal, Chris Boyle, Heidi Walliker,

Reid Broda, and Jason Pierceson. Jamie Ross's able research and editorial assistance were invaluable in completing this manuscript, and Christine Seyller helped with proofreading. I am also indebted to my family for their support and interest in my work, particularly to my wife, Jacklyn, who provided encouragement, helpful suggestions, and a keen editorial eye.

Popular Government and
the Supreme Court

INTRODUCTION

To secure the public good and private rights . . . and at the same time to preserve the spirit and form of popular government, is then the great object to which our inquiries are directed.
—*Madison, Federalist* No. 10

This is a book about majority rule, minority rights, representative government, and the role of the Supreme Court. The debate over majority rule and minority rights is a familiar one. The problematic premise of one side of this debate is that there is a catalog of individual rights beyond the power of governing majorities, and we should look to the Supreme Court, relying on the Constitution, to tell us what these rights are. The proponents of this view regard the Court as the peculiar guardian of these rights. Some ask the Court to go beyond the rights defined in the Constitution in order to protect individuals from overbearing legislative majorities and a too-powerful government. But this is the crux of the problem. When the Court protects rights in the course of creating them, without relying upon the text and the unifying theory and structure of the Constitution, it may undermine the Constitution and substitute government by judiciary for democracy.

It is a formidable task to argue against a Court that stands up for individual rights against government. But this book makes just such an argument, with the qualification that the Court should limit its protection to rights derived from the text or the principles of the Constitution. We should not ask the Supreme Court to be the peculiar guardian of an ever-expanding catalog of individual rights. If we do so, we may sacrifice democratic and representative government, separation of powers, and the genius of a written Constitution that sets forth the powers of and limitations on the ruling majority and the government.

The nomination and confirmation of Supreme Court justices have become media events that illustrate the controversy over nonenumerated rights (rights not defined by the Constitution) and the role of the Supreme Court. Network correspondents ask questions about the candidates' conservatism or liberalism. Speculation begins over whether the nominee will be "Borked" and how the prospective justice will vote on abortion. Interest groups assess the composition of the Court and ask if the nominee fulfills their criteria to occupy a seat on the Court. Public attention to this process in some ways rivals that which attends presidential elections. People realize that the president has only four years to advance the executive agenda, whereas Supreme Court justices serve for the constitutionally prescribed term of "good behavior." Supporters and critics of the Court agree on only one thing: justices behave well and live long lives.

A confused observer of the Court is justified in asking what the role of the Court ought to be. This query, in turn, raises the question of what the Constitution is. If we turn to an authoritative commentary on the Constitution, *The Federalist*, we find that the Court's paramount duty is the "steady, upright, and impartial administration of the laws."[1] Since the Constitution is the paramount legal document of the American political order, judicial duty includes fidelity to the written Constitution. Yet the Court has become the focus of passionately argued issues in American society, many of which are not found in the Constitution's text. The legal resolution of these issues sometimes takes the form of the Court's explicating nonenumerated constitutional rights in order to give legal protection to individual rights, the claims of which lie at the foundation of many contemporary social issues. The judicial creation of these nonenumerated constitutional rights, such as privacy, or of constitutional rights that run counter to the Constitution's text, such as a right against the death penalty, raises the question, if such rights are not in the Constitution's text, where are they to be found?

The appointment and confirmation of Supreme Court justices have become extraordinarily political as attention is increasingly focused on one of the most publicized issues on the Court's docket—abortion (and the more inclusive issue, privacy). The Clarence Thomas confirmation became a game of cat and mouse between Thomas and some senators who attempted to ascertain his views on abortion. Thomas insisted that he had not thought about the issue as he would if he were sitting as a justice on the Supreme Court of the United States. Abortion and other privacy issues were central to the Senate hearings on Ruth Bader Ginsberg and Stephen Breyer, as they will be to subsequent nominees.

In the midst of nominations and hearings, we seem caught between vocal groups, each insisting that serious "rights" are at issue. Pro-choice proponents insist that the courts should protect a woman's right to choose how to use her body against legislative majorities who would vote to take that right away. Pro-life forces are equally vocal, pressing their claim on behalf of the rights of the unborn. But the more subtle and important issue arising from the pro-life position is the right of legislative majorities to decide on the issue unimpeded by the Court, which has made abortion a constitutional right.

The divisive issue of abortion raises a perennial conflict in our constitutional democracy: the role of the Supreme Court in the conflict between legislative majority rule and claims of minority rights. The conflict arises because the Court is undemocratic, a body of unelected appointees holding office for life or good behavior. The Court may declare unconstitutional the democratic will of the people as expressed through their properly elected representatives in the House, the Senate, and the presidency. A similar denial of the democratic will occurs when the Court declares state acts unconstitutional. Although the Court exists in a scheme designed to ensure the independence of judges who are but "a remote choice . . . of the people,"[2] compelling arguments are needed to justify the Court's voiding the democratic, legislative will, particularly when that obstruction is based on neither textual prohibitions nor clear constitutional principles.

Pro-life and pro-choice groups are just examples of contending social groups that attempt to influence judicial action. When such issues are pressed to the Supreme Court, it is asked to decide what rights are embodied in our basic charter of government. The Court then determines the content of our supreme law. It sometimes attempts to do so on the basis of some higher law that is presumed to embrace the Constitution and its specific provisions. Then, as it did with privacy rights in the abortion cases, the Court frequently articulates rights that are presumed to rest on principles higher than those of the Constitution. Because judges and commentators use concepts such as natural rights, human rights, human dignity, and individual liberty to determine policy, we must determine what those rights and liberties are. We are driven back to the origin of the concepts of natural right and natural law in the writings of the architects of modern government, including those who framed the American Constitution.

The modern doctrines of the state of nature, natural right, and natural law were set forth by Thomas Hobbes and incorporated into the political theory of John Locke. We properly regard Locke as responsible for the theoretical foundations of the Declaration of Independence and as the grandfather of the Constitution. Hobbes and Locke are not important just because they are part of our political tradition. They also set forth a sound view of human nature and of our political condition that guides us in analyzing contemporary views, which often rest on a different and more utopian view of human nature. Hobbes, Montesquieu, and particularly Locke, guide us in understanding the Declaration's statement of the ends or purposes of the American political order. Montesquieu set forth a theory of politics that is important to American institutions, the leading feature of which is separated powers. The Declaration is critical to an understanding of our politics and Constitution, but it left much to be done by those who framed a constitution designed to achieve these ends. The Constitution has principles of its own that were derived from earlier political theorists and fulfilled the principles of the Declaration.

This fulfillment is explained in *The Federalist,* the most authoritative commentary on the Constitution, which defends decent and moderate democratic government. The decency and moderation derive from the Constitution's majoritarian foundations, moderated by a system of representation; the large commercial republic, characterized by a multiplicity of economic interests and religious sects; separation of powers, including an independent judiciary; and the doctrine of enumerated powers. Thus, ours is not simply a democracy but a democracy designed to serve both majority rule and individual rights under a carefully structured system of representative government. The Constitution set a moderate course that embraced neither simple democracy, that, if unchecked, can become mob rule, nor unrestrained rights characteristic of the state of nature, which are nearly meaningless within civil society. The Constitution most emphatically did not create a system of government in which a majority of the Supreme Court replaces rule by a majority of the people.

Because the Constitution's principles are formulations of the eighteenth century, it is tempting to regard them as outmoded. Our system of government is particularly challenged by contemporary views that covertly oppose democracy or claim that our system is insensitive to individual rights. Commentators call for standards of judicial judgment that attempt to make the Constitution relevant today. These modern standards are based on natural rights, moral growth, privacy, return to a laissez-faire economic system, correction of nonegalitarian elements of law under our Constitution (which range from reform of representation to abolition of capital punishment), and the failure to provide adequately for disadvantaged groups. Commentators ask the Supreme Court to enforce rights that they consider missing in our system of government. They imply that things would be much better if nine justices of like mind with themselves were on the Supreme Court and could enforce their views of right in the guise of constitutional law. Explicitly or implicitly, modern commentators seek to give constitutional teeth to the rights they define. In contrast to the eighteenth-century call for no taxation without representation, many twentieth-century commentators call for the judiciary to enforce rights to which a majority has not consented. In some respects, these views can be traced to a healthy recognition that majorities may act out of passion or interest, to the detriment of both the public good and private rights. Many commentators believe that courts can correct representative majorities and thereby remedy defects of representative government through enforcement of a higher morality or an ever-expanding catalog of rights that are beyond the power of legislative majorities. This resort to a higher morality leads us back to the question of the standard by which we judge positive law, namely, the doctrines of natural right and natural law.

Recognizing the conflict between judicial power and democracy, many thoughtful commentators have attempted to legitimize the Court's powers. This book examines commentary on the Constitution that represents competing schools of constitutional interpretation. Much of this commentary attempts to legitimize an expansive judicial power at the expense of democracy. This commentary ranges from *The Federalist,* written during the founding period, to commentaries of the last several years. *The Federalist,* unlike much modern commentary, resolves the tension between majority rule and private rights through the rule of law in a properly constituted republic characterized by a multiplicity of economic interests and religious sects, by separation of powers and accompanying checks and balances, and by a doctrine of enumerated powers, all of which are based on a written constitution. The authors of *The Federalist* believed that the Constitution had resolved the issue of majority rule and private rights without the inclusion of a bill of rights, which was added after the Constitution went into effect. It is essential to understand the Constitution's own view of the preservation of rights *without* a tabulation of rights, since the Constitution was designed to reconcile majority rule and individual rights through the representative structures in the original document. By contrast, one example of modern commentary is Michael Perry's prescription of the Court's role in human rights cases, a role largely divorced from considerations of representative government and majority consent. He advocates a judicial role of "prophet," of going beyond interpretive to noninterpretive review, so that the Court can lead the moral evolution that furthers human rights beyond those set forth in the Constitution (thus, noninterpretive review).

Rather than looking at the document to determine the number and meaning of rights, Perry and many other commentators ask the Court to invoke its own standards to protect human rights against overbearing majorities. One problem is how the Court ascertains standards by which to declare acts of a legislative majority unconstitutional. The quick and facile answer is that it should do so when a majority tramples on individual rights. Another question is the number and meaning of these rights. The question of what these rights are is fundamental in defining the Constitution and determining the role of the Court in the separation of powers. And that leads us back to the architects of the modern doctrines of natural right and natural law—Thomas Hobbes and John Locke—whose conceptions of rights are rooted in nature.

An examination of Hobbes, Locke, and Montesquieu will not, however, fully satisfy our quest to understand natural right, natural law, legislative power, and the role of the Court, for these theorists did not found the American political order. We must also examine the Declaration of Independence and its relationship to the Constitution and the place of natural rights and natural law in our political order. The proper and primary focus of our enterprise must be the Constitution and its most authoritative commentary, *The Federalist. The Federalist* explicates the theory underlying the Constitution, the government it constructed, its reliance on majority rule, and the structure and limits it imposes on a government designed "to secure the public good and private rights."[3] Its theory helps us understand the role of the Court under a constitution designed to secure both the public good and private rights, as well as the merits and defects of the various contemporary commentaries on the Constitution, some of which put an extraordinary task before the judiciary. Neither the Bill of Rights nor the important Civil War amendments alter the mechanisms of the Constitution, which were designed to effect republican government that is consistent with both the public good and private rights. *The Federalist* and related theoretical materials remain crucial to understanding the Constitution and the role of the Court, whether we are considering provisions of the original Constitution, the Bill of Rights, or the Civil War Amendments.

This is not a book about abortion or any other single vexing contemporary issue. Rather, it explores how the Constitution secures the public good and private rights in a representative government within a theory and framework designed to endure for ages. The book attempts to answer two questions: What is the Constitution? What is the proper role of the Court in interpreting the Constitution? In addressing these questions, I draw on materials contemporary and antecedent to the ratification of the Constitution and the Bill of Rights. Part I examines the constitutional antecedents of government based on natural right and natural law, including Hobbes, Locke, and Montesquieu. It also examines the Declaration of Independence and the theory of government explained in *The Federalist*. This theory includes the major principles underlying the Constitution that resolved the problem of majoritarian government and individual rights through democratic institutions and structures. Part II examines competing contemporary theories of the Constitution and of the role of the Court in light of the principles explicated in Part I. As we shall discover, much of this modern commentary contradicts the understanding of human nature and government found in the work of Hobbes, Locke, and Montesquieu and in the Declaration of Independence, the Constitution, and *The Federalist*. Moreover, it does so without confronting those theories or offering a coherent alternative. Simply showing the contradiction is not sufficient. I also attempt to demonstrate that the earlier understanding rests on a sounder and wiser conception of human nature, politics, and government than does the often "utopian" theory of contemporary constitutional commentators.

I.
Theoretical Foundations of the Constitution

The analysis of contemporary commentators in Part II will reveal that they generally begin with their own strongly held views of justice and then construct theories of constitutional interpretation that advance policies consistent with their views. In many cases, these views run counter to the republican character of the Constitution. The writers of the Constitution, on the other hand, regarded the republican nature of the Constitution as fundamental to justice. They created a representative regime with sufficient power to meet future exigencies and to secure individual rights but did not incline the political system in one policy direction. The Constitution avoids the extremes of unrestrained democracy on the one hand and the absolutizing of individual rights on the other. Absolutizing individual rights leads us back to the state of nature that Hobbes, Locke, and Montesquieu sought to escape. Avoidance of these extremes is a central theme of the various theorists and the historical materials surveyed in Part I. It is instructive that these theorists and the historical materials provide no support for the sort of judicial supremacy implicit in many of the contemporary commentators examined in Part II.

Hobbes paints a vivid picture of the horrors of the state of nature where rights are both absolute and utterly insecure. He advocates the creation of a commonwealth whose power is nearly absolute and that protects us from one another. Private judgement is subordinated to the commonwealth's determination of what rights are to be actualized. Hobbes's theory does not support a judiciary that is empowered to obstruct the nearly absolute sovereign.

Locke rejects absolute monarchy. Although he is sometimes regarded as a proponent of the view that there is a catalog of natural rights that justify judicial intervention to obstruct the legislative power. I believe that this is a misunderstanding of his theory. Locke, like Hobbes, refrains from setting forth a body of substantive rights that are beyond the power of the legislature. Unlike many commentators who advocate the Court's voiding government action on the basis of a theory of unenumerated substantive rights, Locke depends on consent of the governed and procedural mechanisms to protect individual rights.

Montesquieu is commonly regarded as authority for the separation of powers and an independent judiciary, both of which are important features of the U.S. Constitution and essential to its protection of liberty. Although he separates the judicial power from the legislative and executive powers, he does not advocate the doctrine that a catalog of natural rights justifies the judiciary's voiding governmental action inconsistent with these rights. Institutions are central to Montesquieu's protection of liberty through laws that reserve a wide latitude for legislative discretion and that cannot be limited by absolute rules. Reliance on institutions is an essential feature of the American Constitution. Montesquieu requires judicial independence from the other branches of government, but the judicial power does not rival that of the legislature or executive. Thus, even Montesquieu does not advocate the judicial supremacy characteristic of the commentators treated in Part II.

The Declaration of Independence, which derives from Locke's theory, teaches that there are standards beyond the positive law by which governments are judged; however, its broad principles and statements of the ends of American government do not stipulate that the judiciary is to be the enforcer of the Declaration's inalienable rights. The Declaration requires consent to the form of government that a majority believes will best effect the rights it articulates, but it does not specify the form of this government. The Declaration requires neither an independent judiciary with the power of judicial review nor a judiciary empowered to define and enforce the inalienable rights that legitimize the government to which a majority of the people consent.

The constitutional limitations at the base of our inquiry are rooted in the Declaration's conception of "Laws of Nature and of Nature's God." But these limitations exist within the context of the entire Constitution and its underlying theory, which depends upon procedural mechanisms to secure the public good and private rights. These mechanisms rest on the sound premise that rights are best protected by a strong government. Recognizing the unforeseen exigencies that government will face and the difficulty in balancing considerations of the public good with private rights, the Constitution created a strong government in which the scheme of representation, other constitutional structures, and dependence on the people are the primary securities of the public good and private rights.

Part I reveals that the Declaration, the Constitution, and the commentary of *The Federalist* confront and attempt to resolve the problem of republican government, the public good, and private rights. What is remarkable about these sources is that none of them anticipates that the judges will be the primary protectors of individual rights, and not one of them prescribes a system of judicial supremacy. The Constitution and *The Federalist* depend on a strictly republican form of government in which moderate majority rule is to be achieved through properly structured institutions designed to secure the public good and private rights. Leaving the determination of unenumerated rights to the legislative body and the republican processes preserves the democratic nature of the Constitution and assumes an ultimate trust in the sovereign power under our Constitution. It also underscores the status of the Constitution as law, rather than as a grant of power to the judiciary to define unenumerated rights according to its view of what these rights ought to be.

Chapter One

Constitutional Antecedents:
The Doctrines of Natural Right, Natural Law,
and Separation of Powers

Modern constitutional government is based on the premise that governmental powers should be limited. This immediately raises the question of how these limitations are determined. One way is by those principles embodied in our Constitution, principles that both grant and restrict governmental powers. This seems perfectly sensible, but turns out to be problematic if we are to judge by current constitutional commentary. Contemporary commentators ask the judiciary, particularly the Supreme Court, to judge legislation and impose constitutional limitations by such standards as "human rights," "personal dignity and autonomy," "natural law," "Lockean principles," and "democratic processes." The alert reader will note that these terms are not ones that would appear if one did a "word check" of the Constitution. Commentators propose their own views of new constitutional limitations to prevent government from infringing on what they assert to be individual rights. In other words, they believe that some rights are simply beyond the power of government. In this respect, the proposed constitutional limitations take on the character of natural rights that government was instituted to secure and that are beyond its legitimate power. Because the concept of natural rights, or their modern cousins (enumerated above), so often appears in contemporary constitutional commentary, we must understand what they are and what substantive limitations they and the related concept of natural law put on government. This quest drives us back to the origin of the doctrine of natural right. But we must understand more than what constitutes natural right or natural law in Hobbes, Locke and Montesquieu. We must also understand the forms of government these theorists favored. Since natural right and natural law are not protected in the state of nature, it is essential to construct a form of government to secure rights under government. This quest, which we begin with Thomas Hobbes, culminates in the design of the U.S. Constitution. The Constitution constructs a system of government to secure natural rights in a manner consistent with majority rule, and in this sense, it attempts to square equality with liberty. As we shall see, however, the rights secured under government, although derived from the concept of natural rights, do not have the character of the absolute rights of the state of nature—absolute rights that drove us to escape the utter insecurity of the state of nature in order to secure individual rights and achieve peace under government. Both Hobbes and Locke believed that they had resolved the problem of rights under government. Their resolution of this problem is the most important reason for taking their work seriously and applying their theory to contemporary issues of government.

Thomas Hobbes

Thomas Hobbes graphically poses the relationship of rights and the power of government, or commonwealth, as he calls it. He goes to the root of a preoccupation with rights and hostility toward governmental powers by painting a vivid picture of the horrors of the state of nature, where rights are both absolute and utterly insecure. For Hobbes, these horrors justify the creation of a nearly absolute power in the commonwealth. In his commonwealth, there is no broad catalog of private rights beyond the reach of government, and he advocates the abolition of private judgment, which is given up to the absolute authority of the commonwealth, which is the judge of what rights are actualized.[1] Although there may be good reasons not to adopt his solution, he helps us understand the relationship between rights and the powers of the commonwealth that are necessary to achieve peace.

As a leading architect of the modern doctrine of natural right, Hobbes epitomizes the modern quest to find a basis in the state of nature for political right, one that can give us our bearings in constructing a political order. Our current concern with the powers of and limitations on government can be traced to Hobbes. For him, these bearings come from the state of nature, where there is no common power to keep human beings in awe and, consequently, they are in a state of war. In the state of nature, the individual lives in "danger of violent death; and the life of man [is] solitary, poor, nasty, brutish, and short."[2] There are no restrictions on rights, and "every man has a right to every thing; even to one another's body."[3] The defects of this doctrine of absolute rights in the imaginary state of nature are apparent, and they make a compelling case for forming civil society. The root of Hobbes's civil society is found in the state of nature, in which the "right of nature . . . is the liberty each man hath, to use his own power, as he will himself, for the preservation of his own nature; that is to say, of his own life." The rule of reason remedies the insecurity of the state of nature in Hobbes's first and fundamental law of nature: "*that every man, ought to endeavor peace, as far as he has hope of obtaining it.*"[4] Human beings are inclined to peace by the natural law of reason acting on the root passion, the fear of death.

The second law of nature is *"that a man be willing, when others are so too, as far-forth, as for peace, and defence of himself he shall think it necessary, to lay down this right to all things."*[5] For Hobbes, the doctrine of natural right emanates in a doctrine of natural law that requires giving up the rights of the state of nature in order to achieve peace and self-preservation. This law gives rise to the third law of nature, justice. He defines justice as the keeping of the covenant that is made when people transfer to the commonwealth all those rights that, in the state of nature, hinder the peace of humankind. In the state of nature, no action can be unjust; the law of nature requires that people perform their covenants, and in this "consisteth the fountain and original of JUSTICE."[6] Justice exists only within the context of civil society; only when the covenant is made by which the commonwealth is formed, does justice become possible. To violate this covenant, or any covenant made pursuant to the original one, is unjust.

The background for the rule of democracy is equality in the fear of death, or the desire for preservation, in a commonwealth in which everyone agrees to accept as sovereign that person or persons designated.[7] The power of sovereignty in the commonwealth is absolute, a power that individuals authorize in order to preserve themselves: "anything less than absolute power leaves men still in the state of nature, for they cannot be sure that others will abstain from injustice when they do."[8] In Hobbes's own words, this agreement to form the sovereign is a "covenant of every man, in such manner, as if every man should say to every man, *I authorize and give up my right of governing myself*" to the commonwealth.[9] So that there be no misunderstanding, according to Hobbes, whatever the sovereign commands is "justified by the command."[10] This covenant or contract is each individual's word to be bound by the commonwealth, a contract made for self-preservation. The state of nature is so nasty, according to Hobbes, that the remedy of the natural law of reason is a covenant to form civil society in which individuals agree that the commonwealth is the judge of good and evil and possesses power that is fully obeyed. Individuals give up their private, individual judgments on these matters to the absolute authority of the commonwealth in order to achieve self-preservation. Hobbes's best form of government for the absolute authority of the commonwealth is monarchy in which sovereignty is not divided.[11] This form of government follows from the fundamental law of nature on which all agree, that peace is good.[12]

The legitimacy of the commonwealth rests on the consent each individual gives in accepting the sovereign. The democratic character of the consent follows from the fact that we are equal in the decisive respect of our fear of violent death, a fear shared by all in the state of nature. The right of nature antedates and determines the purpose of civil society; the laws of nature derive from the right of nature.[13] Hobbes's covenant does not deny one's right to defend oneself from force with force. But other than that, one is hard-pressed to find rights that Hobbes reserves to the individual or a code of such rights in the form of a system of natural laws.

In the conclusion to his discussion "Of Other Laws of Nature," Hobbes states that "injustice, ingratitude, arrogance, pride, iniquity, acception of persons, and the rest can never be made lawful. For it can never be that war shall preserve life, and peace destroy it."[14] At other places in *Leviathan,* Hobbes speaks of "equity" (187), no ex post facto laws, (218–19, 231), public hearing before punishment, (230), and other salutary practices.[15] These salutary practices are necessary because they are conducive to peace. In fact, he says at the end of the chapter on other natural laws that these conclusions "are but theorems concerning what conduceth to the conservation and defence of themselves; whereas law, properly, is the work of him, that by right hath command over others."[16] Some actions are more conducive to peace than others, and it appears to be in the interest of both sovereign and subject that the enlightened sovereign act in ways that are conducive to peace. If these theorems are to limit the rule of the sovereign, the sovereign must understand what actions preserve peace and protect against a return to the state of nature, or war. Hobbes does not rely on other external checks on the sovereign, such as the American doctrines of a written constitution and judicial review.

Hobbes also addresses the judges' role in interpreting law. They must not interpret the law according to "the letter, but the intendment, or meaning, that is to say, the authentic interpretation of the law (which is the sense of the legislator) in which the nature of the law consisteth." The judges are to be appointed by the sovereign, or "else, by the craft of an interpreter, the law may be made to bear a sense, contrary to that of the sovereign: by which means the interpreter becomes the legislator" (205). In instances in which the meaning of the law is ambiguous, as it often will be, the judges are to interpret the intention of the law and of the sovereign according to equity: "for it were a great contumely for a judge to think otherwise of the sovereign." Hobbes adds, however, that sentences against the law are not warranted, for judges are not to judge "what is commodious, or incommodious to the commonwealth" (209).He also dismisses commentators who write "books of moral philosophy," though they "be naturally reasonable," because these writers do not have the sovereign power that makes their pronouncements law and because they contain "so many contradictions of one another, and of themselves." The authentic interpretation of the law of nature is the judge who sentences "by authority of the sovereign, whereby it becomes the sovereign's sentence"(205–6).

Hobbes's concern with such matters as equity, trial after public hearing, and avoidance of ex post facto laws arises from his concern with preserving life and seeking peace, which derives from the right of nature and is the first law of nature. As such, these matters are rooted in nature and should be sought in civil society. But Hobbes teaches that peace is best achieved through the sovereign; therefore, to actualize a regime based on natural right and natural law, a people must establish a nearly absolute sovereign. They can hope for a moderate regime only if the sovereign is enlightened, for even the judges who rely on equity in interpreting the law are clearly subordinate to that law and the sovereign who issued it. *The Federalist* explicitly rejects reliance on there being "enlightened statesmen" at the helm and relies on institutions to achieve justice. If Hobbes anticipates an enlightened sovereign, there seems little reason to believe that this anticipation will be realized.

Hobbes's solution to the horrors of the state of nature is the creation of a nearly absolute sovereign. There is no room in his commonwealth for a catalog of private rights beyond the power of government. The role of the judiciary is fidelity to the lawgiver or sovereign. Commentators, who claim to base their views of law on what is naturally reasonable, contradict themselves and one another, and Hobbes dismisses them as being inconsistent with the authority of the sovereign. As helpful as Hobbes is to understanding the horrors of absolute rights in the state of nature and to understanding the relationship of rights to the power of government, he does not answer to Locke's satisfaction the problem of controlling the power of the nearly absolute sovereign.

John Locke

Hobbes's system is harsh. His state of nature is a war of every individual against every other, in which each is the potential murderer of others. The defects of his state of nature are so profound that he justifies a commonwealth, preferably a monarchy, with almost unlimited powers. John Locke, however, rejects absolute monarchy as inconsistent with civil society. He characterizes the state of nature as the source of equality and freedom: "there being nothing more evident, than that creatures of the same species and rank, promiscuously born to all the same advantages of nature, and the use of the same faculties, should also be equal one amongst another without subordination or subjection."[17]

Locke is often regarded as the author of a catalog of natural rights that justify the Court in looking beyond the four corners of the Constitution as it seeks to enforce these rights. I believe that this is a misreading of Locke. He does not set forth *substantive* limitations on government as most commentators do. Instead, he relies on *procedural* limitations that emphasize the supremacy of the legislative power, not the judicial power. A proper understanding of Locke is critical to our task of identifying the limitations on government or, to use Locke's terms, the limitations on, or proper extent of, the legislative power. A careful reading of Locke reveals that he is nearly as cautious as Hobbes in his hesitancy to set forth a body of substantive rights that are beyond the authority of the properly constituted legislative power. Government is sufficiently complex, and its necessity so compelling, that Locke's limitations on the legislative power are almost entirely procedural in nature. Although Locke attempts to correct the problem of an absolute or tyrannical government depriving individuals of the very rights the government was instituted to secure, there is no pharmacopoeia of substantive natural rights in Locke's work that justifies invalidating legislative action. Nor does Locke's system provide for an independent judiciary, much less one with the power to invalidate legislation it regards as denying substantive natural rights that are beyond the power of government. Thus, Locke does not provide authority for the Supreme Court to go beyond the Constitution to protect individual rights by obstructing the legislative will in the name of ever-expanding substantive natural rights that are beyond the power of government. He is sound in insisting that government should be restrained primarily by majority rule and through procedural mechanisms that limit the legislative power.

Locke's concern with natural rights and limited government helps us understand the problematic relationship between private rights and the public good. He makes abundantly clear that the sound resolution of this problem does not result in government by judiciary. To understand Locke's resolution of the problem of private rights and the power of government requires a summary treatment of his conception of the state of nature and the procedural limitations he prescribes to restrain the legislative power.

For Locke, as for Hobbes, the state of nature is a condition from which we should escape. Locke's fundamental right of nature is found in the state of nature, where the primary threat to life is the poverty and hardship of nature. As one commentator describes it, "the source, content, and end of the law of nature" are driven by our desire for self-preservation.[18] We are led out of an unsafe and insecure state of nature by reason, which is the law of nature, acting in pursuit of the natural right of self-preservation:[19] "Thus the law of nature stands as an eternal rule to all men, *legislators* as well as others. The *rules* that they make for other men's actions must, as well as their own and other men's actions, be conformable to the law of nature, i.e. to the will of God, of which that is a declaration, and *the fundamental law of nature being the preservation of mankind,* no human sanction can be good, or valid against it."[20] Natural law is the root of the legislative power. But discerning this law within the context of civil society and translating it into positive law are difficult. As we shall see, Locke refrains from setting forth substantive limits on the legislative power derived from natural rights, but he does enunciate procedural limitations that are designed to bind the legislature and to perpetuate rights within civil society.

Locke's state of nature is less harsh than Hobbes's, but both agree that the law of nature leads us to escape from it through reason, acting on the fundamental right of nature, which is self-preservation. This language is adopted by *The Federalist* in its recurrence "to the great principle of self-preservation; to the transcendent law of nature and of nature's God, which declares that the safety and happiness of society are the objects at which all political institutions aim, and to which all such institutions must be sacrificed."[21] The Lockean and American solution to the defects of the state of nature differs from the Hobbesian. Locke teaches that "*absolute monarchy*, which by some men is counted the only government in the world, is indeed *inconsistent with civil society*, and so can be no form of civil-government at all."[22] Thus, in contrast to Hobbes, Locke attempts to remedy the absolute, or nearly absolute, authority of the sovereign, which is the hallmark of Hobbes's commonwealth.

Equality, derived from the fundamental desire of each individual for self-preservation, is reflected in the formation of Locke's political society, where each member of the society must agree to be a part of the community:

> For when any number of men have, by the consent of every individual, made a *community*, they have thereby made that *community* one body, with a power to act as one body, which is only by the will and determination of the *majority*: for that which acts in any community, being only the consent of the individuals of it, and it being necessary to that which is one body to move one way; it is necessary the body should move that way whither the greater force carries it, which is the *consent of the majority*: or else it is impossible it should act or continue one body, *one community*, which the consent of every individual united into it, agreed that it should; and so every one is bound by that consent to be concluded by the *majority*. And therefore we see, that in assemblies, impowered to act by positive laws, where no number is set by that positive law which impowers them, the *act of the majority* passes for the act of the whole, and of course determines, as having, by the law of nature and reason, the power of the whole. (sec. 96)

Once all individuals form the community, they agree to be bound by the greater force, the consent of the majority, which possesses the power of the whole and exercises its legitimate power through positive law. Individuals give up the natural equality and freedom of the state of nature because it is characterized by fear and continual danger. They join society to preserve their lives, liberties, and estates, which Locke calls "by the general name, *property*" (sec. 123). Once political society is formed, the first and fundamental law of the commonwealth is the establishment of the legislative power, which is supreme, sacred, and unalterable. No other edicts "of any body else, in what form soever conceived, or by what power soever backed, have the force and obligation of a law, which has not its sanction from that legislative which the public has chosen and appointed: for without this the law could not have that, which is absolutely necessary to its being a law, the consent of the society, over whom no body can have a power to make laws, but by their own consent" (sec. 134). In Locke's scheme, the legislative power is of primary importance and legitimacy because the majority consented to this power when it formed the commonwealth. After treating the legitimacy and supremacy of the legislative power, Locke turns to the extent of this power. In his discussion of extent, we hope to find limitations on the legislative power imposed by natural right or natural law. These limitations should explain when the legislative power is illegitimate because it conflicts with natural right or natural law.

The first limitation is that the legislative body, whether consisting of one or more persons, does not have absolute arbitrary power over people's lives and fortunes, for the legislative power can have no more power than individuals had in the state of nature (sec. 135). In some respects, this rule simply restates Locke's view that absolute rule is inconsistent with civil society and with the fundamental right of self-preservation that both justifies civil society and is so deeply implanted within us that it cannot be eradicated. This right justifies rebellion (which we now call revolution) if government uses the power entrusted to it in a tyrannical manner, contrary to the purposes for which people consented to government.[23] Thus, Locke's limitation on "absolute arbitrary power" is not a direct, substantive limitation on the legislative power, but rather restates the extralegal natural right upon which civil society is based and that must be given force through the scheme of government Locke discusses in order to produce the "public good."[24]

Locke's second limit is that the "*legislative, or supreme authority, cannot assume to its self a power to rule by extemporary arbitrary decrees, but is bound to dispense justice, and decide the rights of the subject by promulgated standing laws.*" This is necessary because "the law of nature being unwritten," it is "no where to be found but in the minds of men." Because the law of nature is, as a consequence of "passion or interest," miscited or misapplied, the "community put[s] the legislative power into such hands as they think fit, with this trust, that they shall be governed by *declared laws*, or else their peace, quiet, and property will still be at the same uncertainty, as it was in the state of nature."[25] Although the rule of law is a requirement of natural law, making its substantive content consistent with natural law is problematic for reasons that Locke states. Through "*established and promulgated laws*," "people may know their duty, and be safe and secure within the limits of the law." Without such established and promulgated laws, the means to secure the right of nature remain unclear and we "will be in a far worse condition than in the state of nature," subject to a ruling power by "extemporary dictates and undetermined resolutions" (sec. 137). Locke's statements about the extent of the legislative power restate the rule of law—law that is known by the governed and that emanates from the legislative power established by the majority. However much it contributes to security and safety, the insistence on established and promulgated laws does not substantively limit the legislative power, but rather sets the forms or processes that the legislative power must take if it is to be legitimate according to natural right and natural law.

Locke's third limit on the extent of the legislative power requires that "[t]he supreme power cannot take from any man any part of his property without his own consent." The law of the supreme power, the legislative, can take away an individual's property (meaning life, liberty, and estate) only with that person's consent. Locke then states that the arbitrary taking of property "is not much to be feared in governments where the *legislative* consists wholly or in part, in assemblies that are variable, whose members, upon the dissolution of the assembly, are subjects under the common laws of their country, equally with the rest" (sec. 138).

This is clearly a statement of legislative supremacy, but qualified by a process that makes the legislative power "not much to be feared" if it functions according to Locke's principles. These principles are simple: a numerous legislative body (or "divers persons") that can be dissolved and that is subject, along with other citizens, to the same established laws it promulgates. Adherence to these processes helps ensure that the legislative power will pursue the public good (sec. 143).

In his third principle, Locke emphasizes the role of consent to keep the supreme power from subverting the end of government: actions of government must be with the individual's consent, "i.e. the consent of the majority, giving it either by themselves, or their representatives chosen by them" (sec. 140). When the legislative power is exercised through representatives, it operates as a delegated power of the people. In his reiteration of the "bounds" of the legislative power, Locke states that "These *Laws* also ought to be designed for no other end ultimately but *the good of the People*" (sec. 142). As Richard G. Stevens recognizes in his clear explication of these passages limiting the legislative power:

> The crucial limit is simply this: if the legislative power is vested in a numerous body, which comes from an elective system cleansed of rotten boroughs, if the legislature is for a set period and if its members must again become private citizens after, if the laws enacted by the legislature are general, prospective laws and are promulgated, and if they fall equally on all people, including the ex-legislators and the legislators who made those laws, and if the laws are passed by majority vote after debate and deliberation, then those laws will only take so much life, liberty, or property as they must take to serve the general ends of life, liberty, and property.[26]

If the legislature operates according to the procedural limits Locke prescribes, it "is not much to be feared."[27] The majority determines "the public good" by operating through the legislative power according to the procedural limits Locke discusses. This is not a limitation based on substantive natural rights, but rather states the legitimacy of consent of the governed operating through a properly ordered legislative power.[28] The representative legislative majority must judge.

After treating the extent of the legislative power, Locke immediately turns to treatment "Of the Legislative, Executive, and Federative Power of the Common-wealth."[29] He introduces the doctrine of separating the legislative and executive power in his discussion of the necessity for a *"perpetual execution"* by a *"power always in being"* of laws that are at once, and in a short time, made by the legislative power: "And thus the *legislative* and *executive power* come often to be separated."[30] Later in the *Second Treatise*, Locke states that in "well-framed governments," the "legislative and executive powers are in distinct hands" or are separated.[31] Unless the legislative and executive power are separate, legislators may exempt themselves from obedience to the laws they make. Locke stands for the proposition that where law ends, tyranny begins. However, he makes no provision for a separate branch of government to exercise the judicial power and obviously makes no provision for judicial review.

Apart from the role he accords commerce in politics, Locke's primary contributions are the processes he prescribes for the legislative power in order to make the positive law consistent with its foundations in natural right and natural law. His separation of the executive from the legislative power serves the same purpose. Positive law is necessary because the law of nature is unwritten and found only in the human mind and is miscited and misapplied as a consequence of passion and interest. Thus, the community puts the legislative power into hands that will govern by declared positive laws in order to achieve peace and secure property. Except for the right of self-preservation, Locke does not provide a catalog of private rights, much less an ever-expanding catalog of such rights, that government cannot invade. In fact, he explicitly rejects this view of civil society and politics, a view that might be used to justify an expansive judicial power to enforce such a catalog of private rights. A radical expansion of such rights would lead us right back to the state of nature from which Locke is so intent that we escape. Locke states that "all private judgment of every particular member being excluded, the community comes to be umpire, by settled standing rules, indifferent, and the same to all parties; and by men having authority from the community, for the execution of those rules, decides all the differences that may happen between any members of that society concerning any matter of right."[32] Thus, Locke's solution to natural right and natural law in government leads us back to the legitimacy of the majority, the supreme legislative power, and other elements of the government he describes. Locke believes that where law ends, tyranny begins, and that the best actualization of the natural ends of equality and rights is the political order he prescribes, where these ends are determined under law. The legislative power is supreme in this political order, and his scheme does not rely on a listing of "thou shalt nots" in the form of substantive limitations on that power. His restrictions on the legislative power are procedural in nature and depend on the republican elements of the legislative power and the other procedural characteristics he describes. Locke does not provide authority or argument for an independent judiciary to obstruct the legislative will when the judiciary believes that substantive natural rights are being violated by the legislature, and he most certainly does not rely on such a body to define an ever-expanding catalog of individual rights that are used to obstruct the legislative will. His theory is sound insofar as it preserves legislative discretion to meet unforeseen exigencies and yet limits that discretion through procedural mechanisms designed to preserve equality and rights.

Montesquieu

Whereas Locke provided the philosophical basis for the Declaration of Independence, Montesquieu has the distinction of being cited directly at several places in *The Federalist,* including his statement that of the three powers of government, "the judiciary is next to nothing."[33] My discussion of Montesquieu emphasizes those sections of his work that discuss republicanism, natural right, natural law, and the separation of powers, all of which are important to the American scheme of government, the argument of *The Federalist,* and the role of the judiciary.

Montesquieu is commonly cited as authority for the separation of powers and, thus, an independent judiciary, both of which are important features of the U.S. Constitution and essential to its protection of liberty. The independence of the judiciary is the starting point of much contemporary constitutional commentary, which then urges the independent judiciary to identify rights—whether natural rights, principles of natural law, or other rights—that can be utilized and expanded to void legislative or executive actions to achieve the ends the commentators desire. Although it is true that Montesquieu separates the judicial power from the executive and legislative powers, he does not advocate the doctrine that a catalog of liberty and other natural rights justifies the judiciary's voiding governmental action that is inconsistent with these rights. Instead, Montesquieu argues for liberty under the rule of law and carefully constructs a scheme in which a sovereign parliament, a strong executive, and a jury system protect liberty. Like Hobbes and Locke, he in no sense implies a system of government by judiciary. Montesquieu argues that the content of laws designed to secure liberty will vary from one regime to another. Institutions are essential to the protection of liberty through laws that reserve a wide latitude for lawmakers and that cannot be limited by absolute rules. Laws must take into account the character of the particular regime.

Although liberty is the goal of his regime, Montesquieu is hesitant to impose substantive limitations on government in the name of liberty. As a prelude to the U.S. Constitution's reliance on republicanism and institutions to achieve liberty, it is necessary to examine the role of institutions in Montesquieu's work, the manner in which he protects liberty by power checking power, and the manner in which his system bridges the distance between monarchy and republicanism, a distance important to the Constitution.

Near the beginning of Montesquieu's *The Spirit of the Laws,* he distinguishes his view of the state of nature from that of Hobbes. Unlike Hobbes, Montesquieu characterizes the presocial state as one in which the individual would "fancy himself inferior" and be found "flying from every shadow." An individual would not attack another but rather would think first of "the preservation of his being." The first law of nature is peace. But as soon as humans enter into society, "equality ceases, and then commences the state of war."[34] The preservation of society is threatened by human "ignorance and error" and by the influence of "a thousand impetuous passions"; therefore, we need legislators "to confine man to his duty."[35] Like Hobbes and Locke, Montesquieu believes that civil society is necessary to impose peace on the war of one individual against another. The purpose of the state is the establishment of security and peace:[36] "For Montesquieu, the purpose or nature of government in general is the creation of security, or freedom, for its citizens—freedom from domination and from threat of death or attack by other men."[37] Although the need for preservation is rooted in human nature, and "though all governments have the same general end, which is that of preservation,"[38] laws vary widely in order to suit the needs of the particular regime:[39] "Law in general is human reason, inasmuch as it governs all the inhabitants of the earth: the political and civil laws of each nation ought to be only the particular cases in which human reason is applied. They should be adapted in such a manner to the people for whom they are framed that it should be a great chance if those of one nation suit another."[40] Far from prescribing a code of rules or a catalog of private rights that limit government action, Montesquieu claims a wide latitude for statesmanship in which statecraft and reason determine the character of law that is suitable to a nation.[41] He identifies liberty with a life lived under the rule of law rather than with a code of limitations on government:

> In governments, that is, in societies directed by laws, liberty can consist only in the power of doing what we ought to will, and in not being constrained to do what we ought not to will.
>
> We must have continually present to our minds the difference between independence and liberty. Liberty is a right of doing whatever the laws

permit, and if a citizen could do what they forbid he would be no longer possessed of liberty, because all his fellow-citizens would have the same power.[42]

Montesquieu argues that "political liberty is to be found only in moderate governments," and only when power is not abused: "To prevent this abuse, it is necessary from the very nature of things that power should be a check to power. A government may be so constituted, as no man shall be compelled to do things to which the law does not oblige him, nor forced to abstain from things which the law permits."[43]

The form of law, its universal application, and the checking of power by separated institutions seem more important than the content of the law. Thus, the system must ensure the rule of law in order to achieve security and liberty. Although "the key to liberty is law as formal universality," those who obey despotic laws are not free.[44] In addition to such factors as commerce, which is extraordinarily important to Montesquieu, institutional characteristics of government are essential to the liberty found under the English constitution. He examines the English constitution to pursue the constitution of political liberty—liberty under law in which life is secure and free.[45]

The English regime Montesquieu discusses is mixed, consisting of aristocracy, monarchy, and democracy. The legislative power is composed of an upper house of nobles and representatives of the commoners in the lower house, thereby balancing these factions. Each faction checks the other; the nobles are protected from the "licentiousness of the people," and the people can "oppose any encroachment of theirs." The two bodies have "their assemblies and deliberations apart, each their separate views and interests."[46] The people are represented in their separate assembly by representatives who have the great advantage in "their capacity of discussing public affairs," an activity for which the "people collectively are extremely unfit."[47] The nobles are relatively weaker in the English structure and thereby give the English system a republican character, in contrast to the "monarchical balance of powers in other European countries." Whereas Hobbes feels constrained to choose absolute monarchy, Montesquieu's mixed regime bridges the distance between republicanism and monarchy.[48]

Montesquieu argues that when "the legislative and executive powers are united in the same person, or in the same body of magistrates, there can be no liberty." If the "same monarch or senate should enact tyrannical laws," they may "execute them in a tyrannical manner."[49] If the powers are separated, tyrannical laws may be moderated in their execution. The single monarch, or executive power, gives unity and "despatch" to the English constitution as well as providing a third element of institutional balance to the system. Because the monarch is institutionalized, it identifies with the country as a whole. This is an especially valuable characteristic where foreign policy is concerned, but it is also important in avoiding the monarch's consistent identification with one of the factions represented in the legislative body.[50] In support of balancing institutional power, the monarch is given "a share in the legislature by the power of rejecting," that is, by an unqualified veto power,[51] and the monarch also regulates the time of meeting and duration of the legislative assemblies.[52] The legislature, however, also restrains the executive power. The monarch may not be arraigned by the legislature for the manner in which law is executed, but the monarch's counselors may be impeached by the legislative body representing the people and tried by the body representing the nobility. The impeachment power both protects the rights of the people and exerts an element of republican check upon the executive power.[53] The most important elements in balancing institutional power are the legislature and the executive, not the judiciary.[54]

Montesquieu characterizes the legislative power as the enactment of laws and the amendment or abrogation of laws that have already been enacted. The executive power includes the functions we associate with foreign relations as well as the punishment of criminals and the determination of disputes that arise between individuals. But he immediately separates the latter executive power, which he designates the judicial power, for he argues that "there is no liberty, if the judiciary power be not separated from the legislative and executive." As was observed earlier, compared with the legislative and executive powers, "the judiciary is in some measure next to nothing," and this is as it should be, for the judicial power can be "terrible to mankind," since its function is "trying the causes of individuals"[55] and thereby directly confronting individuals with the power of government. The judiciary is not important to the balance of the two legislative factions and the executive, so its power need not rival theirs, but it must be sufficiently independent to be protected from them. This independence helps ensure the rule of law and protects the individual, as the judiciary applies the law to individuals.[56] Montesquieu further protects the individual from the judicial power by directly involving the people in the application of law to the individual through the jury system. However, he is scrupulous about judgments being "conformable to the letter of the law,"[57] and there is a body of judges to conform the judicial power to the letter of the law.[58]

After treating political liberty in relation to the constitution and the distribution of the powers of government, Montesquieu examines it in relation to "security or the opinion people have of their security." Security arises from "manners, customs, or received examples" and may be encouraged by "particular civil laws." Montesquieu emphasizes the criminal laws, "on the goodness of which . . . the liberty of the subject principally depends." He explains the importance of criminal laws in chapter 4 of book XII, "That Liberty Is Favored by the Nature and Proportion of Punishments.'' Montesquieu recommends laws that do not flow from ''the capriciousness of the legislator, but from the very nature of the thing,'' that is, laws that are moderate or humane.[59] He advocates, for example, that in the context of high treason, nothing is ''more arbitrary than declaring people guilty of it for indiscreet speeches: . . . Words do not constitute an overt act; they remain only an idea.''[60] Although Montesquieu advocates humane and moderate laws, he does not set forth the goals of political life as either unchanging or ever-changing rules. Thus, even the protection against bills of attainder may in some instances be suspended in a republic.[61] Although the civil law should have its foundation in the nature of humankind, ''this guiding natural principle of justice does not have the character of a 'law.' ''[62] Private property is important to his regime of liberty: ''Let us pose as a maxim that, when it concerns the public good, the public good is never that one deprive an individual of his property, or at least that the least possible part is to be taken away by any law or political regulation.''[63] But, as important as he regards private property, the maxim he proposes for its protection is flexible and leaves wide discretion for statecraft.

Montesquieu teaches several lessons. The end of his regime is liberty, but he is unwilling to set forth absolute rules to achieve liberty, even in a particular regime. He reserves a wide latitude for statecraft in actualizing the regime of liberty. He places extraordinary emphasis on institutions to produce the most liberty possible at a particular time and place. As Anne Cohler states: ''The mechanisms that balance this government have two purposes: first, they maintain the division of power by protecting each part of the government from the encroachments of the others; and second, they promote what perhaps can best be called good government—that is, they make it easier, or possible, for the parts of the government to perform their tasks well.'' Montesquieu thereby divides the ruling power.[64] His insistence on the rule of law is manifested in a doctrine of parliamentary sovereignty with important republican components. The powers of the monarch, including the power to reject legislation and regulate the meeting of parliament, indicate the necessity he sees for a strong executive power. Even though he regards commerce as fundamental to the regime of liberty, he shrinks from explicating a code of laws to protect liberty even in commercial matters.

Montesquieu regards moderate and humane criminal laws as necessary to personal security or freedom. In addition to laws, the customs and history of a people are important to that liberty and security. According to Montesquieu, the best a political order can do to actualize liberty is indicated by the centrality of the rule of law, a balanced and mixed regime that represents both nobles and commoners and provides for national unity through the monarch, and an independent judiciary to combat the ''terrible'' potential of the judicial power. There is no judicial review and no written constitution in Montesquieu's scheme. He teaches the essential role of institutions in approximating the liberty and security required by the law of nature. Although peace is the first law of nature, our original social condition is a state of war. Self-preservation, security, and liberty are the result of Montesquieu's structure of government and the resulting rule of law rather than a codification of natural rights or natural law of which the judiciary is peculiar guardian. Security under law is the basis for freedom.

Although Montesquieu's regime of liberty is a mixed regime, one unacceptable to those proposing and ratifying the U.S. Constitution, he makes a number of contributions that can account for *The Federalist*'s reliance on his theory. His theory emphasizes positive law, or liberty under law, rather than an undefined liberty of individuals; the compass for this positive law is liberty, which Montesquieu regards as fundamental. Although his separation of powers is rooted in a mixed regime with monarchical and aristocratic powers, separation of powers is fundamental to the strictly republican U.S. Constitution. The separation of powers makes possible responsible and good republican government. It provides the institutional means by which separated institutions preserve democracy while moderating democracy's undesirable tendencies. Separation of powers is the most important institutional mechanism by which the U.S. Constitution provides the remedy for the diseases most incident to republican government. The Constitution uses the theory of Montesquieu as the basis for government that both builds from and provides a republican completion to Montesquieu's theory.

Hobbes, Locke, and Montesquieu are in agreement that government is a difficult undertaking. Their view of human nature and government is at once hardheaded, demanding a strong government to bring us out of a state of war, and based on a natural compass of liberty under government. Liberty is both rooted in nature and actualized through the rule of law effected by strong government. None of the theorists provides a basis for an ever-expanding catalog of individual rights against government, nor do they provide a basis for a view of government in which peace-loving individuals willingly respect ever-expanding rights of others. For Hobbes, Locke, and Montesquieu, strong government is the antidote for a human nature that resists such government. Strong government provides the conditions of peace, security, and liberty under law, which are the best approximations of the liberty rooted in the conception of human nature underpinning their theories. Each of these theorists regards the utopian right of absolute liberty as the despicable condition from which we should escape as we establish government to actualize the conditions of peace, security, and liberty under law. If we take these theorists seriously in their characterization of human nature and government, the doctrine of ever-expanding rights against government seems to lead us in the direction of the very state of nature from which government allowed us to escape.

Lest the emphasis on the positive law leads the reader to believe that either these theorists or the author of this book dismisses the right or law of nature, several observations are in order. The rule of law, to which these theorists and the U.S. Constitution give central importance, is rooted in natural law. The conjunction of natural law and positive law is illustrated by the prohibitions in Hobbes, Locke, and the Constitution on ex post facto laws. To punish an individual for actions that were legal when they were committed but later made illegal is eminently unreasonable and a violation of the rule of law. Such laws violate both the natural law and the positive law of Article I, section 9 or 10. The prohibition against ex post facto laws by both the theorists and the Constitution is a particular manifestation of the insistence that the rule of law is required by the right and law of nature. The due process clause is yet another illustration of the conjunction of natural law and positive law. Hobbes, for example, specifically refers to the necessity of hearing before punishment. The due process clauses of both the Fifth and Fourteenth Amendments embody the natural law's requirement of the rule of law through the stipulation that deprivations of life, liberty, or property must be in accordance with law.

The Declaration of Independence

The Declaration of Independence sets forth the ends or purposes of government that the Constitution is designed to achieve. Its doctrine of natural or inalienable rights presents the strongest case for commentators who ask the judiciary to decide cases according to such standards rather than on the basis of rights and principles found within the provisions of the Constitution. Yet, as we shall see, the Declaration's own principle is one of consent to the form of government that a majority believes will best achieve the rights it articulates. Since consent of the governed gives the Constitution legitimacy, it is imperative to determine the form of government, the theory, and the provisions contained in the Constitution to which consent was given. If we are to ask the Supreme Court to protect rights beyond those found in the Constitution, it is necessary to show that the frame of government to which consent was given includes such a role for the Court.

The second paragraph of the Declaration sets forth the ends of government, the means for the realization of which are provided by the Constitution:

> We hold these truths to be self-evident, that all men are created equal, that they are endowed by their Creator with certain unalienable Rights, that among these are Life, Liberty and the pursuit of Happiness. That to secure these rights, Governments are instituted among Men, deriving their just powers from the consent of the governed, That whenever any Form of Government becomes destructive of these ends, it is the Right of the People to alter or to abolish it, and to institute new Government, laying its foundation on such principles and organizing its powers in such form, as to them shall seem most likely to effect their Safety and Happiness.''[65]

One is immediately struck by the similarities between this passage from the Declaration and propositions found in Locke's *Second Treatise*.[66] The rights referred to in the Declaration are the reason for government and, ultimately, the criterion for judging government. The self-evident truths from which the Declaration proceeds are truths that contain their own meaning rather than referring to something outside themselves.[67] Human beings have a nature that places them between God and the beasts, and in light of this shared nature, or equality, we ought not assume the nature of either extreme in our dealings with others.[68] Unless we delude ourselves, we "are always able to recognize each other's humanity."[69] We share equally the fundamental Lockean right of self-preservation, which, as we have seen, is the root of the equal right to consent to that form of government by which we will be governed. Since individuals derive their rights from nature, government can be legitimated only when they consent.[70]

The Declaration teaches that there are standards beyond positive law, or law of governments, by which governments may be judged. These standards, or ends of government, are related to "Laws of Nature and of Nature's God" and to "unalienable Rights," including rights to "Life, Liberty and the pursuit of Happiness." The Declaration "reminds us of the old-fashioned proposition that there are standards outside and above the agreements and teachings of men, government, and era, standards superior even to what 'the people' might at any moment believe or choose. In short, the right of revolution implies an insistence upon the supremacy of man's reason."[71]

The revolutionary precedent of the Declaration is exercised in a document in which the reasonableness of the revolutionary act of separation is defended and set forth before the opinions of humankind:

> Not only are 'facts' submitted to a 'candid world,' but there also is advanced a kind of argument starting from self-evident premises and proceeding to probable conclusions. . . . Particularly significant here, not least of all as testimony to the gravity of the 'long train of abuses and usurpa-

tions' which led to the disruption, is the list of more than two dozen 'op-pressions' of the colonists visited upon them or assented to by the British monarch.

Thus there is a right to alter or to abolish a form of government that is destructive of the ends of government, but it is a right which has as one condition the proper exercise of reason: 'Prudence, indeed, will dictate that Governments long established should not be changed for light and transient causes.'[72]

Although the self-evident truths lie at the foundation of government, "the means to effect the ends of government cannot be capable of such certainty."[73]

The first step in forming government is the unanimous consent to act as a body politic. Once this step is taken, the body politic acts to establish a form of government through its consent, and it is bound by the majority as to what form of government to establish. Although the principle of equality requires majority rule in choosing the form of government, it does not require a particular form of government as long as the government chosen is not despotic, that is, is not destructive of their inalienable rights.[74] Human beings "have by nature certain unalienable rights which they secure by establishing government,"[75] and it is up to a majority of the body politic to institute the government that "to them shall seem most likely to effect their Safety and Happiness."[76] The majority determines what form of government will best secure their rights. Once this majority consent is given, only the destruction of the ends of government can justify its withdrawal.[77] Although the government to which consent is given need not be a popular form of government, one can understand why a popular government is likely to be chosen.[78]

The Declaration institutes a form of government based on equality, but it is an equality of rights or equal condition of opportunity rather than one of social condition.[79] It arises out of Locke's state of nature, where each is in a "state of perfect freedom."[80] We derive our inalienable rights in civil society from this "equal perfect freedom" in the state of nature.[81] Lincoln interpreted the Declaration in this way: "The authors of that notable instrument . . . did not intend to declare all men equal in all respects. They did not mean to say all were equal in color, size, intellect, moral developments, or social capacity. They defined with tolerable distinctness, in what respects they did consider all men created equal—equal in 'certain inalienable rights, among which are life, liberty, and the pursuit of happiness.' "[82]

Equality demands consent to the institution of government on the part of those who believe that the proposed government will secure their rights. The majority giving consent to the form of government may consent to the establishment of a Supreme Court or to the establishment of a Senate that is not apportioned to population and is not strictly majoritarian. Such institutions are entirely consistent with the requirement of consent of the governed. Consent is rooted in the right of nature and manifested in the Constitution's frame of government. In the words of *The Federalist:* ''The establishment of a constitution, in time of profound peace, by the voluntary consent of a whole people, is a prodigy, to the completion of which I look forward with trembling anxiety.''[83] Consent is a serious matter and requires an understanding of what the majority of the body politic is consenting to. Thus, we will examine both the institutions created by and the theory underlying the Constitution to which consent was given. The Constitution provides the governmental form and theory that are productive of the ends of government articulated in the Declaration, namely, individual liberty.[84]

The Constitution actualizes the Declaration's ends of government according to the best judgment of those who consented to the form of government. In the government it frames, it takes the additional step of extending the consent of the governed from the founding act to the actual operation of the government. The government founded is representative or strictly republican in character. This strictly republican character is fundamental to understanding the role of the Supreme Court and the judiciary consistent with the Constitution's theory.

The Declaration's self-evident truths and inalienable rights set forth the ends of and justification for American government. The Declaration's level of generality is consistent with these purposes, but it did not provide the means for achieving them. Instead, it relies on the principle of consent to establish these means by forming a government that the consenting majority believes will secure inalienable rights and the other ends of the Declaration. The framers of the Constitution sought to actualize the Declaration's ends of government through a charter of government to which a majority consented. As we shall see, the Constitution did not simply entrust the achievement of the Declaration's general ends, including the preservation of rights, to the discretion of the government it established. Instead, it set forth the powers of and limitations on government in a written Constitution. The written Constitution defines the powers of the judiciary and the Supreme Court. If we are to ask the courts to protect rights beyond those found in the Constitution, it must be shown that the Constitution to which consent was given includes such a role for the Court. That such consent was given would be very difficult to support, given the fact that not even the government as a whole was given such broad powers. It was limited by enumerated powers and other prohibitions, rather than given the power to govern according to the general ends of the Declaration. If the strictly republican government is so limited, it is extraordinarily difficult to support a role for the courts, which are only one part of that government, to decide cases according to the general ends of the Declaration or on the basis of other extraconstitutional rights. Hobbes, Locke, and Montesquieu have in common with the Declaration two clear features: these sources provide neither for a judiciary as the primary protector of rights nor for a judiciary empowered to supplant the legislative authority on the basis of judges' voiding properly enacted legislation on the basis of unenumerated rights.

Chapter Two

The Constitution, *The Federalist,* and Constitutional Principles

---

Natural Rights and the Constitution

Those who ask the judiciary to protect rights beyond those specified in the Constitution must justify this judicial role in light of the Constitution's provisions or theory. Some commentators who advocate such a judicial role link it with the doctrine of natural right, which they see as implying an expansive role on the basis of the Constitution and its theory. This chapter addresses the question of how the Constitution preserves rights. In addressing this question, we will explore the relationship between the natural rights of the Declaration and the rights set forth in the Constitution, relying on *The Federalist.* This question is crucial to the judicial role envisioned by the Constitution. We will discover that the Constitution regards a dependence on the people as the primary safeguard of private rights. *The Federalist* argues that a catalog of rights that may impede government action necessary to secure the safety and happiness of the people is risky. The Constitution and the theory explicated in *The Federalist,* like that of the earlier political philosophers who laid the foundation for the liberal state and republican government, do not regard judges as the primary guardians of private rights. The Constitution, following the lead of earlier theorists, creates a limited judicial power and relies primarily on other means to protect private rights.

The Federalist is central to understanding the balance between the public good and the private rights the Constitution effected. The Constitution's specific provisions partake of a theoretical unity that is best understood by a careful examination of the unified theoretical argument of *The Federalist.* One important example of the necessity of going beyond the provisions of the Constitution to the theory of *The Federalist* is the very power of judicial review. There is no textual provision for judicial review in the Constitution. The necessity for this power is deducible from the theory of a limited constitution and from the specific presumption of this power in *The Federalist* as well as in the debates of the Constitutional Convention.[1] An understanding of the principles and unity of the Constitution's theory is necessary not only to defend judicial review but also to achieve a proper understanding of other constitutional provisions.[2] This theory has direct application to the question of securing rights under the Constitution—both the rights specified in the Bill of Rights and those embodied in subsequent amendments such as the Civil War amendments.

The body of the Constitution contains few unqualified prohibitions on governmental power. Although the Bill of Rights contains a group of reasonably specific rights that are derived from traditional civil rights, it does not contain statements of perpetual maxims or limitations on government. The addition of the Bill of Rights and subsequent amendments to the Constitution does not alter the necessity for a firm reliance on *The Federalist* in order to understand the Constitution. *The Federalist* argues the necessity of giving full scope to powers of government and a dependence on the people through a properly structured system of representation in order to secure liberty. Its design for securing liberty and rights is strictly republican and emphasizes the structure of government and a written Constitution, rather than enlightened statecraft, as the primary means of securing the natural rights set forth in the Declaration. This reliance is reminiscent of Locke's procedural mechanisms for securing such rights. In exploring the question of how the Constitution preserves rights, we will examine the constitutional understanding of natural rights, with a special emphasis on the Bill of Rights, its conception of democracy and representation, and the separation and enumeration of powers. Chapter 3 examines the role of the judiciary.

The Federalist makes little reference to the doctrine of natural rights. It focuses on explaining the need for a strong and properly constituted government. John Jay's early and short-lived contribution to *The Federalist* argues the necessity of people ceding to government certain natural rights in order to vest the government with necessary powers, but this may be the text's only explicit reference to natural rights.[3] *Federalist* No. 10 provides an apt summary of the Constitution and *The Federalist:* "To secure the public good and private rights against the danger of such a faction ['a group acting adverse to the rights of other citizens, or to the permanent and aggregate interests of the community'], and at the same time to preserve the spirit and the form of popular government, is then the great object to which our inquiries are directed" (54, 57–58). Citing the Declaration of Independence, *The Federalist* refers in No. 40 to "the transcendent and precious right of the people to 'abolish or alter their governments' " in order to effect their safety and happiness (257). This statement refers directly to the consent of the governed in judging how safety and happiness shall be obtained. Consent of the governed is the clear manifestation of the Declaration's doctrine of equality and the self-evident truth in light of which judgments are finally made as to whether inalienable rights are abridged.

The Constitution extends the doctrine of majority rule to the operation of the government to which consent is given, for example, in its statement that the Constitution is "founded upon the power of the people, and executed by their immediate representatives and servants."[4] As Irving Brant recognizes, the Constitution itself provides for the "right of the people to amend, alter or abolish the government they live under," thereby constitutionalizing one of the self-evident truths of the Declaration. He aptly characterizes the right of revolution as "a natural, not a constitutional, right. Its legal status is akin to treason except when successfully employed, as it was in our own national beginnings."[5]

As we have seen, the Declaration does not designate the particular form to which the body politic must consent in order to be consistent with its underlying principles. Nonetheless, *The Federalist* devotes much of its argument to establishing that the proposed government conforms to "the true principles of republican government":[6]

> The first question that offers itself is, whether the general form and aspect of the government be strictly republican. It is evident that no other form would be reconcilable with the genius of the people of America; with the fundamental principles of the Revolution; or with that honorable determination which animates every votary of freedom, to rest all our political experiments on the capacity of mankind for self-government. If the plan of the convention, therefore, be found to depart from the republican character, its advocates must abandon it as no longer defensible.[7]

Whatever the theoretical latitude of the Declaration's principles, the genius (Webster defines genius as nature, disposition, bent, wit, or spirit)[8] of the American people requires self-government, government that is "strictly republican" in its operation. The reference to genius is reminiscent of Montesquieu's view that the laws must be consistent with the spirit of a people. But unlike Montesquieu's description of a mixed regime as the means to liberty, Publius insists on a Constitution that is strictly republican.

The Federalist devotes considerable effort to arguing for a government that has sufficient power to govern and to achieve the ends of safety and happiness for whose protection consent is given. It formulates the task of constituting a government in clear terms: "In framing a government which is to be administered by men over men, the great difficulty lies in this: you must first enable the government to control the governed; and in the next place oblige it to control itself. A dependence on the people is, no doubt, the primary control on the government; but experience has taught mankind the necessity of auxiliary precautions."[9] The first objective is to grant government sufficient powers to govern or "to control the governed." Second, the government must be constructed in a manner that will "oblige it to control itself." The primary control on government is its "dependence on the people" rather than explicit restrictions on the actions of government.

If one looks to the body of the Constitution, there are few unqualified prohibitions on the national government.[10] Jury trials are guaranteed in all criminal cases, and titles of nobility, bills of attainder, and ex post facto laws are prohibited. The privilege of the writ of habeas corpus cannot be suspended unless the public safety requires it in prescribed instances.[11] The prohibition on titles of nobility is both an expression of "dependence on the people" and a necessity for the wholly republican character of the Constitution and government. The prohibition on bills of attainder is less a substantive guarantee than a protection of individuals through adherence to the system of separated powers. One is hard-pressed to think of instances in which ex post facto laws (laws making an act illegal after it has already been committed) are justified. Such laws also violate Locke's procedural maxim that laws must be established and promulgated (see Chapter 1). The Constitution is thus based on the premise that the primary safeguard of private rights is a dependence on the people. Since unforeseen exigencies inevitably confront government, it is difficult to set down absolute prohibitions on government that will always be consistent with the public good.

The Bill of Rights

In spite of the observations just made, Alexander Hamilton's argument against a bill of rights presents a problem. Immediately after enumerating rights protected in the body of the Constitution, Hamilton argues: "I go further, and affirm that bills of rights, in the sense and to the extent in which they are contended for, are not only unnecessary in the proposed Constitution, but would even be dangerous. They would contain various exceptions to powers not granted; and on this very account, would afford a colorable pretext to claim more than were granted. For why declare that things shall not be done which there is no power to do?"[12] Why does not this same danger apply to the protections or limitations on government power specified in the body of the Constitution, provisions that Hamilton speaks so positively about in No. 84? Perhaps the answer to this question is that the prohibitions in the body of the Constitution impede the powers of government less than would a bill of rights so dear to the hearts of many Anti-Federalists. Perhaps, too, it is easier for the judiciary to apply the clear reservations of rights in the original Constitution than the rights Hamilton anticipated in a bill of rights. Or perhaps the rights enumerated in the body of the Constitution leave less "latitude for evasion" than those Hamilton believed would constitute a bill of rights, such as the freedom of the press, which he treats at some length in No. 84. Whatever the reason for Hamilton's position, it is clear that rights in the original Constitution relating to habeas corpus, bills of attainder, titles of nobility, and ex post facto laws have not given rise to the extensive litigation that has resulted from many provisions of the Bill of Rights. Particularly numerous are cases arising under the application of these provisions to the states through the Fourteenth Amendment.

Publius addresses the issue of protecting rights through parchment declarations and the difficulty of formulating precise prohibitions in a constitution when he discusses in *Federalist* No. 84 the criticism that the Constitution lacks a bill of rights. In examining the particular rights enumerated in the body of the Constitution, Hamilton refers to the prohibition of titles of nobility as "the corner-stone of republican government," once again affirming the importance of a strictly republican dependence on the people. He distinguishes the Magna Charta from our strictly republican system of government because the former was a stipulation "between kings and their subjects." The Magna Charta was obtained by barons, "sword in hand, from King John." The U.S. Constitution is founded and functions consistent with the Preamble: "WE, THE PEOPLE of the United States, to secure the blessings of liberty to ourselves and our posterity, do *ordain* and *establish* this Constitution for the United States of America."[13] Hamilton regards this as a "better recognition of popular rights, than volumes of those aphorisms"[14] that make up bills of rights. This is a strong statement in favor of the strictly republican character of the Constitution and the government it establishes.

Hamilton directly addresses the issue of the Constitution's lack of a bill of rights: "What signifies a declaration, that 'the liberty of the press shall be inviolably preserved?' " Hamilton responds that such declarations "leave the utmost latitude for evasion." The real security of a free press and other liberties "must altogether depend on public opinion, and on the general spirit of the people and of the government."[15] Hamilton's comments on freedom of the press deserve quotation at length:

> To show that there is a power in the Constitution by which the liberty of the press may be affected, recourse has been had to the power of taxation. It is said that duties may be laid upon the publications so high as to amount to a prohibition. I know not by what logic it could be maintained, that the declarations in the State constitutions, in favor of the freedom of the press, would be a constitutional impediment to the imposition of duties upon publications by the State legislatures. It cannot certainly be pretended that any degree of duties, however low, would be an abridgment of the liberty of the press. We know that newspapers are taxed in Great Britain, and yet it is notorious that the press nowhere enjoys greater liberty than in that country. And if duties of any kind may be laid without a violation of that liberty, it is evident that the extent must depend on legislative discretion, regulated by public opinion; so that, after all, general

declarations respecting the liberty of the press, will give it no greater security than it will have without them. The same invasions of it may be effected under the State constitution which contain those declarations through the means of taxation, as under the proposed Constitution, which has nothing of the kind. It would be quite as significant to declare that government ought to be free, that taxes ought not to be excessive, etc., as that the liberty of the press ought not to be restrained.[16]

The essence of Hamilton's statement regarding a bill of rights is that rights depend on public opinion, elevated and refined through the representative process, and the expression of that opinion through a properly constituted government. Rights are not enclaves of absolute prohibitions; rather, they are determined by prudent judgment through a properly constituted government that rests on public opinion and self-government. Thus, in Hamilton's words, "the Constitution is itself, in every rational sense, and to every useful purpose, A BILL OF RIGHTS." Hamilton's defense of the original Constitution is also firmly anchored in two of the Declaration's self-evident truths. The Constitution adopts both the Declaration's doctrine of consent of the governed and its self-evident truth of the power of the people to alter or abolish the government through constitutional processes. It is difficult to conceive of a clearer statement than this of republican principles and confidence in self-government.

But, as every student of the founding period knows, regardless of his arguments' merits, Hamilton failed to persuade the ratifying conventions and the First Congress—particularly the Anti-Federalists, over whom the Federalists prevailed in the ratification struggle. The Constitution was ratified with the understanding that "widely desired amendments" would be considered.[17] John Marshall provides a good reading of this history in his statement that the Bill of Rights was adopted out of a concern that the expansive powers of the new national government might be abused and was not intended to apply to the states.[18] The claim for a bill of rights can be seen as a shadow of Anti-Federalist opposition to and fear of a consolidated national government. Today, of course, many Americans consider the Constitution as almost synonymous with the Bill of Rights.

It may be difficult to understand why the founders excluded a bill of rights, particularly given the self-evident truths enunciated in the Declaration. But behind Hamilton's defense of the Constitution, as it was reported out of the Convention, several considerations deserve treatment. *The Federalist* and the original Constitution seem securely anchored in Locke's reliance on procedural means to secure rights and Montesquieu's institutional solution (supplanted by the strictly republican Constitution's modification of Montesquieu's mixed regime). Article III provides for an independent judiciary designed for impartial enforcement of the laws that the people's representatives have enacted. As we have seen, the body of the Constitution provides for a number of protections of civil and religious liberty beyond the structural mechanisms of a large commercial republic, separated powers, checks and balances, and enumerated powers. But beyond these considerations is *The Federalist's* concern that ''in framing a government which is to be administered by men over men, the great difficulty lies in this: you must first enable the government to control the governed; and in the next place oblige it to control itself.''[19] This concern with granting the representatives of the people sufficient powers to govern reflects that of both Hobbes and Locke and is a recurrent one in *The Federalist. Federalist* No. 23 opens by asserting the necessity of a Constitution at least as energetic as the one proposed.[20] The same paper refers to powers being granted to the government *''because it is impossible to foresee or define the extent and variety of national exigencies or the correspondent extent and variety of the means which may be necessary to satisfy them.''* This principle holds true for ''every other matter to which its [the national government's] jurisdiction is permitted to extend.''[21]

As Herbert Storing recognizes, the most fundamental issue in the argument over a bill of rights was its potential to weaken the government that was instituted in order to secure rights:

> The final Federalist answer to the question, what harm can a bill of rights do? was the seldom explicitly stated fear that a bill of rights, especially undue emphasis on a bill of rights, might weaken government, which is the first protection of rights and which was in 1787 in particular need of strengthening. The first defense of individual rights is a government able to accomplish the necessary tasks of self-defense, regulation of commerce, administration of justice, etc. Loose and easy talk about rights was likely to distract attention from the difficult but fundamental business of forming a government capable of doing the things that have to be done to protect rights.[22]

This view is expressed clearly by James Bowdoin in the Massachusetts Ratifying Convention: ''The public good, in which [the] private [good] is necessarily involved, might be hurt by too particular an enumeration; and the private good could suffer no injury from a deficient enumeration, because Congress could not injure the rights of private citizens without injuring their own, as they must, in their public as well as private character, participate equally with others in the consequences of their own acts.''[23] The sense of this observation is that reservations of particular private rights in a bill of rights may interfere with the essential project of governing according to the consent of the governed. In Bowdoin's words: ''all governments are founded on the relinquish-

ment of personal rights in a certain degree," and if rights are particularly enumerated, "the government might be embarrassed, and prevented from doing
what the private, as well as the public and general, good of the citizens and
states might require."[24]

As both Bowdoin and Locke remind us, when laws are passed by a legislature that must live under these laws, this provides a substantial protection
against unnecessary interference with private rights. The omission of a bill of
rights was also addressed by Edmund Randolph in the Virginia Ratifying Convention, comparing it with the situation of Virginia, whose bill of rights was
not part of the constitution. Randolph believed that bills of rights produce
mischief by introducing ambiguity for judges as to whether constitutions or
bills of rights are paramount: "A bill of rights, therefore, accurately speaking,
is quite useless, if not dangerous to a republic."[25]

The Federalist's concern with maintaining sufficient powers to govern is reflected in George Washington's advice to the First Congress regarding amendments. He advised "no radical changes which would weaken the powers of
the government." Washington "was solicitous of 'the characteristic rights of
freemen,' and declared that 'a regard for the public harmony will sufficiently
influence your deliberations on the question' of how personal rights could be
'impregnably fortified' while an energetic government was maintained."[26]

The Bill of Rights reflects both Hamilton's argument in No. 84 and Washington's concerns. The Constitution embodies the doctrine of the consent of
the governed in its founding, as consent was understood in the states (relating, for example, to the slave population and to women). This strictly republican character is also embodied in the operation of the government as well as in
its provision for altering or abolishing the government according to constitutional mechanisms. In declaring independence, the Declaration refers to the
self-evident truths of equality, inalienable rights, the consent of the governed,
and the right to alter or abolish the government. The Bill of Rights is both
more sober and more specific in limiting the legislative power and the national
government as a whole. It contains no structural change in the government,
nor does it give back to the states powers of government contained in the
body of the Constitution. Nor does it contain any general maxims or statements of inalienable rights such as those found in the Declaration.

In place of inalienable rights—the Bill of Rights enumerates much more
specific civil rights—civil rights that require prudence and judgment in their
application, but nonetheless rights of a different character from those found in
the Declaration. In place of the Declaration's inalienable rights of "Life, Liberty and the pursuit of Happiness," the Fifth Amendment declares that no
person will "be deprived of life, liberty, or property without due process of
law." The Bill of Rights provision makes it clear that in the business of governing, life, liberty, and property will be taken, but it will be done in a manner

consistent with the prescribed processes of law, including the law of the Constitution.[27] Or, to use another example, the liberty of the Declaration is not set forth in the Bill of Rights as that of absolutely private enclaves beyond the power of government. The Fourth Amendment sets out the requirements of a warrant procedure through which private enclaves may be invaded. The Bill of Rights consists of "specific protections of traditional civil rights." Notably absent from its text are such provisions as those in the Virginia Declaration of Rights of 1776, for example, "[t]hat all men are by nature equally free and independent, and have certain inherent rights, of which, when they enter into a state of society, they cannot, by any compact deprive or divest their posterity; namely, the enjoyment of life and liberty, with the means of acquiring and possessing property, and pursuing and obtaining happiness and safety."[28]

Herbert Storing's balanced treatment of the Constitution, the Bill of Rights, and civil liberty deserves further quotation. As he recognizes, "government *does* 'violate' the natural rights of the individual, at least in the sense that it legitimately prevents him from enjoying the fullness of his rights. The question that always has to be asked is whether individual rights have been unnecessarily or unreasonably abridged. Such questions are not easy to answer, with or without a bill of rights."[29]

Locke's state of nature in which there exists perfect equality and perfect liberty is a condition attended with intolerable difficulties. He recognizes that this condition cannot exist under government when he shows that the true limits on government are procedural, not substantive, as those who misunderstand him would have it (see Chapter 1). With or without a bill of rights, there is wisdom in Hamilton's response to the question of how one defines or actualizes rights which are fundamental to American government.

Hamilton's response, however, was not persuasive to many in the state ratifying conventions. Patrick Henry, in a rhetorically effective statement, asked, if "our rights are reserved, why not say so? Is it because it will consume too much paper?"[30] Luther Martin believed that a constitution had to stipulate the rights of both states and individuals because the proposed constitution extended national power to act both on states and "immediately on individuals" and because the latter power departed from a crucial principle of the confederation.[31] The Anti-Federalists' persistent opposition to a consolidated or truly national government emerged again in the First Congress's discussion of freedom of religion. James Madison suggested the that if the Bill of Rights prohibited the establishment of a "national" religion, it would accomplish the objectives of those pressing for protection of religious freedom. Elbridge Gerry opposed the use of the term "national" on the grounds that it expressed a principle of consolidation that the Anti-Federalists opposed. Gerry argued that the Anti-Federalists had injustice done to them by that title, since the Anti-Federalists were the true Federalists insofar as they favored a federated form of government rather than the national government favored by the Federalists. Gerry said, "Their names then ought not to have been distinguished by federalists and antifederalists, but rats and antirats."[32] Gerry's objection was not to the meaning of what constitutes an establishment of religion but to Madison's use of the word "national," which implied a consolidation of government that Gerry and others opposed. The Federalists wanted strong and effective government in an America that was "all too wont to fall into easy and excessive criticism of all proposals for effective government." They saw in the Anti-Federalist arguments "a drift into the shallow view that Americans could somehow get along without government—without the tough decisions, the compulsion, the risk that government must always involve."[33] There is risk in adopting a bill of rights without knowledge of the exigencies government will surely face in the future. *The Federalist*'s admonition against relying on "enlightened statesmen" to pursue the public good and its reliance on republican consent are both violated if representative government and separation of powers are skirted by a judiciary that becomes the peculiar guardian of civil liberty through extensive interpretive powers.[34]

A part of the Anti-Federalist objective in pressing for a bill of rights was that of supplying a set of maxims or "perpetual standards" around which people might rally.[35] Randolph addresses this issue in the Virginia Ratifying Convention when he asks, "Why have we been told that maxims can alone save nations; that our maxims are our bill of rights?"[36] However, these maxims or standards may undermine the government that is designed to secure liberty:

> Recurrence to first principles does not substitute for well-constituted and effective government. In some cases, it may interfere. Does a constant emphasis on unalienable natural rights foster good citizenship or a sense of community? Does a constant emphasis on popular sovereignty foster responsible government? Does a constant emphasis on a right to abolish government foster the kind of popular support that any government needs? The Federalists did not doubt that these first principles are true, that they may be resorted to, that they provide the ultimate source and justification of government. The problem is that these principles, while true, can also endanger government. Even rational and well-constituted governments need and deserve a presumption of legitimacy and permanence. A bill of rights that presses these first principles to the fore tends to deprive government of that presumption.[37]

The First Congress was able to satisfy the demand for amendments without yielding on the question of the need for strong, effective republican government. The first ten amendments appended to the Constitution did not alter the structure of government, nor did they interfere with either the powers or the republican character of the Constitution. Instead of maxims, perpetual standards, or appeals to natural rights, the Bill of Rights consists of reasonably specific protections of civil rights drawn from historical experience, both in England and in America. Congressman Livermore, supporting an amendment to curtail the taxing power of the United States, characterized the amendments agreed to by the House as having no more value than a "pinch of snuff; they went to secure rights never in danger."[38] It remained for the judiciary, relying in a general way on Chief Justice Marshall's opinion in *Marbury v. Madison,* to prepare the way for the extraordinary judicial role we now associate with enforcement of the Bill or Rights and related amendments. This fact is laced with some irony, given Marshall's statement in the Virginia Ratifying Convention that the Virginia "bill of rights is merely recommendatory. Were it otherwise, the consequence would be that many laws which are found convenient would be unconstitutional."[39]

In spite of Madison's considering himself "bound in honor and in duty" to put desired amendments before the House, in the press of setting up the new government, the First Congress delayed its consideration of a bill of rights.[40] Congressman Goodhue argued against delay "because it is the wish of many of our constituents, that something should be added to the constitution, to secure in a stronger manner their liberties from the inroads of power."[41] But Mr. Vining opposed the amendments because they are "founded merely on speculative theory." He believed that the best way to quiet the public mind would be to "pass salutary laws; to give permanency and stability to constitutional regulations, founded on principles of equity and adjusted by wisdom."[42] Mr. Jackson opposed any amendments as premature. He wanted the benefit of "the sure ground of experience." Jackson argued that Congress should "fit out our vessel, set up her masts, and expand her sails, and be guided by the experiment in our alterations. If she sails upon an uneven keel, let us right her by adding weight where it is wanting." Premature action "may deface a beauty, or deform a well proportioned piece of workmanship."[43] Madison counseled caution in the amending process lest it result in a "re-consideration of the principles and the substance of the powers given" and thereby endanger the safety of the government itself. In a clear attempt to protect the structure and powers of the Constitution, Madison characterized the respectable opposition to the Constitution as animated by concern for "encroachments on particular rights, and those safeguards which they have been long accustomed to have interposed between them and the magistrate who exercises the sovereign power."[44]

The amendments that were passed—the Bill of Rights—are of the same character as those proposed by Madison. The Senate rejected a proposed amendment that would have prohibited states from violating equal rights of conscience, freedom of press, or trial by jury in criminal cases.[45] The states did not ratify two proposed amendments relating to the structure of government and the compensation of Congress. The Bill of Rights satisfied the opposition without altering the structure or powers of the national government, as some Anti-Federalists had wanted. The amendments satisfied Madison's concern that any alterations in the Constitution "give satisfaction, without injuring or destroying any of its vital principles."[46]

The Federalists insisted on giving full scope to the powers of government in order to secure liberty. The cornerstone of this liberty is the Constitution's strict republicanism, or its dependence on the people. It is instructive that freedom of speech, press, and assembly remain among the most cherished rights of the Bill of Rights and are so directly related to the task of enlightened self-government. It is a sober reminder of the republican basis of the Constitution that the document begins with "WE, THE PEOPLE" and the Bill of Rights concludes with a statement of powers reserved "to the people." Even though the Federalists insisted on strong government and were reluctant to rely on first principles in the operation of the government,[47] they still believed in the Declaration as embodying true principles and justification for government, as made clear by their inclusion of some of these principles in the original Constitution. But these fundamental principles should not be resorted to by the people in the everyday business of governing, as they might be if they were included within a bill of rights. To do so would impair powers necessary to effective government. Thus, our Bill of Rights consists of what Madison calls particular rights and safeguards to which the people "have been long accustomed." *The Federalist* tells us that in a nation of philosophers, "reverence for the laws would be sufficiently inculcated by the voice of an enlightened reason," but in every other nation, stability, tradition, and "prejudice" are advantageous to even the most rational government.[48] Madison framed amendments consistent with this aim rather than setting forth natural rights as limitations on government. The Bill of Rights was designed to preserve government's need for "a presumption of legitimacy and permanence."[49] As James Wilson put it, "Liberty has a formidable enemy on each hand; on one there is tyranny, on the other licentiousness."[50]

Patrick Henry, in the Virginia Ratifying Convention, had seen a bill of rights as more necessary "in this government than ever it was in any government before."[51] Colonel Varnum, in the Massachusetts Ratifying Convention, however, asked anyone "to produce an instance where any government, consisting of three branches, elected by the people, and having checks on each other, as this has, abused the power delegated to them,"[52] thereby affirming the necessity for strong government. The first ten amendments were consistent with Varnum's view, not with Henry's.

The Bill of Rights strikes a moderate, middle ground, avoiding maxims or perpetual standards such as reference to natural rights. It is also limited in its application to the national government, although Madison's proposed amendments included provisions that were not agreed to in Congress and that would have limited *state* action where rights of conscience, press, and jury trial in criminal cases were concerned. The Bill of Rights serves as an auxiliary safeguard against the powers of government, which, when enforced by an independent judiciary, helps secure traditional civil rights. To paraphrase Patrick Henry in a manner of which he would disapprove, without the Constitution's dependence on the people and its complex structure of government, the appended Bill of Rights would be worth little more than the paper it is written on. In the end, a bill of rights can neither save a republican people from itself nor substitute for the hard task of governing. Reliance on an independent judiciary to enforce natural rights through expansive interpretive powers refutes the wisdom of Hobbes, Locke, Montesquieu, the Constitution, and *The Federalist*. These all depend on a supreme legislative power to protect individual rights. *The Federalist* relies primarily on a strong national government, a supreme legislative power, separated powers, and a properly structured system of representation for this protection.

Democracy, Representation, and *The Federalist*

The Constitution creates a natural bridge between individual rights and consent of the governed. The framers relied primarily on nonjudicial means to secure popular government and individual rights. In *The Federalist*, Publius defends the apportionment of the members of the House of Representatives among the several states. The agreed standard for apportionment is that the number of representatives of each state should be proportionate to the state's population. This rule of apportionment in the House is "understood to refer to the personal rights of the people, with which it has a natural and universal connection."[53] The House is the most directly republican institution of the national government, a connection that Publius links to personal rights. This linking of republicanism to personal rights is central to *The Federalist*. Forty-eight of the eighty-five papers[54] are devoted to "the conformity of the proposed Constitution to the true principles of republican government."[55] The strictly republican nature of the Constitution is deduced from several considerations. Individuals who feel that their self-preservation and related rights are insecure are a potential threat to the government. If they do not regard their life, liberty, and property as secure, they may resort to rebellion in the name of the very self-preservation that justifies civil society. The arguments of self-preservation, the claim of equality, and the "genius of the American people" are strong arguments for extending the principle of majority rule and consent from the formation of the political order to the operation of the government. The strictly republican character of the Constitution exemplifies this extension in its provision for properly constituted majority rule, elevated and moderated by structures of government that are crucial supplements to representation. The House is most directly republican in nature. Republicanism is modified in the Senate to accommodate the previous sovereignty and equality of states; in the executive, to achieve unity and energy, and for other reasons; and in the judiciary, which is only remotely republican, to secure the "steady, upright, and impartial administration of the laws."[56] The role of the judiciary must be understood within the context of the goals and structures of a Constitution that is strictly republican and derives its powers from majority rule through representation.

The Federalist treats republican government in No. 10, which opens with a discussion of popular government's tendency toward instability and the violence of faction. Pure democracy is the form of popular government in which a small number of citizens "assemble and administer the government in person." A republic is the form of popular government "in which the scheme of representation takes place." A republic differs from a democracy because the responsibility of government is delegated to a number of citizens elected to represent the people. A republic allows for a greater number of citizens and may encompass a greater sphere of territory.[57] Because in a pure democracy all powers are accumulated in the hands of the many, it does not allow for a separation of powers into distinct departments, as does republican government.[58]

Republicanism, or representation, is crucial to the scheme of government developed in *The Federalist.* Because the Constitution frames a popular government, the primary concern of No. 10, and of *The Federalist* as a whole, is to avoid the vices of popular government, the primary of which is faction: "By a faction, I understand a number of citizens, whether amounting to a majority or minority of the whole, who are united and actuated by some common impulse of passion, or of interest, adverse to the rights of other citizens, or to the permanent and aggregate interests of the community."[59] Such factions, acting as unwise or overbearing majorities within a popular government, may act adversely either to the rights of others or to the interest of the community as a whole. The task of the Constitution, and the focus of *The Federalist,* is "to secure the public good and private rights against the danger of such a faction, and at the same time to preserve the spirit and the form of popular government" (57–58). Minority factions are controlled by the regular operation of majority rule. The problem is how to prevent majority factions from acting adversely to the rights of other citizens or to the public good (55).

Publius presents two means of curing the mischiefs of faction. The first is to remove its causes; the second is to control its effects. There are two methods of removing the *causes* of faction. One is to remove the liberty that gives rise to faction. But this liberty "is essential to political life" and must not be sacrificed, just as the air essential to animal life must not be annihilated because it gives fire its destructive capability. The second means of removing the causes of faction is to "give every citizen the same opinions, the same passions, and the same interests." But this is not practical:

> As long as the reason of man continues fallible, and he is at liberty to exercise it, different opinions will be formed. As long as the connection subsists between his reason and his self-love, his opinions and his passions will have a reciprocal influence on each other; and the former will be objects to which the latter will attach themselves. The diversity in the faculties of men, from which the rights of property originate, is not less an insuperable obstacle to a uniformity of interests. The protection of these faculties is the first object of government. From the protection of different and unequal faculties of acquiring property, the possession of different degrees and kinds of property immediately results; and from the influence of these on the sentiments and views of the respective proprietors, ensues a division of the society into different interests and parties.
>
> The latent causes of faction are thus sown in the nature of man. (54–55)

As long as liberty thrives and human nature remains as it is, including the imperfection of our reason, differing opinions will be formed, and opining will be influenced by passions and interests. The diversity of our faculties, including our reasoning faculty, gives rise to "possession of different degrees and kinds of property" (55). The amount and kinds of property we hold influence our sentiments and views. Citizens exercise these sentiments and views by means of their liberty to influence government through representation. The republican form of government is necessarily constructed so that the legislative power will "feel all the passions which actuate a multitude" (No. 48, p. 323).

Madison treats a number of objects of opinion that may result in faction, including religion, attachment to different political leaders, and even "fanciful distinctions" that have resulted in passion and conflict. "But the most common and durable source of factions has been the various and unequal distribution of property" (No. 10, pp. 55–56). This is particularly true in this large, commercial, Lockean republic, in which liberty is exercised in self-preservation and acquisition. Publius argues that unequal distribution of property produces class conflict, which convulses society by producing instability and factional violence between the few rich and the many poor. In a large, commercial republic, various kinds of property exist among "a landed interest, a manufacturing interest, a mercantile interest, a moneyed interest," and "many lesser interests." Economic factions, or interests, result from citizens forming themselves according to the various distribution of property or the type of property held. In a large enough, varied enough country, no one interest or faction constitutes a ruling majority. Publius does not depend on the market to produce the public good; rather, "the regulation of these various and interfering interests forms the principal task of modern legislation, and involves the spirit of party and faction in the necessary and ordinary operations of the government." He rejects as unreliable both "enlightened statesmen" and religious or moral motives to adjust these clashing interests and achieve justice.[60] He also opposes the hereditary monarch, so important to Hobbes and Montesquieu, as "creating a will in the community independent of the majority—that is, of the society itself."[61]

Publius's democratic solution to faction depends on a scheme of representation in a large commercial republic. Tocqueville recognizes that the "social power superior to all others must always be placed somewhere" and that "liberty is endangered when this power finds no obstacle which can retard its course and give it time to moderate its own vehemence."[62] Since the political order created by the Constitution places that social power superior to all others in the people, the solution to faction must first address the operation of the majority principle at the level of the democratic society itself. A pure democracy offers "no cure for the mischiefs of faction," for a "common passion or interest will in almost every case be felt by a majority of the whole."[63]

Relief from the bad effects of faction may be achieved through "ENLARGEMENT of the ORBIT within such systems are to revolve."[64] The Union is such an enlarged orbit. Fractions of it would not measure up to the standard:

> The smaller the society, the fewer probably will be the distinct parties and interests composing it; the fewer the distinct parties and interests, the more frequently will a majority be found of the same party; and the smaller the number of individuals composing a majority, and the smaller the compass within which they are placed, the more easily will they concert and execute their plans of oppression. Extend the sphere, and you take in a greater variety of parties and interests; you make it less probable that a majority of the whole will have a common motive to invade the rights of other citizens.[65]

The principle of representation, combined with enlarging the sphere of government to a large republic, creates the condition for replacing the struggle of classes by a struggle of interests: "The class struggle is a domestic convulsion; the struggle of interests is a safe, even energizing, struggle which is compatible with, or even promotes, the safety and stability of society." Martin Diamond further develops his interpretation of the Madisonian solution to faction by enumerating some of the conditions for its successful operation. The government and society must be profoundly democratic, citizens must be free to seek immediate gain, "there must be no rigid class barriers which bar men from the pursuit of immediate interest," and even the disadvantaged must have hope of economic and social gains.[66] The Great Depression and the New Deal provide the clearest example of the threatened emergence of a class struggle within the United States and the government's response to this through the "regulation of these various and interfering interests."[67]

The Federalist's treatment of representation indicates its posture toward democracy. Publius warns that "enlightened statesmen will not always be at the helm." Thus, he relies on a more dependable means of adjusting clashing interests—that of shifting or temporary majorities. Majorities rule through a scheme of representation in a political order characterized by a multiplicity of economic interests and religious sects, no one of which can command a majority. Nor does Publius depend on enlightened representatives in the legislative body to adjust these interests. Representatives may "refine and enlarge the public views" as they are passed "through the medium of a chosen body of citizens, whose wisdom may best discern the true interest of their country." The refining and enlarging effect may be inverted, however: "Men of factious tempers, of local prejudices, or of sinister designs" may betray the public interests. Representatives elected by the citizens of a large republic are more likely to "possess the most attractive merit." Although it "will not be denied that the representation of the Union will be most likely to possess" the desired "enlightened views and virtuous sentiments," it is principally the greater extent of territory and number of citizens that "renders factious combinations less to be dreaded" in a large republic.[68] In a later paper, Publius argues that no "form of representative government could have succeeded within the narrow limits occupied by the democracies of Greece."[69]

The Federalist does not deny enlightened statesmanship and the elevating and refining effects of representation as benefits of the Union. Instead, it relies primarily on the formation of a majority through the compromise and coalition of a variety of interests and sects that make up the extended territory of the Union. This is the bedrock on which the political order and theory of representation rest, that of conciliation of competing interests and sects through a properly constituted republic. We wish for wise statecraft and elevation and refinement through enlightened representation, but these qualities are not dependable. *The Federalist* instead depends on the principle identified by Tocqueville: "The principle of self-interest rightly understood is not a lofty one, but it is clear and sure. It does not aim at mighty objects, but attains without exertion all those at which it aims."[70]

The U.S. Constitution depends on this clear and sure foundation, a foundation that may be responsible for both our virtues and our shortcomings.

The safety net of our law and politics is provided by the operation of this self-interest and its adjustment through the scheme of representation as well as the auxiliary safeguards of the Constitution. It is unlikely that the law will fall below it, and we anticipate that, periodically, it may rise above self-interest. But self-interest and its representation are the primary protections of private rights and the public good.

If enlightened statecraft is not responsible for identifying and pursuing the public good, and if representatives cannot be depended upon to forsake "local prejudices," "sinister designs," and "factious tempers,"[71] one may properly ask where is the repository of the public good? Publius addresses this issue in the context of his discussion of the Senate in No. 63, in which he states that the Senate, with its six-year terms, may act as "a defence to the people against their own temporary errors and delusions":

> As the cool and deliberate sense of the community ought, in all governments, and actually will, in all free governments, ultimately prevail over the views of its rulers; so there are particular moments in public affairs when the people, stimulated by some irregular passion, or some illicit advantage, or misled by the artful misrepresentations of interested men, may call for measures which they themselves will afterwards be the most ready to lament and condemn. In these crucial moments, how salutary will be the interference of some temperate and respectable body of citizens, in order to check the misguided career, and to suspend the blow meditated by the people against themselves, until reason, justice, and truth can regain their authority over the public mind?[72]

The public good—what Publius regards as resulting from "the mild voice of reason"[73]—finally depends on the public mind. If the public mind is temporarily misled by passion, illicit advantage, or demagogues, the representative mechanism can suspend the blow, but only for about four years when two elections provide the opportunity to replace two-thirds of the Senate. What some call "stalemate"[74] or "deadlock"[75] is more accurately described by Tocqueville: Liberty is endangered if the final social power (under our Constitution, the people) is not retarded and given time to moderate its own vehemence. If the people persist in undermining the public good, neither this nor any other governmental mechanism can save the people from themselves. The repository of the public good is the people themselves, governing through representative institutions. The institutions themselves cannot resist the will of a majority. If that will is sustained for a sufficient length of time, the institutions of government will be ruled by it. Even in the case of the Supreme Court, its legitimacy comes from the appointment and ratification process, and from the Court's carrying out the sober will of the people as represented in the Constitution. Congress has control over the appellate jurisdiction of the Court, and the people can alter or abolish even the Bill of Rights by acting through constitutionally defined mechanisms of majority rule, even if enlightened opinion regards this as unwise.

The process of constitutional ratification sparked conflict over the practical concern of how representation might achieve the public good and private rights. Concern was voiced that House members, elected for two-year terms, were "subject to no instructions" and were otherwise too far removed from their constituents to reflect or replicate accurately the views of those who elected them to Congress.[76] This issue was resurrected in the First Congress when Mr. Tucker moved to insert into the proposed Bill of Rights a provision to protect the right of the people "to instruct their Representatives."[77] A number of objections were immediately voiced to the proposal. It was argued that under the provisions of the Constitution, those elected would know the interests and circumstances of their constituents, and that the division of the legislative power into two houses was a protection against error. Although public opinion is generally respectable, it can issue wrong instructions when the people's passions are excited. It was also objected that a representative body from the whole Union would be more attached to the general interests than would the constituency of a single district, because a partial view is not necessarily conducive to comprehending the common good; instructions would be utterly destructive of an independent and deliberative body. Madison observed that Tucker's objective is sufficiently provided for in protections of speech and press, by which means constituents' sentiments and views may be communicated to representatives. The right to instruct representatives may lead to instructions to violate the Constitution, however. Is a representative "at liberty to obey such instructions?"[78] Mr. Stone objected that the proposal would change the government "from a representative one to a democracy, wherein all laws are made immediately by the voice of the people."[79] The proposal for "instructions" was soundly defeated.[80]

This debate and the theory of *The Federalist* concluded that although "the representative ought to be acquainted with the interests and circumstances of his constituents,"[81] representatives' sentiments and views should not be "an exact miniature of [those of] their constituents."[82] The aim of the Constitution is to have rulers who possess "wisdom to discern and virtue to pursue the common good."[83] According to this view, representation "refines and enlarges the public views."[84] The check on this wisdom and virtue is a limitation on the term of office, or accountability to the electorate.[85] The founders attempted to establish both "reflective" and "refining" representation through "enough popular influence for republican safety and enough refinement and competence for good administration."[86] But this refinement is always subject to the accountability of the people through their sovereignty and through the institutions they establish for actualizing consent of the governed in the operation of government. This consent is for two years in the House, four years in the executive, and six years in the Senate. Whatever "refinement" and "enlargement" can take place within these limitations of popular consent is constitutionally acceptable. To go much beyond this allowance for refinement would violate the strictly republican character of the Constitution and the sovereignty of the people as understood by *The Federalist.* The achievement of justice is problematic, in terms of both discerning it and giving it effect. The ultimate judge of what justice is and how to give it effect is the people, operating within a strictly republican government. The approximations to justice that we achieve under the Constitution are rooted in the conception of private rights, interests, and the public good held by each citizen and formed by reason, with its attending passion and interest, which the structure of the Constitution attempts to moderate and elevate.

The Federalist values the rule of law that is fundamental to the theories of Hobbes, Locke, and Montesquieu. The Constitution reflects the procedural protection of rights found in Locke. The architecture of our constitutional mechanisms is provided by Montesquieu's dependence on institutions to protect liberty, but without the mixed elements found in his regime of liberty. As Madison states in the Constitutional Convention: "the great fabric to be raised would be more stable and durable if it should rest on the solid foundation of the people themselves, than if it should stand merely on the pillars of the Legislatures."[87] Thus, in a departure from earlier theorists and from the English constitution, the people, not parliament, are sovereign under the U.S. Constitution. An indication of lessons learned from Hobbes and Locke is the necessity of a strong government empowered to govern. Although the Constitution is designed to secure liberty, *The Federalist* argues that "that liberty may be endangered by the abuses of liberty as well as by the abuses of power; that there are numerous instances of the former as well as of the latter; and that the former, rather than the latter, are apparently most to be apprehended by the United States."[88] Our system of representative government, in which the representatives are elected, is structured to secure both private rights and the public good. The representative structure is intricately designed because it cannot set forth the precise actions that representatives should or should not take when they confront unforeseen exigencies. It is a fitting conclusion to this treatment of democracy and representation in a large commercial republic to quote Publius on the relationship between representative government and the rights of the people: "[T]he whole power of the proposed government is to be in the hands of the representatives of the people. This is the essential, and after all the only efficacious security for the rights and privileges of the people, which is attainable in civil society."[89]

This is the most profound meaning of a constitution intended to endure for ages. As *The Federalist* shows, the Constitution rejects a number of solutions to the problems of balancing private rights and the pubic good and preventing the violence of faction. It rejects a weak government, it rejects destroying the liberty that gives rise to faction and giving all citizens the same opinions, and it rejects "creating a will in the community independent of the majority."[90] Instead, it adopts a strictly "republican remedy for the diseases most incident to republican government."[91] This is the only security for the rights of the people that is attainable in a republican government.

Separation of Powers

Separation of powers is the leading institutional mechanism of the Constitution through which representative majorities govern. These mechanisms were designed to provide for a strong government and to protect individual rights. The judiciary has a place within these structures and mechanisms that is important to understand if the proper, balanced role of the courts is to be preserved. The judiciary was not by itself entrusted with the solemn task of preserving individual rights, but rather the complex system of government in its entirety was designed to secure the public good and private rights.

Separation of powers is particularly important in defining the role of the judiciary and its relationship to individual rights. The doctrine of separated powers is linked to the Constitution's provisions for a strictly republican system of representation. The former both makes possible and refines the latter.[92] For Montesquieu, the separation of powers provides a place for democracy, aristocracy, and monarchy in a regime with a separated judiciary. In the wholly popular government framed by the Constitution, representation separates the ruling power in a way that would not be possible in a purely democratic political order where a small number of citizens "assemble and administer the government in person."[93] Separation of powers also directly depends on the particular scheme of representation in the Constitution to achieve its ends. Because separation of powers rests on a majoritarian foundation, it is dependent on "a prior weakening of the force applied" against it through the scheme of a multiplicity of economic interests and religious sects, which addresses the problem of faction at the level of the society itself. Once this force is moderated or weakened, the legal mechanisms of separated powers and checks and balances within the legislature provide additional protection by retarding and thus refining (but not preventing) the will of the majority.[94]

One of the ways separation of powers works to refine majority will is through the different constituencies that form the basis for the expression of majority will in the different institutions of government. Majorities are formed in different ways in elections for the House, the Senate, and the presidency. As majorities form within a congressional district, within the statewide senatorial electorate (now, but not originally, a wholly popular election), and in the state-wide electoral college system, shifting majorities elect officials in an expression of popular will that reflects the complexity of popular opinion and interests. This refinement of the popular will is furthered through the differing terms of office for members of the House and Senate and for the president. The result of this mechanism provides for refinement of majority rule, of "that social power superior to all others," and gives it "time to moderate its own vehemence."[95] Moderation rather than prevention of the will of the final social power is the key to the strict republicanism of the system, even to the rather complex mechanisms through which the majority may soberly amend or alter the Constitution itself.

This is well illustrated by the Constitution's protection of religious freedom through the Union's encompassing a multiplicity of religious sects. *Federalist* No. 10 addresses this issue when it argues that the "variety of sects" spread across the proposed Union will prevent the formation of a sectarian political faction.[96] But the separation of powers can work only when the majority political faction is broken at the level of the society itself. If a religious sect captures the spirit and support of a majority, this majority can all too soon become a political faction by electing favored candidates to the House, the presidency, and the Senate. This leaves just the judiciary and the First Amendment's religion clauses to prevent denials of religious freedom. But this same majority, if sufficiently sustained, can indirectly affect the makeup of the Supreme Court or change the First Amendment through the constitutionally required mechanism. Thus, the success of the separation of powers depends on the social and political foundations explained in *Federalist* No. 10.

The familiar explanation of the separation of powers emphasizes the level of government itself. Power is divided so that no one ruling body can deny the citizens' liberty. In the context of discussing Montesquieu and the separation of powers, *The Federalist* equates "the accumulation of all powers, legislative, executive, and judiciary, in the same hands" with "the very definition of tyranny."[97] Separation of powers protects the liberty of the individual in ways that, as we saw earlier, led Locke to recommend separating the legislative and executive powers.[98] Montesquieu regards the judicial power as potentially a "terrible" one because it tries the causes of individuals and deprives them of liberty; therefore, he advocates a tripartite separation of powers in addition to the balancing of social factions in a bicameral legislature.[99] The legislative, executive, and judicial branches must concur in deprivations of individual liberty. The foundation is the bicameral legislature's rule of law, but the executive and judicial branches must play their part as the general and prospective statements of the legislature are immediately executed and retrospectively adjudicated as they focus on the individual. The prospective, immediate, and retrospective perspectives and timing of the three branches of government are important results of separating the institutions of government and tempering the power of government in the interest of a just restriction and protection of liberty. The legislative, executive, and judicial powers were also designed to allow officeholders to judge the constitutionality of the legislation, execution, and adjudication of law as the respective branches of government fulfill their constitutional functions. Rights are thereby protected by this separation, as well as by provisions in the Constitution that limit all three branches of government.

The separation of powers protects against not only "tyranny over the people" but also tyrannical and incompetent government by the democratic majority itself.[100] Bicameralism, the separation of powers, and the features discussed above, as well as checks and balances, moderate the formation of public policy in a valuable way. As George Washington is reported to have said to Thomas Jefferson over breakfast, in response to the latter's protest against a bicameral legislature: " 'Why did you pour that coffee into your saucer?' 'To cool it,' replied Jefferson. 'Even so,' said Washington, 'we pour legislation into the senatorial saucer to cool it.' "[101] Factious or unwise majorities must work through the mechanism of the separation of powers in order to convert their opinion into governing law. The Constitution creates a strong executive that is limited by the representative principle but has sufficient powers set forth in the Constitution to be an important source of energy and power in the national government. The judiciary's independence allows exercise of its function free from undue interference.

Rather than weakening the national government, separation allows for a strong government by making the powerful branches of government safe through both their separation from and their interaction with one another. The famous essay on the separation of powers, *Federalist* No. 51, bases the institutional mechanism on giving the officers of each department "the necessary constitutional means and personal motives to resist encroachments of the others."[102] The constitutional means consist of sufficient legal powers to carry out the functions assigned to each branch of government. The personal motives are given play by ambition countering ambition among the branches of government. Ambition is best understood in the context of Publius's statement that "the love of fame" is the "ruling passion of the noblest minds."[103] Ambition exists within the same rubric as love of fame. Self-interest will prevent officeholders from exercising their powers in ways that are servile or foolish in following the immediate wishes of either a factious or unwise majority or another branch of government. The prestige or fame of the officeholder will be enhanced by the proper action and exercise of constitutional powers.[104] *The Federalist's* discussion of separation of powers is firmly rooted in the view that human beings are not angels. But in the context of this discussion, the primary control of government is "dependence on the people." Separation of powers and checks and balances are "auxiliary precautions."[105] In a strictly republican political order, no mechanism can save a people from itself. In the long run, majority opinion will win out. "Our government," Abraham Lincoln said, "rests upon public opinion. Whoever can change public opinion can change the government practically just so much."[106] *The Federalist*'s view that we are not angels applies to all three branches of government, including the judiciary. It counsels against giving courts powers of "enlightened statesmen" to create unenumerated rights or to enforce rights not reasonably derived from the Constitution's specific provisions.

Besides protecting against an accumulation of the ruling power in the same hands, the separation of powers also secures the public good by providing an institutional home for qualities necessary to good government. Madison enumerates these qualities in *Federalist* No. 37: "Among the difficulties encountered by the convention, a very important one must have lain in combining the requisite stability and energy in government, with the inviolable attention due to liberty and to the republican form."[107] Publius believes that the "genius of republican liberty" requires that the sovereign power of the people be entrusted to representatives for only a short duration and that this trust be placed in a number of hands. This is clearly the case in the House of Representatives. The genius of republican government must be balanced with stability. If stability is to be achieved, the officeholders in whose hands power is placed must continue to serve for a length of time. Terms in the House are two years; in the Senate, six years—a length of term that is healthy in general but particularly necessary to stable international relations. The two houses of the bicameral legislature are designed to be as dissimilar from each other as is consistent "with the genuine principles of republican government" so that they cannot concur in "sinister combinations."[108] Energy comes from the duration of the executive power, the placing of it in a single executive,[109] and the fact that the executive is not elected by the legislature. Energy is of such importance that Publius later refers to it as "a leading character in the definition of good government."[110] The Executive, the House, and the Senate bring needed qualities of republicanism, stability, energy, and competency to government, which are made possible by their "standing on as different foundations as republican principles will well admit," and which are "at the same time accountable to the society over which they are placed."[111] Perhaps because it is not accountable to the society, as are the elected officers of government, the judiciary is not included in this discussion.[112] *The Federalist*'s insistence on accountability to the people through a representative scheme with separated powers undermines the claims of those who advocate a judicial power that goes beyond the provisions of a written constitution, even when this overreaching is motivated by a desire to protect individual rights. Advocacy of such a power is particularly objectionable if it interferes with the elements of good government derived from strong legislative and executive powers.

Separation of powers is a constitutional mechanism through which representative majorities govern and was designed both to provide for a strong government and to protect individual rights. The judiciary is only one part of the system designed to preserve individual rights, and its role must be consistent with the system as a whole in order to provide durable protection for the public good and private rights. Although separation of powers retards and refines majority rule, it was not designed to obstruct it. There is little if any indication from the theory of separated powers that the Supreme Court was intended to be the final judge of all powers of the other branches or of the rights protected by the Constitution.

The judiciary should not act in a manner that either obstructs the strictly republican nature of the Constitution or upsets the balance of powers by using its independence to establish rights that are not fairly inferable from the Constitution and its principles. Although the judiciary must have a measure of independence, it was not designed to be an external force independent of republican principles. Likewise, the legislative and executive powers must have their measure of independence from judicial domination if other salutary features of the government are to be preserved. Public opinion and majority will, properly moderated, are more fundamental constitutional principles than is the claim for completely independent judges. An appreciation of the way in which security of private rights and the furtherance of the public good are promoted through the mechanism of the separation of powers is essential to understanding how the Constitution as a whole protects rights; therefore, it is also necessary to ascertaining the proper role of the judiciary in relation to rights. If the judiciary exceeds its proper constitutional role, it may undermine the delicate system of separated powers, which relies heavily on representation and constitutional structures designed to secure the public good and private rights. But the Constitution's doctrine of enumerated powers and federalism also plays a role in perpetuating individual rights. Judicial overreaching may also erode important benefits of decentralized power—what we call our system of quasi-federalism. Thus, the judicial protection of rights must be understood in relationship not only to separated powers, but to enumerated powers and federalism as well.

Enumerated Powers and Federalism

We have seen that one purpose of a strong national government and separated powers is to preserve rights under government. However seductive visions of the state of nature may be, rights there are utterly insecure. The price of security is limitations on the rights of nature, limitations imposed by the sovereign people as outlined in Locke and in the U.S. Constitution. These limitations are primarily procedural and largely directed toward the legislative power. A powerful national government has been realized through expansive interpretations of enumerated powers by the legislative, executive, and judicial branches, which in some cases have substantially eroded powers of the states and localities. The problem with this expansive interpretation is that the preservation of rights is also an important benefit of enumerated powers and federalism. These doctrines leave some nonenumerated powers not affecting the whole to states and localities, thereby nurturing individual rights in a manner quite independent of a far-reaching national judicial power. An overreaching judicial power may centralize or nationalize many policy issues in the name of preserving rights and thus undermining the political and social basis of the very rights it is attempting to protect. My treatment of enumerated powers will conclude, as did the discussion of separated powers, that the whole of our constitutional fabric is designed to secure rights. Dependence on the Supreme Court as the peculiar guardian of rights may interfere with constitutional principles necessary to nurture and preserve such rights.

I do not argue for some vast reservoir of states' rights that requires stripping the national government of necessary powers in the name of federalism. Indeed, separation of powers and the multiplicity of economic interests clearly require that the national system in which they work possess sufficient powers. If powers essential to this scheme are left to the states—particularly those powers essential to the Constitution's solution of the problem of distributive justice concerning property and related matters—the system is simply a theoretical construct and doomed to failure. But the Constitution does not require that every aspect of our political system or our administration of criminal or retributive justice be nationalized.[113] It designed a system that is partly national and partly federal and serves a number of important political ends, including the preservation of rights.

Publius argues in No. 14 that the powers given to the national government should be unlimited because of the impossibility of foreseeing or defining the exigencies that may confront the nation; consequently, national powers should not be constitutionally shackled. It is essential "to discriminate the OBJECTS, as far as it can be done, which shall appertain to the different provinces or departments of power; allowing to each the most ample authority for fulfilling the objects committed to its charge." It would "violate the most obvious rules of prudence and propriety" if the means of power necessary to the objects of national government were not granted to each department.[114] But the objects of national power are "limited to certain enumerated objects." The subordinate governments, or states, retain "their due authority and activity" where other objects of government are concerned.[115]

As for the "necessary and proper" clause, without the substance of this power, "the whole Constitution would be a dead letter."[116] Publius argues that even without this clause, the substance of the powers it grants would result "by unavoidable implication" (294). If the Congress misconstrues this clause and exercises unwarranted powers, "the remedy is the same as if they should misconstrue or enlarge any other power vested in them" by the Constitution: "In the first instance, the success of the usurpation will depend on the executive and judiciary departments, which are to expound and give effect to the legislative acts; and in the last resort a remedy must be obtained from the people, who can, by the election of more faithful representatives, annul the acts of the usurpers" (294–95). The first check on usurpation is the separation of powers, as the executive and judiciary fulfill their constitutional functions of executing and adjudicating the laws, activities that assume the primacy of law. As John Marshall put it in the Virginia Ratifying Convention, if the government of the United States "were to make a law not warranted by any of the powers enumerated, it would be considered by the judges as an infringement of the Constitution which they are to guard. They would not consider such a law as coming under their jurisdiction. They would declare it void."[117] Marshall is speaking here of the judiciary, but much of what he says also applies to the executive power as it carries out its constitutional function.

Separation of powers may fail to check usurpation of power by the national government. If so, *The Federalist*'s fundamental remedy is the strictly republican one of electing representatives who will restore fidelity to the *"enumerated and legitimate* objects"[118] of national power and the means necessary and proper to achieve them. Although it would be inconsistent with the theory of *The Federalist* to interpret the broad enumerated powers restrictively, there are limits to national power. These limits arise from the constitutional design and are justified both by that design and by the political benefits they produce. Under the Tenth Amendment, the powers neither delegated to the national government nor prohibited by the Constitution's limitations on the states are left to the states or to the people.

Publius presents a centralist view of enumerated powers in *Federalist* No. 17. National powers over "commerce, finance, negotiation, and war" are the objects that "have charms for minds governed" by love of power. Regulating the "mere domestic police of a State" holds out "slender allurements to ambition." Later in this paper, he argues that citizens will be more attached to the governments closer to them than to the Union, "unless the force of that principle should be destroyed by a much better administration of the latter" (101–3).

Judging from the expansive interpretations of enumerated powers—perhaps because of "better administration," perhaps because some powers that appeared in 1787 to have only statewide or local significance have now taken on national significance—the "mere domestic police" powers of the states have been substantially eroded. This erosion has been the result of national legislative, executive and judicial action.

Publius treats enumerated powers in No. 39, where he discusses the objection of the Constitution's adversaries that the Convention ought "to have preserved the *federal form*, which regards the Union as a *Confederacy* of sovereign states; instead of which, they have framed a *national* government which regards the Union as a *consolidation* of the States." There is a substantial element of truth in the admonition of the Constitution's adversaries. Publius later admits in No. 39 that the "national countenance" of the proposed Constitution "seems to be disfigured by a few federal features" (245–48). The truth in the adversaries' objection is directly addressed in No. 23, where Publius argues for the "absolute necessity for an entire change in the first principles of the system" that had operated under the federal structure of the Articles of Confederation (143).

The need for a change in "first principles" in order to achieve the ends of Union is evident from *The Federalist*'s discussion of confederation in No. 9, in which the characteristics of confederation are defined and then dismissed as having caused "incurable disorder and imbecility in the government" (52). In the opening sentence of *The Federalist*, Publius refers to "the inefficiency of the subsisting federal government" (3), that is, the federal government existing under the Articles of Confederation. The characteristics of confederation, or a truly federal government,[119] are, first, "restriction of its authority to the members in their collective capacities"; second, no interference with "any object of internal administration" within the member states; and third, each member state's having an "exact equality of suffrage."[120]

Publius characterizes the proposed Constitution, according to the above definition, as "neither a national nor a federal Constitution, but a composition of both."[121] This composition will subsequently be referred to as a "quasi-federal system."[122] Publius supports his conclusion that the Constitution is a composition of both national and federal characteristics by a careful argument regarding the foundation, the sources from which governmental power is derived, the operation, the extent of power, and the method of amendment prescribed by the Constitution.

The *foundation* of the government is the "assent and ratification of the people of America," who consent to the Constitution through "deputies elected for this special purpose." Because the proposed Union requires "the unanimous assent of the several States that are parties to it" and is based on the voluntary act of the people of each state, Madison describes the *foundation* as federal, not national.[123]

The *sources* from which governmental powers are drawn are national in the case of the House which is elected directly by the people; the Senate, providing for equal representation of each state, is federal. The executive power is derived from a compound of national and federal elements because of the manner in which votes are allocated in the electoral college system and the contingency provision for the House to elect the president through the vote of individual delegations from each state. Publius characterizes the government's *operation* as primarily national because it is empowered to act directly on the individual as opposed to operating only on the states. The *extent* of constitutional powers is federal because "its jurisdiction extends to certain enumerated objects only, and leaves to the several States a residuary and inviolable sovereignty over all other objects." But Publius adds that the tribunal that will ultimately decide on the boundary between national and state powers is national.

The *amending* process is again a compound of national and federal elements. It is not wholly national, because a majority of the people of the Union may not amend the Constitution, only three-fourths of the states qua states. But the concurrence of each state is not necessary, as it would be under a truly federal system. Thus, the amending process in neither truly national nor truly federal.[124]

The *structure* of the national government has some federal elements within it. The most obvious example is the Senate, where each state is equally represented. Publius also points toward other authentic federal elements in the foundation, the sources and extent of powers, and the amending process. In this complex structural mechanism, there is a limited federal influence. No matter what policy is considered by Congress—even policy that surpasses enumerated powers and the "necessary and proper" clause—the Senate possesses a federal character that has the potential to protect the interests of state powers (whether or not it is actually used that way in contemporary matters is a separate question). The executive power is derived from a more complicated structure that partakes of some elements of authentic federalism, although unraveling the effects of this structure would be extraordinarily difficult. What is clear, at least since the New Deal, is that a determined Congress and president are not likely to encounter strong resistance from the judiciary when they effect policy that strains the doctrine of enumerated powers.[125] The Supreme Court is not included in the discussion of the national and federal characteristics of the Constitution, except in the discussion of the national tribunal, which is described as having the power "ultimately to decide" the boundary between the jurisdictions of the national and state powers.[126] This power is essential for the national government if the plan for the large commercial republic is to be protected from state incursions.

The Federalist sets forth a powerful argument for a strong national government with powers sufficient to meet national exigencies. But the residual elements of a federal, or decentralizing, character deserve further treatment.

Martin Diamond is perhaps the most thoughtful analyst of the *The Federalist*'s insistence upon a strong national government and the advantages that arise from the residual powers of the states and the authentically federal structural features of the Constitution. Drawing heavily on Tocqueville, he argues that the political effects of the partly national, partly federal Constitution produce a healthy decentralization of government that serves a number of salutary purposes.[127]

The key to the beneficial effects Tocqueville attributes to the peculiar compound of national and federal characteristics in the Constitution is the delegation of the "general business" of the country to the national government while leaving "the particular affairs of a district" to the people who live there, "people who are always meeting" and who "are forced to know and adapt themselves to one another."[128] Under the doctrine of reserved powers, the states and localities are not just administrative arms effecting national policy; they have the power to both formulate and administer policy as they exercise their constitutionally reserved powers.

Tocqueville treats one beneficial effect of decentralization in his chapter entitled "How the Americans Combat the Effects of Individualism by Free Institutions."[129] Individualism, or isolation of one citizen from another, may result from both equality and despotism. Equal citizens may exist "without a common link" to bind them. Despotism constructs barriers to keep citizens apart and creates an isolationist indifference. Combating the effects of individualism is particularly important in democracy, where despotism is "particularly to be feared." When public officials are elected, self-interest drives the office seeker to "care for his fellows, and in a sense, he often finds his self-interest in forgetting about himself." The free system of elections also "forges permanent links between a great number of citizens who might otherwise have remained forever strangers to one another." This principle is multiplied through state and local elections and through the participation of local citizens in public affairs, a multiplication made possible and meaningful by the Constitution's giving "each part of the land its own political life so that there should be an infinite number of occasions for the citizens to act together and so that every day they should feel that they depended on one another."[130] The reserving to the states and localities of what Hamilton calls "mere domestic police" powers may hold "slender allurements"[131] to Hamilton's notion of ambition, but Tocqueville regards these reserved powers as critical to combating the individualism dangerous to democratic liberty. The content of the policy itself is not the critical consideration, according to Tocqueville. He is concerned that citizens participate in formulating policy and become involved in public concerns, during which process the citizens learn the bearing of public matters on private interests: "Thus, far more may be done by entrusting citizens with the management of minor affairs than by handing over control of great matters, toward interesting them in the public welfare and convincing them that they constantly stand in need of one another in order to provide for it."[132]

The elevation of individualism to a self-interested public concern is closely related to Tocqueville's treatment of rights. The American hybrid of federalism is important both to rights and to combating individualism. He describes rights as "the conception of virtue applied to the world of politics," for rights serve as the very definition of license and tyranny without which society must be governed by "force alone."[133] Rights enjoy security in the United States because they are linked with self-interest, "the only stable point in the human heart." This link depends on the elements of federalism in the Constitution as well as on other features of American society. Through the reservation of powers over state and local matters, citizens participate in government in a manner that teaches them the use of rights:

> One can see how this works among children, who are men except in strength and in experience; when a baby first begins to move among things outside himself, instinct leads him to make use of anything his hands can grasp; he has no idea of other people's property, not even that it exists; but as he is instructed in the value of things and discovers that he too may be despoiled, he becomes more circumspect, and in the end is led to respect for others that which he wishes to be respected for himself.[134]

This same process leads citizens to value the idea of rights as they participate in government. They begin with an attachment to their own rights and then learn respect for the rights of others as local and state governments make policy that affects property and rights. Just as decentralized self-government "makes the idea of political rights penetrate right down to the least of citizens," a widespread conception of property rights results from the dissemination of property across society.[135] The idea of rights is buttressed by the decentralization of the lawmaking power over local and state matters to those most directly affected by policies that do not affect the great national interests. But these rights are anchored in self-interest, out of which grows a recognition of the rights of others. This recognition is the result of deliberation over policy and the knowledge that the interests of others are also affected by government policy. The idea of rights is inculcated, in part, through the decentralization that results from the federal elements in the Constitution, including the doctrine of enumerated powers.[136] But these benefits of the American doctrine of quasi-federalism must be understood in light of the Constitution's predominantly national character. Tocqueville's arguments do not necessarily mean that the Court has a peculiar responsibility for achieving these benefits, but he presents persuasive political reasons for the national government to weigh carefully the benefits of our system of decentralized federalism as it formulates policy that affects the powers of the states.

Both a strong national government with separated powers and a respect for the role that decentralized powers and federalism play in preserving rights are necessary to the Constitution's theory of securing the public good and private rights. State and local powers have been substantially eroded by the national government. In some cases, this is consistent with the Constitution's theory. But widespread erosion of this power may interfere with the good effects of decentralization that Tocqueville so persuasively describes. Congress is most often the proper authority to weigh the salutary effects of decentralizing federalism against national necessities. Although it sometimes falls to the Court to determine the boundary between national and state powers, this determination should give great weight to the coordinate branches of government. The Supreme Court should also be wary of nationalizing state and local matters in the name of expanding the rights of individuals. Such judicial nationalization may destroy important effects of federalism and decentralism, which Tocqueville believes nurture such rights. Judicial nationalization is objectionable unless it is justified by the Constitution's provisions or by other rights established by law. The Constitution is not a blank check that the Court can make payable at its own discretion to litigants claiming that their rights have been violated. To do so upsets the intricate constitutional mechanisms of separation of powers, enumerated powers, and quasi-federalism, all of which contribute to securing the public good and individual rights in a strictly republican political order.

Chapter Three

The Role of the Judiciary

We have examined the Constitution's theory in order to discover the proper role for the judiciary and its relationship to individual rights. This theory provides no support for the Court's power to lay down an absolute rule governing all branches of government or to create individual rights that are not specified in the Constitution. The Court's proper business is to decide cases according to law. This interpretation is supported by the strictly republican theory of the Constitution as presented in *The Federalist*. The following discussion of the role of the judiciary relies heavily on *The Federalist,* the *Records of the Federal Convention,* the state ratifying conventions, and the *Annals of Congress*. The purpose of this examination, following the doctrine of legitimacy derived from the consent of the governed, is to determine the judicial role to which consent was given and that was embodied in the Constitution. This role is not only the product of the consent of the governed; it is also a sound role consistent with the political good and the nature of politics. A proper understanding of this role, coupled with a coherent constitutional theory, should reveal a role for the Court that is consistent with the Constitution's scheme for securing the public good and individual rights within a republican government. The historical record helps define the judicial role to which consent was given.

The sources examined emphasize the Supreme Court's role in statutory construction, constitutional construction, and the balance of powers and its relationship to a strictly republican Constitution. This chapter proceeds from the principle, supported in earlier chapters, that the whole of the political system and its republican character are the primary safeguards of political rights and that the people are superior in power to the legislature and the judiciary, which are products of the Constitution that the sovereign people established. This sovereignty is underscored by the people's power to amend or abolish the Constitution. Although a strong judicial power is essential to a completion of the national government's power, this does not mean that the Supreme Court is empowered to lay down an absolute rule of conduct for all branches of government or to create rights. Certain of the framers intended for the Supreme Court to void legislative acts that were clearly in conflict with the Constitution, and such a power is consistent with the republican theory underlying the Constitution. But the boundaries of this power of judicial review give it a more precise meaning. This power is particularly problematic because it is not easily derived from the Constitution's text; therefore, the Constitution's theory and the recorded statements of those who put the government into motion assume particular importance. Distinctions must be drawn between the power to decide a particular case and that of laying down a rule for the resolution of future cases. The impeachment power deserves explanation and definition, since the term "good behavior" is so broad.

Given the lack of dispositive textual support for judicial review, it is necessary to explore the practices antecedent to the Constitution in which some state courts voided legislative acts. These antecedents were one influence on the framers' understanding of judicial power. Our quest is one of identifying the pure judicial power that was embodied in the Constitution prior to the gloss put on that power by subsequent Court decisions, which we now regard as the authoritative law of the Constitution. Was the judiciary regarded as a body of statesmen, the peculiar guardian of individual rights and justice, that should be guided by standards beyond the specific powers and prohibitions laid out in the Constitution? This is a critical question in a political order repeatedly characterized as strictly republican. In sum, the historical record suggests a pure judicial power that was narrower than that of setting forth absolute rules for all branches of government and creating unenumerated rights of individuals. The historical record upon which this chapter relies so heavily is examined in order to help resolve these issues.

The Federalist and Judicial Power

Federalist No. 81 lays bare the conflict between judicial review and democratic government:

> The power of construing the laws according to the *spirit* of the Constitution, will enable that court [the Supreme Court] to mould them into whatever shape it may think proper; especially as its decisions will not be in any manner subject to the revision or correction of the legislative body. . . .
> In the first place, there is not a syllable in the plan under consideration which *directly* empowers the national courts to construe the laws according to the spirit of the Constitution . . . . I admit, however, that the Constitution ought to be the standard of construction for the laws, and that wherever there is an evident opposition, the laws ought to give place to the Constitution.[1]

The strictly republican character of the Constitution is embodied in Congress, which represents the sovereign people. The Constitution empowers and limits the three branches of government it creates. If the representative Congress is not limited, then the goal of a limited Constitution may be impeded and potentially become a mockery. But Congress, in representing the sovereign will of the people as expressed on the first Tuesday after the first Monday in November, may be thwarted by the Supreme Court. The exercise of judicial review is particularly questionable if its obstruction of the representative will of Congress is not clearly prohibited by constitutional provisions but is simply the Court's preference for a public policy it regards as superior to that enacted by Congress.

The conflict between democratic will and constitutional limitations cannot be resolved by the extremes of either congressional *or* judicial hegemony. It is much easier to reject the extremes than to find a balanced middle ground that is consistent with the theory of the Constitution. My attempt to arrive at a balance consistent with this theory requires substantial reference to and quotation from *The Federalist* and other materials that will assist the reader in weighing the evidence presented. In some instances in which I quote selectively, I have provided fuller contexts in notes so that the reader may better judge whether my interpretation is accurate.

The Constitution makes no direct provision for judicial review. It provides for executive appointment of Supreme Court justices and other federal judges, for Senate confirmation, and for congressional regulation of both the organization of the judiciary and the appellate jurisdiction of the Supreme Court. The brevity of Article III and the Constitution's lack of direct provision for judicial review are two reasons for the extensive commentary on the judicial role, commentary that has ranged from endorsement of a wide latitude for judicial review and for a powerful judicial role to skepticism about how extensive the judicial power ought to be, given its potential inconsistency with democracy. Textual support for judicial review is inferred and tenuous; even that derived from the supremacy clause is ambiguous. As Alexander Bickel demonstrates, the Constitution supports the power of judicial review over state actions much more strongly than it does judicial review of coordinate branches of the national government.[2] In any event, the doctrine of judicial review must be constructed from the Constitution's theory, from *The Federalist,* and from other sources rather than from a strict reading of the Constitution's text.

The Federalist's systematic examination of the judiciary begins with No. 78 and is a continuation of the forty-eight papers that treat "[t]he conformity of the proposed Constitution to the true principles of republican government."[3] Understanding the role of the judiciary requires squaring the role of an appointed body of judges who hold office for "good behavior" with the strictly republican character of the Constitution. Consistent with the theme of republicanism, No. 78 begins with the necessity for a federal judiciary to correct a defect of the Articles, an omission earlier described as a "circumstance which crowns the defects of the Confederation."[4]

Federalist No. 22, in discussing these defects, observes: "Laws are a dead letter without courts to expound and define their true meaning and operation. . . . Their [treaties'] true import, as far as respects individuals, must, like all other laws, be ascertained by judicial determinations" (138). According to this passage, judges act within the law to both expound and define its true meaning as it applies to individuals. Indeed, one might say that the law is incomplete or "a dead letter" without adjudication. Implicit in this passage is the fact that judges have significant powers even when they act within the boundaries set by a legislative body, for the law may be open to differing interpretations—thus the need for a Supreme Court that has the authority to declare a uniform rule through statutory construction. This uniformity is necessary to treaties, particularly "where the frame of government is so compounded that the laws of the whole are in danger of being contravened by the laws of the parts." Although the context of this discussion is foreign affairs, Publius argues the necessity for uniformity in adjudicating treaties and "all other laws" (138–39).

Assuming the necessity of the federal judiciary from the earlier paper,[5] Publius addresses the manner of constituting the judiciary and the extent of its powers. No. 78 turns to a defense of the constitutional provision that non-elected judges hold office *"during good behavior."* Life tenure is characterized as "one of the most valuable of the modern improvements in the practice of government."[6] It is a barrier to the prince's despotism in a monarchy; "in a republic, it is a no less excellent barrier to the encroachments and oppressions of the representative body. And it is the best expedient which can be devised in any government, to secure a steady, upright, and impartial administration of the laws" (502–3). This explanation of the Court as a barrier to oppression and an assurance of "steady, upright, and impartial administration of the laws" within the broader framework of strictly republican theory helps explain *The Federalist*'s view of the proper judicial role. A term of "good behavior" is inconsistent with republican accountability to the people unless the Court operates under the limitations of the Constitution and the rule of law.

Publius regards the judiciary as the branch "least dangerous to the political rights of the Constitution." The Executive dispenses honors and "holds the sword of the community"; Congress holds the power of the purse and the prescription of rules "by which the duties and rights of every citizen are to be regulated." Judges have "no influence over either the sword or the purse; no direction either of the strength or of the wealth of the society; and can take no active resolution whatever. It may truly be said to have neither FORCE nor WILL, but merely judgment; and must ultimately depend upon the aid of the executive arm even for the efficacy of its judgments" (503–4).

For these reasons, the judiciary is the branch "least dangerous to the political rights of the Constitution." Rule through representation constitutes the core of government activity as both Congress and the elected executive exercise the powers Publius enumerates. The primary safeguard of political rights consists in "the genius of the whole system," particularly people's "vigilant and manly spirit" of freedom."[7] The public will is given effect through Congress's general and prospective enactments of law through constitutional forms. The executive branch's execution of the law is immediate and may involve "irregular and high-handed combinations" or groups who would "interrupt the ordinary course of justice."[8] Judges are bound by law as they decide specific cases involving individuals. The general political liberty of citizens rests with the political branches; the judiciary is concerned with individuals in specific cases or controversies.[9] Publius appears little concerned that the judiciary might interfere with other political rights that are within the powers of the legislative and executive branches. He seems not to anticipate that the judiciary will interfere with the representative process itself, except, as he subsequently describes, when state acts or those of other branches of the national government violate constitutional provisions. In such instances, the judiciary adjudicates the law at the instigation of individuals who bring cases or controversies.

In light of his foregoing discussion, Publius believes that he "proves incontestably, that the judiciary is beyond comparison the weakest of the three departments of power; that it can never attack with success either of the other two; and that all possible care is requisite to enable it to defend itself against their attacks."[10] Relying on Montesquieu's observation that the judiciary is the weakest branch, Publius properly adds, "so long as the judiciary remains truly distinct from both the legislature and the Executive."[11] He does not include Montesquieu's observation that it is appropriate for the judiciary to be the weakest, since when uncontrolled, the judicial power can be "terrible to mankind" because it tries the "causes of individuals" as the power of government directly confronts them. Montesquieu relies on the jury system to tame the judicial power by involving citizens directly in this process;[12] through the jury process, a microcosm of the society inserts a representative element into judicial proceedings. Publius argues that within the separation of powers, "individual oppressions may now and then proceed from the courts of justice," but "the general liberty of the people can never be endangered from that quarter; I mean so long as the judiciary remains truly distinct from both the legislature and the Executive."[13] This observation is true only insofar as judges remain confined by law and do not meddle with the political rights that are within the constitutional powers of Congress and the executive. The system also requires judicial fidelity to the strictly republican character of the Constitution, which is the mechanism for protection of the people's political or "general liberty."

Within the context of *The Federalist*'s argument for a judicial role that is safe for the general liberty of the people and confined by law, Publius repeats his insistence on the necessity of a judiciary that is firm and independent because of its "permanency in office." This permanency is extolled because the judicial power is limited. The legislature "prescribes the rules by which the duties and rights of every citizen are to be regulated," and the judicial function operates within these rules and within the law of the Constitution.[14] For the judiciary to go beyond this role is inconsistent with the strictly republican character of the Constitution and its theory.

Publius next turns to the independence of courts, which is "particularly essential in a limited Constitution." He understands a limited Constitution as "one which contains certain specified exceptions to the legislative authority; such, for instance, as that it shall pass no bills of attainder, no *ex-post-facto* laws, and the like." Within this context he makes the classic textual defense of judicial review: that such limitations "can be preserved in practice no other way than through the medium of courts of justice, whose duty it must be to declare all acts contrary to the manifest tenor of the Constitution void. Without this, all the reservations of particular rights or privileges would amount to nothing." Publius's statement supports judicial review of state and national actions insofar as the constitutional prohibitions he specifies are contained in the Constitution's limitations on states or on the United States.[15] The fact that his defense of judicial review immediately follows his discussion of the necessity for a firm and independent judiciary that will not be "overpowered, awed, or influenced by its coordinate branches" makes clear the application of this power to coordinate branches of the national government.

No. 78 also addresses the objection that the power to declare legislative acts void implies judicial superiority to the legislature, an objection that remains a part of our constitutional debates. Publius defends the power on the principle that

> every act of a delegated authority, contrary to the tenor of the commission under which it is exercised, is void. No legislative act, therefore, contrary to the Constitution, can be valid. To deny this, would be to affirm, that the deputy is greater than his principal; that the servant is above his master; that the representatives of the people are superior to the people themselves; that men acting by virtue of power, may do not only what their powers do not authorize, but what they forbid.[16]

We will return to the distinction between powers not authorized by the Constitution and those forbidden by it. Publius rejects the proposition that the legislative judgment of the constitutionality of its own powers is "conclusive upon the other departments," unless this conclusive power is prescribed by a particular provision in the Constitution. Conclusive legislative judgment would substitute the will of the representatives for that of their constituents. Publius argues "that the courts were designed to be an intermediate body between the people and the legislature, in order, among other things, to keep the latter within the limits assigned to their authority." Since the Constitution is fundamental law, and because the judiciary interprets laws, the judiciary ascertains the meaning of both the Constitution and legislative acts. In the case of "irreconcilable variance between the two, that which has the superior obligation and validity ought, of course, to be preferred; or in other words, the Constitution ought to be preferred to the statute, the intention of the people to the intention of their agents" (506).

Far from elevating the judiciary to a position superior to that of the legislature, Publius argues that the principle of constitutional superiority of the legislature reflects the superiority of the people reflected in the Constitution, which created both the legislature and the judiciary. He argues that according to "the nature and reason of the thing . . . the prior act of a superior ought to be preferred to the subsequent act of an inferior and subordinate authority; and that accordingly, whenever a particular statute contravenes the Constitution, it will be the duty of the judicial tribunals to adhere to the latter and disregard the former." Publius raises the possibility of the courts substituting "their own pleasure to the constitutional intentions of the legislature" but dismisses this as an argument against the principle underlying judicial review, since the potential for the courts exercising "WILL instead of JUDGMENT" exists both in applying and construing ordinary laws and in adjudicating conflicting statutory law (507–8). But he does not note an important distinction. If the courts substitute their own will for that of the legislature in the case of an ordinary statute, the recourse is simply for the legislature to pass a new law that restores the legislative will. If the courts substitute their own will in declaring a legislative act void because it conflicts with the Constitution, the remedy is not so simple. This problem will be examined further in the discussion of *Federalist* No. 81. The remedies of altering the rules that regulate the Supreme Court's appellate jurisdiction, changing the organization of the judiciary, impeaching judges, and amending the Constitution have such potential. Although these powers have sometimes been used decisively, they have been used sparingly. *The Federalist* may regard the risk of the judiciary substituting will for judgment as unavoidable to some degree if the courts are to be "bulwarks of a limited Constitution against legislative encroachments" (508).

Publius also addresses the necessity of the judiciary's voiding legislative enactments that are incompatible with the Constitution, the provisions of which arise from the people themselves. If the "ill humors" of the people lead them to act through their representatives in a way that is incompatible with the Constitution's provisions and rights of individuals, the judicial duty is clear, even though it requires uncommon judicial fortitude for judges faithfully to guard the Constitution when legislative invasions of it are instigated by the people themselves. The people, of course, retain their fundamentally republican right to amend or abolish the Constitution, but until this action is taken, judges have a duty to be "faithful guardians of the Constitution" (508–9)

Publius turns from discussion of unconstitutional laws to unjust and partial laws that injure private rights. A permanent and independent judiciary may mitigate the severity and confine the operation of such laws. In addition to judicial moderation in applying the laws, the very existence of this judicial power acts as an obstacle to the legislature, which knows that its laws will be subject to judicial interpretation and application. Individuals feel more confidence in the government knowing that a firm judiciary may moderate unjust or partial laws when they have their day in court. Permanency in office helps prevent judicial reliance on mere popularity and makes more likely the "inflexible and uniform adherence to the rights of the Constitution, and of individuals" (509–10).

A final argument supporting permanent tenure for judges is the "long and laborious study" necessary to acquire knowledge of the rules and precedents that define judicial duty. Publius argues that the "folly and wickedness" of human beings will swell legal precedents to a considerable body; that few will have sufficient legal skills to fulfill the judicial function; and, allowing for the "ordinary depravity of human nature," that still fewer will combine the necessary knowledge with integrity. This consideration concludes the paper's arguments for judicial service during "good behavior" (510–11). These arguments are sound when the courts are working within the confines of the Constitution and laws. They are unpersuasive if the Court enters into the realm of political and social judgments of policy that are not based on the Constitution's provisions or principles.

The Federalist's treatment of the judiciary in Nos. 79–83 provides additional insight into its understanding of the judicial power.[17] No. 80 defends the Constitution's provision for the jurisdiction of the federal courts. The first power Publius addresses is jurisdiction over cases "which arise out of the laws of the United States," laws passed by the legislature "in pursuance of their just and constitutional powers of legislation." This power is necessary to give efficacy to constitutional provisions. Without it, national power would be incomplete under the system of separated powers and less able, for example, to enforce the constitutional restrictions on the state legislatures.[18]

The jurisdictional provision for the federal courts is also necessary to the execution of the Constitution's provisions according to the political axiom that the judicial power should be coextensive with the legislative power of the government. Besides being necessary to complete the powers of the national government, such jurisdiction is also necessary to preserve uniformity in interpreting national laws. Thirteen independent interpretations from state courts would result in contradiction and confusion and be a "hydra in government."[19]

Among the other constitutional grants of power to the judiciary discussed by Publius in No. 80 is that of "all cases in law and equity, *arising under the Constitution* and *the laws of the United States.*" The distinction between cases involving laws of the United States and those arising under the Constitution is explained by example. If states emit paper money in violation of the constitutional restriction prohibiting it, the judicial authority in this case would arise from the Constitution, not from the ordinary laws of the United States. The same is true of other constitutional prohibitions upon the states.[20]

Federalist No. 81 again confronts the tension between democracy and judicial review. Publius addresses the objection that the Supreme Court as a separate and independent body will be superior to the legislature because its "power of construing the laws according to the *spirit* of the Constitution, will enable that court to mould them into whatever shape it may think proper; especially as its decisions will not be in any manner subject to the revision or correction of the legislative body." He argues there is not a "syllable in the plan" that justifies this power but acknowledges that the Constitution is the standard for construing laws, and when there is "evident opposition, the laws ought to give place to the Constitution." This is not deducible "from any circumstance peculiar to the plan of the convention, but from the general theory of a limited Constitution; and as far as it is true, is equally applicable to most, if not all the State governments." Such an objection would "condemn every constitution that attempts to set bounds to legislative discretion."[21]

Publius dismisses the implication of his opponents that the ultimate power of judging should rest in one of the legislative bodies. Giving Congress this power would breach the separation of powers and make it less likely that the final authority would "temper and moderate" the application of bad laws. He argues that neither in the Parliament of Great Britain nor in the states can the legislative power "rectify the exceptionable decisions of their respective courts, in any other sense than might be done by a future legislature of the United States." Publius follows this with an argument that deserves quotation:

> The theory, neither of the British, nor the State constitutions, authorizes the revisal of a judicial sentence by a legislative act. Nor is there any thing

in the proposed Constitution, more than in either of them, by which it is forbidden. In the former, as well as in the latter, the impropriety of the thing, on the general principles of law and reason, is the sole obstacle. A legislature, without exceeding its province, cannot reverse a determination once made in a particular case; though it may prescribe a new rule for future cases. This is the principle, and it applies in all its consequences, exactly in the same manner and extent, to the State governments, as to the national government now under consideration. Not the least difference can be pointed out in any view of the subject.[22]

Publius argues that, in "exceptionable decisions," the legislature is empowered to prescribe a new rule for future cases, although it cannot reverse the Court's determination in a particular case.[23] Lincoln justifies this distinction in his first inaugural address:

> I do not forget the position assumed by some, that constitutional questions are to be decided by the Supreme Court; nor do I deny that such decisions must be binding in any case, upon the parties to a suit, while they are also entitled to very high respect and consideration, in all paralel [sic] cases; by all other departments of the government. . . . At the same time, the candid citizen must confess that if the policy of the Government upon vital questions affecting the whole people is to be irrevocably fixed by decisions of the Supreme Court, the instant they are made in ordinary litigation between parties in personal actions, the people will have ceased to be their own rulers, having to that extent practically resigned their Government into the hands of that eminent tribunal."[24]

Publius seems to anticipate the possibility that Congress may respond to "exceptionable decisions" by exerting its own will and prescribing a new rule for future cases. That this legislative power might be used to prescribe a new general rule in a constitutional case is implied by Publius's statement that the principle "applies in all its consequences" to the national government. If Congress chooses to exercise this power in response to a constitutional decision, one might expect the Court to pause before adhering to its own precedent in a subsequent case, but nothing in the Constitution would prevent the judiciary from persisting in its interpretation if its appellate jurisdiction remains over the subject manner and if other congressional powers over the Court are not exercised. If Congress prevails in its encroachment on powers specifically prohibited by the Constitution, the people have the power to effect their will by electing new representatives.

Publius characterizes the possibility that the judiciary will encroach upon Congress as a "phantom." Although particular misconstructions or contraventions of the legislative will may occur, they will not result in inconvenience or "affect the order of the political system." The reasons Publius gives for this are the nature of the judicial power, the objects of that power, the manner of its exercise, its weakness, and its inability "to support its usurpations by force." To this list, Publius adds "the important constitutional check of impeachment," which alone is a complete security. The impeachment power may be used to remove judges from office if they engage in "a series of deliberate usurpations on the authority of the legislature."[25] Publius argued earlier that "inability" was not cause for impeachment, but persistent and deliberate usurpation is.

After treating the impeachment power, Publius returns to the constitutional provision that makes the Supreme Court's appellate jurisdiction subject to "such exceptions and under such regulations as the Congress shall make." Congress is thereby enabled to modify the appellate jurisdiction of the Court "in such a manner as will best answer the ends of public justice and security."[26] In No. 83, Publius treats the objection that the original Constitution makes no provision for jury trials in civil cases and concludes that this matter is best left to the discretion of Congress. Constitutional provision for jury trial in civil cases cannot be relied upon to preserve liberty: "The truth is that the general GENIUS of a government is all that can be substantially relied upon for permanent effect."[27] This statement from No. 83 underscores the role of Congress in the "strictly republican" view of the judiciary, consistent with the theory of government presented earlier in *The Federalist*. Rather than relying on specific parchment provisions, No. 83 concludes by emphasizing the general genius of a republican government in sustaining liberty, including appropriate roles for both Congress and the judiciary.

Publius's conclusion to No. 83, as well as other statements in earlier papers on the judiciary, brings us back to the tension between democracy and the power we have come to call judicial review. How can this tension be resolved within the broader framework of *The Federalist*'s theory and its view of the judicial power? The defense of judicial review in No. 78 is regarded as the classic statement on judicial review and, therefore, deserves careful examination.

Leonard Levy explains No. 78, and its provision that constitutional limitations must be preserved by "courts of justice, whose duty it must be to declare all acts contrary to the manifest tenor of the Constitution void," as shrewd politics, not as evidence of the framers' intention to establish Supreme Court review over acts of Congress. He argues that No. 78 is a response to the Anti-Federalist "Brutus" (Robert Yates),[28] who argued that the effect of the federal judiciary's powers would result in making the judiciary "an engine for consolidating national powers at the expense of the states." Publius (Hamilton) responded to this charge by attempting to persuade his audience that "the Court's power was intended to hold Congress in check, thereby safeguarding the states against national aggrandizement."[29] But it is not inconsistent for No. 78 to be a response to Brutus while at the same time setting forth an argument for the judicial power to void legislative acts that are "contrary to the manifest tenor of the Constitution."[30]

In support of his argument that historical evidence supporting judicial review is inconclusive, Levy cites the discussion in No. 33 of the "necessary and proper" clause and the Anti-Federalist charge that it would give Congress expansive powers to do whatever it willed at the expense of state powers. He points out that in responding to the question of what body will judge the necessity and propriety of such laws, Publius does not mention the Supreme Court: "Congress in the first instance and the people in the last would judge."[31] Levy is right that Publius does not mention the Court in No. 33. What Publius does say is that "the national government, like every other, must judge, in the first instance, of the proper exercise of its powers, and its constituents in the last."[32] Although one might argue that Publius meant "Congress" when he wrote "national government," that is not how the text reads. Publius previously used the term "national legislature" at least three times in No. 33; he subsequently uses the term "Federal legislature" in the same paragraph. The term "LEGISLATIVE power" is used twice prior to the quoted passage.[33] These usages demonstrate a precision in the text that counters Levy's interpretation. In *Federalist* No. 44, Publius (Madison) addresses the same question—congressional exercise of powers not warranted by the true meaning of the "necessary and proper" clause—and responds: "In the first instance, the success of the usurpation will depend on the executive and judiciary departments, which are to expound and give effect to the legislative acts; and in the last resort a remedy must be obtained from the people, who can, by the election of more faithful representatives, annul the acts of the usurpers."[34] Although this passage does not necessarily recognize a broad and general power of judicial review, it does point to an understanding of the judiciary as necessary to give the laws effect and, thereby, complete the operation of the laws passed by the national government.[35] Judgment of the constitutionality of the laws being adjudicated may be involved in this process. Levy's argument is also weakened by the fact that in No. 33, Hamilton is referring to enumerated powers and the "necessary and proper" clause, not to the specific constitutional prohibitions on the legislature that he uses in No. 78 to illustrate the judicial power to void. This fact may instruct our understanding of the judicial power, but it undermines Levy's assertion. It is curious, in light of No. 78, that when Hamilton discussed his plan for a Constitution in the Convention on June 18, 1787, there was no provision supporting a power of judicial review in it.[36] Hamilton's omission does no more, however, than bring us back to the point from which we departed: that the Constitution itself makes no explicit provision for judicial review. Had Hamilton made such a proposal, and had it been rejected, then there would be evidence of the lack of such a power, at least as that power was understood in the Convention debates.

In his searching discussion of the historical evidence for judicial review, Levy addresses the view of Andrew C. McLaughlin and Edward S. Corwin that judicial review is a natural outgrowth of commonly held ideas at the time the Constitution was established. Levy properly recognizes a difficulty with their view insofar as it "does not account for the definitive power of the judiciary to interpret finally the supreme law, nor does it account for the binding effect of court decisions on equal and coordinate branches of the same government."[37]

One reason for this difficulty may be that the term "judicial review" was coined in the twentieth century and was not used by *The Federalist* in the sense that we currently use it.[38] *Federalist* No. 81 uses the term "review" in discussing appellate review—that is, "the power of one tribunal to review the proceedings of another"—a relationship that presumes a superior and inferior status of the two tribunals involved. This use of "review" applies to review of state court decisions and other lower court decisions, but the presumption of superiority in the reviewing tribunal is precisely the rub in the Court's reviewing acts of coordinate branches of government. The term judicial review is now often understood to mean a sweeping and final judgment of the constitutionality of acts of a coordinate branch of government or of state governments, subject only to the amending power. It is more consistent with *The Federalist*'s understanding of the judicial power to regard the voiding on constitutional grounds of executive or congressional action as arising within the context of deciding a case involving the rights of an individual under law in which the consideration of constitutionality, though important, is an issue collateral to the exercise of the pure judicial power.

During the Constitutional Convention, Madison opposed extending the Supreme Court's jurisdiction "generally to cases arising under the Constitution" and supported limiting it "to cases of a Judiciary Nature." If the cases were "not of this nature," the Court should not have the "right of expounding the Constitution." The Convention agreed to the extension, "it being generally supposed that the jurisdiction given was constructively limited to cases of a Judiciary Nature,"[39] an understanding consistent with the exercise of the judicial power in *Bayard v. Singleton*.[40] One day later in the Convention, however, Madison referred to the prohibition on ex post facto laws, "which will oblige the Judges to declare such interferences null & void."[41] Madison's statement that the Supreme Court's jurisdiction was to be restricted to "cases of a judiciary nature" and the Convention's general supposition that the Supreme Court's jurisdiction was to be restricted to "cases of a judiciary nature," when combined with *The Federalist*'s understanding that the exercise of constitutional review is incidental to the performance of regular judicial functions, suggest an understanding of judicial review in the founding era that may be confirmed by examination of the historical record.

Early Debates on Judicial Review

The Constitutional Convention

The Records of the Federal Convention contains a number of other statements on the judiciary and its reviewing power. Some of these statements support a power of judicial review but not a doctrine of judicial supremacy. Many of these comments were made in the context of considering a Council of Revision, the powers of which included examining acts of Congress before they became operative. The Council proposal, which was rejected in spite of Madison's continued support, included the executive, and the Council's judgments would have been subject to legislative override. Since arguments in favor of a Council of Revision supposed legislative supremacy through override, arguments made in this context are not the equivalent of support for judicial review; however, some statements shed light on delegates' understanding of the judicial power.

Mr. Gerry opposed judicial participation in the Council, "as they [the judges] will have a sufficient check agst. encroachments on their own department by their exposition of the law, which involved a power of deciding on their Constitutionality." Gerry also observed that it was foreign to the judicial power to make it judge policy measures, as it would necessarily do under the proposed Council.[42] Rufus King argued "that the Judges ought to be able to expound the law as it should come before them free from the bias of having participated in its formation."[43] Mr. Bedford opposed the Council as a check on the legislature. He argued that the "Representatives of the People" ought to be under no external control beyond that of the bicameral legislature itself (1:101). Although Gerry's reference to the judiciary's resisting encroachments upon its own powers through its power of deciding on the constitutionality of laws favors some sort of judicial review, it does not presume a sweeping judicial power to lay down a rule of conduct for the government. King's statement seems to be premised on separation of powers issues that do not require judicial review, although William Pierce's account of the debate includes King's argument that in expounding the laws, judges "will no doubt stop the operation of such as shall appear repugnant to the constitution" (1:109). This statement does not necessarily support the broad, contemporary understanding of judicial review, but it does presume constitutional limitations on the legislature. Pierce also records Dickinson as opposing the Council because it would blend the powers of expounding with the execution of the laws (1:110).

James Wilson defended the Council's inclusion of judges. He emphasized the necessity of judges' having power to resist encroachments on themselves as well as on the people. Although in their expository capacity judges would have the opportunity to defend "their constitutional rights," this power is not enough: "Laws may be unjust, may be unwise, may be dangerous, may be destructive; and yet not be so unconstitutional as to justify the Judges in refusing to give them effect" (2:73). His insistence that judges should be able to protect their own constitutional rights emphasizes the role of courts in cases that affect the adjudicatory power but does not support a broad power of judicial review. His use of the term "so unconstitutional" is likewise evidence of a relatively narrow scope for judicial review, perhaps one that applies to clear violations of express constitutional prohibitions.

Nathaniel Gorham argued against the Council because judges are not presumed to have "peculiar knowledge of the mere policy of public measures." Gerry argued against the Council's mixing the legislative and the other departments, which result in "making Statesmen of the Judges; and setting them up as guardians of the Rights of the people." He would prefer to rely on the people's representatives as guardians of the people's rights and interests. Mr. Strong regarded the Council as an improper mixture of making and expounding the laws, which might influence the judges' later expounding of the laws (2:73–75). Luther Martin opposed the Council on the grounds that judges do not necessarily have a better knowledge of humankind than do legislators; furthermore, judges will have an opportunity to judge the constitutionality of laws in their proper capacity, in which "they have a negative on the laws" (2:76). George Mason opposed the Council on the grounds that it would give judges a double negative. In their expository capacity as judges, they could impede the operation of the law in one case: "They could declare an unconstitutional law void. But with regard to every law however unjust, oppressive or pernicious, which did not come plainly under this description, they would be under the necessity as Judges to give it a free course" (2:78). Although he agreed that a check on Congress is necessary, Nathaniel Gorham opposed the Council as leading to judges' carrying prepossessions into the exposition of the laws (2:79). John Rutledge's opposition stemmed from his view that judges should refrain from giving their opinion on a law until it comes before them (2:80).

The statements quoted above support a power of review that is narrower in scope than the ability to set a general rule for the other branches to follow or a judicial prerogative to interpret the Constitution expansively and create individual rights. These statements assume a judicial power to refuse to give effect to legislation that violates specific constitutional prohibitions but not a judicial superiority that would upset the equilibrium of separated powers. The concern for separation of powers is clear in Gorham's statement that judges have no peculiar knowledge of public policy, in Gerry's opposition to making judges statesmen and guardians of the rights of the people, and in Strong's insistence on separating lawmaking from expounding the laws. Martin's statement that judges will have an opportunity to judge the constitutionality of laws follows his observation that judges have no superior knowledge of humankind or of legislative affairs. Mason regards it as proper for judges to declare unconstitutional laws void, but the judge's view that a law is unjust, oppressive, or pernicious is not sufficient ground for such a declaration. The statements of both Gorham and Rutledge defend a pure separation of powers theory that would be violated by the Council. These statements defend a strong legislative power and representative government and do not support a judiciary that sets forth rules of government for the other branches. Nor do they support doctrines that lie at the foundation of judicial supremacy, such as that of unenumerated rights, that is, rights not linked to specific constitutional prohibitions.

Later in the Convention, Madison again introduced the Council of Revision (2:298). Pinckney opposed involving the judges in legislative matters because it might bias subsequent judicial opinions (2:298). Mercer approved of the Council because he believed that laws should be well made and then be "uncontroulable." Judges should not have the authority as expositors of the Constitution to declare a law void (2:298). John Dickinson argued that judicial power to set aside a law should not exist (2:299). Gouverneur Morris observed that the judiciary should not be bound "to say that a direct violation of the Constitution was law," and that this might help guard against encroachments of the legislature (2:299). Sherman wanted to keep judges out of "politics and parties" (2:300). The Council that Madison repeatedly supported in the Convention could be overridden by Congress, so his proposal supports legislative rather than judicial supremacy. Pinckney and Sherman argue on the basis of a pure separation of powers theory that does not necessarily include judicial review. Dickinson's and Mercer's statements are clear in their opposition to declaring laws unconstitutional. Morris argued that judges should not be required to regard a "direct violation of the Constitution" as law. Once again, we see little, if any, support for a sweeping power of judicial review.

Hugh Williamson argued in the Convention in favor of including constitutional prohibitions on bills of attainder and ex post facto laws because "the Judges can take hold" of such prohibitions (2:376). Prohibitions on bills of attainder and ex post facto laws regulate the form of law rather than its objects. Hobbes includes the prohibition on ex post facto laws as among the few limitations on the sovereign,[44] and bills of attainder are a direct violation of separation of powers theory. Neither of these provisions has elicited much litigation throughout the history of our judicial system. Their clarity and importance may be reasons both for their inclusion in the original Constitution and for Williamson's comment.

As we have seen, Madison argued that a grant of power to the Supreme Court to adjudicate cases arising under the Constitution ought to be limited "to cases of a Judiciary Nature." The Convention approved the grant of such jurisdiction, but it was "generally supposed" that it was "limited to cases of a Judiciary nature."[45] One day later, Madison spoke in response to a proposal to prohibit states from retrospective interference in private contracts: "Is not that already done by the prohibition of ex post facto laws, which will oblige the Judges to declare such interferences null & void."[46]

State Ratifying Conventions

Certain statements made in the state ratifying conventions are also helpful in defining the judicial power in the proposed Constitution. As was the case with the Constitutional Convention, statements of some delegates support a limited power of judicial review, but they do not support a doctrine of judicial supremacy in which the Court may create unenumerated rights and lay down an absolute rule for the other branches of government. James Wilson, in the Pennsylvania Convention, argued the necessity of a judiciary coextensive with congressional powers in order that it execute the laws that are framed.[47] Wilson also argued that if Congress passed laws inconsistent with its constitutional powers, the independent judiciary would declare such laws "null and void; for the power of the Constitution predominates. Anything, therefore, that shall be enacted by Congress contrary thereto, will not have the force of law."[48] In the Virginia Convention, Madison defended the Article III provision that the judiciary's jurisdiction included cases arising under the Constitution: "It may be a misfortune that, in organizing any government, the explication of its authority should be left to any of its coordinate branches. There is no example in any country where it is otherwise. There is a new policy in submitting it to the judiciary of the United States."[49] Marshall addressed the same provision, defending it against the proposition that it would extend the national authority to every conceivable case, even those within the power of the particular states: "Has the government of the United States power to make laws on every subject? . . . Can they go beyond the delegated powers? If they were to make a law not warranted by any of the powers enumerated, it would be considered by the judges as an infringement of the Constitution which they are to guard. They would not consider such a law as coming under their jurisdiction. They would declare it void."[50] Marshall later observed, "If a law be exercised tyrannically in Virginia, to what can you trust? To your judiciary. What security have you for justice? Their independence. Will it not be so in the federal court?''[51] This last statement does not necessarily support judicial supremacy over the legislature, but rather judicial power to impede the tyrannical exercise of the law as judges fulfill their adjudicatory role.

Debates in the First Congress

The First Congress's debates are instructive to our inquiry both because of Congress's consideration of a bill of rights and because of the discussion of the role of each branch of government in expounding the Constitution. Once again, we see these debates fail to support a doctrine of judicial supremacy in which the Court is empowered to create unenumerated rights and lay down an absolute rule of conduct for the other branches of government. In the context of a discussion of a bill of rights, Madison argues: ''If they are incorporated into the constitution, independent tribunals of justice will consider themselves in a peculiar manner the guardians of those rights; they will be an impenetrable bulwark against every assumption of power in the legislative or executive; they will be naturally led to resist every encroachment upon rights expressly stipulated for in the constitution by the declaration of rights.''[52] He also believes that a bill of rights would result in the state legislatures' scrutinizing the national government and more effectively resisting the latter's assumptions of power (1:457).

Earlier in congressional debates, the House discussed whether the president could remove the secretary of foreign affairs without the advice and consent of the Senate. Madison argues that the departments should be separate and distinct except insofar as the Constitution makes exceptions that blend them (1:516–17). He then refutes the argument that it would be ''officious'' for the House to expound the Constitution in this matter. He believes that the House has a duty ''to take care that the powers of the constitution be preserved entire to every department of Government; . . . a breach in this point may destroy that equilibrium by which the House retains its consequence and share of power'' (1:519–20). But Madison's greatest objection to the doctrine he is refuting is its implication ''that the legislature itself has no right to expound the constitution; that wherever its meaning is doubtful, you must leave it to take its course, until the Judiciary is called upon to declare its meaning'' (1:520). Madison's statement emphasizes ''equilibrium'' among the branches of government, which necessitates each department's making its own judgment on issues of constitutionality rather than presuming that the judiciary will take care of the determination when the issue reaches it. His extended argument deserves rather lengthy quotation:

> I acknowledge, in the ordinary course of government, that the exposition of the laws and constitution devolves upon the Judiciary. But, I beg to

know, upon what principle it can be contended, that any one department draws from the constitution greater powers than another, in marking out the limits of the powers of the several departments? The constitution is the charter of the people to the Government; it specifies certain great powers as absolutely granted, and marks out the departments to exercise them. If the constitutional boundary of either be brought into question, I do not see that any one of these independent departments has more right than another to declare their sentiments on that point.(1:520).

Madison refutes the view of an exclusive judicial prerogative to lay down an absolute rule of constitutional interpretation for all branches of government. He adds, "[i]n all systems, there are points which must be adjusted by the departments themselves, to which no one of them is competent." If this fails, then the "will of the community" must decide the issue."[53] He uses the terms "equilibrium" and "devolves upon the judiciary" (rather than being the peculiar task of the judiciary) and states that no department has any greater right than another to determine the constitutionality of a policy. This conception of the judicial power to review is narrower than our current understanding. The same is true of his statement that the Court's jurisdiction over cases arising under the Constitution should be limited "to cases of a Judiciary Nature." The current popular understanding of the review power—that the judiciary has power to review acts of Congress and the executive and to lay down a rule of conduct for all three branches of government,[54]—is different from and less subtle than Madison's understanding in this quoted material.[55] It is also important to recognize that the issue Madison is discussing in this quotation relates to the separation of powers, not to any specific constitutional prohibition on the powers of Congress.

Summary of Theorists and Historical Materials

The survey of historical materials suggests a relatively narrow judicial role within a republican system of government, the whole of which was designed to secure the public good and private rights. Insofar as the judiciary acts in ways inconsistent with this republican system, it threatens to undermine the very republicanism that is the bedrock of the public good and private rights. The discussions in the founding period refer numerous times to concern about an overreaching judiciary. Some of this evidence deserves repetition.

The Federalist's discussion of the judiciary is a continuation of the part of that work devoted to the Constitution's conformity to "the true principles of republican government." The defense of a powerful judiciary is rooted in the necessity for a strong judicial power to complete the powers of a strong national government and to achieve uniformity in application of the laws. This defense, which may not on its face require a power of judicial review, certainly does not support a judicial power to lay down an absolute rule of government for all branches or to create rights not reasonably drawn from the provisions or theory of the Constitution. The permanence and independence of the judiciary can be extolled only insofar as the judicial power is limited by and operates within constitutional bounds. *The Federalist* takes pains to refute the proposition that the Constitution creates a judicial power superior to the legislative power. Judges have a duty to be "faithful guardians of the Constitution" until such time as the people amend or abolish the Constitution. Although Publius rejects legislative authority to revise a judicial sentence, the legislature may prescribe a new rule for future cases. He also argues that "if the policy of the Government upon vital questions affecting the whole people is to be irrevocably fixed by decisions of the Supreme Court, the instant they are made in personal actions, the people will have ceased to be their own rulers." Republican government and the representative legislative power are sufficiently important to Publius that "persistent and deliberate usurpation" of the legislative power by judges is cause for impeachment. This potent view of the impeachment power indicates the seriousness of Publius's commitment to the proposition that the true safeguard of liberty is the "general GENIUS of a government."

A limited view of the judicial power is also supported by the constitutional antecedents within the states. Levy argues persuasively that these precedents tended to arise when legislatures tampered with either the normal jurisdiction of the courts or their trial procedures. This view is reflected in Madison's generally supported statement in the Convention that the Court's jurisdiction over cases arising under the Constitution is limited to "cases of a Judiciary Nature." It is instructive that *Marbury v. Madison,* which involved an apparent congressional attempt to enlarge the original jurisdiction of the Court, falls within this description. Madison pursued a related theme in the First Congress when he argued that Congress has a right to expound the Constitution and that no one department of government has more right than another to judge the boundaries of the Constitution. To give the judiciary sole power to make these judgments would upset the constitutional equilibrium.

A number of delegates to the Constitutional Convention made statements supporting a judicial power to void legislation repugnant to the Constitution. James Wilson observed: "Laws may be unjust, may be unwise, may be dangerous, may be destructive; and yet not be so unconstitutional as to justify the Judges in refusing to give them effect." Nathaniel Gorham argued against judges being "statesmen" or being "guardians of the Rights of the people." George Mason argued in a similar vein that although judges could declare an unconstitutional law void, they must give every other law free course, no matter how "unjust, oppressive or pernicious" the law. These statements support a view of judicial power consistent with that expressed in *The Federalist*. Judges may void laws that run afoul of constitutional prohibitions. As for laws that are unjust, unwise, dangerous, or destructive, evidence of judicial authority to void is extraordinarily sparing and is intermixed with arguments that such power runs the danger of transforming a republican constitution into one of judicial supremacy.

These historical records are relevant not just because they are extant. They are also evidence of the strictly republican frame of government and the theory underlying it. The arguments of the framers are sound and reflect a sober understanding of human nature and government that is drawn from Hobbes, Locke, and Montesquieu. Hobbes argues the sovereignty of the commonwealth, Locke argues the supremacy of the legislative power, and Montesquieu argues for a separated judicial power under the rule of law. Locke and the framers take very seriously the act of the people in the creation of the legislative power, and as we have seen, Locke's restrictions on that power are procedural in nature. Hamilton takes up a similar theme in *Federalist* No. 23 when he discusses the necessity for government to meet unforeseen exigencies, an argument that requires a strong national government, legislative latitude, and great care in limiting government.

We see repeated direct and indirect references in *The Federalist* to the strict republicanism of the Constitution. Strict republicanism is just as much a principle of government as are the First or Fourth Amendment's prohibitions on government and is clearly a more explicit principle than that of privacy, human dignity, or any other nonenumerated rights, which characterize so much contemporary constitutional debate. In fact, both republicanism and privacy arise from the Lockean premises of equality and liberty. We have seen the lack of teeth in Locke's limitations on the legislative power, lack of substantive teeth, that is. But Locke is insistent on representation in the legislative process, the supreme power. People want, and are entitled, to control their politics through representation. This is the essence of republicanism and the fundamental principle of the U.S. Constitution.

Judicial review rests on its strongest ground, in regard to both the historical materials reviewed and the theory of the Constitution, when it is limited. Limitations suggested by this analysis include cases and controversies that are of a "judiciary nature"—that is, cases that affect the constitutional place and functioning of the judiciary;[56] cases and controversies that involve clear violations of specific constitutional prohibitions; and, in particular, those specific constitutional prohibitions that are procedural in nature, such as those relating to ex post facto laws and bills of attainder, examples of which are used repeatedly throughout the debates on the Constitution and by Marshall to buttress his argument in *Marbury v. Madison*. *The Federalist,* as well as statements of leading framers, understands judicial review in a way that is generally consistent with Marshall's explication of the power in *Marbury*. Judicial review is not a power to create rights that are not firmly grounded in the Constitution. Nor is it a power to lay down an authoritative rule for all branches of government.

Marbury v. Madison

I have argued that the theory underlying the Constitution and the historical materials surrounding the founding period support a view of judicial power that is more limited than the one assumed by our modern understanding. One such modern judicial understanding is summarized by the unanimous opinion of the Court in *Cooper v. Aaron.*[57] The Court, relying on its interpretation of the statement in *Marbury v. Madison*[58] that "[i]t is emphatically the province and duty of the judicial department to say what the law is," enunciated a sweeping view of the federal judicial role: "This decision [Marbury] declared the basic principle that the federal judiciary is supreme in the exposition of the law of the Constitution, and that principle has ever since been respected by this Court and the Country as a permanent and indispensable feature of our constitutional system."[59] The determination of whether *Cooper v. Aaron* is correct in the role it prescribes for the federal judiciary requires closer examination of *Marbury*. It is not my purpose to engage in a systematic analysis of *Marbury v. Madison,* a task that others have done thoroughly and competently. The focus of this analysis is to compare Marshall's opinion with the theoretical and historical materials presented in previous chapters and with the sweeping power of judicial review that *Cooper v. Aaron* and modern commentators purport to draw from *Marbury* and then prescribe as the proper judicial power.

Marbury v. Madison arose as a result of President Adams's appointment of justices of the peace for the District of Columbia shortly before he left office. At the time Jefferson became president, the formal commissions of appointment had not been delivered by Secretary of State John Marshall. Jefferson ordered James Madison, his secretary of state, not to deliver the commissions. Marbury and others, without going to a lower court first, petitioned the Supreme Court for a writ of mandamus ordering Madison to deliver the commissions.[60] Marbury petitioned the Supreme Court under section 13 of the Judiciary Act of 1789, which provided that "[t]he Supreme Court . . . shall have power to issue . . . writs of mandamus, in cases warranted by the principles and usages of law, to any courts appointed, or persons holding office, under the authority of the United States." The difficulty arose because the Constitution provides for the Supreme Court to have original jurisdiction only in cases affecting ambassadors, ministers, and consuls and in cases in which a state is a party. Marshall argued that the statute conflicted with the Constitution and that Congress had attempted to expand the original jurisdiction of the Supreme Court and, therefore, violated the Constitution.[61]

Marshall begins with the premise "[t]hat the people have an original right to establish, for their future government, such principles, as in their opinion, shall most conduce to their own happiness." These principles are "fundamental" and "permanent" unless altered by the people. The Constitution "assigns to different departments their respective powers" and establishes "certain limits not to be transcended by those departments." If "the legislature may alter the constitution by an ordinary act," the "distinction between a government with limited" and one with "unlimited powers is abolished." Because the Constitution is superior, paramount law, "a legislative act contrary to the constitution is not law: if the latter part be true, then written constitutions are absurd attempts, on the part of the people, to limit a power in its own nature illimitable" (176–77). Marshall continues, in what is the most frequently cited portion of his opinion:

> It is emphatically the province and duty of the judicial department to say what the law is. Those who apply the rule to particular cases, must of necessity expound and interpret that rule. If two laws conflict with each other, the courts must decide on the operation of each.
>
> So if a law be in opposition to the constitution; if both the law and the constitution apply to a particular case, so that the court must either decide that case conformably to the law, disregarding the constitution; or conformably to the constitution, disregarding the law; the court must determine which of these conflicting rules governs the case. This is of the very essence of judicial duty. (177–78)

Marshall's characterization of the Constitution as superior law requires that ordinary legislative acts be bound by that law. If the Court were to close its eyes on the Constitution and give effect only to the legislative enactment, the result would be "that if the legislature shall do what is expressly forbidden, such act, notwithstanding the express prohibition, is in reality effectual." Marshall concludes that "[i]n some cases, then, the constitution must be looked into by the judges. And if they can open it at all, what part of it are they forbidden to read or to obey?" The examples Marshall offers to illustrate the judicial duty to look into the Constitution in applying the ordinary law are instructive. He refers to the prohibitions that " 'no tax or duty shall be laid on articles exported from any state,' " that " 'no bill of attainder or ex post facto law shall be passed,' " and the prohibition that a conviction for treason requires " 'testimony of two witnesses to the same overt act, or . . . confession in open court.' " In the case of the last prohibition, Marshall observes that "the language of the constitution is addressed especially to the courts" (178–79).

It follows from his examples of constitutional prohibitions, and from others that Marshall does not enumerate, "that the framers of the constitution contemplated that instrument as a rule for the government of courts, as well as of the legislature." Marshall concludes his opinion by observing that judges take an oath to support the Constitution, and in that oath the Constitution is first mentioned in the declaration of what is to be the supreme law of the land.[62] Under a written constitution, "a law repugnant to the constitution is void; and . . . courts, as well as other departments, are bound by that instrument."[63]

Some of Marshall's language in *Marbury* is broad. Louis Boudin characterizes Marshall's language as framed "in the broadest terms imaginable."[64] Marshall himself, in the later case of *Cohens v. Virginia,* stated, "in the reasoning of the court in support of this decision [*Marbury v. Madison*], some expressions are used which go far beyond it."[65] Perhaps this helps explain the Court's expansive reading of *Marbury* in *Cooper v. Aaron*[66] and its conclusion that *Marbury* supports a judicial role of supremacy in exposition of the Constitution. But, as Professor Robert Clinton recognizes, Marshall's opinion does not support an exclusive judicial power to interpret the Constitution.[67] In fact, the portion of Marshall's opinion quoted above makes it clear that he regards the Constitution as "a rule for the government of courts, as well as of the legislature," and in some instances, *both* courts and legislatures must look to the Constitution when judging the constitutionality of legislation,[68] for "a law repugnant to the constitution is void; . . . courts as well as other departments, are bound by that instrument [the Constitution]."[69]

Boudin makes some other instructive observations regarding *Marbury v. Madison:*

> *So far as the decision in* Marbury v. Madison *established any precedent, it only went to the extent of deciding that under a written constitution establishing three independent and co-ordinate branches of government, and prescribing limitations upon the power of the legislature, and establishing a court the powers of which are expressly defined in the constitution, the legislature has no power either to diminish or to increase the powers of that court; and if it attempts to do so, that court has a right to disregard such act of the legislature.*[70]

Boudin emphasizes that the statute under consideration in *Marbury* was not just an ordinary act of legislation but a law that related particularly to the judicial power—a power defined with some specificity in the Constitution. Marshall's opinion proceeded from this particular factual situation. Boudin observes that "[o]ne may very well concede that under such circumstances the

Legislature has no right to diminish, and no power to increase, the powers of this court as defined by the Constitution,—and that an attempt to do so may be disregarded by that court—without at all being bound to concede that the Judiciary has a general right to declare invalid *any* law of the Legislature repugnant to the Constitution." Boudin further argues that "*each department of the government* [according to the theory of Madison and Jefferson] *had a right to construe the Constitution independently of any other department in so far as its own action was concerned.*"[71] Apart from some of the broad language in Marshall's opinion, Boudin characterizes the decision itself as a relatively narrow and proper one in which the Court defines its own constitutional powers in a way that precludes legislative expansion.[72]

Although he does not adopt this definition of judicial review, Alexander Bickel makes an argument similar to Boudin's. In dealing with Marshall's example in *Marbury* of the constitutional requirement that convictions for treason require two witnesses to the same overt act or confession in open court, Bickel observes that "this may mean only that it is the judiciary's duty to enforce the Constitution within its own sphere, when the Constitution addresses itself with fair specificity to the judiciary branch itself."[73] Bickel also argues that "[t]he same might be true as well of other clauses prescribing procedures to be followed upon a trial in court and also of the provisions of Article III setting forth the jurisdiction of the courts." *Marbury* falls under this category.[74]

Bickel also addresses Marshall's reliance on the fact that judges are bound by oath or affirmation to support the Constitution. This oath is also required of senators, representatives, and other governmental officers. Bickel therefore believes that the oath is the strongest textual argument against Marshall, since "it would seem to obligate each of these officers, in the performance of his own function, to support the Constitution" and entitle each "to construe the Constitution with finality insofar as it addresses itself to the performance of his own peculiar function."[75]

The narrow interpretation of *Marbury*—that judicial review is limited to cases in which the Constitution specifically addresses itself to the judiciary—has a number of virtues. It avoids the doctrine of the judiciary being the final judge of all powers of the three branches of the national government—that is, of the judiciary having the power to lay down "an absolute rule of conduct for the entire government of the United States"[76]—and thereby restrains the actions of "the least dangerous" branch.[77] This interpretation, limiting the judiciary's power to void to constitutional provisions specifically directed at it, fits Marshall's treason example but does not fit the forbidden procedures of ex post facto laws and bills of attainder. Nonetheless, these two prohibitions are relatively clear, and because they are procedural in nature, they do not involve judicial interference in the substance of legislation. Marshall argues that if bills are passed that constitute ex post facto laws or bills of attainder, a court should not enforce them and thereby condemn "those victims whom the constitution endeavors to preserve."[78]

What Marshall seems to be saying, and what seems to be an inevitable conclusion under a written constitution with express prohibitions directed toward the legislative power, is that the judiciary should not enforce clear violations of these prohibitions. Of course, this is precisely the issue. Most often, legislation is not passed that constitutes clear violations of constitutional prohibitions. As Charles Grove Haines recognizes, determining the validity of a law is "a delicate and difficult question frequently with serious political implications on which lawyers and statesmen may well disagree."[79] There has been little litigation of the prohibitions on bills of attainder and ex post facto laws because these provisions are relatively clear. If there is an honest difference of opinion between the legislative and the judicial judgment of express constitutional provisions, Marshall's opinion supports the judiciary's giving substantial weight to the legislative judgment; the actual decision in *Marbury* is restricted to those instances in which the Constitution provides a "direct rule for the courts."[80]

This relatively narrow decision in *Marbury* is consistent with much of the historical and theoretical material considered earlier and does not support a sweeping judicial power. The actual decision in *Marbury* takes seriously the strictly republican nature of the Constitution, as explicated in *The Federalist*, and the necessity for a strong legislative power that is accountable to the electorate. Even the broader language of *Marbury*, which is sometimes used to justify a far-reaching judicial power, is framed in such a way that people are unmistakably regarded as sovereign, that is, "the people have an original right to establish, for their future government, such principles, as, in their opinion, shall most conduce to their own happiness"; and "the authority [the people] from which they [the principles] proceed is supreme, and can seldom act, they [the principles] are designed to be permanent."[81] In speaking of the dangers of a legislative power unrestrained by the Constitution's provisions, Marshall refers to acts that are "expressly forbidden" by the Constitution.[82]

Perhaps most fundamentally, Marshall's opinion in *Marbury* rests on the premise that the Constitution is law: "The constitution is either a superior paramount law, unchangeable by ordinary means, or it is on a level with ordinary legislative acts, and, like other acts is alterable when the legislature shall please to alter it."[83] Marshall recognizes that his argument for judicial voiding of legislative acts depends on this premise that the Constitution is law that binds both legislators and judges. Whether one adopts the narrow interpretation of *Marbury* based on the decision itself or the broader interpretation implicit in some of the opinion's language, interpretations of judges are limited by the permanent principles of the Constitution. Even the broad interpretation of the judicial role under *Marbury* does not justify the interpretive theory of many modern commentators who dismiss the Constitution as law and substitute for constitutional principles their own conceptions of justice, which allow nearly unlimited latitude for the Supreme Court as it decides constitutional cases. Deciding constitutional cases on the basis of concepts such as "equal concern and respect,"[84] laissez faire economic theory,[85] moral evolution,[86] or personal dignity and autonomy[87] is not consistent with even the broadest possible reading of *Marbury*. Part II of this volume examines theories of contemporary constitutional commentators and focuses on their inconsistency with the theory and permanent principles of the Constitution.

II.
Contemporary Constitutional Commentary

P art II examines competing contemporary theories of the Constitution and of the role of the Court in light of the principles explicated in Part I. As we shall discover, much of this commentary contradicts the understanding of human nature and government found in the work of Hobbes, Locke, and Montesquieu and in the Declaration of Independence, the Constitution, and *The Federalist*. Moreover, much modern commentary rejects these previous theories without confronting them or offering a coherent alternative. Simply demonstrating contradictions between the Constitution and its theoretical antecedents is not sufficient. I also argue that the earlier understanding rests on a sounder and wiser conception of human nature, politics, and government than does the often utopian theory of many modern commentators.

A body of appointed judges who hold office for life or good behavior and who make important policy judgments exists in an uneasy tension with a political order that is fundamentally democratic in nature. Constitutional commentary, directed in part to resolving this tension, has been an important part of our political life since the publication of *The Federalist*. Because the Constitution was intended to endure for ages and, for the most part, laid out only fundamental political principles, the tradition of and necessity for constitutional commentary, begun by the Constitution's architects, has continued throughout our history. The early commentary sought to give meaning to the Constitution's broad principles by working within its confines to illumine the principles of government in a way that gave life and application to the Constitution's theory, but always within those confines.

Joseph Story, associate justice of the United States Supreme Court from 1811 to 1845, warns the reader of his respected *Commentaries on the Constitution of the United States* not to expect to find "any novel views, and novel constructions of the Constitution" in its pages.[1] Story's "first and fundamental rule" of interpretation is that the Constitution, as law, is to be interpreted according to the sense of its terms and "the intention of the parties." The parties to the Constitution are the people: the Constitution "was made by the people, made for the people, and is responsible to the people" (1:382–83). Story argues that when the words of the Constitution are clear, there is ordinarily no need for recourse to other sources of interpretation. In cases of ambiguity arising from the words used, from the sense of words used in other clauses of the instrument, or between the words used and "the apparent intention derived from the whole structure of the instrument, or its avowed object," interpretation is necessary (1:384). This interpretation is properly confined to the "nature and objects" and the "scope and design" of the Constitution "viewed as a whole, and also viewed in its component parts" (1:387). In addressing contemporary construction of the Constitution, Story observes: "It can never abrogate the text; it can never fritter away its obvious sense; it can never narrow down its true limitations; it can never enlarge its natural boundaries" (1:390). Story eschews "loose interpretations and plausible conjectures" as canons of constitutional interpretation (1:391–92). Most important for our purposes is Story's premise that the Constitution is law. His rules of interpretation all derive from the Constitution and do not attempt to reform or give new meaning to the Constitution and its underlying theory, but rather to guide application of the Constitution as law.

The last two decades have given rise to scores of commentaries on the Constitution and "speculations of ingenious minds" that construct novel theories of the Constitution (1:392). Many of these contemporary commentaries are extended essays on jurisprudence that attempt to reform government and society, often through novel interpretations of the Constitution that advance the author's purposes. Some of these interpretations can be understood as attempts to reconcile the author's reforms with a system of government that provides for majority rule, elective branches of government, and a judiciary appointed for life or good behavior. Much of this modern commentary searches for a unifying theory that will give a meaning to the Constitution that supports the commentator's proposed reforms. The authors of these commentaries attempt to square the Constitution with their views of the nation's contemporary needs. They generally neglect serious study of the Constitution's theory and principles, as those are illumined by the political theory of Hobbes, Locke, Montesquieu, the Declaration of Independence, and *The Federalist*. Modern commentators also often fail to give serious attention to the justification for majority rule, which lies at the foundation of the Constitution, and to the political theory that informs it.

This theory, particularly that of *The Federalist*, provides my basis for analyzing the competing theories of constitutional interpretation. Part II of this book focuses on the assumptions about democracy, the Constitution, and the role of the judiciary in each of these commentaries. The commentators chosen are well known and influential, but they also represent nearly the entire range of contemporary constitutional interpretation—from that of judicial restraint to judicial activism, from conservative to liberal to critics of the very enterprise of liberalism. I have organized the pairs of commentators into sections, each of which focuses on one constitutional principle. Analysis of each commentator's work emphasizes the constitutional principle on which I focus, but fair treatment requires examining other aspects of each commentator's theory as well. For example, Philip Kurland is identified with his advocacy of judicial restraint. My treatment of Kurland includes this doctrine, but from the perspective of his emphasis on the institutional features of the Constitution. The theory of the Constitution postulated by the selected commentators directly affects the role each prescribes for the Court. Part II compares and criticizes the various judicial roles prescribed by the commentators.

The Federalist is crucial to this enterprise because it explains the underlying theory of the Constitution as a whole, a theory that gives meaning to the particular provisions of the document and explains the way in which the Constitution is designed to secure the public good and private rights. The Declaration of Independence regards the security of inalienable rights as the justification for government. *The Federalist* demonstrates how the Constitution, based on a multiplicity of interests and a doctrine of enumerated and separated powers, secures these rights and the public good under a republican government. The Constitution provides a balance between its dependence on the people and its auxiliary safeguards: it is fundamentally democratic in character, but it protects republican liberty by restraining the majority. These restraints are consistent with democratic theory because they are the result of the majority's decision to restrain itself. It is within the context of these restraints that democratic rule is made consistent with liberty and other inalienable rights demanded by the Declaration as the ultimate justification for government; it is within this same context that the judicial power is justified.

Many contemporary constitutional commentators call for standards of judicial judgment that attempt to make the Constitution relevant to today. Among these modern standards are natural rights, moral growth, privacy, return to a laissez-faire economic system, equality in an egalitarian sense (such as reform of representation), and standards that the commentators believe will remedy disadvantaged groups. Some commentators simply reject the current constitutional system. Commentators ask the Supreme Court to enforce rights that they see as missing in our system of government. They imply that things would be much better if nine justices of like mind with themselves were on the Supreme Court and could enforce their views of right in the guise of constitutional law. In many respects, the views of modern commentators arise from a healthy recognition that majorities may act out of passion or interest, to the detriment of both the public good and private rights. Many commentators believe that courts can correct representative majorities and thereby remedy defects of representative government. Recognizing the conflict between judicial power and democracy, many thoughtful commentators have attempted to legitimize the Court's powers. Part II examines contemporary commentary that represents competing schools of constitutional interpretation, many of which attempt to legitimize an expansive judicial power at the expense of democracy.

Much of the modern commentary on the Constitution and the role of the Court reminds one of Thomas Hobbes's dismissal of "books on moral philosophy" that may be reasonable but whose authors do not have the sovereign power to make their pronouncements law and whose work contains "so many contradictions of one another, and of themselves."[2] Many of these commentators also reject Locke's reliance on securing the rights of nature through procedural requirements that legitimize the law as pronounced by the supreme legislative body. Finally, many commentators reject the strictly republican character of the Constitution and *The Federalist*'s treatment of the judiciary in the series of papers devoted to the true principles of republican government. Fundamental to this republican theory is the doctrine of consent to a Constitution that is designed to secure the public good and private rights through a popular government in which opinion is elevated and refined through representative structures.

As we have seen in Part I, those who framed the Constitution did not provide for a far-reaching judicial role in which judges would be free to rule on the basis of the strongest moral argument in the pursuit of equal concern and respect, to act as the voice of natural law, to be moral prophets, to enforce a laissez-faire economic system, or to reform representation and the Constitution in the name of an egalitarian conception of equality or a theory of socialism. The theory of the Constitution is inconsistent with this nearly unbounded judicial role. Instead, it created a system of government as a whole that rests on the sovereignty of the people and representative institutions to secure the public good and private rights. The sovereign people established a Constitution that delimits the powers of the judiciary as well as those of the executive, Congress, and the states. The historical record and theory of the Constitution are consistent with a judicial power narrower than that of setting forth absolute rules for all branches of government and deciding cases on the basis of unenumerated rights. Publius argues in *Federalist* No. 81, for example, "that the Constitution ought to be the standard of construction for the laws, and that wherever there is an evident opposition, the laws ought to give place to the Constitution."[3] This justification for judicial review assumes a judicial power far narrower than that advocated by many modern commentators. As we shall see in the analysis of ten modern commentators, they often impose their own theories of morality on the Constitution's principles and, unlike Joseph Story, go outside the boundaries of the Constitution to seek theories of interpretation that they believe are necessary to reform the system of government. Most often, these commentators seek to reform the Constitution without serious effort to understand its theory and its wisdom in resting government on the strictly republican principle, elevated and refined through a representative system of separated powers.

Chapter Four

The Concept of Rights and Natural Law as Fundamental Constitutional Principles

Ronald Dworkin and Archibald Cox stand out among contemporary constitutional commentators, not simply because they regard rights as important but because their understanding of the Constitution is preeminently concerned with rights. Ronald Dworkin argues that the Constitution consists of highly abstract concepts, that the root of the Constitution is the abstract principle of "equal concern and respect," and that *principles* are limited to individual rights and exclude broader social, political, or economic goals. Principles, and therefore rights, are the peculiar province of courts. The proper standard of judgment for the courts, and the only immediate restraint on their judgment, is the strongest argument that supports these principles. Thus, the proper work of judges is articulating the strongest argument from those available to moral philosophy and constructing these arguments in a manner that is articulately consistent, that is, in a manner "consistent with principles embedded in Supreme Court precedent and with the main structures of our constitutional arrangement."[1]

Archibald Cox explicates a theory of the Constitution and the Supreme Court that is both more constitutionally based and more sensitive to representation and traditional standards of legitimacy than that of Dworkin.[2] Cox views the Constitution as a natural law document and an expression of natural rights. He sees a conflict between the Constitution's commitment to natural law and its implicit conviction that "the people are the source of all legitimate power, that governments are the people's agents, and that the people, expressing themselves through the majority, have the right to work their will." Cox describes state and federal legislatures as the elements of popular sovereignty in the political order; the Supreme Court, as enforcer of constitutional restrictions in behalf of the individual, is "the voice of natural law."[3] Although he advocates a powerful judicial role, his work is also devoted to the legitimate wielding of judicial power in a manner that is consistent with the sovereignty of the people and with the constitutional powers of the other popular institutions of government. In this regard, Cox is more attentive to other constitutional principles than is Dworkin. Cox regards the most important quality of law in a free society as that of maintaining the community's acceptance and support.[4] Yet, in some respects, Cox's conception of the judicial role leads to some aspects of the judicial role that Dworkin advocates. Although Cox is much more cautious than Dworkin in unleashing the judicial power, the theories of both ultimately undermine the republican character of the Constitution that is fundamental to its operation.

A Theoretical Approach to Rights: Ronald Dworkin

Ronald Dworkin is perhaps the foremost proponent of rights among contemporary constitutional commentators. The outline of his jurisprudential argument is disarmingly simple, although as he presents it, it assumes textual complexity, complete with a vocabulary that is tailored to his underlying theory. Dworkin derives his preeminent role for judges from his definition of "principle," which is limited to individual rights, and from his understanding of the structures of our constitutional arrangements. He believes that the contemporary Court ought to interpret constitutional concepts according to current conceptions of the Constitution's highly abstract concepts. He argues that the Supreme Court is the Constitution's legitimate and sole expositor when principles and rights are concerned, even in hard cases. His scheme results in giving the Court a practical monopoly on determining what constitutes individual rights.[5] I will argue that even by Dworkin's own standards of "articulate consistency" and "constitutional integrity," his argument for extension of the judicial power fails. He abstracts the Bill of Rights from the body of the Constitution and undermines the Constitution's provision for democracy through representative government and through its scheme of separated powers, a scheme that ultimately rests on democracy.

Dworkin presumes that judges have the authority and the ability to understand, articulate, and enforce answers to the hardest constitutional and social questions. By limiting the definition of "principles" to claims for individual rights, he excludes the Constitution's root principle of popular or representative government in which the people are sovereign. By limiting "principles" to individual rights and by characterizing the Constitution as a "Constitution of principle," he sunders the body of the Constitution from the Bill of Rights. Dworkin thereby minimizes the principle of separated powers, which is designed to effectuate a republican form of government in a manner that helps ensure a representative, energetic, and stable government that is consistent with individual rights. His scheme obscures the important question of who is to decide hard cases of government and individual rights, gives that authority to the judicial system, and constrains judicial judgment in cases involving individual rights only by the tenet that the Court decide according to the strongest moral argument. His theory undermines a written and limiting Constitution, a Constitution arising out of the recognition that determining the strongest moral argument is extraordinarily difficult. Ultimately, Dworkin rejects democracy and representation.

Dworkin sidesteps the Constitution's reliance on representation and the separation of powers and constructs his "Constitution of principle" in a manner that establishes judicial hegemony. I will examine his theory of rights and principles and his doctrine of articulate consistency, illustrating his argument and its shortcomings in the context of constitutional issues related to pornography, church and state, capital punishment, and abortion. Although the Court does have an appropriate role in a scheme of republican government, separated powers, and individual rights, it is not the exclusive role Dworkin advocates. In fact, even before the adoption of the Bill of Rights, the body of the Constitution was designed to secure individual rights at the same time it sought to provide the means for achieving the public good. Dworkin disregards the role played by the body of the Constitution in securing the public good and private rights and focuses his theory on the Bill of Rights and related individual rights.

There is yet another difficulty with Dworkin's principle of "equal concern and respect." He purports to draw this principle from our Constitution and system of government, but his arguments in this regard are not persuasive. One could just as easily argue for a fundamental constitutional premise of limited government, democracy, limited equal liberty, or security. A more plausible premise than these (and more plausible than that of Dworkin) is Joseph Story's view of the Constitution as the will of the people and supreme law. Story argues that the Constitution should be interpreted by ascertaining the "true sense and meaning" of the Constitution. Story continues that the Constitution "is not an instrument for the mere private interpretation of any particular men" and that it should be judged by "common sense, and not by mere theoretical reasoning."[6] Although Story believes in the fundamental premise of republican (representative) government, he believes that this principle is defined in the legal instrument established by the people—the Constitution. Story's teaching, which is sounder than that of Dworkin, is that theoretical premises of any individual must give way to the legal terms, or words, of the Constitution. Dworkin dismisses such an interpretation as a bogus "Constitution of detail," for Story's rules of interpretation would prevent Dworkin from imposing his own theory on the Constitution and the Bill of Rights. Another difficulty with departing from the terms of the Constitution into abstract moral theory is that because of its high level of abstraction, it is not helpful in deciding cases. This same difficulty presents itself in other abstract premises that attempt to supplant the terms of the Constitution.

Ronald Dworkin presents his theory of rights in his book *Taking Rights Seriously.*[7] His theory rejects the doctrine of natural rights, characterizing it as one of the "ghostly forms" (xi), but he later adopts a theory of individual rights that exist above the authority of legislation, convention, or hypothetical contract (176). In one of the most persuasive parts of his work, he rejects the doctrine of legal positivism, which holds that legal truth is simply derived from the rules adopted by social institutions and from explicit political decisions. His general critique of positivism centers on the fact that positivism "stops short of just those puzzling, hard cases that send us to look for theories of law." He particularly objects to positivism's retreat from hard cases and its taking refuge in the discretion of a judge "to decide the case either way." This doctrine of discretion "leads nowhere and tells nothing" (45, 81). Law, in contrast, presupposes that there are right answers, and Dworkin is persuasive that we must examine the moral principles that lie at its foundation. He argues from the premise that "our intuitions about justice presuppose not only that people have rights but that one right among these is fundamental and even axiomatic." He calls this most fundamental right "a distinct conception of the right to equality," the "right to equal concern and respect" (vii–xii).

Dworkin's Theory of Rights, Reflective Equilibrium, and Subjective versus External Preferences

Dworkin derives his theory from our immediate intuitions or moral reactions from which general principles are constructed—principles that give structure to these intuitions. A state of "reflective equilibrium" results from a two-way process that moves "back and forth between adjustments to theory and adjustments to conviction until the best fit possible is achieved" (164). This repeated movement results in general theories of justice, or a coherent theory of morality, which Dworkin calls the right individuals have to "equal justice and respect in the design and administration of the political institutions that govern them" (160, 168, 180). He dissociates his theory of rights from the "disqualifying metaphysical associations" of the traditional natural rights doctrine and argues that his theory of rights is not "metaphysically ambitious." He characterizes his theory of rights as that of protecting "individual choices as fundamental, and not properly subordinated to any goal or duty or combination of these" (176–77). The reflective equilibrium that results from movement between intuition, or conviction, and tentative principles and back again provides a systematic justification for our own intuitions that is consistent with intuitions of others. Intuitions inconsistent with the constructed principles resulting from reflective equilibrium are rejected.[8]

Dworkin admits that his principle of equal concern and respect is highly abstract and, therefore, open to various interpretations.[9] He attempts to resolve this abstraction or ambiguity by specifying a system of equality of condition. He bases this system of politics and rights on personal rather than external preferences. He defines "personal preferences" as those pertaining to our own enjoyment of goods or opportunities; "external preferences" pertain to the assignment of goods and opportunities to others (234). Under his scheme, "individual rights to distinct liberties must be recognized only when the fundamental right to treatment as an equal can be shown to require these rights. If this is correct, then the right to distinct liberties does not conflict with any supposed competing right to equality but on the contrary follows from a conception of equality conceded to be more fundamental" (273–74).

Central to Dworkin's theory of rights and the role of judges is his distinction between policy and principle. He defines "policy" as that which sets forth a goal to be reached in the form of an improvement in economic, political, or social features of the community. A "principle" is a standard that is observed not because of its economic, political, or social benefit but because it is required by justice, fairness, or some other moral concept (22). Arguments from principle are "arguments intended to establish an individual right; arguments of policy are arguments intended to establish a collective goal. Principles are propositions that describe rights; policies are propositions that describe goals" (90). A political right is an individualized political aim; goals are non-individualized political aims (91). Justice is separated from economic, political, or social benefits. Furthermore, Dworkin regards the justifications for constraining liberties as being very limited.

One of Dworkin's justifications for constraining individual rights, an argument of principle as opposed to policy, is that a right may be limited if it injures the distinct right of someone else. The utilitarian argument for policy, that some overall political goal will be furthered by constraints on an individual's liberty, is rejected because it "assigns critical weight to the external preferences of members of the community" and thus "will not be egalitarian in the sense under consideration. It will not respect the right of everyone to be treated with equal concern and respect" (274–75).

Having addressed utilitarian objections to his theory, Dworkin considers "ideal arguments of policy," that is, the good of the community understood as resulting from policy that will bring the community closer to an ideal community and thereby justify constraining individual rights. He rejects this justification for constraining rights in the name of his "liberal conception of equality." He argues that such justification is valid only if the policy in question is without controversy within the community (274). There is one ideal, however, that he believes is not controversial, that of "a more equal society"; this ideal is linked to the fundamental right to "equal concern and respect."[10] Equality of condition supersedes equality of opportunity; according to Dworkin's understanding, greater equality within society does not deny the right of anyone to be treated as an equal.[11] Exemplary of rights that should not be constrained, however, are liberties of free expression and of free choice in personal and sexual relations, rights he articulates in his treatment of "What Rights Do We Have?"[12]

Property Rights

As a kind of afterthought to this section of his work, Dworkin dismisses property rights. He argues, for example, that laws limiting a right to liberty of contract "do not give effect to external preferences, and in that way offend the right of those whose liberty is curtailed to equal concern and respect."[13] His dismissal of property rights is summary and, for Dworkin, apparently dispositive. He subordinates property rights of individuals to an egalitarian welfare policy, the goal of which is equality of condition.[14] The alternative explanation—that property rights, like other rights, are problematic to actualize and in the end depend on the judgment of a properly constituted majority acting within the constraints of a written constitution—would open the door to compromising other rights that Dworkin prefers to defend as individuated rights based on principle and that are thereby protected from any compromise required by policy goals designed to effect the public good.

Unlike Dworkin, *The Federalist* regards property rights and interests as important to the liberty, dignity, and respect underlying the Constitution's theory. Property rights spring from the conceptions of equality and liberty underlying the Constitution, as do other individual rights. These rights, however, are not absolute in the sense that they are determined by the private judgment or personal preferences of individuals. Property rights stem from the exercise of liberty and from the diverse and unequal faculties of individuals. But they are subject to regulation by a properly constituted public judgment of their extent and limitations: "No man is allowed to be a judge in his own cause, because his interest would certainly bias his judgment, and, not improbably, corrupt his integrity."[15] Personal preferences or interests are not reliable judges of what constitutes justice or the public good, although such personal preferences are inevitably important to the process by which justice and the public good are determined.

Regulation of property often rests on those very external preferences that Dworkin rejects as fundamentally illegitimate. Questions such as welfare policy, progressive taxation, regulation of imports, and government subsidies rest on considerations of what is good for others (external preferences) or on conceptions of what policy will produce a better way of life for others and the public. Dworkin's summary dismissal of property rights is unjustified. A sounder view of these rights is that they are subject to regulation even though they are rooted in the same theoretical principles as those rights Dworkin elevates and defends in the name of equal dignity and respect. To admit that property rights are related to other personal rights, that regulation of property rights involves external preferences, and that such rights are regulated in order to serve justice or the public good would seriously undermine Dworkin's thesis. The dichotomy he draws between property rights and other personal rights is not justified by his broad premise of "equal concern and respect." One can only conclude that Dworkin wishes for property rights to be regulated, but for other rights to be virtually free from such regulation, and he tailors his premise to justify this conclusion.

Principles, Individual Rights, and Articulate Consistency

The Federalist and Dworkin agree that there are right answers to questions of law and individual rights. But *The Federalist* is much sounder in its view that these rights must be determined through a constitutional system that entrusts them to a properly constituted and structured majority that defines them in a context that accords importance to the permanent and aggregate interests of the community. *The Federalist*'s principles give the judiciary an important role in determining rights, but not the nearly exclusive role that Dworkin does.

Dworkin attempts to bring unity and coherency to his theory by limiting his definition of principles to arguments that support individual rights. *The Federalist*'s broader and sounder conception of principles includes a written constitution, representation, separation of powers with a strong legislative power, an independent judiciary, and the characteristics of energy and stability. All these principles are necessary to govern and to define and secure individual rights. By limiting his conception of principles to rights of individuals, Dworkin dispenses with much of the framework necessary to govern and to secure the very rights he defends. His theory seems more compatible with the state of nature described by Locke or Hobbes than with the civil society they argued was necessary in order to escape the difficulties of private judgment and unfettered rights found in the state of nature. Dworkin denies the principles of natural rights and the law of nature, which serve as the compass of Hobbes, Locke, and the U.S. Constitution. Dworkin also comes perilously close to denying the means for effective government through his standard of personal preferences, which is the principle he uses for judging the legitimacy of law.

Dworkin links his "rights thesis" and judicial use of precedent in hard cases to "articulate consistency," a concept that is fundamental to his scheme of rights and the role of judges. The doctrine of articulate consistency condemns decisions that "seem right in isolation, but cannot be brought within some comprehensive theory of general principles and policies that is consistent with other decisions also thought right," including "a constitutional theory" that justifies the Constitution as a whole.[16] In another work, he describes the closely related concept of constitutional integrity, one in which judges decide cases according to principle in a way consistent with "Supreme Court precedent and with the main structures of our constitutional arrangement." A judicially adopted principle must be applied in all cases, "even in apparently unrelated fields of law."[17] Articulate consistency assumes primary importance in judicial decisions. Judicial decisions, which should be based on principle as opposed to policy, are legitimate only if they have a principled basis that is consistent with earlier precedents and with other decisions the court is prepared to make in hypothetical circumstances.

Dworkin's thesis acknowledges the important role of both precedent and institutional history in deciding hard cases, but judges may be confronted with hard cases in which precedent does not produce a just result. It then becomes their duty to depart from wrongheaded precedents and enforce the right to win the lawsuit.[18] In the course of analyzing statutes, precedents, and principles, a judge may discover that more than one theory fits the case at hand. In this case, Dworkin's hypothetical judge, Hercules, must develop a comprehensive theory that justifies the Constitution as a whole: "In that case Hercules must turn to the remaining constitutional rules and settled practices under these rules to see which of these two theories provides a smoother fit with the constitutional scheme as a whole."[19] Articulate consistency requires the judge to "develop a theory of the constitution, in the shape of a complex set of principles and policies that justify that scheme of government."[20] This turns out to be largely a creative enterprise.

Given this view, it seems extraordinary, at first blush, that Dworkin spends almost no time attempting to establish the theory and principles of the U.S. Constitution by examining the substantial body of theory surrounding its creation.[21] He spends little effort establishing the basic principles and theory of the Constitution as framed because he regards these conceptions as largely irrelevant. In his formulation, contemporary judges should be guided not by the *conceptions* that the framers had in mind but rather by the *concept,* for example, that architectonic principle of fairness they had in mind when they framed constitutional provisions. Rejecting both historical materials and the theory of the Constitution expounded at the founding, Dworkin characterizes the framers as setting up a constitution in which they charge posterity with the responsibility of defining and actualizing the concept of "fairness" in politics. His scheme makes the judiciary responsible for defining and actualizing the concept of fairness and the principled rights he sets forth.

The Judicial Role and Judicial Application of Dworkin's Theory: Hercules Unleashed

THE ESTABLISHMENT CLAUSE. The lawyer-judge "Hercules" provides one example of Dworkin's view of constitutional adjudication in a case involving the First Amendment's religion clauses. The constitutional question is whether the legislature's granting of free busing for children who attend parochial schools violates the establishment clause. Hercules would resolve the issue first by accepting the Constitution and the political scheme as justified by the criterion of "fairness," a scheme accepted until it is modified by discrete amendment or by revolution. Dworkin then requires Hercules to construct "a full political theory that justifies the constitution as a whole" and that fits constitutional rules. Hercules' problem is that more than one fully specified theory may fit the provisions of the religion clauses. One such theory may provide that an established church will produce social tensions and, therefore, it is wrong for the legislature to establish a religion. Another theory, however, may rely on "a background right to religious liberty, and therefore argue that an established church is wrong, not because it will be socially disruptive, but because it violates that background right." Hercules must then determine which of the two theories fits more smoothly with the whole constitutional scheme.[22]

Hercules' decision that the establishment clause is justified by a right to religious liberty rather than the goal of social order does not end his inquiry. He must still determine the nature of this liberty: whether religious liberty requires only that one religion must not be preferred over another, or whether it requires that taxes cannot be used for any purpose that benefits religion in general. Since institutional rules and practices may not rule out either of these conceptions of religious liberty or clearly justify one conception over the other, Hercules must turn to political philosophy and "decide which conception is a more satisfactory elaboration of the general idea of religious liberty."[23] This is necessary if Hercules is to finish the project he began, namely, determining the constitutionality of the legislative enactment providing free busing for parochial school children. The project of Hercules, however, requires that the judge determine what religious liberty requires even in close or hard cases in which there seems little advantage in setting the legislative judgment aside. Dworkin assumes that it is the role of the judge to override the legislative judgment in hard cases, even when there is admittedly substantial support for that legislative judgment. He will later explain why it is legitimate for Hercules, or even for a judge less philosophic and talented than the son of Zeus, to substitute his judgment for that of the legislature.

Dworkin's treatment of the establishment clause presents an opportunity to examine the application of his central premise of "equal concern and respect." His premise is not helpful in resolving the question of publicly subsidized busing on city buses to both private and public schools. Whose equal concern and respect is to prevail under his theory? The application of Dworkin's premise and theory of rights is not nearly so clear as he would have us believe. In the context of busing all children, regardless of the type of school they attend, a number of questions need to be resolved. Are we concerned with the equal dignity and respect of parents who pay taxes for public schools but choose to have their children attend private schools? Is the dispositive issue that the private schools in question are, in fact, parochial schools? Is the issue the equal concern and respect for taxpayers who would subsidize the transportation of all schoolchildren, not just those who attend the subsidized public schools? Is the equal concern and respect determined by the "private moral universe" of schoolchildren who choose to attend parochial schools, some of whom may have determined that they wish to devote their lives to religious service? Should the equal concern and respect of atheists who believe that religion is a delusion prevail? Should the issue be determined according to the views of civil liberties lawyers who believe that their views should determine public policy on this issue, or should it be determined by the views of private school administrators who have an important stake in this issue? Dworkin does not answer these questions. Nor does he answer the alternative view that, given the problematic mix of rights and the public good, this issue should be determined by a democratic system in which all parties who claim that their views are based on justice (or equal concern and respect) should determine public policy.[24] Dworkin's premise of equal concern and respect is simply too vague to be helpful in resolving the issue of the establishment clause, an example he relies on to explicate and defend his own theory.

THE DEATH PENALTY. The Constitutionality of the death penalty is yet another example of Dworkin's constitutional theory. Once again distinguishing "conception" from "concept," he argues that it is a mistake for the Court to be much influenced by the fact that the prohibition against cruel and unusual punishment was put into the Constitution at a time when capital punishment was acceptable. The framers' acceptance of the death penalty—indeed, the explicit reference to the death penalty in the text—would be decisive if the framers had intended to lay down a specific "conception" of cruel and unusual punishment. But Dworkin argues that they did not do this; rather, they laid down a "concept" of cruelty, leaving successive generations to fill in the details or, more specifically, leaving the Court to fill in such detailed "conceptions."[25]

Dworkin's analysis of the death penalty is open to a number of objections. First, his theory presumes a judicial prerogative to ascertain rights from principle, which is not found in the theory or text of the Constitution. He presumes a burden of proof falling on those who support the death penalty, for example, in his statement, "Can the Court, responding to the framers' appeal to the concept of cruelty, now defend a conception that does not make death cruel?"[26] Granted, the Constitution does not require the death penalty; its assumption of the death penalty in the due process clauses of the Fifth and Fourteenth Amendments indicates only that if there is a death penalty, it must be administered according to due process of law.[27] Legislative bodies are not required by the Constitution to legislate the death penalty. Legislative, not judicial, discretion over the matter is more consistent with the text and theory of the Constitution than is Dworkin's presumption that it is simply the province of the Court to determine whether the death penalty is cruel or unusual. It is difficult to see a justification for Dworkin's position beyond his own opposition to capital punishment. He may be justified in this opposition, but the Constitution does not make this judgment the exclusive province of the Court. If judges are free to disregard this clearly stated conception in the Fifth and Fourteenth Amendments, a written constitution places little effective limitation on judges.

The validity of Dworkin's distinction between "conceptions" and "concepts" of fairness depends on its degree of abstraction. It is difficult to quarrel with the proposition that the concept of unreasonable search and seizures should apply to electronic communications, even though the framers obviously were not thinking of the application of Fourth Amendment principles to the telephone or computer technology in their conception of that amendment. But the defect of Dworkin's analysis is his moving from concepts embodied within constitutional provisions to vague and abstract rights, namely, those of equal concern and respect. He then uses the right of equal concern and respect to give judges the authority to create their own conceptions and applications of justice. He would have judges use these concepts to become the peculiar guardians of justice, even when these concepts contradict the explicit language of the Constitution, as he believes they do in the case of the death penalty. He asks judges to impose these conceptions on state governments, on the other branches of the national government, and ultimately on the ruling majority itself. At its foundation, Dworkin's doctrine of rights seems designed to allow judges to impose their own conceptions of justice on the democratic branches of government, all in the name of individual rights and principles, which Dworkin's scheme makes the peculiar province of the judiciary. Rights and principles become the creatures of judicial discretion, a discretion that Dworkin assumes will most often be used to take rights seriously and to decide hard cases properly.

Dworkin's scheme of principles versus policy, and his subordination of the latter to the former, has a number of flaws. At one level, it is a means to justify judicial supremacy. At a more basic level, it puts a Herculean burden on judges to determine how competing goods are to be resolved, all within the rubric of rights. Absent is that hardheaded conception of politics found in Hobbes and Locke and *The Federalist,* which views the state of nature with its absolute rights as an abominable place, utterly incompatible with the political necessities of civil society. Or, in the words of *The Federalist,* the rights of citizens must be reconciled with "the permanent and aggregate interests of the community."[28] Dworkin's regime is a regime of subjective moral preference in which individual determinations of what is right reign supreme.

The political order established by the Constitution has succeeded in balancing these two goods with its underlying recognition of the difficult task of governing and the necessary accommodation of individual rights to the public good. Dworkin rejects the concept of the public good in his formulation that individual rights trump other considerations, including that of the public good. The Lockean scheme and contributions made by the Constitution have produced a contemporary political order upon which Dworkin tries to impose his regime of uncompromising individual rights. In doing so, Dworkin neglects the difficulty and necessity of governing individuals and focuses almost entirely on individual rights. The success of the Lockean view embodied in the Constitution has produced a stable political order in which the very basis of the Constitution's scheme for an energetic and democratic government is in some respects obscured. Government seems a simpler matter than it actually is because of the very success of the Constitution. It has succeeded because it recognizes the necessity for energetic government and is not entirely devoted to a strictly individualistic view of government. The original constitutional scheme embodied this view in the body of the Constitution and in a form of government designed to secure both the public good and private rights. The Bill of Rights appended reasonably specific rights to protect individuals from feared abuses by the central government. In protecting the public good and individual rights in the body of the Constitution and subsequently specifying certain individual rights in the Bill of Rights, the Constitution has resulted in a stable and successful form of government that secures both private rights and the public good. The Constitution's success masks the inherent difficulty in governing. Its success is one of the reasons that Dworkin's theory of individual rights appears even plausible. If he were not heir to a constitutional system that secures rights through energetic government and that accounts for both the public good and private rights, his proposal for trumping the public good with his theory of rights would appear utterly unattractive and unrealistic.

Dworkin's theory rests on an individualistic or self-regarding understanding of government.[29] Its compass is the individual's private judgment. Both Hobbes and Locke subordinate private judgments to public judgments about what the law should be, and they recognize the necessity for government to subordinate private judgments as a primary justification for civil society. The Constitution and *The Federalist* depart from Hobbes in important respects and add to Locke's theory a written constitution and an independent judiciary with the power of judicial review. But *The Federalist* retains their view of the necessity of subordinating private judgment to the judgment of a properly constituted government.[30] *The Federalist* regards private rights as justifying government, but it also recognizes the problematic task of actualizing these rights within a political order. It recognizes that "[a]s long as the reason of man continues fallible, and he is at liberty to exercise it, different opinions will be formed." Uniformity of opinions and interests is also obstructed by the "diversity in the faculties of men from which the rights of property originate."[31] Individuals "have an equal right to personal safety and the free use of their 'diverse and unequal' capacities for acquiring property and for pursuing their own conception of happiness."[32] Diverse and unequal faculties contribute to the formation of differing political opinions and are the origin of the rights of property, to the latter of which Dworkin accords little importance. These are some of the reasons that private judgment is not trustworthy to achieve justice. This conclusion does not rest on skepticism about the existence of justice or the desirability of pursuing it but is skeptical of private judgment's ability to achieve justice or to be the authoritative judge of what is just.

With full confidence in the existence of justice and individual rights, *The Federalist* explains how the Constitution sets out to achieve these elusive goals. Private judgment about public things is subordinated to a properly constituted and moderated public judgment, which results from an intricate constitutional structure and process that are fundamentally democratic in nature. The private realm and the public realm are defined by the public judgment because private judgment is not trustworthy. The public judgment will err, but it is a more dependable means of achieving the public good and private rights than is private judgment, particularly the private judgment of human judges who do not embody the mythical qualities of Dworkin's Hercules. When this judgment errs, or is about to err, the constitutional system is designed to give the democratic will the opportunity to correct itself through mechanisms that are fundamentally democratic in nature.[33] These mechanisms include a proper role for the judiciary, but not the Herculean role advocated by Dworkin. Neither the judiciary nor private judgment was designed to have a monopoly on defining and actualizing the principles of constitutional restrictions on government. Dworkin departs from the constitutional design in relegating these judgments to the private judgment and to the judiciary for sole and final resolution.

Dworkin's theory of individual rights regards those rights as indissolubly linked to principles. The judicial role he advocates deals with principles, and his definition restricts principles to issues dealing with rights. The private judgment that his theory seeks to protect is based on rights and on the judiciary's being the peculiar guardian of these rights. Dworkin's scheme replaces democratic will with judicial rule in the name of private judgment and individual rights, even when these rights are clearly inconsistent with constitutional presumptions, as they are in the case of a judgment that the death penalty is cruel and unusual punishment.

PORNOGRAPHY AND THE FIRST AMENDMENT. Regulation of pornography offers another helpful application of Dworkin's constitutional theory.

Regulation deriving from "ideal arguments of policy" cannot be defended on the basis of elevating the community, "because that argument would violate the canon of the liberal [Dworkin's] conception of equality that prohibits a government from relying on the claim that certain forms of life are inherently more valuable than others."[34] Dworkin's liberalism supposes that government must be neutral as to what constitutes the good life.[35] He applies his theory to the constitutional issue of regulating pornography. He rejects the rationale that holds that pornography portrays a way of life or nurtures attitudes that are "demeaning or bestial or otherwise unsuitable to human beings of the best sort." He then proffers a defense of pornography regulation that is consistent with personal rather than external preferences and that avoids "ideal arguments of policy" embodying ideas of how human beings should live. Dworkin supposes the possibility that all forms of literature, including pornography, Shakespeare, and the Bible, may be sufficiently powerful emotionally to influence conduct and contribute to crime.[36] Yet, under this argument, Shakespeare or the Bible need not be suppressed. For the sake of argument, he attempts to distinguish pornography from literature such as Shakespeare or the Bible while avoiding any judgment that pornography presents an unsuitable way of life, a judgment that would involve the forbidden external preferences. Rather than admit that pornography encourages and embodies a way of life that society may discourage or forbid—an admission that would undermine his theoretical premise—Dworkin turns to an alternative defense for its regulation.[37] Suppression of pornography might be made consistent with his "equal dignity and respect" thesis because, unlike Shakespeare or the Bible: "The judgment in question—that pornography does not in fact contribute enough of literary value, or that it is not sufficiently informative or imaginative about the different ways in which people might express themselves or find value in their lives, to justify accepting the damage of crime as the cost of its publication—is not the judgment that those who do enjoy pornography have worse character on that account."[38] Thus, Dworkin attempts to justify suppression of pornography because, unlike the Bible or Shakespeare, it fails to supply information about a wide range of lifestyles.[39]

It is not surprising that Dworkin does not use this halfhearted argument to support his own view. In the context of feminist attacks on pornography, Dworkin responds that free speech "is the core of the choice modern democracies have made, a choice we must now honor in finding our own ways to combat the shaming inequalities women still suffer."[40] In Dworkin's principled egalitarian society, even pornography without ideational content is a part of the pornographer's and consumer's "moral environment" to which they have an equal right that cannot be "locked out" by law.[41]

Quite apart from the questionable premise in his hypothetical defense of pornography regulation—that it does not supply information about a wide range of lifestyles—Dworkin's proffered rationale for suppression of pornography obscures the reason that majorities, as well as the Supreme Court, believe regulation of pornography to be justified. Pornography is offensive to community standards, appeals to the prurient interest, and lacks serious literary, artistic, political, or scientific value.[42] The Supreme Court's rationale for regulation of pornography is, of course, inconsistent with Dworkin's "right to moral independence"[43] and his premise of equal concern and respect.

Robert George offers yet another criticism of Dworkin's position on pornography. George argues that pornography regulation in actuality preserves the interests of those individuals who would desire to use pornography if it were freely and legally available. He persuasively argues: "Dignity and beauty in sexual relationships (and a supporting cultural structure) are no less goods for them [those who are inclined to use pornography] than for anyone else."[44] Thus, quite contrary to Dworkin's argument that pornography regulation denies equal concern and respect, George argues that such regulation shows concern and respect for those very individuals who would be inclined to use pornography. George's argument rests on the sensible distinction between the immediate satisfaction of desires through pornography and the higher dignity and beauty of sexual relationships, which pornography regulation nurtures through its restrictions.[45] Regulation of pornography also sets a standard through the public law that reinforces the view that some ways of life contribute more to dignity and respect than others and are a part of the moral environment from which we draw our private standards of what is deserving of dignity and respect.[46]

Dworkin's tortured defense of pornography regulation, in trying to be consistent with his theory, attempts to avoid using external preferences. His theory presents another problem. He moves his analysis from a conception of what constitutes human virtue or the good life to considerations constructed within the framework of "equal concern and respect." This is a problematic position for one who regards "intuition" as a cornerstone of his theory of rights and who rejects the tenets of legal positivism. Dworkin supposes that individuated rights exist beyond positive acts of a society or a political order, yet he denies that there is any way of life more intrinsically valuable than any other. His hypothetical defense of pornography regulations not only is in tension with his view of individual rights and right answers but also belies the very intuition or conviction on which his theory of rights rests. Dworkin himself must finally reject his hypothetical defense of pornography regulation in favor of his own premise that every individual has the equal right to "moral independence," to contribute to the "moral environment," even if that contribution is offensive and contains no ideas.

Dworkin's premise invalidates our intuition or judgment that the lives of Abraham Lincoln, Franklin Roosevelt, and Winston Churchill are intrinsically more valuable than those of purveyors of pornography or those who commit treason for private gain. It denigrates virtues such as courage, magnanimity, liberality, and justice to merely personal judgments, utterly subjective and without objective merit and based on an egalitarian "right to moral independence."[47] Dworkin sidesteps the question of whether or not his view would enjoy the support (the intuition or conviction) of any significant segment of the liberal society on whose convictions his enterprise of establishing rights purports to rest. And sidestep it he should, for liberal democracy does presume that there are right answers to questions of the highest human concern and how we should live our lives. It confers honors, dispenses justice, rewards truthfulness, and punishes lies. But if Dworkin granted this and allowed pornography to be punished for the reasons the Supreme Court has articulated, it would undermine his thesis of moral independence. Yet the intuition shared by citizens supports government and society both in rewarding good ways of life and in dishonoring or punishing base ways of life. Such intuition or moral reaction, which runs counter to Dworkin's general theory or principles, would, according to his own doctrine of "reflective equilibrium" and "articulate consistency," require altering his underlying principle of "moral independence" and avoiding "external preferences."[48] In short, according to Dworkin's own rule of articulate consistency, intuitions or moral reactions that contradict "equal concern and respect" require modification of his fundamental premise.

Dworkin is right to equivocate as to whether his theory of rights is a theory of natural rights. It cannot be a traditional theory of natural rights, for he rejects the proposition that any way of life is intrinsically more valuable than any other and instead relies on contemporary intuition and "moral independence" rather than what is natural to human beings. He wishes, however, to construct a standard beyond that of legal positivism. To do this, rather than relying on Hobbes, Locke, or their conceptions of natural rights within the U.S. Constitution, he turns to intuitions or convictions arising within liberal democracy. Rather than justifying liberal democracy or natural rights as intrinsically valuable, he presumes their validity as consistent with his conception of contemporary intuition and his theory built from that conception. To achieve effective government, Hobbes and Locke subordinated private judgment to law. Locke and, more dramatically, the American Constitution insisted on majority rule and the proper structuring of that majority through institutions of government to make sound decisions regarding the relative weight of private rights and "the permanent and aggregate interests of the community."[49]

Dworkin's hypothetical defense of pornography regulation, abstracted both from legislative judgment and from any conception of preferred ways of life, becomes tortured and ultimately fails as he attempts to base it on his theory of external versus subjective preferences. This defense cannot stand up to his fundamental right of egalitarian "moral independence." His "right answer" to the question of pornography is that there is no right answer to be enforced through law and that pornography's status is to be determined by the market and by the consumer's subjective, private morality. According to his premise, regulation of pornography is inconsistent with "equal dignity and respect." Dworkin does not answer the question of how a political order that cannot embody in law the view that there is a right answer to the status of pornography can sustain the sentiment or intuition that there are right answers to questions of justice on which his entire scheme rests. Although Dworkin insists that there are right answers in hard cases, he dismisses the "right answer" thesis in the context of fundamental questions of law and how we should live within political society.[50]

The Supreme Court has taken a more moderate course by embodying First Amendment principles within its decisions and also allowing some legislative latitude to regulate in the interests of contemporary community standards to reach the patent offensiveness and prurient interest of pornography. Although the Court's standards are far from Victorian, its decisions recognize the desirability of the law's giving guidance as to how we should live. Court decisions reflect concern with freedom of speech and the press and with the legislative determination of how these values are to be weighed against the competing value of a moral community. The Court seems properly hesitant simply to impose its own views on the legislative bodies that attempt to regulate pornography. This limited deference to legislative will reflects caution in imposing judicial supremacy upon the legislative judgment and a recognition that regulation of pornography should be subject to both legislative will and judicial review in a way that is consistent with separated powers. The Court's decision has the additional virtue of recognizing that there are right answers to the question of how we should live our lives, as problematic as it may be to balance these answers with applicable First Amendment provisions.

ABORTION. The link between Dworkin's theory of rights and his dependency on the judiciary to promulgate these rights brings us to the role he describes for the judiciary and the Supreme Court in the abortion controversy. Dworkin's latest book, *Life's Dominion,* devotes much of its analysis to the question of abortion and individual rights. He also undertakes sustained analysis of the judicial role in the abortion controversy. This analysis reveals his view of the proper role of the Court and the proper mode of constitutional interpretation. The major premise of Dworkin's analysis is that the issue has been incorrectly framed. Rather than proceeding from the question of whether a fetus is a person with rights and interests, he argues that the controversy should be grounded in the commonly held view that life has an intrinsic value and, therefore, should be resolved on the basis of "our common commitment to the sanctity of life.''[51] He properly objects to many critics and proponents of the abortion decisions who form their view of "what kind of constitution they want by asking what kind would benefit their side of the abortion argument; they treat that issue as a litmus test of any constitutional theory's adequacy" (124).

Dworkin contrasts the view of bitter critics of *Roe v. Wade* who say the Court licensed murder with the view of more sophisticated critics who argue that the Court "had no business ruling on the matter at all, because the Constitution gives democratically elected state legislatures, not unelected judges, the power to decide whether and when abortion will be legal" (102). He cites Robert Bork as one of those constitutional scholars who believe that whatever one thinks about the merits of the abortion argument, a right to abortion is simply not found in the Constitution (103). It turns out, however, that Dworkin does not think that these critics are sophisticated after all.

He begins his refutation of the argument of the sophisticated critics by examining the issue of whether fetuses have rights according to his standard of articulate consistency. This standard states that the Supreme Court is "obliged to make its decisions consistent, so far as this is possible, with the broad constitutional traditions established and respected in its past decisions" (106). His treatment of the constitutional tradition begins with *Griswold v. Connecticut,* a 1965 case that outlawed prohibitions on the sale of contraceptives to married persons on the grounds that such laws violated a constitutional right to privacy.[52] He argues that if one accepts that case as good law, it follows that the principle of privacy includes the decision not only whether to beget but also whether to bear children.[53] He spends substantial time establishing and supporting the proposition that fetuses are not constitutional persons; therefore, they do not possess the attendant constitutional rights (113). In response to Professor John Hart Ely's argument that the government has a legitimate right to protect the interests of creatures who are not persons, for example, by forbidding cruelty to dogs, Dworkin relies on Laurence Tribe's argument that "government does not have the power to do this in ways that make the exercise of a fundamental constitutional right impossible" (113). The presumption that there is a fundamental constitutional right to abortion persists both as a premise and as a conclusion throughout his treatment of the issue. It leads him to contrast two different modes of constitutional interpretation.

The preferred mode of constitutional interpretation raises for Dworkin the question of what kind of Constitution the United States should have. He posits two modes of interpretation, the first of which is a "constitution of *principle* that lays down general, comprehensive moral standards that government must respect but that leaves it to statesmen and judges to decide what these standards mean in concrete circumstances." He believes that this requires all citizens to be treated with "equal concern and respect." The other mode of interpretation is a "constitution of *detail*," which expresses "only the very specific, concrete expectations of the particular statesmen who wrote and voted for them." Dworkin regards the "constitution of detail" as a "collection of independent historical views and opinions unlikely to have great unity or even complete consistency." He discusses the Bill of Rights (including the post–Civil War amendments) but does not address the body of the Constitution, the legislative power, or the separation of powers (119).

Dworkin, of course, prefers the mode of interpretation embodied in his constitution of principle, dismissing the other alternative as a "postage-stamp collection" of nonunified, inconsistent historical views. Recognizing the abstraction intrinsic to his view, and admitting that "philosophers, statesmen, and citizens have debated for many centuries with no prospect of agreement" on these issues, Dworkin readily accepts the unbridled judicial authority he sees implicit in his theory of the Constitution (119–20, 143). He believes that judges' interpretations of abstract principles such as "equal concern and respect" will be grounded in the "principle and integrity" of arguments that are subject to the professional critique of the legal profession and, finally, to the judgment of the public, "whose influence should be felt when presidents nominate judges." His corrective to judicial abuse of this authority is the amendment process or waiting until "age, death, or change produces a different Supreme Court with different convictions" (120). Dworkin is confident that a Herculean Court will decide cases of highest moral principle on the basis of abstract concepts such as "equal concern and respect" and that the stronger moral argument will prevail. Although he is content to rely on more specific principles such as freedom of speech or press when the constitutional text provides such principles, he will not allow his theory to be constrained by even these principles of an intermediate level of abstraction, for it would constrain the Court from enforcing principles of morality beyond those embodied in specific constitutional provisions.

Dworkin believes that there are right answers to questions of rights, that these answers are ascertainable by Herculean judges, and that it is their duty to enforce them on democracy until the democracy responds through the amendment process or through the only remotely democratic process of Supreme Court nominations. Because Dworkin discredits the intent and conceptions of those who propose and ratify constitutional amendments, this turns out to be no limitation at all. Judges can merely circumvent such amendments through appeal to a more abstract principle, which they support through argument and therefore justify as the law of the Constitution. Much the same can be said of the appointment process. If a seat on the Supreme Court amounts to a blank check to impose the justices' views of such abstract principles as "equal concern and respect" upon the democracy, then the nomination process amounts to little more than a designation of which embodiment of Hercules is to wear the robe and write the judicial opinions that will impose the justices' philosophy upon the democracy.[54] Dworkin argues that we should strive for government "not by men and women, or even under law, but government under principle."[55] He regards the law as properly subordinated to judges' conceptions of principle: "We must abandon the pointless search for mechanical or semantic constraints and seek genuine constraints in the only place where they can be found: in good argument" (145).

Dworkin has now set the stage for making a strong argument in favor of a right to abortion, which, according to the model he has constructed, should be the argument the Supreme Court enforces as constitutional law. Indeed, his argument should be taken into consideration as society and lawmakers assess the competing considerations involved in this issue. But this is not sufficient for Dworkin. He believes that judges have a duty, once his argument is made, to enforce it as the law of the Constitution. This is the very question in controversy: do judges have a duty to decide hard cases such as this when the Constitution provides little or no guidance in this task and they must resort to the doctrine of unenumerated rights to assume this authority? Dworkin argues unequivocally that they should, and that the liberty guaranteed by the due process clause of the Fourteenth Amendment contains a right to abortion. The right is established by the strength of the arguments favoring such a right, not by "bogus arguments about original intention and unenumerated rights" (144). These bogus arguments should give way to a more sweeping judicial role: "The Constitution insists that our judges do their best collectively to construct, reinspect, and revise, generation by generation, the skeleton of freedom and equality of concern that its great clauses, in their majestic abstraction, command" (145). He believes that the choices in the mode of interpretation consist of his preferred view of a principled constitution on the one hand and on the other a constitution of detail that leaves the legislature and executive "legally free to disregard fundamental principles of justice and decency" (123). Principles of justice and decency are appealing and fundamental concepts, but Dworkin gives us little clue as to where or how the Constitution insists that the judiciary is the proper body to ascertain what they are. More accurately, Dworkin insists that this is the proper judicial role according to his theory; but the Constitution and its theory provide for no such role.

Conclusion

LIMITING PRINCIPLES TO INDIVIDUAL RIGHTS. The abortion issue exemplifies Dworkin's preference for a constitution of principle that requires the judiciary to articulate and enforce constitutional principles. According to his constitution of principle, the judiciary is responsible for enforcing the stronger argument as constitutional law, whether the issue is abortion or any other right. He supports his preference by contrasting his view with the bogus constitution of detail, "a postage-stamp collection" of constitutional provisions that frees the legislature and executive to disregard principles of justice and decency fundamental to a constitution of principle. On the surface, this is an appealing view. But it runs counter to the theory of the Constitution that, absent constitutional prohibitions, it is the right of the majority to determine what is the stronger argument, even on those occasions when the majority errs by making non-Herculean judgments, as it inevitably will.

At its most basic level, Dworkin argues that the Supreme Court ought to enforce rights, including a right to abortion because abortion and these other rights are required by his "right to equal concern and respect." Abortion and any other rights supported by strong argument deserve judicial enforcement, even though they are not included in constitutional provisions or in what Dworkin calls the constitution of detail. This is the level at which Dworkin's argument is most vulnerable, because it disregards the principle of consent, runs counter to the principle of separation of powers, and is contrary to the principle of representative government. These are legitimate constitutional principles and are more fundamental than the rights that are the sole depositories of principle according to Dworkin's argument. By calling rights principles and relegating considerations of consent, representation, and separation of powers to a subordinate status, Dworkin buttresses his theory in a way that sunders it from the theoretical foundations of our system of government. His theory is inconsistent with even his own test of articulate consistency—that decisions be consistent with "principles embedded in Supreme Court precedent and with the main structures of our constitutional arrangement."[56]

Contra Dworkin, a root principle of the Constitution is democratic representation. The Constitution is built on this principle and on the need to moderate and elevate public opinion as that opinion becomes public law. We have reviewed the mechanisms and structures designed to achieve this end (see Chapter 2). Achieving justice, or approximating justice, is extraordinarily difficult. The constitutional theory aims to do this through properly constituted majority rule in which a vision of justice, or the stronger argument, must be accommodated to the consent of those who are governed. If the majority errs, the system has mechanisms to correct this error before majority opinion becomes public law. If bad laws are passed, there is provision for majority correction through the process of representation.

The Supreme Court has a proper role in this process, and the Constitution has designated areas of political life that allow the Court latitude in determining and enforcing constitutional rights. Areas such as free speech, a standard of reasonableness where searches and seizures are concerned, and an impartial jury are not simply "postage stamps" with no unifying principle. They are principles of intermediate or tolerable generality, which judges must apply to changing circumstances. Free speech applies to telecommunications, for example, but Dworkin's level of abstraction of liberty or "equal concern and respect" removes all impediments to judicial sovereignty, except that judges are bound by the stronger argument. It is no coincidence that in the contexts discussed above, the stronger argument turns out to be the argument Dworkin favors.

There are good reasons for the legislative authority to prevail except when there are specified restrictions on that authority in the Constitution. Hobbes argues against judges being bound by views having no authority other than that of "books of moral philosophy," though they "be naturally reasonable."[57] To justify such judicial power, which undermines the sovereignty of both the Constitution and the legislature, Dworkin must show that such judicial sovereignty is consistent with the underlying theory of the Constitution and with a sound system of representative government. Although he asserts this as a matter of moral philosophy, he makes little effort to establish such an intention by those who established the Constitution or to show that his theory corrects the mistakes they made.

Dworkin's interpretation also contradicts Locke's characterization of the legislative power. Locke argues that the force and obligation of law rest on the "sanction from that legislative which the public has chosen and appointed: for without this the law could not have that, which is absolutely necessary to its being a law, the consent of the society, over whom no body can have a power to make laws, but by their own consent."[58] The Court cannot claim consent as the legislature can, and unless the Court can point to constitutional prohibitions to which consent was given, judicial invalidation of legislative law violates Locke's principle. Dworkin's reliance on the "stronger argument" as the limitation on judges also violates Locke's principle of "established and promulgated laws" within which people are safe and secure within the law,[59] as well as Montesquieu's principle that the rule of law is essential to security and liberty.[60] If judges are not restrained by the law of the Constitution and are bound only by the principles of moral philosophy and selective reliance on their own precedents, they are beyond the restraint of law. No citizen can be secure when the judicial anchor in the Constitution's text is removed because of a preferred moral philosophy. We may be pleased when this moral philosophy coincides with our own sentiments, but when it does not, there is little recourse. As was observed earlier, given Dworkin's canon of interpretation, amendment to the Constitution becomes nearly meaningless, since amendments are to be interpreted according to the principle of "equal dignity and respect," and the conceptions or intent they embody are irrelevant. The remotely democratic process of judicial nomination lauded by Dworkin is no substitute for the consent that Locke requires.

The principle of consent also applies to the U.S. Constitution. First, it was necessary to give legitimacy to the act of founding; that is, the legitimacy of the frame and theory of government embodied in the Constitution rested on the consent of the governed. Second, the Constitution and its theory are strictly republican in nature. Not only the act of framing the government but also the actual operation of the government is based on the principle of consent through representation. Thus, the principle of consent is carried from the act of founding to the actual operation of our institutions. Dworkin emphasizes the "main structures of our constitutional arrangement" as central to his concept of articulate consistency and constitutional integrity.[61] Yet, in the context of individual rights, he fails to acknowledge the importance of the "strictly republican" principle of the Constitution. He thereby sunders the body of the Constitution from the Bill of Rights. By limiting his definition of principles to individual rights and characterizing the document as a "constitution of principle," he eliminates by definition those important principles contained in the body of the Constitution, the most important of which are representation and the separation of powers.

Dworkin's case for judicial activism, the authority of the Court to give final answers in hard cases, is illustrated by his equating the framers with the father and the Court with children.[62] As Stanley Brubaker recognizes, Dworkin presents the framers as "ontologically confident" in the existence and importance of the concepts they embodied in the Constitution; Dworkin believes that the framers were "epistemologically skeptical" of their capacity to know the implications of these concepts and skeptical of the "enduring significance of their own conceptions."[63] Thus, according to Dworkin, it is the duty of the Supreme Court as responsible children to give contemporary meaning (articulate conceptions) to the concepts the framers embodied in the Constitution. Brubaker properly argues that there is a flaw in Dworkin's illustration. There are really two sets of children present in this scenario: the Court and the legislature, "each pleading to the father [the framers] that *its* conception is better" (513). Dworkin would have the Court follow the framers' mind-set and, therefore, become the contemporary father of the Constitution by refining the framers' concepts into contemporary and binding conceptions. In this process, the Court determines and enforces right answers according to its conceptions of the framers' concepts and thereby binds the legislature to these conceptions. Although the framers had examples in mind of what they meant by the concepts embodied in the Constitution, Dworkin contends that they did not intend these concepts to be limited to those examples. He argues that future children will face situations the framers did not anticipate; furthermore, some particular actions that the framers thought acceptable may not be so regarded by future children (513).

Brubaker persuasively argues that Dworkin's scenario supports a doctrine of judicial restraint. The Court should be reluctant to negate laws that the legislative children can reasonably argue are consistent with the framers' concepts and constitutional provisions. One may fully accept Dworkin's view that there are right answers to hard questions without accepting the proposition that judges fully grasp those answers (513–14). Judges should pay deference to the reasonable claims legislators make to "right answers," that is, if one takes representative democracy seriously.

HERCULEAN OR HUMAN JUDGE? THE ROLE OF REPRESENTATION AND CONSENT. Dworkin justifies substitution of judicial judgment for that of the legislature or society in his examination of the right of the majority to determine questions of political morality. He assumes that many decisions of his hypothetical judge, Hercules, determine legal rights on the basis of political theory—determinations that other judges or the public might make differently. But he dismisses this objection. The reason for his dismissal is that even if a judge defers to a legislative body or some other authority, the judge is relying on a conviction or judgment to justify this deferral. Thus, judges have to rely on their own convictions as to when they should defer to some other authority. Dworkin believes that his judge does not face this problem, for Hercules uses the Constitution as a means of finding the legal rights of the parties based on the concepts of the Constitution, and "when that judgment is made nothing remains to submit to either his own or the public's convictions." Dworkin believes Hercules is justified in reaching a decision independent of the public's or the legislature's convictions because Hercules does not approach the law as being limited by what it explicitly requires and uses "an independent discretion to legislate on issues which the law does not reach."[64] Dworkin seems to forget that the mythical Hercules is celebrated for his strength rather than his wisdom. But in one respect, his use of Hercules is justified, since Dworkin wishes to supplant the power of popular government with a powerful judiciary that will be supreme in his theoretical system.

Instead of relying on majority opinion, Hercules relies on the community's moral traditions, "at least as these are captured in the whole institutional record that it is his office to interpret." If "no justification of the earlier constitutional cases can be given that does not contain a liberal principle sufficiently strong to require a decision in favor of abortion," Hercules must rule in favor of abortion no matter how strongly the practice is condemned by popular morality. Dworkin explains that this view is a consequence of an individual's "institutional right," that is defined by the "community's constitutional morality," one that "Hercules must defend against any inconsistent opinion however popular" (125–26). In other words, the institutional right as embodied in earlier Court decisions must prevail over specific legislative or popular opinion that, though intensely held, is inconsistent with the institutional right of the individual. Hercules is justified in correcting the "ordinary man's opinion" as expressed through legislative or popular will in light of the "institutional rights" that constitute community morality (126–29). Thus, judges determine the community morality, which is based on principles that extend beyond the explicit requirements of the law as set forth in the Constitution. Dworkin admits that when Hercules decides cases of contested concepts such as "fairness or liberality or equality," his decisions will be controversial. Dworkin resolves this problem by using his inevitable example of abortion and due process. He argues from a supposition that earlier due process cases can be justified on the basis of human dignity, but that they are unclear as to whether such dignity requires a right to abortion: "If Hercules sits in the abortion cases, he must decide that issue and must employ his own understanding of dignity to do so" (126–27).

Dworkin anticipates the criticism that although the judicial role he prescribes might be appropriate for Hercules, it is not proper for ordinary human judges, who will inevitably make mistakes and disagree with one another. He responds that although we (ordinary humans and social critics) "know that mistakes will be made, we do not know when because we are not Hercules either." His answer to this objection is that the techniques of adjudication and the process of selecting the most competent judges should be improved (130).

But where is the pool of Herculean candidates to be found? Are we not limited to the non-Herculean stuff of which humans are made? This is the issue that persuaded the framers to rely on representative government as the final source of authority in government. Dworkin's admission that, because we are not Herculean, we do not know when judges make mistakes does not, in itself, undermine his thesis that there are right answers in hard cases. But is this not an argument for moderation in what we expect from judges? Non-Herculean judges ought to be bound by law and exercise judgment in a manner consistent with the moderation that is fundamental to the regime. This is precisely the type of regime that Publius describes in *The Federalist* after observing in No. 1 that "the causes which serve to give a false bias to the judgment" are numerous, and as a consequence, we see "wise and good men on the wrong as well as on the right side of questions of the first magnitude to society." Realization of these characteristics of human nature, Publius argues, "would furnish a lesson of moderation to those who are ever so much persuaded of their being in the right in any controversy."[65] One of the consequences of this moderation is a written constitution that limits the powers of government, including that of the judiciary. Publius describes a limited constitution as "one which contains certain specified exceptions to the legislative authority."[66] The non-Herculean judges within this constitution were not given the authority to reason constrained only by their own decisions and the strongest moral argument. This would violate Publius's understanding of the limits of human nature and judgment, his insistence on representative government, and his understanding of a limited, written constitution.

By Dworkin's own standards of articulate consistency and constitutional integrity, one questions why he does not take representative democracy seriously. It is a fundamental principle of the "main structures of our constitutional arrangement" from which his articulate consistency is derived.[67] As was established in Part I of this work, the constitutional structure was established on the premise that "dependence on the people is, no doubt, the primary control on the government,"[68] and representation of individuals has a "natural and universal connection" with the "rights of the people."[69]

Dworkin's dependence on Herculean judges to decide all hard cases of individual rights presumes a confidence in judicial reason and a rejection of republican principles, which runs counter to the Constitution's underlying theory. *The Federalist* rejects this antirepublican solution in a number of respects, all of which dismiss moral motives or "enlightened statesmen" as reliable means to achieve justice.[70] The framers and ratifiers of the Constitution present no evidence of the far-reaching, Herculean role for judges advocated by Dworkin. Their concept of the Constitution was based on the representative principle as the most reliable protection for individual rights.

The Federalist and other founding documents refute Dworkin's premise of judicial supremacy. *The Federalist* characterized "a series of deliberate usurpations on the authority of the legislature" as cause for impeachment. James Wilson's comment in the Constitutional Convention refutes Dworkin's view of judicial supremacy: "[l]aws may be unjust, may be unwise, may be dangerous, may be destructive, and yet not be so unconstitutional as to justify the Judges in refusing to give them effect."[71] Madison's limitation of the review power to "cases of a judiciary nature" and Mason's view that laws, "however unjust, oppressive or pernicious," that are not plainly unconstitutional must stand support a theory relying on republican principle rather than on the Supreme Court as moral guardian of the political order.[72]

In explaining the "main structures of our constitutional arrangement,"[73] Publius devotes forty-six of the eighty-five papers in *The Federalist* to the "conformity of the proposed Constitution to the true principles of republican government."[74] This evidence of the constitutional structure, together with other evidence presented in Part I of this book, refutes Dworkin's view. He would empower the Court to overturn decisions of representative bodies by standards abstracted from constitutional provisions and arising out of the strongest arguments provided by the judge's understanding of moral philosophy, grounded only in the abstract concepts of "equal dignity and respect."

The Bill of Rights excludes general or abstract maxims from its protections, such as those in the Virginia Declaration of Rights of 1776: "That all men are by nature equally free and independent, and have certain inherent rights, of which, when they enter into a state of society, they cannot, by any compact deprive or divest their posterity; namely, the enjoyment of life and liberty, with the means of acquiring and possessing property, and pursuing and obtaining happiness and safety."[75] This exclusion, and the character of those rights protected by the Constitution, shows a due regard for republican government that is inconsistent with Dworkin's theory. Instead of setting forth inalienable rights in the Bill of Rights, the framers enumerated specific civil rights. These rights require prudence and judgment in their application to specific factual situations and to changing circumstances, but they are of a different character than the rights central to Dworkin's theory, which are bounded only by the strongest moral argument advancing "equal concern and respect." The concern and respect for individuals resulted in a written constitution based on representative government, separation of powers, constitutional limitations, and a judiciary with a role much less far-reaching than that prescribed by Ronald Dworkin.

Dworkin shares with Archibald Cox a belief that the Court should go beyond the explicit provisions of the Constitution in order to protect rights. Unlike Dworkin, Cox grounds his belief in the natural law that he sees underlying the Constitution. Cox is also much more cautious than Dworkin in prescribing the proper judicial role. Cox regards legitimacy, consent of the governed, and institutional considerations of separated powers and federalism as much more important than Dworkin does. This importance is reflected in the role Cox sets forth to guide the judicial power.

Judicial Reform under a Written Constitution: Archibald Cox

The Constitution as the Embodiment of Natural Law

Archibald Cox views the Constitution as an expression of natural rights or as a natural law document. He sees a conflict between this commitment to natural law and the conviction implicit in our Constitution that "the people are the source of all legitimate power, that governments are the people's agents, and that the people, expressing themselves through the majority, have the right to work their will."[76] Cox describes state and federal legislatures as the elements of popular sovereignty in the political order; the Supreme Court, as enforcer of constitutional restrictions in behalf of the individual, is "the voice of natural law."[77]

The brevity of Cox's treatment of the Constitution qua constitution requires that his understanding of the document be drawn primarily from the role he prescribes for the Court, particularly that part of his work dealing with the legitimacy of Supreme Court decisions. This will help determine what Cox means by the "relevant body of ever-changing, ever-constant law" upon which he believes justices should base their decisions.[78]

Cox's view of the Constitution rests on the premise that constitutionalism requires the "observance of the rule of law"[79] as a substitute for power and as the means to freedom.[80] Necessary to this end of freedom and to observance of the rule of law is the people's habit of voluntary compliance and their understanding of the relationship between freedom and the rule of law. Much of Cox's view of the Constitution and the Court can be understood as an inquiry into the means necessary to retain compliance with the rule of law embodied in the Constitution. This capacity to secure compliance to the rule of law is what Cox calls legitimacy. His view of the rule of law that is embodied within the Constitution includes not only the principle of "law-abidingness" but also that of natural law or natural rights as the measure of what is appropriate to abide by. With this addendum, it is appropriate to say that Cox views the Constitution as the rule of law, but it must be understood that his view is more subtle than is indicated on the surface of this statement.[81]

Probing this subtlety requires analysis of his criteria that constitute the appropriate grounds for Supreme Court decisions. In defining the appropriate role for the Court, Cox argues that it should decide cases "according to law, according to a continuity of principle found in the words of the Constitution, judicial precedents, traditional understanding and like sources of law."[82] He seems to regard the Constitution itself as only one source of judicial authority that is to be supplemented by other sources in a way that involves the impartial judicial application of principle. Cox implies that these additional sources of judicial authority enjoy a status equal to that of the Constitution, or perhaps they are an implicit part of the Constitution. He regards the Court's application of reason to the problems that confront the political order as an essential part of the very definition of the Constitution. The Court's reasoning should be guided by freedom or the natural rights of individuals.[83] The Constitution is a natural law document, but in a sense, it is an incomplete one, according to Cox. It must be supplemented by a Court that acts as the "voice of natural law" and thereby completes the Constitution.

Implicit in the rule of law as the central element of the Constitution is Cox's insistence that Court decisions rest on a principled basis rather than on fiat or the merely personal preferences of the justices.[84] This insistence on principled adjudication is also a significant element in achieving the legitimacy that helps ensure the people's acceptance of Court decisions. Such acceptance is necessary to prevent the degeneration of law into mere exercises of power—a degeneration that would mean an end to the freedom toward which the Constitution is aimed.

The Supreme Court as the Voice of Natural Law

Cox regards cases as properly within the Court's authority to rule only insofar as the traditional characteristics of the judicial power are preserved. He specifies such requirements as a real controversy, standing, and the avoidance of moot issues and advisory opinions as desirable limitations on the judicial power as the Court decides cases according to law. A judge should decide cases not by "personal predilections or even by his own superior wisdom as to what is just or right or desirable but by an inherited legal wisdom and the long-range ideals and customs of the community." But Cox believes that the "law is meaningless and will not long survive unless it serves the present needs of men."[85] He approvingly quotes Judge Learned Hand, who argues that a judge must cloak "himself in the majesty of an overshadowing past; but he must discover some composition with the dominant trends of his times."[86] Cox sees the importance of keeping "the law in tune with the current needs of the community," particularly where constitutional law is concerned. Cox's concern for keeping the law in tune with the current needs of the community leads to his emphasis on legitimacy as he explicates his prescribed role for the Court.

One role of the Court regards the relationship of the state and national governments, the separation of powers, and "the necessity for an umpire to resolve the conflicts engendered by our extraordinarily complex system of government."[87] Cox sees the Court as having "responsibility for the framework of our government."[88] An aspect of the Court's umpire function is the judicial resolution of competing claims of state and national governments. He treats this topic in his analysis of the Burger Court's rulings on federalism, in which he emphasizes the benefits of variation and experimentation in advocating "deference to local judgment . . . in the determination of what forms of procedure due process requires."[89] In his discussion of access to federal courts where matters affecting state administration of criminal justice are concerned, he fears that the "too-ready intervention of federal courts" may stunt the growth of state constitutional law and decrease the responsibility and sensitivity of state tribunals.

Cox, however, advocates a role for the federal courts in constitutional litigation to "reform pervasive misconduct of governmental programs and institutions," notwithstanding the value of encouraging local responsibility. His treatment of the state's sovereign immunity from federal regulation focuses on *National League of Cities v. Usery.*[90] He objects to this case because it establishes an "unprincipled exception to the general rule of federal supremacy" and rests on the grounds of "pragmatic and particularistic policy-making" rather than supplying a general rule of decision.[91] It is clear that in the area of state laws that burden interstate commerce, Cox is sensitive to the balancing of pragmatic concerns, which he sees as guiding the Burger Court's failure to build a body of law to instruct lower courts and guide its own adjudication. But he criticizes decisions of both the Warren and the Burger Courts, which pay "too little thought to the long-run institutional consequences of successive majorities imposing their inconsistent pragmatic judgment upon the country on ever-debatable questions of public policy. 'Law' implies more than a claim of superior wisdom wearing judicial robes. The protection which constitutionalism gives to liberty depends upon continued pursuit of the ideal of the rule of law."[92]

In discussing federalism, Cox emphasizes pragmatic concerns, but always with a view toward principles that give them coherence. However, he does not attempt to justify principles such as national supremacy by going beyond them to an underlying constitutional theory. As is the case with his discussion of the Court's role as the voice of natural law, he emphasizes the rule of law, voluntary compliance, and legitimacy much more than the question of theoretical standards to guide the Court's decisions. Although the subject matter differs, most of the standards Cox prescribes for the umpire function also apply to issues of individual liberty.

Cox's second role for the Court derives from his view that the Constitution is the embodiment of the rule of law, including natural law. The Court's role requires consistency with the rule of law. More specifically, he sees one important role for the Court as that of "the voice of natural law." This role becomes most important in "enforcing constitutional restrictions in the interest of the individual." Judicial supremacy in constitutional questions is justified, in his view, because "the Constitution, the Court, and judicial review . . . express and partially realize the deep-seated human conviction that there are fundamental individual liberties, chiefly in the realm of the spirit, that should be beyond the reach of any government—not just beyond a king or an elected executive, but beyond *any* government, including even the majority of a representative legislature."[93]

Cox explores the conflict between natural rights and majoritarianism in his treatment of state and federal legislatures, which he properly regards as elements of popular sovereignty in the political order.[94] This conflict between natural rights and majoritarianism pervades his entire work. He uses it to justify the Court's going beyond the specific contours of the Constitution in pursuit of natural law, at least insofar as it can retain legitimacy and the compliance on which the rule of law and constitutionalism are dependent.

His discussion of legitimacy emerges in the conflict between the Court as the voice of natural law and the popular sovereignty underlying the legislative function. Cox argues that the law's most important quality in a free society is commanding the community's acceptance and support so that force will be unnecessary.[95] This requires the people to believe that the Court is acting in a legitimate manner, for although courts control neither purse nor sword, their decrees often run against other branches of government and against the states. Thus, the people's compliance is dependent upon their belief that the courts are legitimately fulfilling the judicial function.[96]

Cox cites a number of sources for this legitimacy, chief among which is history. For example, he sees history as justifying much of what the Court has done, and the Court's role as umpire of the federal system has become an accepted part of its function. But he objects that history is limited insofar as it fails to legitimize a new judicial role in the eyes of either the judges or the people. Furthermore, humankind's dull and traditional habits give greater weight to those who challenge new judicial decisions as usurpations.[97]

Since history will not explain or legitimize any innovations or reform on the part of the Court, additional sources of legitimacy are necessary: "At the core of the Court's strength is impartiality and independence," qualities that should be used to "serve our society's long-range fundamental values appropriately expressed in constitutional law."[98] If decisions are formulated in terms of "principles referable to legal precedent and other accepted sources of law," they are more likely to be accepted and supported.[99] Courts must also be sensitive to the "moral sense of civilization," "the needs of men," "ethical sensibilities," and "the deeper lasting currents of human thought that give direction to the law" as they determine whether to adhere to precedent or to reform the law.[100]

Judicial departures from history or precedent are ultimately justified or legitimized by natural law, a concept that increases in importance as constitutional adjudication is increasingly utilized as an instrument of reform.[101] Cox's view of the proper judicial use of natural law can be partially understood in his rejection of the argument that if a neutral principle lacks connection with values the Constitution has specified, then the principle is not a *constitutional* one and the Court should not impose it.[102] Cox responds by saying that within the context of the due process clause, decisions must be made "with no real guidance from the document." He links this open-ended adjudication under substantive due process with "our natural law inheritance" and regards it as inevitable under our Constitution.[103] The abortion issue illustrates this aspect of Cox's theory. His criticism is not that *Roe v. Wade* was decided with no real guidance from the document; he objects that "the Court failed to establish the legitimacy of the decision by articulating a precept of sufficient abstractness to lift the ruling above the level of a political judgement based upon the evidence currently available from the medical, physical, and social sciences."[104] He apparently regards the development of abstract principles from which decisions can be derived as sufficient justification for judicial reform and the transformation of natural law into constitutional law: "Constitutional rights ought not to be created under the Due Process Clause unless they can be stated in principles sufficiently absolute to give them roots throughout the community and continuity over significant periods of time, and to lift them above the level of the pragmatic political judgements of a particular time and place."[105] The

Court may endanger its legitimacy if its decisions, rather than proceeding "bit by bit," go "too far too fast."[106]

Cox anticipates two criticisms of his prescription for judicial reform through a greater political role for the judiciary. He rejects Judge Learned Hand's objection that such a political role transforms the Court into a Council of Platonic Guardians and denies citizen participation in government.[107] The ground for Cox's rejection of Hand's position is that "modern government is simply too large and too remote, and too few issues are fought out in elections, for a citizen to feel much more sense of participation in the legislative process than the judicial."[108] Thus, Cox finds Hand's criticism of judicial activism unpersuasive.

A second criticism of Cox's prescribed role for the Court can be drawn from a view articulated by James Bradley Thayer. Thayer argues that when courts exercise judicial review, they correct legislative mistakes and thus cause the people to lose the political experience and moral responsibility that would result from the people's correcting their own errors.[109] Cox responds by suggesting that the "Court at its best assist[s] in the process of education," that the "opinions of the Court seem to me to help to make us what we are by telling us what we may be." He argues that "[t]he Court must know us better than we know ourselves." By basing its decisions and the "aspirations"[110] it voices on roots that are already in the nation, the Court can help "shape our national understanding of ourselves" in a way that will elevate society and at the same time command a consensus.[111]

Cox's prescription for the Court puts that institution in the position of exercising statecraft over the political order. He is willing to do this because of his conviction that "reason, moral right, and justice" need expression by our political institutions, and the best place for this expression, "even though imperfect, is the judicial branch and ultimately the Supreme Court." His confidence in the Court is based on his view that "on the average and over the years, courts will be a great deal firmer and also wiser than legislatures in interpreting constitutional guarantees protecting essential liberty."[112] Combined with the conception of natural law he sees as central to legitimizing judicial activism or reform—activism that does not need the support of specific formulations in the Constitution—this role, indeed, leads to the judicial discretion that we associate with a Council of Platonic Guardians. The primary control over these guardians cannot be the ballot box; Cox sees this control implicit in the various elements constituting "legitimacy."

Analysis of Cox's Commentary

Although Hand and Thayer level two criticisms at Cox's position, there are even more profound problems implicit in that position. Fundamentally, Cox wants the Court to issue principled decisions consistent with natural law and to be mindful of the need for legitimacy so that the people will acquiesce in these decisions. There is no doubt that Cox rejects the mere "edicts of a council of wise men" as relying too much on judicial subjectivity. He insists that such subjectivity be minimized by adherence to principled decision making.[113] This adherence will, in his judgment, result in a "coherent body of law" that can limit the subjectivity of justices.[114] Cox assumes that the Court will issue wiser decisions than those forthcoming from the popular branches of government and suggests that decisions from this body of judicial statesmen will usually be in accordance with the law of nature and thereby elevate the character of the political order.[115]

Decisions such as *The Slaughterhouse Case*,[116] *Dred Scott*,[117] *Plessy v. Ferguson*,[118] *Buck v. Bell*,[119] and many cases thwarting New Deal legislation cast grave historical doubts on Cox's optimism regarding the Court's positive influence as the voice of natural law. In Leonard Levy's words, "the pernicious, highly undemocratic influence of the series of decisions in which the Court crippled and voided most of the comprehensive program for protecting the civil rights of Negroes after the Civil War" and "paralyzed or supplanted legislative and community action" led to "bigotry and played a crucial role in destroying public opinion that favored meeting the challenge of the Negro problem as a constitutional—that is, as a moral—obligation."[120] The legislative efforts to govern and secure rights embodied in legislation that the Court quashed, illustrated by the decisions above, should make us wary of trusting the Court as the voice of natural law and the sole guardian of our liberties. The appropriate question in this context is not the existence of rights but, as *The Federalist* reminds us in No. 84, how these rights are to be defined as a strong and energetic government goes about the necessary business of governing—a process that in itself secures liberty. The reliance on natural law, which Cox sees as necessary to the role he desires for the Court, is incompatible with the constitutional theory of the leading framers whose work is authoritatively expressed in *The Federalist*. There are a number of reasons articulated in this work that counsel against granting the Court the broad authority advocated by Cox. *The Federalist* trusts a properly structured republic to provide for competent government and individual liberty; it distrusts any particular institution of government as being the sole protector of civil liberty. Perhaps it would not be surprising to Publius that the Court in which Cox places so much trust has not consistently supported equality and liberty. Constitutional history casts grave doubts on the thesis that the Court will better protect individual rights in such matters as racial discrimination than will the elective branches of government, and in some instances, the Court has done worse.

NECESSITY OF A STRONG NATIONAL GOVERNMENT AND REPUBLICAN MECHANISMS TO SECURE RIGHTS. Central to the Constitution's wisdom is its provision for a strong but properly structured national government, a provision resting on the conviction that a strong national government is necessary to secure rights. Cox regards the Court as "umpire" of these issues of federalism and separation of powers. The key he advocates for appropriate judicial umpiring is principled and consistent decision making. Although principle and precedent are important legal values, the Constitution contains theoretical guidance that goes beyond these values. The framers, guided by experience with the Articles of Confederation, believed that a strong national government is necessary because republican liberty is not safe within the smaller sphere of each state government.[121] In order to overcome the defect of small republics, a properly structured scheme of representation is necessary. This scheme is based on self-interest and requires a coalition among a multiplicity of interests in order to form a governing majority. Representative government also provides a mechanism for elevating and refining public opinion before that opinion becomes public law. Our system of bicameralism, staggered elections, and other constitutional mechanisms contribute to this elevation and refinement.

The argument of *The Federalist* emphasizes the importance of the Union to the theory of the Constitution and the "insufficiency of the present Confederation to preserve that Union."[122] The theory of representation underlying the new Constitution demanded a large, commercial republic as a barrier against domestic faction and insurrection.[123] The national government encompasses sufficient diversity or multiplicity of interests to control faction and thereby secure individual rights.

Cox's theory of the Constitution and the judicial power undermines the role of representation by pitting popular government against the doctrine of natural rights and concluding that the two are logically inconsistent. As a result, his understanding of the Constitution asks the Court to assume a special responsibility for the protection of natural rights, rights that he sees as being at odds with majority rule and the Constitution's representative principle.[124] His emphasis on natural rights and the rule of law, though in some respects appropriate, conceals the Constitution's concern for the elements of government that are essential to a government directed toward republican liberty. Resolving the inconsistency that Cox sees necessitates examining how the remotely democratic Court fits into the wisdom of the Constitution's theory. The reconciliation of democratic government with individual liberty is the theme of our constitutional theory. This problem is so fundamental that the entire constitutional scheme of separation of powers and multiplicity of interests is designed to resolve it.

As we have seen, *The Federalist* argues that certain of the elements essential to good government do not reside in the judicial branch. Through a properly constructed legislature, the framers intended to supply an important remedy to the disease most incident to republican government—a majority acting in a manner "adverse to the rights of other citizens, or to the permanent and aggregate interests of the community."[125] Because of the makeup of the legislature—the very institution in which the ruling majority is formed—the framers did not see an inconsistency or contradiction between popular government and the natural rights or law of nature on which the government is based. In fact, the framers insisted on the necessity of maintaining the link between representative government and the preservation of rights toward which the entire frame of government is directed. The framers regarded it as necessary to submit the Constitution to the people of the United States for their consent. The element of democratic consent was also central to the operation of the government embodied in that Constitution and its capacity to secure individual rights. Cox's prescribed role for the Court undermines the necessity for such consent. His interpretation of the Constitution rejects this crucial relationship between republican government and natural rights by viewing the two as logically contradictory. He resolves this problem by giving the Court the role of the voice of natural law in which it protects the natural rights of individuals.[126]

SEPARATION OF POWERS AND REPRESENTATION. Separation of powers theory includes an independent judiciary that, in the exercise of its proper function, enforces the exceptions the majority has specified in the Constitution, including the Bill of Rights and subsequent amendments. Such enforcement is consistent with democratic theory only insofar as it operates on the basis of these exceptions to majority rule that the majority itself has embodied within the Constitution. Otherwise, the Court functions in a manner inconsistent with the Constitution's premise of majoritarian government. The judicial supremacy involved in such a function means that the judiciary assumes a legislative function severed from the requirement for majority rule. Such judicial usurpation of power forecloses the constitutional design of a properly constructed legislature that balances the competing interests of a strong and responsible government and civil liberty. Depending on the Court as the primary guardian of civil liberty pits republican government against individual liberty in the context of a lawsuit—a lawsuit attended with many disadvantages.[127] If courts take constitutional principles to extremes or insert into the Constitution *judicially* created exceptions to the legislative power that are not rooted in the Constitution, a problem warned against in *Federalist* No. 63 may result: "[T]hat liberty may be endangered by the abuses of liberty as well as by the abuses of power; that there are numerous instances of the former as well as of the latter; and that the former, rather than the latter, are apparently most to be apprehended by the United States."[128]

Congress is designed to be a much more effective register of the competing goals with which government is perpetually confronted than is the Court. This realization should limit the role assigned to the Court and counsel restraint in asking the Court to judge what groups are properly represented in government.[129] This same restraint is appropriate in judicial protection of minorities and individuals from the majority. The Court is justified in protecting minorities and individuals only when Congress has exceeded its constitutional powers over such individuals and groups. When an activist Court makes broad pronouncements of public policy not rooted in the Constitution, even with the intention of protecting individuals or minorities, it thwarts much of the Constitution's protective scheme of representation and the balance between the power of the other branches of government and the states and that of the judiciary. Insofar as the judiciary assumes legislative or executive powers, *The Federalist* recognizes an obvious problem relative to separation of powers theory: "Were the power of judging joined with the legislative, the life and liberty of the subject would be exposed to arbitrary control, for *the judge* would then be the *legislator.* Were it joined to the executive power, *the judge* might behave with all the violence of *an oppressor.*"[130] Broad judicial policy making may both violate separation of powers and deny a democratic check on policy making. When the Court assumes legislative powers, even when its decisions are informed by principle in the way Cox prescribes, it bypasses that process of coalition and compromise among the multiplicity of interests in the legislative branch. This process is essential both to democratic consent and to the moderating and elevating effects of the multiplicity of interests discussed earlier.

To include within the Court's role an undefined power to quash legislative enactments may also constitute an obstacle to effective government that actually supports the principles of equality and liberty Cox embraces. Exercises of legislative power may be necessary not only to meet unforeseen exigencies such as the Great Depression but also to give reality to rights of minorities. It is clear from some of the Supreme Court cases cited above that the Supreme Court has thwarted congressional actions that are supportive of the principles Cox advocates. He responds to the criticism that the Court has made some "misguided" decisions by arguing that " '[w]rong decisions' can be corrected by time, debate, and judicial reconsideration, or by constitutional amendment as in the cases of Dred Scott and the Income Tax."[131] To dismiss the *Dred Scott* decision as one that was simply corrected by a constitutional amendment is a gross oversimplification of the historical record, a record that includes the Civil War and the greatest acts of statesmanship (by Lincoln) since the founding. Furthermore, if the correction of previous errors is a desirable feature of government, then the greater ease with which legislative errors may be corrected is actually an argument against judicial activism.

A reformist or political Court such as the one Cox advocates is at odds with the Constitution's fundamental "dependence on the people" as "the primary control on the government."[132] The reasons for this dependence go beyond the reasons Cox acknowledges and dismisses—the fact that rule by a Council of Platonic Guardians would be "irksome" or that such a council would result in deadening the people's "sense of moral responsibility."[133] The Constitution rests on the assumption of an enlightened voting population that must finally be the seat of sovereignty within the political order. There is no assumption of wisdom in the population at large, but there is a dependence on an enlightened citizen body. The form of government embodied in our representative system makes the distinction between enlightenment and wisdom that underlies the Declaration. We believe that although our enlightenment falls short of the excellence represented by wisdom, it is so firmly wedded to our self-interest that it is a better source of authority for our lives than the utmost wisdom unalloyed by self-interest.[134]

Such a system of representation rests on the possibility of the people's denying re-election to representatives who, in the people's opinion, are not serving their interests. The Constitution contains numerous qualifications of the principle of majority rule, but it finally rests on this view of representation. Thus, the principle of representation is different in its operation where states and nation are concerned; where the Senate, House, and executive are concerned; and where the proposing and ratifying of amendments are concerned. Yet the Constitution fundamentally rests on this connection between the people and their representatives. The Court is not representative in the ordinary sense of that term, since its members are only a remote choice of the people and hold office for life or good behavior. The intention of the framers and the principles of the charter of government they framed justify judicial enforcement of the "specified exceptions to the legislative authority."[135] Hamilton argues that courts have a duty, in enforcing these exceptions, "to declare all acts contrary to the manifest tenor of the Constitution void."[136] He adds in a later paper, however, that there is "not a syllable" in the Constitution that "*directly* empowers the national courts to construe the laws according to the spirit of the Constitution."[137] This argument supports the view of the Court as having authority to enforce those limitations on the legislative authority contained in the Constitution (or added in amendments) but provides no support for judicial enforcement of natural law except insofar as particular manifestations or interpretations of that law are singled out for specific protection in our charter of government. This, a more limited view of the judicial power than that held by Cox, is also supported by the democratic or representative character of the Constitution as a whole. The people, through the elevating and moderating processes of governmental mechanisms, are to be the enlightened judges of the wisdom of their representatives. Since justices are not elected, the people cannot exercise enlightened judgment over the wisdom of judicial decisions through the usual mechanisms of the electoral process. Any enlargement of the judicial function beyond that involved in enforcing the specific provisions of the Constitution, because of the unelective nature of the Court, short-circuits this enlightened judgment of the people.

JUXTAPOSITION OF POPULAR SOVEREIGNTY AND INDIVIDUAL RIGHTS. Yet another difficulty with the judicial role Cox proposes is his juxtaposition of the elements of popular sovereignty and individual rights in a way that assumes mutual hostility. By severing the Court from the principles embodied in the Constitution and allowing the Court to proceed on its own judicially created principles, Cox indeed introduces tension between the Court's articulation of rights and the seat of sovereignty in the American people, the people themselves. He attempts to moderate this tension by counseling the Court to take the ''common will'' into account as it articulates the people's aspirations.[138]

Replacing constitutional principles with judicially created principles severs the link that is necessary to true legitimacy in this democratic political order. This link is not only theoretically important but also practically necessary, so that the citizenry can know that the Court is acting consistently with the Constitution's democratic theory. Furthermore, if the Court simply imposes its views on the nation—without properly linking them with the Constitution—it quashes the will of democratically elected representatives and creates a dangerous possibility. Individual rights that are imposed on the sovereign people by the Court and are not rooted in the minds and souls of the people rest on a fragile foundation. The Court's role as a principled adjudicator exists in a precarious relationship with the democratic principle of the Constitution, even when the Court adjudicates principles found within the Constitution; when it goes beyond the Constitution, this relationship is severed. We then see the potential for true hostility between the democracy and the Court if the Court acts counter to the will of the people with no persuasive constitutional basis. It is doubtful that a constitutional democracy can survive if its institutions proceed on a basis that is inconsistent with its foundations. In any event, Cox readily admits that the democratic element is sufficiently strong in this political order that legitimacy is a concern. One may take the argument one step further. The American political order is so fundamentally democratic that, in the long run, popular will prevails. Any theory of the judicial power that does not recognize this as fundamentally important misunderstands the appropriate role for the Court.

Other aspects of the Constitution and its theory also support the view of a limited judicial power. Cox urges the justices to pursue the law of nature in the exercise of their power. Yet the entire Constitution was constructed out of a distrust of government's pursuing a general and undefined natural law. Far from bestowing such a broad commission on the Court, the Constitution did not envision even the government as a whole acting in pursuit of a general law of nature. The Constitution was structured to avoid reliance on those holding any governmental office as a Council of Platonic Guardians. The legislative power is not exercised in pursuit of the dictates of the law of nature but rather under the doctrine of enumerated powers. This distrust of any general governmental power to pursue natural law lies at the foundation of the famous discourse on faction in *Federalist* No. 10—a discourse that is directed toward a system of government that will preserve individual rights. *The Federalist* refuses to rely solely on statecraft to adjust the clashing interests that inevitably emerge in a free government.[139] Instead, it relies on properly structured self-interest so that it will operate in the service of the public good. This structuring of self-interest operates both in the multiplicity of factions, which we associate most directly with the legislative branch of government, and in the separation of powers, which seeks to harness this self-interest by connecting the interest of the officeholder with the duties of the office.[140] Although *The Federalist* does not deny the possibility of or necessity for such statecraft, its genius lies in structuring a political order based on self-interest in which the representative principle plays a crucial role. The potential for statecraft exists within this theory, but since statesmen are elected, their wisdom must have the consent of those they represent. Thus, from the view of *The Federalist,* the representative principle and doctrines such as that of enumerated powers restrict the potential for officeholders to pursue the law of nature broadly in the course of their exercise of statecraft. Democratic consent limits the potential for tyrannical abuses of power. Conversely, this consent may also confine the potential for statecraft. But the Constitution is distrustful of statecraft that is not exercised in accordance with its principles and that is not dependent on the consent of the governed.

LEGITIMACY. Cox emphasizes legitimacy in his discussion of the law of nature he asks the Court to pursue, but his conception of legitimacy is not equivalent to consent of the governed. His concern for the Constitution as the rule of law leads him to emphasize the need for compliance with the law. Cox's concept of legitimacy becomes most important in securing acquiescence or acceptance when the Court hands down decisions.[141] He sees this acceptance as a consequence of the widespread opinion that the Court is acting legitimately and as a product "of the opinion of the legal profession, of attitudes in the Executive and in Congress, of the response in State governments, of the press, and of public opinion."[142] Essentially, these are all measures of what these groups will accept rather than measures of the consistency of the Court's action with the Constitution.[143] In fact, Cox argues that "the Framers provided no charter by which to measure the legitimate scope and nature of constitutional adjudication."[144] Consequently, he turns to other sources of legitimacy, such as history and established practice, judicial impartiality and independence, principled decision making "referable to legal precedent and other accepted sources of law," and finally "our natural law inheritance."[145] Although the content of the Constitution is one accepted source of law, it seems clear that it is not the primary source of legitimacy for Cox.

Cox's concern with legitimacy is appropriate, but it is an incomplete measure of true legitimacy as that term applies to the American political order. He emphasizes the Constitution's embodiment of the rule of law. It is clear that the rule of law is crucial to the U.S. Constitution, but without an inquiry into the constitutional mechanisms that produce this law, much of the wisdom implicit in the Constitution is obscured. Therefore, many of the Constitution's protections of liberty and its provisions for the stability we associate with the Senate, the energy we expect from the executive, and the competency we demand of a strong government are undermined. The concern with the rule of law leads Cox to emphasize the need for compliance with the law. True legitimacy, according to the Declaration, requires that the government operate in a manner consistent with the consent of those who founded the government and subsequently with the tacit consent of those governed. Acquiescence to or toleration of particular laws or decisions of the Court does not constitute the tacit consent necessitated by true legitimacy. We understand that as members of this political order, we are legally bound by public declarations of law. The Declaration's meaning of consent does not imply that we grant approval or give consent to *particular acts* of the government or the judiciary. The meaning the Declaration attaches to consent is more fundamental than that of mere obedience to whatever law is pronounced by government.[146] Consent to be governed by the political order to which we belong is not the same as legitimacy in the sense in which Cox uses this term. The people may accept judicial rulings that are inconsistent with the Constitution's grants of and exceptions to governmental power and ultimately inconsistent with their "unalienable rights."[147] This acquiescence would not make these actions legitimate.

A theory of judicial review cannot run counter to the underlying character of the Constitution and be legitimate in any meaningful sense. Cox's advocacy of the judiciary's acting as "the voice of natural law" is, in his words, "logically inconsistent [with the] conviction that the people are the source of all legitimate power, that governments are the people's agents, and that the people, expressing themselves through the majority, have the right to work their will."[148] Given the inconsistency Cox sees, one questions why he does not propose a role for the Court that would be more nearly consistent. In fact, there is no intrinsic conflict between the principle that "the people are the source of all legitimate power" and the "commitment to individual rights."[149] This conflict emerges when a role for the Court is advocated that is inconsistent with the manifest tenor or specific provisions of the Constitution. The judicial role Cox desires—adjudication informed by natural law and then further legitimated on the basis of whether or not the people acquiesce—exacerbates this inconsistency.

This potential inconsistency is minimized when the Court reasonably acts within the provisions of the Constitution that are based on the consent of the people, a people who are, according to the Declaration, the "source of all legitimate power."[150] If, in framing the Constitution, the people as source of all legitimate power set down reasonably specific limits to the Court's legislative power, and if the Court acts in judicious accordance with these limits, there is no logical inconsistency with the political theory underlying the U.S. Constitution. The people have set down reasonably specific limitations on themselves in the Bill of Rights and in other parts of the Constitution. The people set down no authorization for the government to pursue the law of nature or for the Court to be the "voice of natural law," even if it pronounces the dictates of this law of nature in a principled manner. Rather, the people of the United States sought to safeguard inalienable rights on which the law of nature is based by granting enumerated powers to government and by making certain exceptions to these powers. The weaker the link between the provisions and principles of the Constitution and principles enunciated by the Court, the greater the inconsistency between the people as the source of all legitimate power and the practice of judicial review. The role Cox prescribes for the Court as the "voice of natural law" dramatically weakens this link.

In addition to straining the consistency of judicial review with the doctrine of the consent of the governed at the time of the founding, such a judicial role works at odds with the representative principle and its foundations in enlightened self-interest. Just as importantly, a role for the Court that prescribes that it adjudicate in a principled manner without basing those principles on the integrated theory of the Constitution and the political order puts the Court in the position of selectively refounding the political order as it decides cases. There is wisdom in Cox's wanting the Court to help educate us, to transform our principles into political reality through the adjudication of cases, and in his recognition that the Court must apply principles to changing circumstances. But observing the traditional canons of judicial decision making is not sufficient to secure the democratic character of the political order and its auxiliary safeguards if the Court does not securely found its decisions in the Constitution's principles and theory.

Conclusion

My analysis is firmly based on the view that there is an integrated and fundamental theory within the Constitution. Cox's work subordinates or obscures important aspects of the wisdom inherent in the Constitution. This oversight or misinterpretation opens the way for a judicial role that is inconsistent with our constitutional theory. Cox clearly favors judicial activism. He relies on the Court as "the voice of natural law" as it protects individual rights, even if the right involved "lacks connection with any value the Constitution marks as special."[151] Although his criteria of legitimacy qualify this activism, Cox prescribes a judicial role that is in some respects contrary to the constitutional theory outlined above. This activism contradicts the theory that requires a balance between democratic rule and the auxiliary safeguards because it bypasses the necessary reliance on majoritarian-imposed exceptions to the legislative power specified within the Constitution.

A virtue of Cox's work is that he does not divorce the Constitution from the doctrine of natural rights, which is its "ultimate source and justification."[152] Cox properly argues that the doctrine of natural rights is central to the American scheme of government; he is wrong in short-circuiting the complex constitutional features that secure these rights and instead advocating that the Court decide cases by resorting to first principles of natural rights.

The absence of a broad statement of natural rights in the Bill of Rights—as a declaration of broad first principles—illustrates several points. Such broad statements might interfere with the primary task necessary to securing freedom, that of establishing and conducting strong and competent government. Power to govern competently necessarily interferes with the unfettered rights that exist in the state of nature. But governments may abuse their legitimate powers. Although the primary protection against such abuses are representation and the political and social checks discussed earlier, a bill of rights can provide supplementary security. The Bill of Rights contains more specific protections than those that might have embodied the broad principles of the Declaration. These narrower civil rights are sufficiently defined so that they can be effectively (though not unproblematically) enforced. But these narrower principles are rooted in the doctrine of natural rights. As one analyst put it, our Bill of Rights is "an echo of the earlier declarations of natural rights." The First Amendment, for example, "might be described as a statement in matter-of-fact legal form of the great end of free government, to secure the private sphere, and the great means for preserving such a government, to foster an enlightened citizenry."[153] The Bill of Rights contains traditional civil rights that are formulations of principles of justice ultimately rooted in the doctrine of natural rights. The founding majority gave its consent to the more specific and traditional rights embodied in the Bill of Rights; therefore, Cox's advocacy of the Court's reaching beyond these rights in adjudicating cases is inconsistent both with sound government and with the principle of the consent of the governed. The Bill of Rights sets forth generally objective and enduring principles in the form of traditional civil rights.[154]

The strength of Cox's analysis is his advocacy of principled decision making and the rule of law. In pursuit of this end, he insists on observance of traditional characteristics that define the judicial role, such as the role of precedent, the requirements of a real controversy, and standing. The weakness of his theory of the Constitution and the Court is his failure to link the Court's role with the Constitution's theory and that theory's fundamental reliance on self-government and representation tempered by auxiliary safeguards, of which an independent judiciary is only one element. His emphasis on the Court as the protector of natural rights obscures the Constitution's provision for energetic, competent, and stable government through a complex system of representation that elevates and refines self-interest and democratic rule. Individual rights are thus to be preserved through this complex system of self-government. The constitutional design does not simply trust the perpetuation of individual rights to an independent judiciary. Indeed, the history of the Court counsels against relying on the Court as the voice of natural law and as the peculiar guardian of liberty.[155] The Constitution did not simply trust this task to the Court, but instead carefully constructed an entire frame of government to pursue this noble objective.

Cox desires greater constraints on the judicial power than does Dworkin. Cox's attention to legitimacy and consent is particularly important to the role he prescribes for the Court. Nonetheless, he would have judges adjudicate according to their interpretation of natural law and act as the voice of natural law. In this respect, although Cox is more pragmatic than Dworkin and emphasizes legitimacy and consent, Cox points toward Dworkin's nearly unrestrained view that constitutional interpretation ought to be in accordance with the strongest moral argument.

Chapter Five

Property Rights and Human Rights

Richard A. Epstein and Michael Perry focus their work on particular aspects of the rights doctrine. Epstein emphasizes economic rights as the cornerstone of the Constitution, and Perry emphasizes "human rights." Epstein's theory requires fidelity to the text of the Constitution, a text that he believes has a reasonably clear meaning. Perry understands the Constitution as embodying the best aspirations of the American people and asks the Supreme Court to serve as the prophet of these aspirations as it leads the way in a process of moral evolution that advances human rights. Although Epstein's conservative view of government and the Constitution differs dramatically from Perry's liberal view, both ask the Court to protect us from self-government by obstructing the representative branches of government when the representatives act in a manner inconsistent with these commentators' respective constitutional theories.

Richard Epstein equates his view of law and economics with the "takings" clause,[1] the provision in the Fifth Amendment that private property may not be taken for public use without just compensation. This specific provision informs Epstein's entire constitutional theory.[2] Epstein's interpretation of Locke translates into a firm view of the Constitution that puts teeth in its provisions, particularly the takings clause, which is his basis for interpreting the Constitution as a whole. In his chapter titled "The Integrity of Constitutional Text," he justifies his view of the Constitution by asserting its foundation in his interpretation of Locke's natural rights doctrine. Epstein then uses this theory to empower the judiciary to declare much legislation unconstitutional, with little support or no support from the Constitution's provisions.

Michael Perry explicates his theory of human rights in a book entitled *The Constitution, the Courts, and Human Rights*.[3] Perry focuses on what he calls "extraconstitutional policy making," particularly in the area of human rights. Extraconstitutional policy making is his term for judicial rulings that go "beyond the value judgments established by the framers of the Written Constitution" (ix). He believes that the judiciary should impose on the democracy a vision consistent with our highest moral aspirations (99).

The judicial role Perry desires—prophetic adjudication aimed toward moral growth—exacerbates the tension between judicial power and democracy. He believes that Congress's power to limit the jurisdiction of the federal courts constitutes a sufficient democratic check on the extraordinary judicial power he advocates (128). This check, I will argue, is not sufficient to legitimize the role of the Court as "prophet," with the power to rule according to the highest aspirations of the American people (97–99).

Property Rights and Judicial Activism: Richard A. Epstein

Richard A. Epstein systematically sets forth his view of economics and law in a book entitled *Takings: Private Property and the Power of Eminent Domain.*[4] In spite of the title, it would be a mistake to view the scope of this book, and his theory, as narrow or particularistic. Epstein accurately describes the book as an extended essay "about the proper relationship between the individual and the state."[5] He begins his treatment of the relationship between law and economics with his interpretation of Lockean political philosophy. The takings clause—"nor shall private property be taken for public use without just compensation"—is simply the vehicle for an overarching theory of constitutional interpretation and policy analysis, which includes topics ranging from "The Integrity of Constitutional Text" to "Taxation" and "Transfer Payments and Welfare Rights."[6] He follows where his political views lead as he applies in a Euclidean manner his understanding of the philosophy of Locke and his theory of the Constitution to each of these subject areas. Epstein states clearly, "It will be said that my position invalidates much of the twentieth-century legislation, and so it does."[7] His book is far-reaching in scope and includes his understanding of the Constitution, constitutional interpretation, and the role of the Court.

Epstein's Constitution—The Constitution as the Embodiment of Lockean Political Philosophy

Epstein postulates the common-law view that "no one owned the external things of the world until the first possessors acquired them." He relies on related Lockean propositions that the "organization of the state does not require the surrender of all natural rights to the sovereign" and that the "state can acquire nothing by simple declaration of its will but must justify its claims in terms of the rights of the individuals whom it protects." Private rights "are preserved as much as possible even after the formation of civil society, modified only to secure the internal and external peace for which the political power is necessary." Private property has a crucial role in the scheme of government insofar as it represents what individuals get to keep outside the control of the state. "The state gets what it needs to rule—its costs—and nothing more." The relationship between the sovereign and the individual must provide "both for the monopoly of force and for the preservation of liberty and property." Although individuals cannot enjoy the absolute protection of their property, when the sovereign takes an individual's property, provision must be made for just compensation (10–15). This is Epstein's understanding of the cornerstone of the Constitution, the takings clause of the Fifth Amendment. He regards the eminent domain approach to the Constitution as offering "a principled account of both the functions of the state and the limitations upon its powers" (331).

In Epstein's chapter titled "The Integrity of Constitutional Text," he justifies his view of the Constitution by asserting its foundation in his interpretation of Locke's natural rights doctrine. The principled meaning of the Constitution, which is of particular importance to judicial interpretation, according to Epstein, is dependent on language "clear and precise enough to bind even those who disagree with what it says, for the mission of constitutional government must soon founder if judges can decide cases as freely with the Constitution in place as without it" (19–20).

Epstein finds the provision of the Fifth Amendment "nor shall private property be taken for public use without just compensation" both clear and precise. Words have "regular, disciplined meanings," meanings that can best be discerned from the "internal intellectual integrity" of the provisions themselves rather than from the intention of those who drafted or ratified the document or from the purposes the framers may have believed the provision served (20, 26, 28). The term "private property," for example, "carries the same meaning for the Marxist who wants to abolish it, for the social democrat who wants to limit it, and the Lockean who wants to protect it. The Marxist has good reason to keep the Takings Clause out of his constitution" (25). In short, Epstein believes that the meaning of constitutional provisions does not change over time. To ask that such provisions be interpreted anew by each generation in light of changing circumstances invites destruction of the rule of law: "If the next generation can do what it wants, why bother with a constitution to begin with, when it is only an invitation for perpetual revision?" (24).

Epstein draws his understanding of the Constitution from the "constitutional text and the underlying theory of the state that it embodies" (31). He begins with his interpretation of Locke: that government derives its rights and powers from the individuals who are governed. From this, Epstein deduces that "all arrangements between the state and private individuals are broken down into a network of relationships among different individuals," a deduction that he regards as critical to both the meaning of and the justifications for taking private property (31).

The income tax provides a useful paradigm for understanding Epstein's theory of the Constitution. He opposes the modern view that the power of taxation is plenary. Rather, he argues that the elements necessary to analyze takings also emerge in the context of taxation. He undertakes a unitary analysis of taxes and takings and in a manner characteristic of the book as a whole, builds his theory of the Constitution from the takings clause (283–85). A target of his analysis is the progressive income tax. His standard of judgment is whether an income tax produces a disproportionate impact and whether it enlarges the overall economic pie (295). He dismisses a per capita tax, which in principle could exceed the full amount of an individual's income, as running counter to the takings clause because it is an illicit redistribution to the rich (297).

Epstein objects to the progressive tax on a number of grounds. It would be defensible if benefits from government increased as an individual's income rose, but he sees no evidence to support that conclusion. Public benefits are hard to define in economic terms that can be related to a just tax. Tax rates could be left strictly to the legislature, despite the fact that taxation is a taking of private property, but Epstein refuses to adopt this solution. Instead he argues for the proportional tax on the grounds that it minimizes the mismatch between taxes imposed and indirect benefits received. He believes that the proportional tax gives a respectable match between taxes and benefits and thereby best meets the proportionate burden test, which is critical to this area of eminent domain law. The progressive tax is redistributive in nature and requires a choice among what Epstein calls "arbitrary progressive schedules." Furthermore, it invites factions to fight for economic gains by advocating redistribution through various forms of progressive taxation. He sees no "real cost" to an interpretation of the eminent domain clause that requires a proportional or flat tax, for it does not inhibit the legislature and executive in the discharge of their functions, nor does it place a revenue constraint upon government (297–300).

Epstein argues: "The case for the progressive tax is not 'uneasy.' It is wrong." He applies this to estate and gift taxation as well, where he sees a redistributive motive as explaining the highly progressive structure of taxes. He is particularly critical of a statement in *Magoun v. Illinois Trust & Savings Bank* that the "right to take property by devise or descent is a creature of the law, and not a natural right—a privilege, and therefore the authority which confers it may impose conditions upon it"[8] Epstein characterizes this statement as naked positivism, inconsistent with the natural law account of property that lies at the foundation of limited, constitutional government. He sees no principled distinction between property and the attending rights of possession, use, and disposition. The rights of private property, the Constitution, and taxation are intertwined and governed by the principles of the takings clause.[9]

Epstein on the Proper Role of the Court

Epstein's view of the Constitution as embodying natural rights leads him to advocate a role for the Court that seems uncompromising in its requirements.

In his words: "It would be nice if we could avoid the difficulties of judicial mischief by following a simple principle of judicial restraint. But the Constitution does not allow so simple an escape or so tempting a shortcut in its effort to establish justice. That business requires all public officials, including judges, to understand the permanent and sound principles of government on which our Constitution rests."[10]

Epstein advocates a "level of judicial intervention far greater than we now have, and indeed far greater than we ever have had." But he denies basing this intervention on "a belief in judicial activism in cases of economic liberties." He relies instead upon "necessary implications derived from the constitutional text and the underlying theory of the state that it embodies."[11] Stated differently, he seems to draw his theory more from specific constitutional provisions than from an overall theory of representative government and separation of powers. He uses Locke primarily to support the very strict theory of private property that is central to *Takings*.

Epstein's theory of taxation illustrates his application of constitutional theory to adjudication and to the realities of a policy that long ago departed from the views he advocates. He also believes that it is a good place to begin the overhaul of current law mandated by his interpretation of the takings clause. The highest marginal tax bracket has been gradually reduced by legislative enactment from over 90 percent in the 1950s to its present level, although admittedly inflation has brought more people into the highest bracket. There is no reliance interest (as there is in the case of Social Security, for example), which

> prevents a responsible court from demanding that Congress not increase the levels of progressivity in future years. Indeed, only the persistence of transfer payments makes it difficult to strike down a progressive tax. With the frequent changes in brackets, there is surely no powerful reliance interest in the current tax structure as it relates to the tax rates for future income, even that arising out of past transactions. It is quite possible to invalidate the whole pattern of special exactions, like the windfall profits tax, that have luxuriated in the absence of any judicial supervision.[12]

Epstein would not stop judicial intervention at taxation. He sees no reliance interest preventing, for example, the immediate invalidation of what he regards as an unconstitutional minimum wage. He supports this argument by asserting that no one has suggested that claims of reliance and private property prevent the introduction of or increase in the minimum wage, even though the effects of it are to drive certain firms out of business. After laying the groundwork for judicial intervention with the progressive tax and moving to the minimum wage, he raises the question: "Why then stop with the minimum wage?" Using his economic analysis and its emphasis on private property and market mechanisms, he advocates judicial intervention in such areas as striking down the National Labor Relations Act, lifting price controls on oil and gas, and finally addressing what he calls "the ultimate citadel of welfare programs."[13]

His analysis of welfare programs is instructive insofar as it demonstrates the results of his economic analysis. He advocates a principled case for holding the line with Social Security payments because of a reliance interest. But he believes that as a result of the reforms he has outlined, the political process and the economic structure will be influenced for the better:

> Production will rise; taxes will, in general, fall; the tradeoff between welfare and productive labor will shift in a favorable direction so that even if benefit levels remain the same, fewer people will demand them. That result in turn will reduce the taxes needed to fund them, which implies greater levels of productivity. If one has the courage to follow a course of action to its conclusion, then the process can be expedited to provide overall gains so large that they will swamp any distributional losses.[14]

Professor Herman Schwartz clearly summarizes Epstein's view of the positive effects of rolling back much existing social and economic legislation: "Under this scheme, the poor and disadvantaged will ultimately be better off because the termination of excessive governmental control will free up energy and initiative, increase the amount of goods and benefits available for all, and increase private charity."[15]

Epstein does not believe that there is a political will to carry out the reforms he advocates, either on the part of the legislature or in the courts. Even though present social and economic programs "cannot be wholly dismantled," he believes that his theory can lead to some change in the proper direction. He seems content to rest his advocacy of the takings clause, law, and economic theory on the proposition that the stakes are so high that even some shift in doctrine can have important and salutary consequences.[16]

Epstein's Treatment of Locke's Theory

Since Epstein derives his interpretation of the Constitution and the role of the Court from John Locke, it is with Locke that a critique of Epstein's theory of law and economics must begin. First, and most obviously, there is no provision for a judicial branch of government nor for a power of judicial review in Locke's frame of government. Instead, Locke examines, in chapter 12 of his *Second Treatise of Government*, the legislative, executive, and federative powers of the commonwealth.[17] The preceding chapter of the treatise is titled "Of the

Extent of the Legislative Power." It is here that we must look for Locke's views regarding protection of private property. If we read Locke rather than Epstein's interpretation of Locke, we discover that the

> *legislative* is not only the supreme power of the commonwealth, but sacred and unalterable in the hands where the community have once placed it; nor can any edict of any body else, in what form soever conceived, or by what power soever backed, have the force and obligation of a *law*, which has not its *sanction from* that *legislative* which the public has chosen and ap- pointed: for without this the law could not have that, which is absolutely necessary to its being a law, the consent of the society, over whom no body can have a power to make laws, but by their own consent.[18]

If the legislative power is supreme, then what are the limitations on its power, apart from the public's choosing the legislature? If we were to be in- structed by Epstein, we might expect Locke to provide specific and substan- tive limitations on the legislative power, among them perhaps a version of the takings clause. Locke specifies that the legislature rule not by extemporary de- cree but by promulgated standing laws. Locke adds, in response to the possi- bility that the legislative power might dispose of the estates of subjects arbi- trarily, that "this is not much to be feared in governments where the legislative consists, wholly or in part, in assemblies which are *variable,* whose members upon the dissolution of the assembly are subjects under the com- mon laws of their country, *equally with the rest.*"[19] In regard to subjects' prop- erty, government may not take it, in whole or in part, without the subjects' consent. This consent comes from "the consent of the majority, giving it ei- ther by themselves, or their representatives chosen by them." Without such consent, the government violates "the fundamental law of property."[20] Fi- nally, the legislative power must govern for the good of the people and not be transferred to another body.[21]

Within the framework of the American system of government, Locke's cri- teria, to the extent they explain the Constitution, would be satisfied by a legis- lative body that serves for limited terms, is subject to the very same laws it passes, and does not transfer its legislative power to any other body. Finally, the people must be the judge of whether the legislature is serving the public good; if not, the people's remedy is to turn the legislators out of office. In simple terms, these are Locke's limitations on government in the name of property. Locke makes no provision for what we call judicial review and im- poses no further specific or substantive limitations on the legislative power.

The U.S. Constitution should not be definitively interpreted according to the political theory of John Locke. We must look to the Constitution itself to understand its meaning. But the above analysis of Locke is sufficient to refute the interpretation of Locke that Epstein attempts to superimpose on the Constitution in order to reconcile it to his theory of law and economics. The limitations that he would have the judiciary impose on the legislative power are not those of John Locke. They are those of Richard Epstein.

Epstein's emphasis on property is consistent with that of the Constitution and its exposition in *Federalist* No. 10, where Madison summarizes the Constitution's purpose as that of securing the public good and private rights against the danger of faction,[22] while at the same time preserving the spirit and form of popular government (57–58). He tells us that "the most common and durable source of factions has been the various and unequal distribution of property" (56). In a civilized nation, diverse property interests will result; "regulation of these various and interfering interests forms the principal task of modern legislation, and involves the spirit of party and faction in the necessary and ordinary operations of the government" (56). The regulation of these interests in a way that prevents such a faction from ruling, yet preserves popular government, goes far toward explaining the ends of the Constitution and its exposition in *The Federalist*. This regulation takes place through an extensive and properly structured popular government. There are remarkably few prohibitions on the legislative power in the original document.

There are links of necessity and constitutional design among the self-interests of the citizen body, the legislative body, and the process of legislation that regulates property interests. The process of majority rule through coalition of these competing interests is the fundamental principle of the Constitution. The doctrine of majority rule is not symbolic window dressing simply to be trotted out on the Fourth of July, Constitution Day, and the first Tuesday after the first Monday in November. Majority rule is the animating principle of our political life, the backbone of the body politic. It is the means of linking private rights and property interests to the public law.

Given this fundamental characteristic of American political life, *The Federalist* turns its attention to structuring the democratic form of government in a way that minimizes injustice and preserves the democratic nature of the government: "In the extent and proper structure of the Union, therefore, we behold a republican remedy for the diseases most incident to republican government" (62). Democratic rule, properly extended and structured, is not an obstacle to be hurdled. It is a governing principle to be limited only by means consistent with itself. In the words of Publius, "in republican government, the legislative authority necessarily predominates."[23] Limitations on this power must be undertaken with a recognition that they limit the most republican branch of government. Such limitations must be consistent with the fundamental principle of the regime—majority rule.

As Hamilton states in *Federalist* No. 78, however, there are constitutional limitations on the legislative authority: "By a limited Constitution, I understand one which contains certain specified exceptions to the legislative authority. . . . Limitations of this kind can be preserved in practice no other way than through the medium of courts of justice, whose duty it must be to declare all acts contrary to the manifest tenor of the constitution void."[24] These limitations were placed in the Constitution with the consent of the governed and thus gained their legitimacy. They serve as the cornerstone of the classic defense of judicial review.

Epstein asks that the judiciary use the power of judicial review to negate much of the legislative agenda of the twentieth century. His is not a novel idea. It lay at the center of the invalidation of much of the New Deal by the "Horse and Buggy Court." What that Court and Epstein do not seem to understand is that the Constitution established not only a free government but, just as importantly, a government powerful enough to deal with unforeseen exigencies and competent to a broad range of tasks.[25] During the period of the New Deal, ordinary majorities regulated property in a way that Epstein regards as objectionable, but they did so through the process of consent, just as that process was described by Locke and prescribed by the Constitution. The due process clauses, for example, which were used to invalidate much social and economic legislation, state that individuals may be deprived of property by law if that deprivation is with due process. What constitutes the public good is to be determined by properly constituted majorities. Through his interpretation of the takings clause, Epstein attempts to transform the nature of American democracy in the interest of his favored theory of law and economics. In the area of taxing and spending and regulation of commerce, for example, one looks in vain for ironclad constitutional limitations on these legislative powers. *The Federalist* described the Constitution's taxing power, for example, in this way: "The federal government must of necessity be invested with an unqualified power of taxation in the ordinary modes."[26] In more general terms, *Federalist* No. 23 addresses the question of limitations on the power of the national government: "The same must be the case in respect to commerce, and to every other matter to which its jurisdiction is permitted to extend. . . . Not to confer in each case a degree of power commensurate to the end, would be to violate the most obvious rules of prudence and propriety, and improvidently to trust the great interests of the nation to hands which are disabled from managing them with vigor and success."[27]

Epstein extends the reach of the takings clause to enable him to insert his own view of law and economics into the Constitution. Such an extension of the clause, with a resulting straitjacket on the legislative power, is justified neither by Locke nor by the theory of the Constitution as revealed in *The Federalist*. In the name of strict construction and a claimed "interpretivism" that smuggles his own views into the Constitution, Epstein seeks to justify judicial imposition of his views on the other branches and levels of government. Such a constitutional theory represents a conservative effort to make an end run around the Constitution and the representative theory of democracy it embodies. In this sense, Epstein has much in common with Michael Perry, who is a liberal proponent of a similar end run.

Constitutional Aspiration and Judicial Prophecy: Michael Perry

The essence of Michael Perry's work is contained in *The Constitution, the Courts, and Human Rights,* a book that he describes as "an essay in constitutional theory."[28] Perry focuses on what he calls "extraconstitutional policy making," particularly in the area of human rights. Extraconstitutional policy making is his term for judicial rulings that go "*beyond* the value judgments established by the framers of the Written Constitution." Since he excludes as democratically indefensible "contraconstitutional" policy making that "goes *against* the framers' value judgments,"[29] the object of his analysis is the reconciliation of extraconstitutional policy making with democracy.

Perry defines the Constitution as "a complex of value judgments the framers wrote into the text of the Constitution and thereby constitutionalized" (10). The issues Perry addresses are structural ones dealing with federalism and separation of powers and those that limit the powers of government in the interest of individual rights. His explanation of interpretive and noninterpretive review explains these competing theories:

> The Supreme Court engages in *interpretive* review when it ascertains the constitutionality of a given policy choice by reference to one of the value judgments of which the Constitution consists—that is, by reference to a value judgment embodied, though not necessarily explicitly, either in some particular provision of the text of the Constitution or in the overall structure of government ordained by the Constitution. Such review is "interpretive" because the Court reaches decision by interpreting—deciphering— the textual provision (or the aspect of governmental structure) that is the embodiment of the determinative value judgment. The effort is to ascertain, as accurately as available historical materials will permit, the character of a value judgment the framers constitutionalized at some point in the past.
>
> The Court engages in *noninterpretive* review when it makes the determination of constitutionality by reference to a value judgment other than one constitutionalized by the framers. Such review is "noninterpretive" because the Court reaches decision without really interpreting any provision of the constitutional text (or any aspect of governmental structure)— although, to be sure, the Court may explain its decision with rhetoric de-

signed to create the illusion that it is merely "interpreting" or "applying" some constitutional provision. (10–11)

Perry defines the theory of *interpretivism* as the view that "only interpretive review is legitimate" (11). Legislative and executive actions exceeding constitutional bounds and constitutional *policy making* by the judiciary (as opposed to judicial *interpretation* of the Constitution) are illegitimate as well. Interpretivism demands that the boundaries of legislative, executive, and judicial action be determined by judicial interpretation; for the Court to act as a policy maker both blocks the will of elected officials acting within proper constitutional bounds and is an act of lawlessness on the part of the judiciary (28–29). The theory of *noninterpretivism* holds that "at least some noninterpretive review . . . is legitimate too" (11). Perry argues just this point, which leads us to his discussion of federalism, separation of powers, and human rights.

Perry believes that he has set forth a standard of review for issues of federalism and separation of powers that fits within his definition of interpretivism. In areas affecting the relationship between the national government and the states, he uses the commerce clause and the power to tax and to spend as examples of broad grants of power to Congress. As Perry puts it, "the framers intended to grant Congress a great deal of legislative authority—perhaps all the legislative authority Congress would likely need . . . to deal effectively with whatever problems might arise which the states individually would not be competent to handle" (41). He regards the Court's decisions in the pre-1937 period that struck down congressional legislation on the grounds of federalism as exemplary of noninterpretive review: that is, the Court invoked its own judgment rather than that of the framers. Perry sees no justification in either the text or the history of the Constitution for such noninterpretive review; nor does he see functional considerations offering support for noninterpretive review in cases involving issues of federalism. In his opinion, both houses of Congress are sufficiently linked to their respective states to ensure that, from a functional point of view, the national government will be sensitive to local and state interests; thus, functional considerations do not justify noninterpretive judicial review in such cases (41–43).[30]

Perry searches for a legitimate functional basis for noninterpretive review where separation of powers issues are concerned. In summary, he sees no functional justification for noninterpretive review of interbranch issues involving separation of powers when Congress and the executive agree. But when the "legislative and executive branches disagree as to whether the challenged federal action is within the jurisdiction of the branch that took it," functional considerations justify an activist stance and the consequent exercise of noninterpretive review (52–53).[31] Perry believes that such review is defensible in terms of its functional desirability in resolving conflict between the legislative and executive branches. He tries to resolve the problem of democratic legitimacy by arguing that whichever side the judiciary takes in such conflict, it is supporting a democratically accountable branch of government.[32] Thus, Perry believes that in the areas of federalism and separation of powers, his theory of review is defensible against interpretivist criticisms.[33]

With the important exception of "human rights" issues as he defines them, Perry sees the Constitution as a grant of fulsome powers to the political branches of government where issues of federalism and separation of powers are concerned. He also defers to the democratic nature of the political order by allowing broad play to the Constitution's grants of power to the legislative and executive branches, and in his seemingly novel justification of noninterpretivist review of interbranch conflicts. According to his account, the Constitution and its theory provide minimal guidance to the functioning of the system, except for setting in motion the structures of separated powers and federalism. He thereby dismisses the theoretical guidance rooted in the Constitution, theory used by Chief Justice Marshall in such important cases as *Marbury v. Madison*[34] and *McCulloch v. Maryland*.[35] In an important case such as *Youngstown Sheet and Tube Co. v. Sawyer*,[36] which Perry would regard as an interbranch dispute, it presumably would not make much difference to him how the Court held.

Noninterpretive Review in Human Rights Cases

Perry's theory of noninterpretive review in human rights cases is the core of his work.[37] He argues that where human rights are concerned, determination of constitutionality by reference to a value judgment other than one constitutionalized by the framers (noninterpretive review) is justified by functional considerations. In Perry's judgment, the "stakes are very high" in terms of justifying noninterpretive review in human rights cases, for "precious few twentieth-century constitutional decisions striking down governmental action in the name of the rights of individuals . . . are the product of interpretive review" (92).

In rejecting the source of the framers' values, Perry identifies and then rejects other standards for noninterpretive review, including tradition, contemporary consensus, and principled interpretation of traditional values. Having failed to identify "a source of values (other than the set constitutionalized by the framers) that can serve as a reservoir of decisional norms for human rights cases," Perry turns to his own formulation of the "irreducible feature of the American people's understanding of themselves." He refers to this conception as *religious*, but he uses the term "to refer to a binding vision—a vision that serves as a source of unalienated self-understanding, of 'meaning' in the sense of existential orientation or rootedness"—rather than as a sectarian, the-istic or metaphysical term (97). Perry's view of the "irreducible feature of the American" people is not derived from the Declaration of Independence as effected by the Constitution but is a result of the American people's being a "chosen" people in the "biblical sense of that term." A chosen people guided by this vision, Perry posits, "need[s] to be called to judgment—provisional judgment—in the here and now. That is the task of prophecy" (97–98).

Perry moves from the religious foundation he identifies to the associated concept of prophecy to the review function of the Court: "The function of noninterpretive review in human rights cases is prophetic; it is to call the American people—actually the government, the representatives of the people—to provisional judgment." Central to his conception of the review function of the Court is his notion of "moral evolution," which is a result of the nation's incessant struggle to achieve a broader and deeper moral understanding. Although he relies on this religious interpretation and moral evolution to help explain and clarify noninterpretive review in human rights cases, he does not regard these factors as the root justification for such review (99).

Perry's primary justification for noninterpretive review by the judiciary is his objection that members of the executive and legislative branches are dependent on their constituencies and concerned with incumbency to a degree that interferes with their being committed to moral evolution, particularly where the legislature is concerned: "Over time, the practice of noninterpretive review has evolved as a way of remedying what would otherwise be a serious defect in American government—the absence of any policymaking institution that *regularly* deals with fundamental political-moral problems other than by mechanical reference to established moral conventions" (100–101). Perry believes that noninterpretive review in human rights cases enables the independent federal judiciary to move us in the direction of right answers to political and moral questions because it is not encumbered by the conventional, by the problem of being accountable to the established public opinion through the electoral process (102). He refers to the Court as "an institution that resolves moral problems not simply by looking backward to the sediment of old moralities, but ahead to emergent principles in terms of which fragments of a new moral order can be forged" (111).[38]

Perry's prescribed role for the judiciary raises the case of what limits exist over judicial discretion, an issue he addresses in raising the hypothetical case of a judge who believes that porpoises, because of their intelligence, should be treated as persons, or that any imprisonment of a human being is immoral. He responds to his own hypothetical at one level by observing that courts do not have an unlimited supply of political capital to expend on controversial issues; second, he observes that constitutional law should be developed incrementally in order to preserve a stable and productive dialectical relationship between noninterpretive review and electoral accountability.[39]

In searching for constitutional means of reconciling noninterpretive review in human rights cases with electoral and democratic accountability, he rejects both the impeachment power and the legislative power over the judiciary's budget. He then settles on a means that, in his opinion, apparently does not strike with such a blunt edge as the budget power and is not as cumbersome as the impeachment power, namely, the congressional power to control the jurisdiction of the federal courts (128). This jurisdiction-limiting power of Congress, subject to the usual check of presidential veto, is the democratic touchstone of Perry's noninterpretive review in human rights cases.

Congressional control of jurisdiction in cases involving human rights is a legitimate constitutional weapon, according to Perry, only when the Court has exercised noninterpretive review (130). If the Court exercises noninterpretive review and Congress wishes to oppose such a judicial decision, Congress is acting constitutionally and legitimately, according to Perry, if it acts to limit jurisdiction over such cases. Furthermore, such congressional action is not itself subject to noninterpretive review on the part of the judiciary; otherwise, such jurisdiction-limiting action would be an impotent exercise of power on the part of Congress subject to the Court's own value judgments (132).

In Perry's scheme, the jurisdiction-limiting power of Congress emerges as the thread giving legitimacy to noninterpretive review in human rights cases. As such, it is the democratic component in the process of moral evolution that Perry advocates. Perry applauds the sluggishness of the jurisdiction-limiting power. But the cumbersome nature of this power and the fact that it strikes with a blunt edge are similar to characteristics of the impeachment and budget powers and thereby undermine its role as a means to reconcile democracy with the judicial power Perry advocates (135).

Perry's Role for the Judiciary

The role of the Court and the judiciary in general, according to Perry, is one of taking the lead in the process of moral evolution, at least in the area of human rights.[40] The fact that he leaves the concept of human rights largely undefined presents a problem to his theory and for the judiciary. Whether or not his solution to democratic accountability is anything other than a theoretical exercise in resolving the tension between a judiciary that decides cases involving human rights by noninterpretive review (according to its own value judgments) and a political order based on majority rule is a question he does not resolve. The nation's experience with the jurisdiction-limiting power of Congress is scant. Perry presents little persuasive argument that his dialectical scheme is an improvement over the subtle scheme of separation of powers, checks and balances, and a judiciary that attempts to ground its decisions on the principles of the Constitution rather than on its own value judgments. Indeed, some may question whether his solution of jurisdiction limiting as a control over a noninterpretive judiciary does not undermine the very interplay among branches of government that Perry desires; after all, it constitutes a broadside approach to a separation of powers scheme that was designed to be subtle and intricate. Some may wonder, as well, whether the broadside approach of jurisdiction limiting is a sound means of legitimizing noninterpretive judicial review, since it would simply remove jurisdiction over classes of cases, some of which may involve issues begging for judicial resolution.

Perry's theory is deceptive. He claims that he does not advocate contraconstitutional policy making by the Court, that is, policy making that "goes against the framers' value judgments."[41] But he proposes a role for the Court that gives it discretion to form a new moral order.[42] He proposes an extraordinary judicial power that polices itself, subject to the limitations that it should not go against the framers' value judgments and that it be subject to the jurisdiction-limiting power of Congress.

Perry frames his argument for extraconstitutional review around particular constitutional issues in which he argues that the Court acts legitimately if it does not go against the framers' value judgments. But he does not satisfactorily address the issue of the very powerful role he advocates for the Court itself, running counter to the framers' "value judgments." Absent a specific constitutional provision to the contrary, the Court seems free under his theory to advance its own general view of morality, subject only to the chance that Congress may remove its jurisdiction over the type of case in question. Perry advocates a judicial power that goes beyond even the powerful legislative role provided in the Constitution. The legislature is limited to broad enumerated powers and by specific constitutional prohibitions. The role Perry advocates for the Court limits it only by the latter, subject to a kind of veto power through the jurisdiction-limiting power.[43] Thus, Perry advocates a judicial role that does not rest on constitutional grants of power, like those upon which the legislative power rests, and, of course, does not have the democratic check crucial to the legislative and executive powers—a dependence on the electorate—which is the fundamental limitation on the elected branches.

Perry tries to justify this broad judicial power by invoking the jurisdiction-limiting power of Congress to give it democratic legitimacy. There are relatively few restrictions on the legislative or executive power and few grants of power to the judiciary in the Constitution. Perry's proposal for expanding the judicial power, and thereby limiting the legislative and executive powers, constitutes a refounding of the Constitution. It substitutes government by judiciary for the constitutional government set in motion by the theory and actions of those who framed and ratified the Constitution and thereby undermines the democratic foundations of government. Thus, what Perry attempts to justify as noninterpretive review or *extra*constitutional policy making is in reality *contra*constitutional policy making writ large because of the role it establishes for the Court.

Perry takes up the argument over the role of the Court in a later book, *Morality, Politics, and Law,* as he analyzes democratic arguments that run counter to the judicial role he advocates.[44] He dismisses as "question begging" the argument that nonoriginalist review is illegitimate because it was not authorized by the ratifiers of the Constitution.[45] Perry seems to assume that the judicial role authorized by the framers is somehow disconnected from their theory of democracy and separation of powers and has no relevance to modern government. He does not deem it necessary to explore this proposed judicial role nor to investigate the underlying theory of which it is a part. He asks: "*Why* is government morally obligated to act consistently with original beliefs?" He dismisses, with the same inattention to democratic theory, the argument that government is bound to obey originalist decisions but not nonoriginalist decisions: "Indeed, it is counterintuitive to suppose that today's public officials are morally obligated to defer to the beliefs either of the long-dead and mostly WASP men who ratified the original Constitution and the Bill of Rights or of the long-dead and mostly WASP men who ratified the second Constitution—the Civil War amendments."[46] It is unclear whether Perry dismisses these beliefs because those who espoused them were mostly WASP men or because they are long dead. What is clear is that he does not regard the Constitution and its amendments as law, and he deems it unnecessary to determine whether the theory underlying the Constitution is a sound theory of government. If the Constitution is not law, an important foundation for judicial review is eroded. Given Perry's lack of concern for the principle of consent of the governed or for representation that is undermined by the judicial role he advocates, it is ironic that he dismisses the Constitution because it was proposed and ratified with an insufficiently broad base of representation.

Perry expresses little concern with the question of whether the modern, nonoriginalist judicial role is undemocratic. He posits, instead, the claim to justice that he sees coming from nonoriginalist judicial policy making. Implicit in this position is the idea of the judiciary's becoming more aggressive in imposing its view of justice on the democracy or, as he puts it, imposing the aspirations of the American tradition on the democracy. Perry focuses on the period since about 1954, during which time he believes that the Court has done an effective job of keeping faith with the tradition's aspiration to justice:

> My suggestion, which concededly is speculative (but speculation is all we have to go on here), is that what the tradition is likely to gain in terms of justice—in terms, that is, of the correct mediation of the past of the tradition with its present—from a judicial role of the nonoriginalist sort the Court has (often) played in the modern period, more than offsets what the

tradition is likely to lose, in terms of "responsiveness" and "accountability."[47]

Recognizing that nonoriginalist theory will likely result in a nearly unrestrained Court, Perry sets forth some guidelines that nonoriginalist judges should impose on themselves. He argues that judges should not invalidate a legislative policy unless their choice to invalidate is the result of a "relevant aspiration."[48] Judges should not make decisions about relatively unimportant issues that would involve a disproportionate "expenditure of institutional capital," nor should they decide even more important issues if such decisions would "precipitate a societal crisis and perhaps even impair the Court's capacity to function effectively." Perry concludes that even nonoriginalist judges should act "moderately rather than imperially or precipitously in deciding whether a policy choice regarding some matter is to be invalidated."[49]

In spite of these cautions against excessive imperial or precipitous policy making, Perry's speculative role for the Court should not be underestimated.[50] It transforms the regime and allocates the role of statecraft to the Court. In the end, we must ask: Who is to determine what America aspires to in the name of justice and the American tradition? The answer must be the people who have given their consent to government under constitutional principles. Any other answer is inconsistent with the Constitution's "dependence on the people" as the "primary control on the government."[51] The exceptions to the legislative power and the judicial power are among those "auxiliary precautions" that control government, but as *The Federalist* reminds us, the primary control is that of majority rule expressed through its representatives.

Conclusion

Perry and Epstein are both impatient with the role the Constitution assigns the legislature. Neither the body of the Constitution nor the Bill of Rights sets down broad and nearly limitless statements of morality to justify the power Perry desires for the Court. Perry advocates extraconstitutional review to justify this power—a power he wants used to pursue an undefined moral growth. Epstein wants the Court to enforce strictly the view of law and economics that he thinks should be in the Constitution. To accomplish this, he imposes an extraordinarily broad interpretation on the takings clause, an interpretation that he spends almost no effort establishing as the original meaning of the clause. Instead, he uses the clause as a vehicle for his own interpretation of law and economics and then uses the clause to inform his theory of the Constitution as a whole. Perry is correct that rights and morality are central to the American scheme of government; he is wrong in advocating that the

Court decide cases by acting as prophet of the new moral order. Epstein is right to emphasize the provisions and principles of the Constitution and its theory; he is wrong in imposing his own view of law and economics upon a particular constitutional provision and applying that view to the Constitution as a whole.

The Bill of Rights contains more specific protections than those that might have embodied the broad principles of the Declaration—certainly much more specific protections than those set forth by Perry.[52] Its provisions are not as far-reaching as the interpretation Epstein gives to the takings clause, however—an interpretation that he does not base on substantial historical analysis. The narrower civil rights in the Bill of Rights are sufficiently defined so as to be effectively (though not unproblematically) enforced. But these narrower principles are rooted in the doctrine of natural rights, which is the cornerstone of the political order and our founding—not in an undefined new moral order advocated by Perry, and not in the economic views held by Epstein. The founding majority gave its consent to the more specific and traditional civil rights embodied in the Bill of Rights; therefore, Perry's and Epstein's advocacy of the Court's reaching beyond these rights to adjudicate cases is inconsistent both with sound government and with the principle of consent of the governed.

Perry sees a conflict between moral evolution and the conviction implicit in the Constitution that dependence on the people is the primary control on government. He believes that the imperative of moral growth, or prophecy, justifies the Court's going beyond the Constitution in pursuit of this growth. Epstein's justification for the judicial role he prescribes is his impatience with what he regards as the foolish course much economic legislation has taken during the twentieth century. Perry assumes that the Court will issue wiser decisions than will the popular branches of government. He believes that judicial supremacy will produce moral growth and elevate the character of the political order. Decisions such as *Dred Scott v. Sandford*,[53] *Plessy v. Ferguson*,[54] *Buck v. Bell*,[55] and many cases thwarting New Deal legislation cast grave doubts on his optimism regarding the Court's capacity as the prophet of moral growth.

Perry proposes that the Court function not by looking backward at the "sediment of old moralities" but by looking ahead to a new moral order that can be forged from emergent principle.[56] Epstein wants the judiciary to undo much of this century's legislative agenda. The judicial roles that both advocate are at odds with the Constitution's dependence on the people as the primary control on government.[57] The reasons for this dependence go beyond the familiar maxims that rule by a Council of Platonic Guardians would be irksome[58] or that such a Council would result in deadening the people's sense of moral responsibility.[59] The Constitution rests on the premise that the people are sovereign.

The Declaration and Constitution do not assume wisdom in the population at large, but they are confident in the ability of the people to govern through a properly constituted representative government. Representation rests on the self-interest of the electorate, which, if not a lofty principle, is extraordinarily reliable. Our system of government is based on the conviction that reined and elevated self-interest is a better foundation of government than a presumption of the government's or, a fortiori, the Court's dispensing wisdom.[60] In other words, the framers believed that people generally know their own best interests better than do intellectual elites or judges. Our system of representation rests on the possibility of the people's denying reelection to representatives who are not serving the people's interests. The Constitution contains numerous qualifications of the principle of majority rule, but it rests on this view of representation. The principle of representation operates differently in states and the nation; in the Senate, House, and the executive; and in the proposing and ratifying of amendments. Yet the Constitution fundamentally rests on this connection between the people and their representatives. The Court is not representative in the ordinary sense of that term, since its members are only a remote choice of the people and hold office for life or good behavior. An important authority for judicial review comes from the underlying theory of the Constitution as set forth in *The Federalist*, which was written during the period of ratification. Judicial review departs from the principle of representation, understood as popular control through election. The sanction for this departure arises from the consent of those who framed and ratified the Constitution and who put principled limitations on the ruling majority.

The intention of the framers and the principles of the charter of government justify judicial enforcement of the "specified exceptions to the legislative authority."[61] Hamilton argued that courts have a duty, in enforcing these exceptions, "to declare all acts contrary to the manifest tenor of the Constitution void."[62] He added later in *The Federalist*, however, that there is "not a syllable" in the Constitution that "*directly* empowers the national courts to construe the laws according to the spirit of the Constitution."[63] This argument supports the view that the Court is authorized to enforce those limitations on the legislative authority that are contained in the Constitution or its amendments; it provides little support for judicial enforcement of natural law except insofar as particular manifestations or interpretations of the law are identified in the Constitution. This more limited view of the judicial power than that held by Perry is also supported by the democratic or representative character of the Constitution as a whole. It is supported, as well, by the reality that judges are not necessarily wiser than other governmental officials, nor are they necessarily wiser than the citizen body. The people, through the elevating and moderating processes of governmental mechanisms, are to judge their representatives. Since the judiciary is not elected, it is not accountable to the usual mechanisms of the electoral process. Because of the non-elective nature of the judiciary, any enlargement of the judicial function beyond that involved in enforcing specific constitutional provisions short-circuits this accountability to the people.

Other aspects of the Constitution and its theory also support this limited view of the judicial power. The Constitution was constructed out of a distrust of government's pursuing a general and undefined morality or a wiser economic policy than that which results from the scheme of representation. The Constitution was structured to avoid reliance on those holding governmental office as a Council of Platonic Guardians. The legislative power is not exercised in pursuit of the dictates of the law of nature or an undefined morality, but rather under the doctrine of a written constitution. The distrust of any general governmental power to pursue natural law lies at the foundation of the famous discourse on faction in *Federalist* No. 10—a discourse directed toward a system of government that will preserve individual rights. It rejects reliance on statecraft to adjust the clashing interests that inevitably emerge in a free government.[64] Instead, it relies on the proper structuring of self-interest so that it will operate in the service of the public good. The structuring of self-interest operates both in the multiplicity of factions that we associate most directly with the legislative branch of government and in the separation of powers that seeks to harness this self-interest by connecting the interest of the officeholder with the duties of the office.[65] Although *The Federalist* does not deny the possibility of or necessity for statecraft, its genius lies in structuring a political order based on self-interest in which the representative principle plays a crucial role. Thus, although statecraft is not precluded, it is not regarded as essential to the ordinary operation of the government and, in the end, is accountable to democratic consent. According to *The Federalist,* the representative principle and constitutional provisions restrict those holding office; they are not free simply to pursue the law of nature or a general view of morality. In this sense, the Constitution is distrustful of statecraft that is not securely anchored within its grants of power to government and is not dependent on the consent of the governed.

Perry provides for a check on the judiciary's role as prophet and agent of moral evolution in the form of the jurisdiction-limiting power. But this check does not constitute consent of the governed. As sketched by Perry, this check is more akin to a veto power—one that has almost never been used effectively throughout our history, and one fraught with both practical and theoretical difficulties. Perry's veto is exercised by an elective body over a nonelective one. This is unlike the presidential veto over Congress, which allows one elective official to veto legislative actions, but whose veto can in turn be overridden by the legislature. To use the jurisdiction-limiting power as a substitute for consent of the governed turns the Constitution on its head.[66]

A theory of judicial review that runs counter to the underlying character of the Constitution is contraconstitutional. The judicial role Perry desires—prophetic adjudication aimed toward moral growth and then legitimated if the Court's jurisdiction is not removed—exacerbates the tension between judicial power and democracy. Epstein seems unconcerned with the tension between his theory of law and economics and democratic consent, perhaps because the wisdom he sees in his theory is its own justification. The tension in both Perry's and Epstein's theories is minimized when the Court acts in accordance with the constitutional principles based on the consent of the people who are the source of legitimate power. If, in framing the Constitution, the people as the source of all legitimate power set down reasonably specific limits to the legislative power, and if the Court acts in judicious accordance with these limits, the principle of democracy is preserved. The people have set down reasonably specific limitations on themselves in the Bill of Rights and in other parts of the Constitution. However, the people did not authorize the government as a whole, much less the Court, to pursue unbridled moral growth or wisdom without consent. Rather, the people of the United States sought to safeguard inalienable rights by granting enumerated powers to government and by making certain exceptions to these powers. Impatience with representative government and the Constitution does not justify commentators' imposing their own views on the Constitution, whether that commentator be liberal or conservative. The touchstone of the Constitution is not liberalism or conservatism, but constitutionalism and the representative system of government it embodies.

Chapter Six

Representation and Democratic Theory in the Constitution

Both John Hart Ely and Robert Bork emphasize the democratic foundations of the Constitution and its representative structures. Ely believes that the theory of equality underlying the Constitution requires reforms such as those that have been undertaken in reapportionment cases. But Ely does not limit his theory of equality to representation and reapportionment. Equality also informs his entire constitutional understanding, including the meaning and application of rights specified in the Bill of Rights and other parts of the Constitution. Bork accepts the "original understanding" of the constitutional system of representation and the legitimacy it accords majority rule and rejects reforms that Ely would impose in order to further egalitarianism.

Ely emphasizes the role of process in the Constitution. He rejects the view that the Constitution is concerned with "general values" and argues instead that the choice of substantive values is left almost completely to the political process. He believes that the Constitution is primarily concerned with procedural fairness to individuals and with ensuring broad participation in both "the processes and distributions of government."[1]

Robert Bork critiques the judicial role that he believes has resulted from judges' choosing their own versions of justice in preference to applicable statutory law or provisions of the Constitution. Judges who yield to this temptation substitute their own views of justice for the "American form of government," usurp the legislative power, and politicize both the courts and the Constitution.[2] He argues that the "democratic integrity of law" is entirely dependent "upon the degree to which its processes are legitimate." Legitimate exercise of the judicial power requires a judge to begin the decision-making process with "recognized legal principles" and to reason "in an intellectually coherent and politically neutral way to his result." Bork contrasts the judicial role he regards as legitimate with the view of those who succumb to "the temptation of results without regard to democratic legitimacy."

These two contrasting views rest on different conceptions of the Constitution and law: "Either the Constitution and statutes are law, which means that their principles are known and control judges, or they are malleable texts that judges may rewrite to see that particular groups or political causes win."[3] Bork argues that judges should be bound by the doctrine of *original understanding,* that is, by the principles of the constitutional (or the statutory) text as the text was generally understood by those who ratified the document when it was enacted.[4] His theory has a number of strengths, notably his opposition to an unelected judiciary making important political decisions without support from constitutional provisions and his insistence on maintaining the democratic or representative character of the Constitution.

The Constitution as Process: John Hart Ely

Ely's Understanding of the Constitution

Ely's understanding of the Constitution reflects his interpretation of most of its component parts and defines his view of the proper role for the judiciary. He describes the Constitution as follows:

> [C]ontrary to the standard characterization of the Constitution as an "enduring but evolving statement of general values," is that in fact the selection and accommodation of substantive values is left almost entirely to the political process and instead the document is overwhelmingly concerned, on the one hand, with procedural fairness in the resolution of individual disputes (process writ small), and on the other, with what might capaciously be designated process writ large—with ensuring broad participation in the processes and distributions of government.[5]

This understanding of the Constitution supports the view Ely prescribes for the Court and, unlike the rival "value-protecting approach," is consistent with his underlying premises of American representative democracy (88). Ely seems confident that he has identified the quintessential feature of the U.S. Constitution and its system of government. His argument regarding the nature of the U.S. Constitution begins, quite appropriately, with the Declaration of Independence. He attaches great importance to the Declaration's statement of the self-evident truth that governments derive their just powers from the consent of the governed (89–90).

Ely argues that consent, understood as democratic process, is the central theme of both the Declaration and the Constitution (82–83); however, the archetype of Ely's theory of the Constitution did not appear until after the Civil War, namely, the equal protection clause of the Fourteenth Amendment. Ely believes representation is the keystone of the Constitution (82–83). Consequently, he considers the equal protection clause a dramatic embodiment of the ideal that minorities must be represented and accorded "equal concern and respect in the design and administration of the political institutions that govern them."[6] He treats many provisions, ordinarily assumed to embody fundamental values or rights, as protecting the processes of representation (83–84). For example, he interprets First Amendment protections of speech, press, and assembly as preeminent protections of the representative process rather than safeguards of substantive rights (93–94). He attempts to demonstrate that this concern with processes is characteristic of most of the provisions in the Bill of Rights. He interprets the cruel and unusual punishments clause and the Fourth Amendment, both of which he admits have substantive-value implications, in procedural terms (96–97).

Ely's characterization of the Constitution as most fundamentally informed by a principle of equality is reinforced by his view that the primary goal of the U.S. Constitution is greater egalitarianism—an actualization of its fundamental principle that has resulted in an increasingly democratic and more legitimate form of government. Factors responsible for enlarging the concept of representation were that "[s]ignificant economic differences remained a reality" and "the institution of slavery" persisted (81).

Ely believes that the equal protection clause encompasses a concept of virtual representation: "But even the technically represented can find themselves functionally powerless and thus in need of a sort of virtual representation by those more powerful than they" (84). This view provides great latitude for the judiciary's interpretation of the Constitution and its equal protection clause.

Ely views the Constitution as a movement toward greater democratic participation, as is evidenced by amendments extending the franchise to previously excluded groups (99).[7] He derives his view of the Constitution as democratic process from a theory of representation that he traces from colonial America through the amendments extending the franchise (98–99). The concept of equality underlying this theory, and most clearly expressed in the equal protection clause, constitutes his most fundamental political and constitutional value. His emphasis on equality and the Constitution's progressive march toward greater egalitarianism transforms the foremost constitutional concern from one of rights to that of representative process.

Ely considers fundamental values in the context of the need for some standard to give content to the Constitution's open-ended provisions (39–41). To qualify for such a role, he requires both that the standard was intended as the appropriate end of the constitutional enterprise and that it remains so. He rejects natural law on both counts (48–54). Ely argues that "[a]lthough there were during both relevant eras people who expected the Constitution to be informed by natural law, this theme was far from universally accepted and probably was not even the majority view among those 'framers' we would be likely to think of first" (39). He asserts that the leading framers (and their Reconstruction counterparts) did not have natural law in mind when they authored and ratified the Constitution and its amendments; furthermore, the document nowhere adverts to the term (49). Ely dismisses the Declaration's reliance on natural law as an attempt "to throw in arguments of every hue" so as to make the Declaration rhetorically more effective (49). He believes that he has discredited the view that the Constitution rests on, and is directed toward, the end of rights or law rooted in nature.

But even if the framers of the Constitution did intend specific rights to be embodied in the charter, Ely questions the relevancy or democratic legitimacy of such intent, since it represents "the voice of people who have been dead for a century or two" (11). Although he seeks to discover a principle of equality as a foundation for his theory of representation, he does not seriously address the theory of the Declaration or the Constitution as articulated by its framers. He dismisses the Declaration as a "brief" (49) and characterizes *The Federalist* as "propaganda" (5). His justifies his diminution of these two sources of American political theory with his view that a contemporary majority neither proposed nor ratified these documents, thereby undermining their democratic bona fides (5).

Ely's view as to whether the concept of natural rights or natural law is an appropriate contemporary standard is unequivocal: "The idea is a discredited one in our society, however, and for good reason" (50). He focuses his criticism on the doctrine's vagueness: "You can invoke natural law to support anything you want" (50). This vagueness leads Ely to believe that all "attempts to build a moral and political doctrine upon the conception of a universal human nature have failed," and that the concept of natural law is nearly absent from American discourse (51–52). Consequently, Ely concludes that society rejects the idea that there is a discoverable and objectively valid set of moral principles that justifies a court's quashing the will of elected branches of government (54).

Ely deals with yet another aspect of legitimacy as it relates to consent of the governed. He understands the Declaration's consent of the governed to necessitate democratic form in the process of governing after the government is founded. This is a misunderstanding of the Declaration's meaning. The Declaration merely declares that majority consent is necessary to establish or institute the government and that such government is intended to preserve our inalienable rights. The Declaration does not require a particular form of government.[8] Thus, the Declaration does not require the people to set up popular governments.[9]

Ely's interpretation of the Declaration is the first step in his interpretation of the Constitution as a document preeminently concerned with representative process and equality. But Ely fails to acknowledge that the Constitution is legitimate only insofar as it meets the standard set forth in the Declaration, namely, that of securing "the unalienable rights possessed equally by all men, but which no man without government can adequately secure."[10] Without this source and justification for government, there is no standard by which to measure the legitimacy of the representative process or of the legislative policy in question. Representative process as embodied in the Constitution is defensible only in terms of the natural rights specified in the Declaration.

Although Ely properly regards equality as a fundamental American political principle, he dissociates equality from the doctrine of natural rights and fails to appreciate the foundations of the American conception of equality in such rights. But in fact, "the equality of the Declaration . . . consists entirely in the equal entitlement of all to the rights which comprise political liberty, and nothing more."[11] This necessary foundation of equality in the doctrine of the natural rights of individuals is essential to a proper understanding of not only American equality but also the nature of the U.S. Constitution and its representative institutions.

If equality is properly understood as equality in the possession of natural rights, then consent of the governed to institutions that preserve such rights but are not representative in an immediate or radical sense is eminently justifiable. A majority may, by this principle, make exceptions to the democratic operation of the government by providing for an institution, such as the Court, that is only remotely democratic and by making constitutional exceptions to the legislative power. This is precisely what the framers did. They inserted, largely through the Bill of Rights, "specific protections of traditional civil rights."[12] Although the framers, contrary to Ely's view, understood the Constitution as aimed toward and justified by the doctrine of natural rights, the constitutional manifestations of these rights took the form of the traditional civil rights enumerated with reasonable specificity both in the body of the Constitution and in the Bill of Rights. Ely is correct that there is no broadly based natural law provision or protection of general natural rights within the Bill of Rights.[13] But he fails to see that these specific protections within the Bill of Rights, though not general protections of natural rights, are specific formulations of civil rights that are justified by and derived from the doctrine of natural rights. These protections of individual rights, along with the doctrine of properly structured and enumerated powers, are the constitutional means employed to achieve the ends outlined in the Declaration. Any effort to sunder the Constitution from the Declaration attempts to separate the means (the Constitution) from the ends (the Declaration) that justify the government created under the Constitution.

Ely's presentation of the Constitution as a document that is concerned with representative process is only partially correct. The people also set certain fundamental rights apart, thereby making exceptions to the legislative power. Thus, Ely's view distorts the Constitution insofar as he presents it as a document that is concerned simply with representative process. The strength of his position is that he affirms the necessary role of representation and a dependence on the people in the Constitution's plan for securing rights through a properly structured representative democracy. He emphasizes the relationship between self-interest and representative government that is so necessary to understanding the multiplicity of interests and separation of powers principles of the Constitution. But he severs these principles from the ends of the Declaration that they are designed to serve and interprets specific constitutional limitations on governmental power as protections of representative process rather than as traditional protections of civil rights. The implications of the respective constitutional views just analyzed will become clearer as the role of the Court within the constitutional system is described and analyzed.

Ely's Prescribed Role for the Court

Although Ely recognizes the need to reconcile the Court's authority with a representative form of government, he misunderstands some aspects of the proper judicial role under the Constitution. The framers who prevailed in the Constitutional Convention set forth a view of the Court's role in a democratic republic that is consistent with representative government and the theory of the Constitution as a whole.

The fundamental issue relevant to Ely's work is how the role of the Court, which is only remotely democratic, fits into the wisdom of the Constitution's theory. The reconciliation of democratic government with individual liberty is the theme of our constitutional theory. This problem is so fundamental that the entire constitutional scheme of separation of powers and multiplicity of interests is designed to resolve it. The separation of powers theory includes an independent judiciary that enforces the exceptions the majority has specified in the Constitution, including the Bill of Rights and subsequent amendments. Such judicial enforcement is consistent with constitutional principles and democratic theory only insofar as the judiciary operates on the basis of these exceptions to majority rule that a more sober majority made a part of our fundamental charter of government. Otherwise, the Court functions in a manner inconsistent with the Constitution's premise of majoritarian government, since it assumes a legislative function severed from the requirement for majority rule. Such judicial usurpation of power forecloses the constitutional design of balancing the competing interests of strong and responsible government and civil liberty through the properly constructed legislature. Depending on the Court as the peculiar guardian of civil liberty pits republican government against individual liberty in the context of a lawsuit—a lawsuit attended with many disadvantages.[14] If courts take constitutional principles to extremes or create constitutional exceptions to the legislative power, a problem warned against in *Federalist* No. 63 may result: "liberty may be endangered by the abuses of liberty as well as by the abuses of power; that there are numerous instances of the former as well as of the latter; and that the former, rather than the latter, are apparently most to be apprehended by the United States.''[15]

Congress is designed to be a much more effective register of the competing goals with which government is perpetually confronted than is the Court, thereby requiring restraint in asking the Court to judge what groups are properly represented in government and in protecting minorities and individuals from the majority. The Court is justified in protecting minorities and individuals only when Congress has exceeded its constitutional powers over such individuals and groups. When an activist Court makes broad pronouncements of public policy, even with the intention of protecting individuals or minorities, it thwarts much of the Constitution's protective scheme. Insofar as the judiciary assumes legislative or executive powers, *The Federalist* recognizes an obvious problem relative to the separation of powers theory: ''Were the power of judging joined with the legislative, the life and liberty of the subject would be exposed to arbitrary control, for *the judge* would then be *the legislator.* Were it joined to the executive power, *the judge* might behave with all the violence of *an oppressor.*''[16]

Broad judicial policy making violates the separation of powers and denies a democratic check on policy making. When the Court assumes legislative powers, it bypasses the check provided by a multiplicity of interests in the legislative branch. This check is essential to both democratic consent and to the moderating and elevating effects of the multiplicity of interests discussed earlier (see Chapter 2). The strength of Ely's theory is his recognition of the democratic nature of the Constitution. The weakness of his theory is the subordination of other constitutional principles that were defined to secure rights to his fundamentally egalitarian view and his insistence that the Court enforce this view on the other branches of government and on the states.

The Court as Reinforcer of Representation

Ely's prescribed role for the Court is aimed at reconciling judicial review with his theory of the Constitution. He believes that the Constitution is fundamentally concerned with representation, the concept from which he derives the Court's role.[17] The Court functions as both a reinforcer of the Constitution's emphasis on representation and an agent for the virtual representation of those who are ''technically represented'' but who are ''functionally powerless'' (84). This latter role is necessary because functionally powerless groups are not protected by the representative system from ''the community that is doing them in'' (84). Ely believes that his theory of judicial review is consistent with the democratic assumptions of the Constitution, particularly its underlying theme of representation (vii, 87–88). This justification also helps him reconcile the power of an appointed body of judges who hold office for life or good behavior with democratic theory. Judicial review is justified because it protects popular government and protects minorities from denials of equal concern and respect. Both protections arise "from a common duty of representation" (86–87). More specifically, the Court's role should be oriented toward participation and should reinforce representation because, as experts on process and as political outsiders, courts can claim superiority to other political officials (86–88).

Ely's reliance on the concept of virtual representation is also important to the judicial role he prescribes. Although his theory of representation is sufficient to explain judicial actions such as reapportionment decisions, it is insufficient where "functionally powerless" minority groups are concerned. For example, virtual representation becomes important in the protection of minorities from discrimination. Even when barriers to minority participation in the political process have been removed, the majority may vote themselves advantages at the expense of others or refuse to take the minority's interests into account. Equal representation in the sense of one person, one vote does not guarantee equality of treatment, as evidenced by society's treatment of blacks, who, even after gaining official access to the process, still suffered from majority-enacted discrimination (135). What we traditionally refer to as the problematic conflict between majority rule and individual rights, Ely treats as a problem of virtual representation of minorities. He believes that if the Court acts as an agent for the virtual representation of minorities, it can avoid both the judicial subjectivity and the inconsistency with democratic theory implicit in the fundamental rights approach.

Although he explicitly directs his theory to the Constitution's open-ended provisions, such as the Ninth Amendment and the privileges and immunities clause, Ely argues that most of the Constitution's protections can be understood on the basis of a representative principle, which he apparently derives from equality (100–101). Thus, either "reinforcing representation" or "virtual representation" of minorities serves as Ely's standard for the Court's interpretation of most of the Constitution's provisions (93–104).

The role of the Court as reinforcer of representation is spelled out in a chapter of *Democracy and Distrust* entitled "Clearing the Channels of Political Change" (105–34). Ely concentrates his analysis and the illustration of his theory on freedom of speech, voting rights, and reapportionment. He emphasizes First Amendment protections because they are essential to an "open and effective" representative process through which political change takes place, and because the legislative and executive "ins" may want "to make sure the outs stay out" by inhibiting their speech (105–6). This seems to be the primary connection between his theory of the Constitution, the role he prescribes for the Court, and the First Amendment protections he treats as central to the Court's role.

Given the claims Ely makes for his theory, one would expect it to apply to First Amendment issues in a way that derives explicitly from that theory and offers significant guidance to the Court. His analysis of the First Amendment does neither. His thesis that First Amendment freedoms are important to the political process is persuasive, but not particularly insightful. He concludes that when state officials seek to silence a message that they believe is dangerous, that message must fall within a narrow and specific category designated in advance as unentitled to protection (112). Although one may have difficulty quarreling with this proposal, it seems to say little more than that the regulation of speech and related rights ought to proceed upon a principled basis and that these principles should be articulated in advance.

The insistence that tests of constitutionality be articulated in advance does not remove the need for sound judicial judgment in interpreting specific constitutional provisions. Ely's prescribed role for the Court—that of reinforcer of representation—provides little guidance to the Court as it engages in the difficult task of reconciling individual rights with exercises of governmental power. He acknowledges that, in First Amendment cases, the Court is inevitably involved in "assessing the importance of the interest the state adduces to support its regulation" (106). His theory offers little help in assessing this interest and, therefore, offers no essential advantage over the fundamental rights approach to constitutional freedoms. The advancement and promulgation of the arts and sciences, morality, religion, and truth are central to the ends of human freedom, but their importance is subordinated in Ely's theory primarily because he displaces the judiciary's traditional role as enforcer of individual rights and substitutes a role as reinforcer of representation.

Although Ely acknowledges that the First Amendment is not, by its own terms, limited to political speech, such limits are implicit in the representation theory he uses to explain the tenor and consistency of the Constitution (94). If his theory does not explain important applications of the First Amendment to situations other than those that are directly political in nature, then one is driven to find a theory that will explain such application.

Ely's emphasis on process leads to the other primary aspects of the Court's reinforcement of representation—the right to vote and reapportionment. This is the area of judicial activity that derives most immediately from his theory. In Ely's words, "unblocking stoppages in the democratic process is what judicial review ought preeminently to be about, and denial of the vote seems the quintessential stoppage" (117). Voting rights cases are peculiarly appropriate for resolution by the judiciary because they involve rights "essential to the democratic process" (117). These issues are not safe with our elected representatives because those officials have an interest in maintaining the status quo (117).

Ely dismisses the claim that the political nature of the reapportionment issue precludes the creation of administrable standards for deciding these cases (120–21). He believes that "one person, one vote" is eminently administrable. Furthermore, Ely asserts that the standard adopted by the Court, although having the superficial appearance of intruding upon the states, is actually not so intrusive in practice because its clarity and predictability require fewer judicial inquiries into individual apportionment cases (121).

Ely approves of the line of Supreme Court cases that effected the one person, one vote rule, including *Lucas v. Forty-fourth General Assembly.*[18] In *Lucas,* the Court struck down an apportionment scheme in which only one house of the state legislature was to be apportioned strictly on the basis of population (relying on the federal analogy).[19] This scheme had been approved by voters in a statewide referendum.[20] To Ely, the decision by a majority of voters to depart from the standard of strict majority rule, as understood by the one person, one vote standard, is inconsistent with the Constitution's theory. He characterizes this case as one that compelled judicial intervention.[21]

Ely's discussion neglects a most important aspect of the political character of representation. He incorrectly assumes that the Constitution, and even the Declaration, implies his preferred form of representation. By accepting Ely's view of representation and government as mere process, it becomes much easier to justify the Warren Court's standard of one person, one vote. However, the Declaration's and the Constitution's principles of consent of the governed and representation are much more complex than Ely assumes.

An analysis of Ely's theory of representation and its application to apportionment cases requires a return to his understanding of the Declaration of Independence and the Constitution. He interprets the Declaration's reference to "consent of the governed" as a recognition of the critical role of democratic process.[22] The Declaration contains no such requirement. The end is political liberty; the Declaration leaves open the question of which form of government best secures this liberty (see Chapter 1).

Ely, by understanding "consent of the governed" as necessitating democratic process, is led to a misunderstanding of the Declaration's central teaching regarding rights and to a simplification of the Constitution's meaning of representation. The Constitution understands suffrage and representation as means of securing rights; Ely presents the processes of suffrage and representation as ends in themselves and thus severs them from the inalienable rights that justify the process of representation and the principle of majority rule.

Ely's view of representation concentrates on a purely quantitative understanding which, if radicalized, nearly denies the possibility of individual rights. His view emphasizes the process of majority rule while neglecting the character of this rule relative to the rights the political order was designed to secure. His primary concern is that a quantitative majority—a majority measured by the one person, one vote standard rather than by the quality of government this majority produces—be the sole and immediate animating force within the political order.

Ely's assessment of the reapportionment cases, particularly *Lucas,* rests on a view that representation ought to be simply a reflection of the views and interests of those represented. This seems evident from the very terms he uses in discussing the Court's role in voting rights cases—one of unblocking stoppages in the democratic process so that these views and interests will be reflected.[23]

The framers who prevailed in the Constitutional Convention did not share Ely's view of representation. It is true that a dependence on the people through a carefully structured system of representation is the primary safeguard they relied on to protect individual rights. However, in order to moderate excesses in majority rule and to help ensure both competent government and individual rights, this system of representation was coupled with auxiliary safeguards.[24] The framers designed a system of representation that required a large commercial republic that would allow for the possibility of refining and elevating the public view rather than merely reflecting it.[25] Those Anti-Federalists who favored the small-republic theory of government, which would simply mirror the views of the population at large, lost the argument. Such elevation and moderation are possible because our system of representation does not immediately and precisely reflect the public views.[26]

Important mechanisms were inserted into the Constitution in an attempt to remedy defects of majority rule, but they were thought to be consistent with the republican form of government. Among these mechanisms are the separation of powers, bicameralism, the doctrine of enumerated powers, federalism, and even the practice of judicial review. The U.S. Senate, for example, is not controlled by a national popular majority. It requires that all national legislation pass through an institution in which states, qua states, are represented in an attempt to protect important interests and rights to which a national popular majority might not be sensitive. Yet very few level the charge that the Senate's character disqualifies the national government as democratic. One could make much the same argument relative to the Supreme Court's exercise of judicial review. Certainly this institution is neither democratic nor representative in the ordinary sense. Yet Ely and most other commentators do not object to an appropriate role (as they define it) for this institution.[27] A problem with the Court's decision in the reapportionment cases is well illustrated by the particular factual situation in *Lucas.*[28] If a majority of the people of a state can establish a state supreme court to protect their rights, there is little ground for arguing that a majority of the people of Colorado cannot apportion one house of their state legislature on a basis other than population, with a view toward the same end of protecting minority rights and interests. The same argument applies with even greater force to the legitimacy of the U.S. Supreme Court. As Ely reminds us, those who originally consented to the Court's role have been dead for several generations.[29] Where *Lucas* is concerned, this Court is quashing the action of a contemporary popular majority of a state on the basis of a principle that will not sustain the legitimacy of its own action.[30]

Ely's emphasis on majoritarianism and his denial of fundamental rights rooted in nature make it difficult to discern a principle that will sustain judicial intervention in the representative process. This concern is underscored by Ely's rejection of natural rights.[31] Once that doctrine is rejected, the American idea of equality as expressed in the Declaration loses its traditional and fundamental source of philosophic support; it then becomes possible to regard the principle of equality itself as merely a subjective preference. One must pose two questions: How long can the Court sustain its authority in view of its elevation of the pure majoritarianism implicit in *Lucas* and other reapportionment cases to which the foundation of its own authority runs counter? How can the principle of equality persevere when it is severed from its necessary conjunction with the doctrine of individual rights?

Since Ely rejects the concept of individual rights rooted in nature as the foundation of the constitutional prohibitions he discusses, he is driven to some other basis for those prohibitions. He believes that the "representation-reinforcing approach to judicial review, unlike its rival value-protecting approach, is not inconsistent with, but on the contrary (and quite by design) entirely supportive of, the underlying premises of the American system of representative democracy" (88). The basis he constructs to supplement the Court's role as reinforcer of representation is that of virtual representation. This latter concept is apparently his explanation for the constitutional provisions and for the role of the Court in areas that cannot be directly drawn from the concept of representation reinforcement: "The existing theory of representation had to be extended so as to ensure not simply that the representative would not sever his interests from those of a majority of his constituency but also that he would not sever a majority coalition's interests from those of various minorities" (82).

There are problems with Ely's attempts to interpret and clarify the Court's role, even when his constitutional theory of participation or representation is directly related to the issues in question, that is, the First Amendment and reapportionment. Ely also attempts to incorporate other provisions of the Constitution into his theory that are much less obviously related to it (93–101). He interprets the Bill of Rights as process oriented in content and as reinforcing representation (93–101), presumably in an attempt to free the Court from the difficulties of the interpretivist theory in adjudicating constitutional provisions that are facially value laden in their concern with individual rights. Ely wishes to avoid the subjectivity of the fundamental rights approach. His theory interprets the Bill of Rights within a framework derived from the Fourteenth Amendment's equal protection clause (93–101). In determining his theory's validity, an analysis of it within the context of both the Bill of Rights and the equal protection clause is required.

Ely's assertion that much of the rationale of the Eighth Amendment's ban on cruel and unusual punishment lies in the realization that there is tremendous potential for arbitrarily inflicting severe punishments on people of a particular class is exemplary of his interpretation (97). This interpretation is consistent with Ely's view that the Fourteenth Amendment is aimed at discrimination by the legislature ("us") against a minority class ("them").[32] In the context of cruel and unusual punishments, Ely's argument seems to be that "we," the legislature, will be more likely to inflict cruel and unusual punishments on "them" because legislators do not really believe that these punishments will be inflicted on "us," the law-abiding legislative majority. Consequently, the Court has the duty, arising out of virtual representation, to represent "them."

Ely's group-oriented interpretation does not provide an underlying principle to guide adjudication under the Cruel and Unusual Punishment Clause. Judicial analysis of a most speculative nature is required to reveal the bad motives or perhaps even the subconscious motives necessary to discern the legislative dichotomy between "them" and "us." His test provides little help to a judge who must decide difficult cases, such as a death penalty case involving a second electrocution after the first failed due to a mechanical malfunction;[33] a divestiture of citizenship of a natural born citizen;[34] or the proportionality between the punishment of fifteen years at hard labor, perpetual surveillance, or loss of all civil rights, and the offense of falsifying public documents.[35] It is much more intelligible to view the clause as a particular manifestation of the conception of justice underlying our Constitution and political system rather than as a provision rooted in process that reinforces representation or demands the Court's virtual representation of a minority group. Viewing the clause as conferring a right on an individual to be free from unnecessary cruelty[36] or a right to be free from "punishments which by their excessive length or severity are greatly disproportioned to the offences charged"[37] is a particular civil manifestation of the law of nature on which our Constitution is based. Viewing the clause as a personal right does not ensure its automatic application, but it does provide more direct and intelligible guidelines than does Ely's theory. These guidelines provide a more effective constraint on judicial judgment by insisting that judges be bound by the explicit meaning of the amendment stated in principled and unchanging terms, that is, a constitutional right to be free from unnecessary cruelty or nonproportional punishment. A view of the amendment as a particular manifestation of the natural rights doctrine provides important elements of judicial guidance without setting the judges free to roam, at large, in natural law theory.[38]

Ely's emphasis on process, the "us" and "them" group view of legislation, and the role of the Court as both reinforcer of representation and agent for virtual representation are fundamental to his understanding of the equal protection clause. The application of Ely's theory in the area of affirmative action is paradigmatic of the theory's application in the other areas he discusses. Essentially, Ely argues that "[t]here is nothing constitutionally suspicious about a majority's discriminating against itself."[39] Since whites are well represented in the legislative process, this is not an instance of the legislative "us" discriminating against "them." "Whites are not going to discriminate against all whites for reasons of racial prejudice" (170). Thus, the bad motivation element is lacking. Predictably, Ely's analysis in this area takes on a group orientation rather than an individual orientation. It follows that he subordinates individual rights to the process of representation. Consequently, since whites as a class are well represented, the process appears to be functioning well. This majority will not "deny to whites generally their right to equal concern and respect" (170). In the same context, Ely defines the function of the equal protection clause as "largely to protect against substantive outrages by requiring that those who would harm others must at the same time harm themselves—or at least widespread elements of the constituency on which they depend for reelection" (170).

Equal protection, then, is reduced to the process of representation of majority and minority groups in which the Court's role consists of both reinforcement of majority representation and virtual representation of minorities. Equal protection as a right of a person, as it is defined in the Fourteenth Amendment, is transformed into the process of representation of groups in the legislative and judicial process. It becomes a simple task for Ely, given the elements of his theory, to justify "reverse discrimination" (170–72).

Ely's understanding of equal protection as directed toward groups rather than individuals is not consistent with the Constitution and its underlying theory. Although he is obviously correct that the equal protection clause grew out of the mistreatment of blacks in this country, and blacks are an identifiable minority group, this is not the decisive issue. The injustice and contradiction in the American political order's tolerance of slavery resulted from the denial of the personal rights enumerated in the Declaration. The fundamental injustice of slavery is the denial of the natural rights of life, liberty, and property that define our equality as human beings. The principle of individual rights, not group representation or process, condemns slavery and justifies the equal protection clause.

Ely's theory denies this fundamental, self-evident truth. Ely's argument that a legislative body or a board of regents will not "deny to whites generally their right to equal concern and respect" (170) is not the relevant point. It is the individual, not the group generally, who suffers the immediate impact of discrimination. The Fourteenth Amendment specifies the "person" as the entity entitled to equal protection. The regents of a university are not promulgating a rule applicable to themselves but one applicable to candidates for admission to the University of California Medical School at Davis, for example.[40] Ely's argument that the white majority will not discriminate against itself is irrelevant. The problem is not discrimination against itself as a group but against the individual applicant who happens, in a general sense, to be a member of the white majority to which Ely refers. The effect of reverse discrimination is a denial of the very individual rights that lie at the foundation of the American idea of equality. These same individual rights are the basis on which slavery was condemned.

Ely's process-oriented theory is attractive, both because of the claims he makes on its behalf and because of his proper emphasis on the importance of representation to the process of government implicit in our Constitution. However, his attempt to sunder the Constitution from its fundamental concern with individual rights rejects important aspects of the Constitution's theory of representation and distorts individual rights protected by the Bill of Rights and the Fourteenth Amendment.

Conclusion

The critique of Ely and other commentators is based on the view that there is an integrated and fundamental theory within the Constitution. Like many other commentators, Ely overlooks important aspects of the wisdom inherent in the Constitution. Although his theory purports to serve democracy and representation, it is inconsistent with the theory of the Constitution.

Ely rejects the rights approach advocated by many other commentators, primarily because of the inconsistency he sees between this approach and the underlying democratic assumptions of the system.[41] But his theory, although rooted in his view of the proper criteria of representation, is not that of our constitutional system. In the name of participatory democracy, he would have the Court deny the decision of a majority to restrain itself through measures such as those the Court invalidated in *Lucas*.[42] Such restraints are important parts of the American system of government. Although Ely properly emphasizes representation as important to our system of government, he raises it to an end in itself and obscures the elevating and refining qualities of representation. These qualities are important to securing individual rights. Ely misunderstands the constitutional theory of representation and sunders this theory from the doctrine of natural rights, which lies at the foundation of the Constitution's theory. In asking the Court to proceed from his theory of the Constitution, Ely is essentially asking the Court to reform the constitutional system in a way that departs from the framers' constitutional theory. This is judicial activism "writ large," which asks the Court to act as a continuously functioning constitutional convention. Although Ely is correct in that specific provisions of the Constitution should be interpreted in a manner consistent with the tenor of the entire Constitution, his interpretation departs from that wisdom implicit in the framers' theory.

Ely rejects the doctrine of natural rights for a number of reasons, but primarily because it frees justices to insert their subjective values into the Constitution.[43] The framers' theory of the Constitution rests on the doctrine of natural rights, but it also encompasses the concern with process that defines Ely's theory. He is correct that the Constitution and Bill of Rights do not set down the first principles of natural rights, but he is wrong in divorcing the Constitution from its "ultimate source and justification."[44] The Bill of Rights sets forth generally objective and enduring principles in the form of traditional civil rights.[45] Ely's attempt to view these rights as "process" is misleading and is not helpful in making the difficult choices all free governments must make as they attempt to govern competently and preserve individual liberty.

The strength of Ely's theory is his recognition of the importance of process in the constitutional system and his acknowledgment that much of the responsibility for securing rights rests with the process of representation and legislative judgment. His theory of representation obscures the constitutional mechanisms for elevating and refining the democratic will and asks the Court to redefine the entire Constitution to make it consistent with his theory. His emphasis on equality and representation also abstracts the Constitution's processes from the ends they were designed to serve, the securing of the public good and private rights. Ely is sound in rejecting a role for the Court in which it usurps the legislative power and decides cases on the basis of natural rights, but he asks the Court to restructure the system of representation on which the Constitution rests and to interpret constitutional rights according to his view of equality. This view sunders constitutional rights from their foundations in nature and obscures the great purposes of a Constitution designed to effect a number of great ends, one of which is to "secure the Blessings of Liberty to ourselves and our Posterity."[46] The concept of equality on which Ely's theory of representation and constitutional interpretation is utterly dependent derives its fundamental legitimacy from the "Laws of Nature and of Nature's God," which Ely unequivocally rejects.[47]

Interpretivism, Democracy, and the Constitution's Original Understanding: Robert Bork

Robert Bork, unlike the other commentators examined, has authored a best-seller—*The Tempting of America*. He is well known because of the controversy over his nomination to the U.S. Supreme Court. One of the primary criticisms voiced by those opposed to Bork's nomination was that his constitutional views were outside the mainstream.[48] The fact that the centerpiece of his constitutional commentary is also a popular book presents some problems to an analyst, for it may preclude some of the subtlety or depth necessary to a fair analysis of his theory. Therefore, although this analysis focuses on *The Tempting of America*, it also includes some of his law review articles and other scholarship.

The temptation Bork eschews is that of judges' choosing their own versions of justice in preference to applicable statutory law or provisions of the Constitution. Judges who yield to this temptation substitute their own views of justice for the "American form of government," usurp the legislative power, and politicize both the courts and the Constitution.[49] He argues that the "democratic integrity of law" is entirely dependent "upon the degree to which its processes are legitimate." Legitimate exercise of the judicial power requires a judge to begin the decision-making process with "recognized legal principles" and to reason "in an intellectually coherent and politically neutral way to his result." Bork contrasts the judicial role he regards as legitimate with the illegitimate view of those who succumb to "the temptation of results without regard to democratic legitimacy." These two contrasting views rest on different conceptions of the Constitution and law: "Either the Constitution and statutes are law, which means that their principles are known and control judges, or they are malleable texts that judges may rewrite to see that particular groups or political causes win."[50] Bork argues that judges should be bound by law, which means the same thing as being bound by the principles of the constitutional (or the statutory) text as the text was generally understood by those who ratified the document when it was enacted; that is they should be bound by the "original understanding."[51] Although he believes that judges make law when they decide cases, this should be "minor, interstitial lawmaking."[52]

Bork's theory has a number of strengths, notably his opposition to an unelected judiciary's making important political decisions without support from constitutional provisions and his insistence on maintaining the democratic character of the Constitution. He regards the Constitution as law, and he attempts to ground his doctrine of original understanding in the Constitution's text. Unlike many other commentators who impose their own theories on the Constitution, he is deeply suspicious of moral theories that pervert the constitutional text as understood by those who ratified it. Although such theories may be appropriate objects of analysis for politicians and academics, they are not the proper basis for judicial decisions. Bork acknowledges the existence of rich historical sources that help illumine the original understanding, but he does not often rely on these materials to support his doctrine. This failure causes difficulty for him, for example, in justifying the doctrine of judicial review on which his theory depends. Theory and history also give meaning to the Constitution and inform our understanding of the relationship of the Constitution's provisions to its underlying and unifying theory. Without this theory, the Constitution may become merely a collection of provisions abstracted from the context of its underlying purposes.

Bork believes that the Constitution was designed to resolve the "Madisonian dilemma." This dilemma consists of opposing principles: the first is that majorities are entitled to rule "simply because they are majorities," and the second is that there are "some things majorities must not do to minorities, some areas of life in which the individual must be free of majority rule."[53] Bork resolves the Madisonian dilemma he posits between majority rule and minority rights in favor of judicial supremacy, which he believes will protect individual rights. In this respect, he is in the mainstream of contemporary constitutional commentators, allied at a fundamental level with many of those who opposed his nomination and who favor judicial supremacy as the best protection for individual rights. Bork is saved from the characteristic excesses of many other judicial supremacy advocates by his doctrine of "clause-bound interpretivism," that is, by his focus on the text of particular constitutional provisions as the standard by which to decide cases. His "clause-bound interpretivism"—confining the Constitution to the meaning of its various clauses—has substantial merit as a principle of adjudication. But I will argue that clause-bound interpretivism is an inadequate interpretive theory, even by Bork's own standards of interpretation, which properly rely on the "text, structure, and history" of the Constitution to give it meaning.[54]

Bork's Doctrine of Original Understanding

The status of the Constitution as law leads Bork to his "philosophy of original understanding, and the associated idea of political neutrality in judging."[55] The rule of law is fundamental to his constitutional doctrine. The apparent key to his understanding of the Court's role is what he calls the "Madisonian dilemma"—the tension between the principle of democracy (or majority rule) and the principle that there are some aspects of an individual's life that should be free from majority rule. This tension exists because "neither majorities nor minorities can be trusted to define the proper spheres of democratic authority and individual liberty." Placing "that power in one or the other would risk either tyranny by the majority or tyranny by the minority."[56] Bork believes that the Constitution deals with this problem by limiting the powers of the federal government, by staggering elections for the elective branches, and by including a Bill of Rights in the Constitution. The Bill of Rights "is the only solution that directly addresses the specific liberties minorities are to have." Bork argues that "[w]e have placed the function of defining the otherwise irreconcilable principles of majority power and minority freedom in a nonpolitical institution, the federal judiciary, and thus, ultimately, in the Supreme Court of the United States."[57] He also argues that the Court should discern the powers of Congress and the president when they come into conflict and define "the respective spheres of national and state authority."[58] Considerations of national supremacy and uniformity of constitutional interpretation, as well as the theory of the large commercial republic treated in Part I of this book, support Bork's view where the respective spheres of national and state authority are concerned. Judicial umpiring between Congress and the president does not rest decisively on these considerations, although it may sometimes be supported by other considerations.

Bork's broad view of the judicial power is similar to that of many he criticizes, but he disagrees fundamentally with many other commentators about how the judicial power should be exercised. In spite of Bork's doctrine of original understanding, he has adopted the mainstream understanding of the judicial power rather than one firmly anchored in the original Constitution. It is far from clear that the original understanding regarded the Court as the ultimate arbiter of the issues of separation of powers and individual rights, which Bork places within the judicial power.[59] He is saved from the excesses of judicial supremacy advocated by many commentators by other elements of his doctrine.

Central to Bork's doctrine of original understanding is his prescription of neutrality in "deriving, defining, and applying principle," a prescription that distinguishes him from many other commentators. He does not argue that the principles of the Constitution are neutral, for the Constitution favors some principles over others. He believes, for example, that "the concept of original understanding builds in a bias toward individual freedom." But *judges* should be neutral in finding the principles of the Constitution and not "create new constitutional rights or destroy old ones."[60] In this instance, as in many others, Bork's standard for adjudication is sound and helps avoid judicial excesses and preserve the democratic character of the Constitution.

Neutral definition of principle is crucial, particularly in cases involving general principles of the Constitution, such as the First Amendment protection of speech. In spite of this general prohibition, "no one has ever supposed that Congress could not make some speech unlawful or that it could not make all speech illegal in certain places, at certain times, and under certain circumstances."[61] Judges must reasonably determine speech and freedom as they define the First Amendment principle. In defining constitutional principles, a judge "must not state the principle with so much generality that he transforms it." In finding the appropriate level of generalization or abstraction of a constitutional principle, Bork relies on "the level of generality that interpretation of the words, structure, and history of the Constitution fairly supports."[62] The words, structure, and history of the Constitution are sound sources of interpretation, and Bork stands in sharp relief to those commentators who largely disregard these factors in imposing their own theories on the Constitution. It remains to be seen whether text, structure, and history can be applied properly without some reliance on principle and theory.

Bork illustrates his precepts of interpretation in his treatment of the equal protection clause of the Fourteenth Amendment. He relies on the historical evidence and the text to establish the appropriate scope of equal protection. Although the clause was adopted with recently freed slaves in mind, its general language applies to all persons. Bork argues that the judge is required to look to history to determine whether, for example, the equal protection clause requires only that "blacks should be treated by law no worse than whites," or whether whites were protected against "discrimination in favor of blacks." Proper disposition of Bakke's "reverse discrimination" case[63] turns on this distinction, one that Bork would make from the historical record. In cases of gender and sexual orientation, Bork argues that since we do not know the original understanding, the general language of the clause simply requires that statutory distinctions be reasonable.[64]

Bork applies his doctrine to the decision in *Brown v. Board of Education,* which found legal segregation of public schools to be unconstitutional.[65] He supports the decision in this case, but not the reasoning by which the Court reached it. He argues that the decision of the Court—"a great and correct decision"—was right because the principle of the Fourteenth Amendment is equality, and legal segregation denies that equality in contemporary America. He objects to the Court's reasoning because it focused on the "feeling of inferiority" fostered by segregated schools. He does not regard this as a principled basis for the decision, relying as it does on social science and psychological studies that do not live up to his standard of principle.

Bork confronts the problem that those who ratified the Fourteenth Amendment did not intend it to apply to segregated public schools, but he nonetheless regards *Brown* as a "great moment in constitutional law."[66] He argues that *Brown* was correctly decided, in spite of the fact that the Fourteenth Amendment's specific intention was not to outlaw segregated schools. Even though segregation did not lie at the "central meaning" of the equal protection clause, he believes that the central principle of equality required holding that legally segregated schools were unconstitutional. Indeed, he argues that the decision in *Brown* "is compelled by the original understanding" of the Fourteenth Amendment.[67] History yields to principle in his treatment of *Brown.*

Bork's defense of the decision in *Brown* accepts the contradiction that those who ratified the Fourteenth Amendment intended black equality but also assumed legal separation of the races and, therefore, left state segregation laws in place. The equal protection clause does not mention segregation, but rather makes equality under law its primary goal. Therefore, equality must prevail over segregation. Bork further argues that by 1954 it had become clear that segregation did not produce equality, since school facilities for blacks were inferior to those provided for whites—a proposition demonstrated in a number of previous Supreme Court cases. He believes that the Court's choice in *Brown* was either to abandon "the quest for equality by allowing segregation or to forbid segregation in order to achieve equality." Since either choice "would violate one aspect of the original understanding," and equality is the principle articulated in the Fourteenth Amendment, the Court ruled properly in forbidding segregation in order to achieve equality.[68] Bork might well have cited the first Justice Harlan's dissent in *Plessy v. Ferguson,* in which Harlan observed that the primary purpose of segregation was to exclude blacks from railroad coaches assigned to white persons, not to exclude whites from coaches assigned to black persons.[69] Given the history of the United States, Harlan's observation seems compelling and illustrates the necessity of combining history and principle in interpreting the Constitution.

In his analysis of *Brown v. Board,* Bork makes *principle* the decisive consideration. In this case, principle is the standard by which he interprets the text. The principle of equality also trumps the historical fact of segregation and thereby subordinates the history of the Fourteenth Amendment's meaning to the principle of equality it contains. At least in this case, Bork adds principle to the precepts that guide constitutional interpretation. This may well be justified because *Brown* is an extraordinary case that goes to the root of the Constitution's fundamental principles, but it is hard for us to know from Bork's writing when reliance on principle subordinates text or history and when it does not.

Although Bork supports the Court in its decision to invalidate state school segregation laws, he objects to the Court's applying this principle to the national government in *Bolling v. Sharpe*[70] because the Fourteenth Amendment's equal protection clause is directed to the states, not to the national government. For the Court to hold that the due process clause of the Fifth Amendment forbids the national government to segregate schools in the District of Columbia transforms the meaning of the Fifth Amendment's due process clause (the Fifth Amendment, which applies to the national government has no equal protection clause). This transformation is undertaken in order to achieve the ends desired by the Court and thereby usurps the legislative power in a way Bork finds objectionable. Because it is "unthinkable, as a matter of morality and of politics," for the national government to segregate schools while states are forbidden to do so, he argues that Congress would not have allowed this "ugly anomaly to persist" and would have repealed the District's segregation laws.[71] This conclusion is consistent with Bork's strong textual emphasis in constitutional interpretation and also recognizes that it is not the peculiar duty of the Court to define rights.

One of Bork's greatest strengths is his emphasis on judicial neutrality in enforcing the Constitution and law. Neutrality is rooted in his view of the proper role of judges as interpreters of the law and in his rejection of the judiciary's revising the Constitution in order to keep it current with the times as judges superintend the legislative power. Judicial neutrality is also linked to his strong textual orientation and his view that the text of the Constitution means what it says. His discussion of neutrality focuses much more on principle than on text, structure, or history. Neutrality in the application of principle requires a judge to apply the derived and defined principle without regard to prejudice for or against the parties to the lawsuit. Neutral application requires applying a principle found in the Constitution, not one specially tailored so that the judge can achieve a result that is desirable for reasons extraneous to the Constitution. Bork uses the case of *Shelley v. Kraemer* to illustrate a violation of the neutral application of principle.[72] This case struck down racially restrictive covenants. Property owners had signed agreements that restricted sales to white persons. In spite of the restrictive covenants, some whites sold to blacks, and other property owners sought to enforce the covenants. Applying common-law rules, the state courts enjoined the black buyers from taking possession of the property. Since these were private agreements, the Supreme Court was faced with the problem that the Fourteenth Amendment applies only to state action. But the Supreme Court regarded the state judicial enforcement of the restrictive covenants as constituting state action, which satisfied the Fourteenth Amendment requirement.[73]

Bork believes that the standard of state action embodied in *Shelley v. Kraemer* cannot be neutrally applied; therefore, it should not have been used to decide this case. However much he admires the decision in *Shelley* on moral grounds, the case involved private action that the state courts had enforced according to a rule that applied to private agreements and that the Court would be unwilling to give neutral application in other cases. Bork's primary objection to the Court's standard of state action in *Shelley* is that almost anything, no matter how frivolous, may result in state court action, subjecting virtually all private conduct to Fourteenth Amendment scrutiny. Bork observes that such a result would "be both revolutionary and preposterous" if *Shelley* were applied neutrally, which it has not been. Subsequently, the Court upheld the post–Civil War civil rights acts that outlawed racially discriminatory private contracts.[74] Bork supported this result in the brief he filed as solicitor general. He thinks that Congress has the power to outlaw such contracts, but the Court does not.[75]

Bork regards the judicial role he describes as consistent with the original understanding of that role and with the republican system of government framed by the Constitution. The original understanding "does not countenance . . . a judiciary that decides for itself when and how it will make national policy, [and] when and to what extent it will displace executives and legislators as our governors."[76] He believes that the only exceptions to democratic rule are those few but important instances in which the Constitution has placed prohibitions on the majority. He refers briefly to statements in the Constitutional Convention and in *Federalist* No. 78 to support his view that the courts were not intended to have a political role. Even if such statements of the framers were not extant, he believes that the judicial role he describes is "a necessary inference from the structure of government apparent on the face of the Constitution."[77]

Although Bork's argument for relying on the structure of government provided by the Constitution is sound, he could strengthen his case for democracy and the judicial role he favors through the use of history and political theory. John Locke's work, which was the basis for the Declaration, is an important theoretical source for understanding the inference Bork draws from the structure of government and from the face of the Constitution. Locke makes clear that the act of instituting a government follows the establishment of a political community of which each member of society agrees to be a part. Once every individual has consented to be part of the political community, that community acts through the consent of the *majority:* "And therefore we see, that in assemblies, impowered to act by positive laws, where no number is set by that positive law which impowers them, the *act of the majority* passes for the act of the whole, and of course determines, as having, by the law of nature and reason, the power of the whole."[78] Once political society is formed, the first and fundamental law of the commonwealth is the establishment of the legislative power, which is "supreme . . . sacred, and unalterable in the hands where the community have once placed it; nor can any edict of any body else, in what form soever conceived, or by what power soever backed, have the force and obligation of a *law,* which has not its *sanction from* that *legislative* [power] which the public has chosen and appointed: for without this the law could not have that, which is absolutely necessary to its being a *law.*"[79]

Once the people consent to become a community, they act through a majority to establish the legislative power. The legislative power in the United States is established through the Constitution. Locke regards the judicial power as derivative from the legislative power. Although the American judicial power is not derivative in the Lockean sense, the Constitution, according to Publius, creates a judicial power that is consistent with the strictly republican character of the Constitution. Publius defends the judicial power in that part of *The Federalist* that treats "the conformity of the proposed Constitution to the true principles of republican government."[80] Consent of the governed is required by equality. A majority of the political community, acting on this same principle, establishes the legislative power. It is crucial to understand the Constitution and the role of the judiciary to which consent was given. Bork is correct to object to commentators who impose their own theory on the Constitution, but his attempt to interpret the Constitution with so little attention to its theory and history is problematic.

Bork's Responses to Criticisms of Original Understanding

In defense of his doctrine of original understanding, Bork articulates critics' objections and responds to them. These responses are sound and answer certain criticisms of some of the commentators in this volume. His responses to the following claims are closely related: (1) The original understanding is unknowable. (2) We cannot understand the principles of the Constitution because those who enacted them "lived in an entirely different society." (3) The original meaning is unknowable because of the passage of time. (4) The Constitution must change as society changes. (5) The living should not be governed by the dead.[81]

Bork argues in response to these critics' claims that the requirement that a judge know the specific intention of the lawgiver would destroy all law:

> [A]ll that a judge committed to original understanding requires is that the text, structure, and history of the Constitution provide him not with a conclusion but with a major premise. That major premise is a principle or stated value that the ratifiers wanted to protect against hostile legislation or executive action. The judge must then see whether that principle or value is threatened by the statute or action challenged in the case before him. The answer to that question provides his minor premise, and the conclusion follows. (162–63)

Bork acknowledges that two judges using this method may not agree in their conclusions, but this is true when judges apply any law. The task for judges is to seek "the best understanding of the principle enacted" (163). If they adhere to the principles of the historic Constitution, judges will find that many issues "are placed off-limits for judges" and left to democratic resolution.

Bork contends that if we cannot understand the principles of the Constitution because those who enacted them "lived in an entirely different society" (164), the National Bank Act of 1864 and the Sherman Act of 1890 would be reduced to "gibberish" and we would be unable to understand the concept of judicial review established in *Marbury v. Madison*.[82] Understanding particular provisions of the Constitution is aided by rich historical materials, which include the constitutional text, records of the Philadelphia convention, records of ratifying conventions, the newspaper accounts of the day, the Federalist Papers, the Anti-Federalist Papers, the constructions put upon the Constitution by early Congresses in which men who were familiar with its framing and ratification sat, the constructions put upon the document by executive branch officials similarly familiar with the Constitution's origins, and the decisions of early courts, as well as treatises by men who, like Joseph Story, were thoroughly familiar with the thought of the time.[83]

In addition to these rich historical materials (which he utilizes only sparingly), Bork regards the structure of the Constitution and the government that John Marshall relied on as another source of judicial enlightenment. These aids to original understanding result in a good deal of knowledge about some parts of the Constitution, only some knowledge about other parts, and little or no knowledge about others. He believes that the privileges and immunities clause of the Fourteenth Amendment falls into this last category, that judges cannot make out the meaning of this clause, and that it should be considered an "ink blot" on the Constitution. Since this clause is a mystery, judges should disregard it (165–66). The proper course of action for the judiciary, if his critics' claim is true and the Constitution has no discernible current meaning, is to "let current majorities rule, because there is no law superior to theirs" (166–67). Bork does not explain why there is no law superior to that of majorities. He might have relied on the Declaration's adoption of Lockean theory, which explains the legitimacy of consent and its roots in equality, as well as on the framers' conception of the legislative power and the judicial power in a strictly republican Constitution. These sources, as well as the text, history, and structure of the Constitution, support the view that on most occasions, public policy should be left to majorities. There are exceptions to the legislative power that are specified in the Constitution and require judicial enforcement. The Constitution's exceptions to the legislative power distinguish the American system from a parliamentary system.

In responding to the claim that the Constitution must change as society changes, Bork argues that the philosophy of original understanding produces neither a "rigid Constitution" nor "a mechanical jurisprudence"; rather, it preserves the Constitution's relevancy and integrity as it controls the development of constitutional doctrine. The boundaries of the Constitution's provisions are not "self-evident," and judges must "discern how the [f]ramers' values, defined in the context of the world they knew, apply to the world we know." Contemporary application of the framers' values justifiably takes account of changing circumstances, such as those in the technological or legal environment. He rejects leaving such adjustments to the legislature, since to do so would "render constitutional guarantees meaningless" (167–68). But would leaving such adjustments to the legislature really render constitutional guarantees meaningless? It is more accurate to say that leaving such guarantees to the legislature would undermine the doctrine of judicial supremacy. The legislature regularly creates legal rights in response to the changing technological and legal environment. Bork himself argues for the legitimacy of congressional action to enforce the Constitution's provisions in outlawing discriminatory restrictive covenants and for the illegitimacy of judicial action to accomplish this same end (153). It is more consistent with the original understanding to say that the Court has a role in enforcing constitutional guarantees in cases of a judiciary nature, but it is not the exclusive branch of government to give constitutional guarantees meaning.

Bork's rebuttal to the claim that there is no reason for the living to be governed by the dead also relies on the analogy to the Sherman Act, the National Bank Act, and the parts of the Constitution delineating the powers of the branches of government, all of which would be invalid under this claim. He believes that those who argue that dead men have no authority to govern us are really asserting that the "courts should be free to write into the Constitution freedoms from democratic control that the framers omitted." Bork turns this argument against its proponents, however, in observing that the dead-men argument might also be used "as an excuse for a judge who decided not to enforce the Bill of Rights because James Madison and his colleagues are no longer among us," a conclusion none of those making the dead-men argument wants to reach. Bork argues that the proper and democratic means of creating new freedoms through law is constitutional amendment or simple legislation (rule by living majorities), not judicial creativity (170–71, 173).

Yet another claim of those who oppose the doctrine of original understanding is that the Constitution is not law, a claim usually advanced by those who wish to expand judicial governance. Bork observes that the Constitution is not law merely because it asserts that it is. Both the Constitution and statutory law gain their legitimacy from the fact that the people assume that our lawmaking process is legitimate; however, Bork believes that there is no "ultimate philosophic reason" to support this presumption of legitimacy (171–74). This statement would surprise those who framed the U.S. Constitution. As Part I of this book argued, there is a substantial philosophic justification for the rule of law, for equality, and for the consent of the governed, which lie at the foundation of the Constitution. However, Bork's view that the Constitution is law is sound, as is his response to critics that if the Constitution is not law, there is no reason that the decisions of the Supreme Court should be legitimate or binding (175).

Regarding the claim that the Constitution is simply what the judges say it is, Bork responds that, practically speaking, this is true. But his critics err in disregarding the normative meaning of the historical Constitution as it was understood by those who enacted it (176). Bork's view was stated better by Abraham Lincoln, who clearly expressed this distinction and emphasized the democratic character of the Constitution in his first inaugural address:

> I do not forget the position assumed by some, that constitutional questions are to be decided by the Supreme Court; nor do I deny that such decisions must be binding in any case, upon the parties to a suit, while they are also entitled to very high respect and consideration, in all paralel [*sic*] cases, by all other departments of the government. . . . At the same time, the candid citizen must confess that if the policy of the Government upon vital questions affecting the whole people is to be irrevocably fixed by decisions of the Supreme Court, the instant they are made in ordinary litigation between parties in personal actions, the people will have ceased to be their own rulers, having to that extent practically resigned their Government into the hands of that eminent tribunal.[84]

The crucial difference between regarding a judicial ruling as binding in a particular case and regarding it as fixing the meaning of the Constitution goes to the root defect of the claim that the Constitution is simply what the judges say it means. The Constitution has a meaning independent of what judges may say it means in any particular case.

Ronald Dworkin and others claim that the choice to resort to original understanding in itself involves judges in political choices. Although not denying that the doctrine of original understanding has political consequences, Bork argues that the doctrine is saved from the claim of its critics because it does not have "political intentions." The choice to adhere to original understanding is one of adhering to the political choice made by those who framed the Constitution. Thus, original understanding simply perpetuates the design of the Constitution and the republic. The proper judicial task is to apply the morality of the framers and the law into a rule that governs unforeseen circumstances. Such judicial restraint is "important to American liberty," and it embodies the view that "[t]he Constitution assumes the liberties of self-government, not merely those liberties that consist in being free of government." A restrained judiciary also allows the political community the "freedom to control the environment—physical, aesthetic, and moral—in which they and their families live."[85] The essence of this last argument is that, unless constitutionally designated by specific prohibitions, rights are to be determined through the electoral system and through legislative and executive processes.

The final claim against original understanding is the impossibility of "clause-bound interpretivism" (confining the Constitution to the meaning of its various clauses), on which Bork's original understanding rests. John Hart

Ely argues from this claim in his book *Democracy and Distrust*. Ely argues that the Constitution itself contains provisions that require looking beyond the rights specified therein. Bork characterizes this as "a claim that the *law* of the Constitution commands judges to find rights that are not specified in the Constitution," a view that gives the judiciary a much stronger role than it is commonly supposed the framers had in mind.[86]

Bork agrees with Ely that the due process clauses do not warrant the creation of additional constitutional rights, for due process is simply a procedural right, not one forbidding government from acting in certain substantive areas. Ely believes that the due process clauses do not authorize the judicial creation of nonenumerated rights, but the privileges and immunities clauses do: "the most plausible interpretation of the Privileges or Immunities Clause is, as it must be, the one suggested by its language—that it was a delegation to future constitutional decision-makers to protect certain rights that the document neither lists, at least not exhaustively, nor even in any specific way gives directions for finding."[87] Bork objects to making the judiciary the future constitutional decision makers who have license under this interpretation to create new, unenumerated rights. He objects to this view as creating an unbridled judicial discretion. Bork interprets privileges and immunities as directed to legislators and executives, not to judges: "Before legislating, signing legislation, or taking action, legislators and executives are to think about what they would regard as privileges and immunities (meaning 'liberties') that ought not to be infringed."[88] The privileges and immunities clause of the Fourteenth Amendment, then, is not quite an "ink blot" as he suggested earlier.[89] Rather, according to his understanding, it is a provision that legislatures and executives enforce.

Although Bork does not utilize this argument, his interpretation of privileges and immunities is strengthened by the fact that Congress is given authority to enforce the Fourteenth Amendment through appropriate legislation in section 5 of the amendment. Bork could very well argue, in support of his interpretation, that Congress is the appropriate body to define privileges and immunities of citizens of the United States.[90] This would clearly save him from his "ink blot" explanation, one that regards the clause as without ascertainable meaning according to his doctrine of original understanding.

Ely regards the Ninth Amendment as another invitation for the judiciary to enforce rights beyond those specified in the Constitution.[91] The amendment reads: "The enumeration in the Constitution, of certain rights, shall not be construed to deny or disparage others retained by the people." Ely regards this amendment as being directed to the judiciary. Bork responds that although the history of the amendment is sparse, it does not authorize judges "to create constitutional rights not mentioned in the Constitution." If such a meaning had been intended, the amendment might easily have been drafted in clear language to indicate such a judicial role. He believes that a more sensible interpretation of the Ninth Amendment is that rights promised by state constitutions and laws are not to be denied or disparaged by the national government.[92] This is a sensible interpretation, so long as rights promised by state constitutions and laws to citizens in their relationship with the state governments are not allowed to interfere with the national government's exercise of its enumerated powers or with the supremacy clause of Article VI. It hardly seems likely that Madison and others who were so concerned that the national character of the Constitution not be altered by the addition of amendments would have authorized state constitutional or statutory obstructions of national powers through the Ninth Amendment. Madison provides insight into the meaning of the Bill of Rights, including the Ninth Amendment:

> What use then it may be asked can a bill of rights serve in popular Governments? I answer the two following which though less essential than in other Governments, sufficiently recommend the precaution. 1. The political truths declared in that solemn manner acquire by degrees the character of fundamental maxims of free Government, and as they become incorporated with the national sentiment, counteract the impulses of interest and passion. 2. Altho' it be generally true as above stated that the danger of oppression lies in the interested majorities of the people rather than in usurped acts of the Government, yet there may be occasions on which the evil may spring from the latter sources; and on such, a bill of rights will be a good ground for an appeal to the sense of the community.[93]

In this passage, Madison clearly does not view the judiciary as the sole guardian of rights, even those rights specified in a bill of rights. I certainly do not mean to argue, however, that the judiciary should not enforce the specific prohibitions of the Constitution. Madison states in the First Congress that "enumerating particular exceptions to the grant of power" in the Constitution will result in courts being "an impenetrable bulwark" against legislative or executive encroachments upon the rights stipulated. Madison also argues in the First Congress that a bill of rights specified in the Constitution will enable state legislatures to guard more effectively the rights of the people.[94] Madison sees the prohibitions in the amendments he proposed, which became the Bill of Rights, as providing a means for judicial enforcement and a textual reminder to the states and other branches of government of the rights the Constitution was designed to secure. He regards the prohibitions of the first ten amendments as serving purposes beyond that of providing a means for judicial enforcement. In referring to the provision that would become the Ninth Amendment, Madison argues in the First Congress: "It has been objected also against a bill of rights, that by enumerating particular exceptions to the grant of power, it would disparage those rights which were not placed in that enumeration; and it might follow, by implication, that those rights which were not singled out were intended to be assigned into the hands of the General Government, and were consequentially insecure.'' Madison adds that a bill of rights will provide a means for the state legislatures to ''watch the operations'' of the national government and ''to resist with more effect every assumption of power.''[95]

A sensible interpretation of the Ninth Amendment is that the inclusion of specific rights in the first eight amendments does not imply that the national government should open season on private rights that were not specified. The fact that the Bill of Rights includes a right to a grand jury and not a right to marriage does not mean that the Constitution's framers, by implication, intended to authorize Congress to abolish marriage. Madison seems to be arguing that the government is founded on private rights, and it is suitable to remind both the sovereign people and their representatives of the importance of these rights—to incorporate them in the ''national sentiment.'' Such incorporation will serve a salutary purpose when acts of the sovereign people or their representatives resolve issues involving the public good and private rights. Madison characterizes the Bill of Rights as directed to the people as well as to the courts and presumes that the people are sovereign in his reference to ''the sense of the community'' to which appeal can be made when private rights are unduly violated. Madison's hesitancy to place strict and numerous limits on the power of government seems clear in this statement: ''It is a melancholy reflection that liberty should be equally exposed to danger whether the Government have too much or too little power, and that the line which divides these extremes should be so inaccurately defined by experience.''[96]

It is ironic in light of Madison's comments regarding the Ninth Amendment as directed at state governments that Ely and other commentators would argue, contra Bork, that the Ninth Amendment authorizes the Supreme Court to define the rights of citizens relative to their state governments and to do so with no specific constitutional guidance. An important element of this irony is the fact that the first ten amendments were originally directed to the national government, not to the states. Bork's interpretation of the Ninth Amendment seems consistent with his standards of the Constitution's text, history, and structure.

Bork's response to his critics is generally sound. He argues persuasively that the Constitution is law, and he believes that judges should adhere to it. The primary difficulty with his clause-bound interpretivism is that it decisively weakens the case for judicial review and the role of judges in the system of government. Bork is also sound in not using either the privileges and immunities clause of the Fourteenth Amendment or the Ninth Amendment as a means to convert the Constitution to a judicial ''blank check'' for the creation of rights that judges regard as important. Such an expansive reading of specific provisions of the Constitution would transform the nature of the political system and undermine the separation of powers and the democratic character of the Constitution. In the case of the privileges and immunities clause, there are substantial arguments for an interpretation that regards it as the power of Congress to specify such privileges and immunities. Both this clause and the Ninth Amendment must be interpreted in light of the Constitution and its theory as a whole, not as isolated textual provisions.

Evaluation of Bork's Theory of the Constitution and the Judiciary

Bork is sound in rejecting the conclusion that the judiciary, regarded by Publius as the least dangerous branch, is justified in overriding decisions of the democratic branches on the basis of authority "outside the written Constitution," authority that judges have used to insert their own political views into the Constitution. His conclusion that clause-bound interpretation of the Constitution is possible, however, presents some problems even for his own theory. A proper understanding of the Constitution requires an understanding of the Constitution's theory and purposes, not just the clauses that compose it. Indeed, the very institution of judicial review on which Bork relies rests on shaky foundations if one limits its justifications to clause-bound interpretivism. Judicial review is not provided for in any clause's specific grant of power and thereby fails the test of clause-bound interpretivism. Judicial review is justified by the structure of government, the theory of limited government, the rule of law, and the principle of equality which requires consent of the governed.[97] Hamilton, in *Federalist* No. 81, attributes the power of judicial review not to "any circumstance peculiar to the plan of the convention, but from the general theory of a limited Constitution."[98] Hamilton's influential defense of judicial review is not based on clause-bound interpretivism.

Bork warns readers of *The Tempting of America* that the book is not about legal theory.[99] But one cannot properly explicate the Constitution without reference to its ends or purposes and without inquiry into its underlying theory. The Constitution's purposes and its theory give unity to its various provisions and aid in the proper construction of those provisions. Much of what Bork says about the proper judicial role is consistent with the theory of the Constitution as a whole, but his analysis stops short of that theoretical and historical analysis necessary to defend the constitutional system. For example, he derives the legitimacy of the Madisonian system from the fact that it is consistent with what "the people of this nation assume to be ways of making law." Bork states that he knows of no ultimate philosophic basis for this assumption.[100] This is not the answer Madison would give. The Constitution provides for a system of government derived from the consent of the people, and the system to which consent was given was a representative one based primarily on a properly constituted legislative power with a derivative role for the judiciary. To explain the role of the judiciary in this system requires a sound understanding of the entire constitutional scheme for securing the public good and private rights, a scheme that depends on the intricate system of representation and the separation of powers. Bork would strengthen his argument if he devoted more of his work to these issues.

Bork emphasizes the case of *Dred Scott v. Sandford*[101] in his history of the genesis and development of judicial usurpation. The factual situation of that case was as follows:

> Dred Scott had sued for his freedom in the slave state of Missouri, where he had returned, after having been taken by his master to live in Minnesota Territory, in which slavery had been prohibited by the Missouri Compromise legislation of 1820. Scott claimed his freedom on the ground that he had been taken by his master to reside (he was not a runaway), and had resided, in a federal Territory in which slavery had been prohibited by federal law. But Taney's opinion declared that the 1820 legislation had been unconstitutional, because Congress had no lawful power to deprive a slaveowner of his property, merely because he had exercised his constitutional right to migrate to a United States Territory. To do so would violate the Fifth Amendment's prohibition against depriving a person of his property "without due process of law." Congress had no power over slavery in the Territories, said Taney, other than "the power coupled with the duty of guarding and protecting the owner in his rights."[102]

Bork describes this case as one in which the "the politics and morality of the Justices combined to produce the worst constitutional decision of the nineteenth century."[103] Chief Justice Roger Taney's opinion can be criticized on a number of grounds, but Bork regards its fundamental defect as that of using the doctrine of substantive due process to overturn the will of Congress as expressed in the Missouri Compromise:

> How, then can there be a constitutional right to own slaves where a statute forbids it? Taney created such a right by changing the plain meaning of the due process clause of the fifth amendment. He wrote "[T]he rights of property are united with the rights of person, and placed on the same ground by the fifth amendment to the Constitution, which provides that no person shall be deprived of life, liberty, and property, without due process of law. And an act of Congress which deprives a citizen of the United States of his liberty or property, merely because he came himself or brought his property into a particular Territory of the United States, and

who had committed no offence against the laws, could hardly be dignified with the name of due process of law."[104]

Bork believes that Taney was wrong to transform the procedural meaning of the due process clause of the Fifth Amendment into a substantive protection of property, which Taney used to declare unconstitutional the congressional action in the Missouri Compromise. Bork argues that Taney's opinion not only produced a terrible decision in *Dred Scott* but also set in motion the objectionable doctrine of substantive due process, which "created a powerful means for later judges to usurp power the actual Constitution places in the American people."[105] Whatever criticisms one may make of Bork's analysis of *Dred Scott,* adherence to his interpretation of the due process clause, which limits it to procedure, might have avoided a decision which almost all agree was one of the worst in the history of the Supreme Court.

Apart from Bork's criticisms, Taney's interpretation of substantive due process in *Dred Scott,* as well as other parts of his opinion, exhibits a number of fundamental problems. First, a right to property follows from the fact that we are persons, that is, personhood is the justification for property. The very justification for property is inconsistent with violating the liberty of another human being by holding that individual as property. Taney used the Declaration as additional justification for his opinion. He argued that "the legislation and histories of the times, and the language used in the Declaration of Independence, show, that neither the class of persons who had been imported as slaves, nor their descendants, whether they had become free or not, were then acknowledged as a part of the people, nor intended to be included in the general words used in that memorable instrument."[106] Taney's fundamental error is his presumption that both the Declaration and the Constitution regarded slaves and their progeny as nonpersons. The Fifth Amendment due process clause on which Taney relies states, "[N]or shall any *person* . . . be deprived of life, liberty, or property, without due process of law."[107] The constitutional restriction on Congress's prohibiting the slave trade refers to "[t]he Migration or Importation of such *Persons* as any of the States now existing shall think proper to admit, shall not be prohibited by the Congress prior to the Year one thousand eight hundred and eight."[108] This provision thereby makes it clear that it regards slaves as persons. Although the Three-Fifths Compromise modifies its reference to *persons* with the adjective *free,* its very use of the modifier and its avoidance of the term *slaves* indicates its understanding that slaves are persons.[109]

Under Taney's substantive interpretation of due process, the definition of person to include or exclude slaves and their descendants is critical, and his understanding of the Declaration and the Constitution is flawed in this regard, the compromises of the Constitution regarding slavery notwithstanding.

But Bork cannot avoid the same definitional difficulty even by limiting the meaning of due process to procedure. One must determine who is a person in order to determine who has a Fifth Amendment right to due process. Even the narrower interpretation of due process as *procedure* necessitates determining who has a right to such process, including the judicial process of access to the federal courts. The determination of who is a person and the relationship between personhood, liberty, and property seems necessary even to the limited application of the due process clause, which in its own terms protects the processes by which a person may be deprived of life, liberty, or property. For Bork to apply the procedural protections of the due process clause, it seems necessary to do more than just apply the words of the clause itself, for such application would produce an impasse between the liberty of a person and the property of a person, an impasse requiring judicial determination of which one is subordinate to the other. Such a determination requires a theory that explains the relationship of property to liberty and personhood, a theory that can be derived from a proper understanding of the Constitution, the Declaration, and John Locke.

The Tenth Amendment offers an example of the need to go beyond clause-bound interpretivism in order to understand the Constitution. The amendment reads: "The powers not delegated to the United States by the Constitution, nor prohibited by it to the States, are reserved to the States respectively, or to the people." Bork argues that "[t]he tenth amendment is clearly a guarantee of federalism,"[110] a guarantee that the Court ignored in such cases as *Wickard v. Filburn*.[111] This case justified penalties on wheat grown in excess of government quotas. The excess wheat, intended for consumption on the farm, affected interstate commerce. If it had not been grown, the farmer would have had to purchase wheat elsewhere or reduce the amount sold. Bork objects to this permissive attitude of the Court toward congressional power as "a manifestation of judicial activism."[112] Perhaps the governmental action in this case was unwise, but it hardly constitutes *judicial* activism. It is unclear how Bork could limit the commerce power by the doctrine of federalism and still avoid the political role for judges to which he so strongly objects. The Constitution empowers Congress to regulate commerce among the states with no explicit reservation of state autonomy. The commerce power is limited implicitly by the structural principles of the Constitution, including the equal representation of each state in the Senate.[113]

The difficulty with Bork's view of clause-bound interpretivism is that the Tenth Amendment depends on the meaning of the whole Constitution and its integrating theory.[114] The Tenth Amendment cannot, for example, tell us anything about the power to regulate commerce without an understanding of the scope of the grant of power in Article I, section 8 of the Constitution, or the meaning of other constitutional prohibitions that limit that power. One has great difficulty understanding the commerce power without an understanding of the theory's justification, which is explicated in *The Federalist* and in other sources. If Bork's proposition that the Tenth Amendment guarantees federalism is to be persuasive, a careful argument is needed to support that view, for on its own terms, the Tenth Amendment supports the proposition that the remainder of the Constitution simply means what it says.[115] Bork emphasizes the importance of text, structure, and history in interpreting the Constitution, but his reliance on clause-bound textual interpretivism in the case of the Tenth Amendment does not employ the whole text, the structure of the Constitution and government, and the theory of the enumerated powers presented by history. Text, structure, and history are sound precepts of interpretation, but he does not use them well in the case of the Tenth Amendment.

Chief Justice Stone in *United States v. Darby* described the Tenth Amendment as "a truism that all is retained which has not been surrendered," as "declaratory of the relationship between the national and state governments as it had been established by the Constitution before the amendment."[116] This interpretation is like that of Chief Justice John Marshall in *McCulloch v. Maryland*. Marshall's interpretation of the "necessary and proper" clause in *McCulloch* accorded particular importance to the fact that the Tenth Amendment did not use the term "expressly delegated" in reference to national constitutional powers. The adverb "expressly" might have obstructed important national powers necessary to the successful implementation of the Constitution's underlying theory had it been included in the Tenth Amendment.[117]

Given Bork's concern for state powers and the doctrine of federalism, it is curious that he makes no attempt to resolve the controversy concerning the application of the Bill of Rights to the states through the Fourteenth Amendment, a doctrine that rests on shaky historical and theoretical foundations.[118] This application has resulted in much of the judicial lawmaking that he finds objectionable. Perhaps he regards the application of the Bill of Rights provisions to the states as so central to his conception of the judicial function that it is justified by practical, if not by historical, reasons. The Fourteenth Amendment would provide Bork with an excellent opportunity to treat the virtues of legislative action as opposed to judicial action, since Congress is charged in section 5 with the enforcement of the Fourteenth Amendment's provisions. Bork is a proponent of judicial supremacy where the Bill of Rights is concerned, whether in application to the national government or to the state governments. His objections arise when the Court uses either the Fourteenth Amendment or the Bill of Rights to create unenumerated rights. In this, and in some other respects, he adopts the view of Justice Hugo Black.[119]

Bork rejects the mode of interpretation that ultimately relies on political theory or on sources beyond the Constitution, such as the Declaration of Independence. His primary objection is the bad use of such reliance in the past.

Taney's reliance on the Declaration to buttress his opinion in *Dred Scott v. Sandford* resulted in a decision that many regard as the most infamous in American Constitutional history and that perverted the meaning and principles of the Declaration.

The Court also invoked the Declaration of Independence in its opinion invalidating a Georgia apportionment scheme in *Gray v. Sanders:* "The conception of political equality from the Declaration of Independence, to Lincoln's Gettysburg Address, to the Fifteenth, Seventeenth, and the Nineteenth Amendments can mean only one thing—one person, one vote."[120] The somewhat complex county unit system in Georgia weighted rural votes more heavily than urban votes and the votes of smaller rural counties more heavily than the votes of larger rural counties.[121] One difficulty with the Court's reasoning is that neither the method for electing U.S. senators nor the electoral college squares with the "one person, one vote" standard. The election of senators and the mechanism of the electoral college, however, were specified in provisions of the Constitution, a Constitution designed to effect the ends of government articulated in the Declaration. The framers regarded these provisions as both republican and consistent with the Declaration's principles.

In spite of the Court's opinion to the contrary, the county unit system invalidated in *Gray* is consistent with the framers' view of an acceptable republican mechanism, one similar to that embodied in the national government's electoral system. *Gray* met the requirements of republican government as understood by the framers. Thus, in both *Dred Scott* and *Gray,* invocation of the Declaration's principles resulted in decisions inconsistent with the original understanding. The Court's reasoning in *Gray* was extended in *Lucas v. Forty-Fourth General Assembly* to invalidate a Colorado apportionment scheme that included geographic districting, analogous to that of the U.S. Senate, and which had been overwhelmingly approved by Colorado voters in a referendum.[122] These reapportionment cases are exemplary of decisions that Bork finds objectionable because they run counter both to historical practice and to the Constitution's own provisions for representation in the U.S. Senate.[123] Thus, *Gray's* reasoning, relying in part on the Declaration of Independence, led to wrong results in *Lucas.*

Bork would decide reapportionment cases on the basis of the history, structure, and provisions of the Constitution. Indeed, the provisions of the Constitution and its structure and history seem entirely consistent with the Colorado scheme. Bork believes that when the Court goes beyond these sources, the sort of judicial legislation involved in *Lucas* is inevitable. Although the Court is wrong in arguing that the Declaration requires "one person, one vote" (indeed, each person did have one vote, the objection was to the political effect of each vote), Bork believes that expanding the authority of the Court to go beyond the text, history, and structure of the Constitution opens the door to just this type of judicial legislation that claims to be the law of the Constitution. In this discussion, Bork forgoes the opportunity to discuss the distinction between consent to form the government and the nature of the representative institutions to which that consent was given and that were embodied in the Constitution. It is clear that democratic consent was given to a Constitution that does not meet the egalitarian standard of the reapportionment cases—for example, the creation of a Supreme Court that is only remotely democratic in its operation.

Bork's defense of the Constitution is thoughtful and, in most respects, persuasive; however, it stops short of the justification and explication of the Constitution as a whole, which is necessary to support his view of the proper judicial role. This shortcoming is manifested in his clause-bound interpretivism and in his emphasis on ratification as opposed to intent. He argues that "constitutional law has very little theory of its own,"[124] but in fact there are rich sources for such theory that he uses only sparingly.[125] The intention and principles of the Constitution would be illegitimate and simply an exercise in political theory without the necessary process of ratification and consent. There is, however, a deep well of theoretical and historical material that illumines the Constitution's meaning in subtle and profound ways that go beyond the understanding of the ordinary citizen who played a crucial role in the ratification process. The work of Publius and other public figures during the founding provides keys to the theory and unity of the Constitution. These sources are important not just because they came from the pens of notable individuals but because they lead us toward the principles of the Constitution and the Declaration, which have an intrinsic merit and which the framers both explicated and justified in their work. Bork's restriction of his focus to ratification sacrifices the wisdom of those whose statecraft formed the coherent system the people ratified. Although he properly asserts that a secret letter from George to Martha Washington should not be decisive in interpreting the Constitution, this objection paints with too broad a brush.[126] The intentions and theory of the framers are indispensable to us in understanding the true meaning of the Constitution. *The Federalist* is a part of the ratification process as Bork defines it (for example, *Federalist* No. 1 makes it clear that it and successive papers are directed "To the People of the State of New York").[127] But beyond their direct role in the ratification process, *The Federalist* and related materials are also a great help to us in understanding the ends, structure, and meaning of the Constitution. They help us understand the ideas of which the Constitution is the manifestation and legal statement.

Understanding these ideas and principles is of indispensable help to a judge, even one who regards the proper judicial role as similar to that prescribed by Bork. For example, properly resolving the issue of the one-house legislative veto of executive decisions in *Immigration and Naturalization Service v. Chadha* requires invoking the theory underlying separation of powers, including the issue of whether this is an appropriate judicial question.[128] Theory and principle are also necessary to resolve issues such as the extent of enumerated powers; conflicts between specified rights, such as those between free press and fair trial; and tension between the establishment and free exercise of religion. A proper application of the First Amendment's speech or press provisions requires reflection on the purpose of that amendment and its relationship to republican government and other considerations. Thus, even when staying within the four corners of the Constitution in deciding constitutional issues, judges must rely on theory and principle to resolve them.

The Constitution's specific provisions necessarily leave substantial latitude for the invocation of theory and principle in their application, including a judgment of whether the interpretation of Court, Congress, or the executive should prevail. The Court is sometimes driven to theory and principle in the proper resolution of constitutional cases, as it was in the extraordinary case of *Marbury v. Madison.*[129] But even the ordinary work of the Court in cases of a judiciary nature requires resort to theory and principle in explicating the Constitution's provisions. This is a different enterprise, however, from allowing judges to go beyond the provisions of the Constitution to enforce rights that are not specified. Bork properly disagrees with judges imposing their own views on the Constitution, whether they purport to base these views on natural rights or on any other doctrine. He is right to limit the judicial role to the provisions of the Constitution. But this properly delimited judicial role requires judges to understand the Constitution as a whole and employ the standard of justice in applying and interpreting constitutional provisions.

Bork's writings have led many to characterize him as a legal positivist. In spite of his reassurances that he is not, parts of his writing may lead to that conclusion.[130] Bork quotes with approval, for example, Oliver Wendell Holmes's famous response to Learned Hand's calling upon Holmes to do justice. Holmes responded: " 'That is not my job. It is my job to apply the law.' "[131] Bork's own formulation is that judges should "administer justice according to law," which is not the same thing as saying that judges should ignore justice in applying the law.[132] But, putting Hand, Holmes, and Bork aside, it is clear that the framers were not legal positivists. One can reject legal positivism without making judges the peculiar guardians and interpreters of the rights and law of nature. The framers did not hold this view of the judiciary. When judges have engaged in this role, the results have often been undesirable, for example in *Dred Scott v. Sandford.*[133] *Dred Scott* is an extraordinary case, and resolution of the issues underlying it go to the fundamental principles of the political order. The objectionable feature of Taney's opinion is not the use of political theory but his bad use of that theory.

There are other examples of the Court's obstructing the will of Congress, sometimes on the basis of judicially created rights—a judicial role that Bork properly finds objectionable. *United States v. Harris* declared unconstitutional the 1871 Anti-Lynching Act, which had made it a federal crime to conspire to deprive a person of equal protection of the law.[134] *The Civil Rights Cases* declared the Civil Rights Act of 1875 unconstitutional and voided its prohibition on segregation and racial discrimination in public accommodations and other public places.[135] *Adair v. United States* held that the Fifth Amendment barred the government from preventing interstate employers from firing union laborers.[136] *Hammer v. Dagenhart*, using the doctrine of "dual federalism," struck down the first child-labor law.[137] *Adkins v. Children's Hospital* held that a minimum-wage law for women in the District of Columbia violated the Fifth Amendment.[138]

Bork and other analysts are justified both in questioning the constitutional legitimacy and in lamenting the results of these cases—cases resulting from a doctrine of judicial supremacy and often resting on unenumerated rights. Publius observed in *The Federalist* that the public good results from "the mild voice of reason," which finally depends on the public mind.[139] Bork is justified in questioning whether the judiciary should attempt to impose this "mild voice of reason" upon the properly constituted republican branches of government when that reason is not firmly anchored in the Constitution's provisions. One can fully reject the doctrine of legal positivism without embracing the doctrine of judicial supremacy to enforce unenumerated rights. Many originalists are also proponents of natural law.[140]

Conclusion

An important element in the Senate's refusal to confirm Robert Bork's appointment to the Supreme Court was the charge that his theory of constitutional interpretation was out of the mainstream. His theory of interpretation resulted in his rejecting the constitutional rights to privacy and abortion. Many of his opponents tenaciously opposed his views on these issues. However, his view of the judicial role is similar in a number of respects to many of those views his opponents apparently regarded as defining the contours of the mainstream. Although Bork often argues for majority rule, he posits a "Madisonian dilemma," based on his belief that the Constitution has "placed the function of defining the otherwise irreconcilable principles of majority power and minority freedom" in the judiciary, and ultimately in the Supreme Court. He also argues that the Court should determine the powers of Congress and the president when they come into conflict and define the proper spheres of national and state authority.[141] A fair reading of those materials relating to the "original understanding" that Bork embraces does not support this broad judicial power (see Part I). The original understanding depended primarily on the strictly republican sense of the people and their carefully constituted legislative representatives to secure rights rather than on the superintendency of the Supreme Court. If Bork is out of the mainstream in some respects, he certainly shares the mainstream's rejection of reliance on the strictly republican character of the Constitution and that mainstream's adoption of judicial supremacy. It is ironic in an age in which so much labor and treasure are devoted to the exportation of democracy that the sense of the people expressed through their representatives is accorded so little respect.

Bork's endorsement of judicial supremacy is qualified by his insistence that exercise of the judicial power be contained within the specific clauses of the Constitution, a policy of containment that the Court has not followed. In addressing the First Amendment, for example, Bork would accord constitutional protection "only to speech which is explicitly political."[142] Recognizing that the "sins" of the Court have changed the law of the Constitution from that required by the original understanding, he addresses the question of how the Court should proceed in order to be consistent with the original understanding. His basic admonition to judges: " 'Go and sin no more.' "[143]

If judges wish to avoid further deforming the Constitution, he offers additional advice on how they should handle precedents that have departed from the original understanding. He agrees with Justice Frankfurter that " 'the ultimate touchstone of constitutionality is the Constitution itself and not what we [the justices] have said about it.' " But Bork properly believes that prudence prevents the Court from overruling all precedents that he believes depart from the original understanding (156). In determining which precedents are wrong, he accords particular respect to those that were set within a few decades of the ratification by judges who, presumably, had a better understanding of the original meaning of the Constitution than is available to current judges (157). Claims of stability and continuity support respect for good-faith efforts of previous Courts to arrive at the original understanding, particularly when contemporary judges reflect that they, too, are subject to error. Practical considerations, such as the possibility of interrupting modern governmental practices and throwing us into chaos, also affect the decision to overthrow or abide by precedent. On the one hand, Bork believes that overruling New Deal and Great Society programs, which were enacted pursuant to the commerce, taxing, and spending powers, would have that effect in many instances. On the other hand, "it will probably never be too late to overrule the right of privacy cases, including *Roe v. Wade,* because they remain unaccepted and unacceptable to large segments of the body politic, and judicial regulation could at once be replaced by restored legislative regulation of the subject" (158). He would not overrule the privacy right of married couples to use contraceptives established in *Griswold v. Connecticut,* however. Since no jurisdiction would enforce such a law, it has little practical importance, but he would not extend the privacy right into new areas. Even in such areas as commerce, taxing, and spending, however, the Court need not repeat earlier mistakes by affirming congressional regulation of new subject areas (158–59).

Bork's treatment of precedent offers useful insights into how the Court should apply those precedents that depart from his theory of original understanding. As in other areas of his constitutional doctrine, the decision to adhere to precedent depends on more than the practical considerations he so ably treats. Determining when the Constitution, "the ultimate touchstone of Constitutionality," justifies departing from precedent requires understanding the unifying theory of the Constitution, which illumines the Constitution's most fundamental purposes. Central to this inquiry is recapturing the "strictly republican" character of the Constitution and its representative mechanisms. These mechanisms elevate and refine public opinion as it undergoes the process necessary to its becoming public law. In some respects adopting the premises of other commentators he criticizes, Bork rejects reliance on the people and regards the judiciary as the peculiar guardian of individual rights.

The theory of the Constitution explicated in Part I of this volume rejects the notion of the judiciary as the peculiar guardian of rights and instead regards the whole of the government it creates as the only reliable security for the public good and private rights. Careful treatment of this theory is essential to recover the proper judicial role. Important elements of American history also counsel against relying on the judiciary as the peculiar guardian of the public good and private rights and as the authoritative umpire of the powers of the national government. Dependence on the Court as the peculiar guardian of individual rights was ill placed in *Dred Scott v. Sandford*. It was left to the statecraft of Abraham Lincoln to lead the democracy toward a proper resolution of the problem of slavery. Congressional efforts to stop lynching and to protect civil rights following the Civil War were blocked by the Court. The Court's preservation of federalism as Bork understands that doctrine finally gave way to the democratic will of the executive, Congress, and the people in the New Deal's redefinition of the national government's powers.

We are so accustomed to relying on the judiciary to protect rights that we often discard the understanding of the Constitution's theory of republican government, which rests primarily on a refined and elevated public opinion. Although Bork laments this fact, his own theory accepts important elements of judicial supremacy.[144] His proposed limitations on the judicial power would be much more persuasive if, in his reliance on the text, history, and structure, he plumbed the depths of the Constitution's theory and the importance of self-government to those who framed a constitution designed to secure the public good and private rights.

There is some inconsistency in Bork's work as to when he relies on "text, structure, and history," when he relies on "clause-bound interpretivism," and when he relies on principle. Clause-bound interpretivism or text will not support the doctrine of judicial review that he supports and that is central to his constitutional theory. The justification for judicial review is based in history (for example the theory explicated in *The Federalist*, which was part of the ratification process) and in the theory of limited government and a written constitution. In discussing *Brown v. Board*, he rejects the historical fact of racial segregation at the time the Fourteenth Amendment was ratified and relies on the principle of equality to ascertain the root meaning of the equal protection clause. In interpreting the Tenth Amendment, he relies on clause-bound interpretivism rather than on the structure and meaning of the Constitution as a whole.

Bork seems ambivalent regarding the status of the Declaration's "Laws of Nature and of Nature's God." This leads him to favor the legislative power and majorities in his doctrine of original understanding. A sounder defense of the power of the legislature and majorities is consistent with the fundamental truths about which Bork expresses ambivalence. One may fully accept the status of the laws of nature in the Declaration while favoring the system of legislative supremacy the Constitution embodies. Legislative supremacy rests on both the fundamental doctrine of equality and the consent of the governed. Analysis of the theory recorded in the history of the founding period is necessary to determine the proper judicial role in enforcing the Constitution's exceptions to the legislative power. These exceptions were specified in the act of the people's consenting to the form of government they regarded as most conducive to their safety and happiness. Recognition of the proper legislative role and restricting the judicial role to the Constitution's provisions are not synonymous with embracing the positivism that sometimes emerges in Bork's work. His defense of a restrained judiciary would be much more compelling if he followed the course that is rooted in the theory and history of the Constitution. One may fully embrace the laws and rights of nature and yet argue for the actualization of that law through a system of republican government in which the judiciary is not their sole guardian. Much of Bork's theory is consistent with such a view. If one were to suggest improvements for his theory, it would be to apply with greater fidelity the "text, structure, and history" of the Constitution, which he regards as so important, and which are sufficient to decide most constitutional cases. These interpretive precepts, at least as he utilizes them, fall short of justifying judicial review, and they do not account for the extraordinary cases that give shape to the Constitution's principles such as *Marbury v. Madison, Dred Scott v. Sandford*, and *Brown v. Board of Education*. His precepts are sound insofar as they take the Constitution seriously and support a judicial role that is largely consistent with the strictly republican government the Constitution embodies.

Chapter Seven

Separation of Powers, Federalism, and Other Institutional Considerations

Philip Kurland is an advocate of judicial restraint. He believes that such restraint avoids supplanting the power of a representative legislature with that of an unelected judiciary that is responsible only to itself. He regards the central concepts of the U.S. Constitution as the rule of law and limited central authority. The institutional considerations of enumerated powers, federalism, and separation of powers are essential to maintaining these limits.[1] A restrained Court helps preserve these institutional features necessary to limit central authority. Laurence Tribe neither shares Kurland's desire for a restrained Court that defers to democracy nor accords institutional considerations the importance that Kurland does. Institutional considerations are subordinate to advancing justice as he defines it. Tribe rejects outright the assumptions of those such as Kurland who regard the Court's highest mission as that of conserving ''judicial credibility.''[2]

Kurland's theory of the Constitution contains several themes: ''Because experience and not textual analysis has given meaning to the Constitution, it has been possible for a single document to provide what has been, in effect, three different constitutions, without the political chaos that usually accompanies the making of a new constitution.''[3] The dramatic constitutional changes that have evolved require a subtle and incremental judicial role, which leads him to argue that ''the Court should abandon its activist role.''[4]

Among the reasons Kurland advances to support a restrained role for the Court is that judicial activism ''is undemocratic.'' Second, judicial activism ''undermines the public faith in the objectivity and detachment of the Court. . . .'' At the root of this objection is Kurland's fear that the Court will be undermined by a loss of public confidence—a loss that is the consequence of judicial activism.[5] He regards the institutional considerations of enumerated powers, federalism, and separation of powers as essential to limiting central authority. In spite of the importance he accords these institutional considerations, he characterizes the Constitution as a document of compromise without discernible principle. In his view, the Constitution means ''whatever the Justices of the Supreme Court want it to mean . . . subject to the acquiescence of the American people.''[6]

In spite of their differences, Tribe and Kurland share the view that the Constitution is a document of compromise rather than coherent principle, and that it has acquired its meaning through evolution. Tribe believes that his analysis "can provide a coherent foundation for an active, continuing, and openly avowed effort to construct a more just constitutional order"[7] and help form " 'a more perfect Union' between right and rights within that charter's necessarily evolutionary design." Tribe's fundamental goal is the advancement of constitutional justice as he defines it, irrespective of the particular institution that does the advancing. Institutional considerations assume subordinate importance in Tribe's work insofar as he rejects outright the assumptions of those such as Kurland, Justice Frankfurter, and Professor Bickel, who regard "the highest mission of the Supreme Court" as conserving "judicial credibility."[8]

Tribe's jurisprudence, presuming the living development of constitutional justice, raises the questions of the ends toward which this justice should move. He identifies these at a number of points in the treatise as he discusses various constitutional provisions. Among these ends are "human freedom rightly understood,"[9] "personal autonomy,"[10] and the "human need for closeness, trust, and love."[11] One difficulty with these ends of constitutional justice toward which Tribe would have us aim is their ambiguity or imprecision, which does little to inform our constitutional understanding.

The Doctrine of Judicial Restraint and Institutional Considerations: Philip B. Kurland

Philip Kurland has been described as "the most astute living student of the United States Supreme Court."[12] He addresses important questions that transcend narrow limits of legalism and devotes a significant amount of his prolific analysis to matters that have traditionally occupied political scientists whose chosen subfield is public law. Two of his book titles indicate the political character of his work. *Politics, the Constitution and the Warren Court* analyzes the role of the Warren Court in a federal system of separated powers and enumerates the problems of a political court.[13] A second example of the political character of Kurland's work is his book *Watergate and the Constitution*. His treatment of Watergate includes the powers of each branch of government, an explicit treatment of separation of powers and checks and balances, and an assessment of reform in American government. These two major works, as well as his other books and numerous articles, provide sufficient sources for constructing Kurland's views of the Constitution and politics.

Kurland's Constitution

Kurland's understanding of the Constitution may be gathered from a number of his writings, but perhaps the most concise and unified treatment of his views is found in an essay entitled "American Systems of Laws and Constitutions." In this essay, Kurland argues that the Constitution is nearly independent of textual constraints: "Because experience and not textual analysis has given meaning to the Constitution, it has been possible for a single document to provide what has been, in effect, three different constitutions, without the political chaos that usually accompanies the making of a new constitution." The first U.S. Constitution can be measured temporally from the establishment of the Union to the Civil War; the second followed the Civil War and lasted until Franklin Roosevelt's accession to the presidency, and the third originated in the New Deal and is still in the process of operative change.[14] It is necessary to define these constitutions in order to discover the foundations of Kurland's understanding.

The period of the first Constitution, from 1789 to the Civil War, was characterized by debate as to whether the Constitution was a "compact" from which the parties (the states) could withdraw or a "deed of power" from the people to the central government that could be withdrawn only by the people of the United States. Kurland regards the controversy as having been capable of resolution not "by contending theorists but only through the clash of arms." The issue was, of course, settled by the outcome of the Civil War, which "established the nationalists as the predominant force in the country once and for all." The Civil War put an end to "claims of State sovereignty," and "Federalism was to become an empty slogan for rhetorical rather than practical use" (142–43).

Kurland properly views the Supreme Court as a powerful influence on the nationalization of government during the period of the first Constitution. The Court used a number of constitutional provisions for "transmogrifying the 'sovereignty' of the several states into the sovereignty of the nation." Among the most important of these were the supremacy clause, the "necessary and proper" clause, a broad view of the negative implications of the commerce clause for state power, and the invocation of the power of judicial review over state actions (143).

The period of Kurland's second Constitution—from the Civil War to the New Deal—was one in which "the role of government was belittled and the powers of both state and national governments were restrained by the courts whenever they were exercised in such a way as to interfere with the control of the market. . . . The guarantee of due process of law set out in the Fourteenth Amendment as well as in the Fifth was found to include Social Darwinism as the highest law of the land" (143). During this period of our constitutional history, Kurland describes the rights of personal liberty and property as conjunctive; "*laissez-faire* dominated constitutional doctrine" (146).

It is difficult to quarrel with Kurland's thesis that freedom of contract was a fundamental judicial standard during this period. Kurland labels the second

Constitution as that period in which "[e]ssentially . . . the Court thought that government regulation of business activities was unnatural and, therefore, unconstitutional. If such regulation was indulged by the states, it violated the Fourteenth Amendment's protections against infringement of life, liberty, or property without due process of law. If attempted by the nation, it was found to be beyond the powers specifically granted by the Constitution and an invasion of those that the Tenth Amendment reserved to the States and the people" (146).

These Court-imposed restrictions on government action changed with the coming of the Great Depression and the government's response to it. Kurland states, "without a single word in the document being changed," the same Constitution that had prevented government interference with business suddenly became a license for such laws. The third Constitution was characterized by the end of judicial restraint of the national government's efforts to regulate the economy, the decline of federalism, the era of the service state, and the "development of non-property rights of persons." Much of this development of personal rights came through the application of the Bill of Rights to the states through the Fourteenth Amendment (146–47).

In each of these three periods, Kurland defines the Constitution as what the Court has said about the document. His analysis maintains a predominantly descriptive posture, a posture that simply summarizes the various epochs of the Court's interpretations. He then equates these judicial interpretations with the Constitution itself. Such a definition of the Constitution effectively denies the existence of any independent body of constitutional principles or theory and reduces to Chief Justice Charles E. Hughes's view that the Constitution means whatever the Justices of the Supreme Court want it to mean. In fact, Kurland explicitly adopts this view and appends to it his own addition: "It is experience—history if you will—that demonstrates what Hughes forgot to add, that the Justices' interpretations are only the penultimate ones, for they are in fact subject to the acquiescence of the American people" (141).

In spite of his fluid view of the Constitution, however, Kurland understands the document to embody two fundamental concepts. The first is the "concept of the rule of law, as a right of the people and an obligation of government." The second is the "need for limited government and more particularly for limited central authority" (141). Reduced to its quintessence, Kurland's view amounts to this: the Constitution is whatever the justices of the Supreme Court want it to mean, subject to the acquiescence of the American people; but the Constitution embodies two root concepts, the rule of law and that of limited government.

In order to address Kurland's argument at the level of its basic assumptions, it is necessary to examine the Constitution to determine whether it has guiding principles and, if so, what they are. This examination relates most directly to the period of constitutional government that Kurland refers to as the first Constitution—from 1789 to the Civil War. Although Kurland is correct that the competing views of the nature of the regime under the first Constitution were resolved by the clash of arms, the issues that framed the Civil War were theoretical ones. What Kurland fails to acknowledge is that the Federalists won the theoretical argument over the nature of the regime at the time of the founding. As one political scientist put it: "Finally, the Constitution was real to the Federalists and Antifederalists, which is why they fought so vigorously over it, and why, when it was adopted, some of them knew they had won and some of them knew they had lost."[15]

The winning of the argument at the time of the founding indicated that the supporters of one set of constitutional principles prevailed over their opposition. Although it is clear that the finished documents contained some compromises with those we call the Anti-Federalists, the Constitution contained a theory of government that rested on the transfer of sovereignty from the people of the states to the people of the United States. The theory required transferring certain powers from the states to the new nation, especially the commerce power. The leading theorists that favored the Constitution, and who prevailed in the Convention and ratification process, had a vision for the United States which required the unfolding of the constitutional history of the United States in a particular way. It was left to subsequent statesmen such as John Marshall and Joseph Story to play the essential role of applying this constitutional theory to the practical realm of politics. Unlike Kurland, who sees this epoch merely as a rivalry between two views of the Constitution, these justices understood the Constitution's underlying theory. This understanding guided their constitutional jurisprudence and allowed them to rise above mere partisanship. From the perspective of a constitutional analyst, the question of which side should prevail in the clash of arms is dependent on understanding the political theory underlying the Constitution.

Reconstruction of a portion of the constitutional theory that relates to the need for a strong national government, as opposed to a mere compact among the states, is necessary in order to assess Kurland's thesis of three Constitutions. The central importance to the constitutional theory of union as opposed to mere compact is indicated in the first line of *The Federalist*. It refers to the "unequivocal experience of the inefficiency of the subsisting" government under the Articles of Confederation. The argument presented in *The Federalist* emphasizes the importance of union to the theory of the Constitution and the "insufficiency of the present Confederation to preserve that Union."[16] It is also useful to recall that the Preamble to the Constitution of the United States begins with the statement, "WE the People of the United States . . . do ordain and establish the CONSTITUTION for the United States of

America. This clearly indicates that the nation was not designed to be a mere compact among the states.

At a more substantive level, the theory underlying the new Constitution demanded a large commercial *nation*—rather than a compact—as a barrier against domestic faction and insurrection. The "ENLARGEMENT of the OR-BIT" within which the system would revolve was crucial to the very nature of the regime as explained in *The Federalist*.[17] Among the advantages of a strong union is its tendency "to break and control the violence of faction."[18] The factions that plague popular governments are to be less dreaded under the new Union. The greater diversity of parties and interests in this expanded sphere "make it less probable that a majority of the whole will have a common motive to invade the rights of other citizens."[19]

A defect in Kurland's discussion of these three Constitutions is that he concentrates his analysis on the *events* that transpired between 1789 and the present. He does not relate the theory underlying the Constitution to the various epochs he identifies. The concepts he sees embodied in the U.S. Constitution are the rule of law and limited central authority.[20] One cannot quarrel with the first concept as fundamental to the U.S. Constitution, but it applies to any truly constitutional government. The second concept of limited central authority is not accurate. *Federalist* No. 51 states that the first task of founding is to "enable the government to control the governed." Only then can framers turn to the task of obliging the government to control itself.[21] Contrary to the view Kurland presents, the first objective of government is to give the government sufficient *power* to control the governed. Only then does it become necessary to control or limit the government.

Although it is true that the federal government is one of enumerated powers, *Federalist* No. 23 tells us that the authority entrusted to the national government under these broad powers should be unconfined.[22] Because the government may face exigencies that are beyond the capacity of the founders to predict, the powers of government must be sufficient to meet these exigencies.[23] The question arises whether these powers should be lodged in the states or in the nation. The Constitution rests on the need for the nation to possess essential powers, for the national government is the one that encompasses sufficient diversity or multiplicity of interests to control faction and thereby render a strong government safe for individual rights. There exists in the Constitution a theory independent of the manner in which a specific Court interprets it during any epoch of American history.

A limited central authority is not, properly speaking, the goal of the separation of powers. Nor is the federal system of divided powers, as originally and properly understood, a means to diminish or limit the power of the national government. Rather, the powers given to the national government may safely exist because this government is an extensive republic that is properly structured through its utilization of the multiplicity of economic interests and religious sects and the separation of powers. This strong national government is controlled primarily through internal mechanisms so "that its several constituent parts may, by their mutual relations, be the means of keeping each other in their proper places."[24] The limitations that were added to the Constitution, such as the parchment barrier of the Bill of Rights, are given effect through these internal mechanisms.

Kurland might respond by saying that *The Federalist* did not take cognizance of the Bill of Rights, which was added to the Constitution later and supports his constitutional concept of limited central authority. It is true that these amendments were designed to protect individual rights as well as to lessen fears about the new national government. But the Bill of Rights does not supplant the theory of *The Federalist*. Rather, *The Federalist* has much to teach about the political reality of the subsequent application of the Bill of Rights.

In spite of these additional limitations on government that were added in the form of the Bill of Rights in 1791, their use by the Court to limit the power of the national government has been infrequent.[25] Perhaps a part of the reason for this infrequency is the difficulty of determining when the competing claims of individual liberty should give way to other pressing public needs. *The Federalist* argues that if the government is properly structured, the legislature will make responsible judgments in this regard. Implicit in this proper structuring is the transfer of significant powers to the national government—that level of government under which individual liberty will be safe. The check on the national legislature presupposes a strong government able to meet unforeseen exigencies, but one that is controlled by the mechanisms of multiplicity of interests and religious sects and separation of powers. This aspect of the Constitution is central to our system of government and must be emphasized before one can describe our government as one of limited powers. Characterizing the government simply as one of limited powers obscures the theory implicit in the Constitution and explicated in *The Federalist*. Much of this theory was actualized by the generation of justices that sat on the Supreme Court during the period of Kurland's first Constitution. Thus, although the Constitution was what the Court said it was, and to a certain extent the people acquiesced in what the Court said, this definition of the Constitution set forth by Kurland is insufficient. What is most significant to the Constitution and constitutional law is that during the epoch of Kurland's first Constitution immediately following the founding, many important aspects of the constitutional theory explicated by *The Federalist* were effected in a way that was faithful to the integrity of the Constitution.[26]

As was demonstrated in my discussion of Kurland's first Constitution *The Federalist* presents a theory of government that makes a sound and integrated whole of the Constitution. Much of the Court's activity described by Kurland under the second Constitution is inconsistent with a proper understanding of the commerce clause, the due process clauses, and the Tenth Amendment. The major defect of this era is a judicial misunderstanding of the necessarily broad powers possessed by the national government. Kurland identifies the emergence of the third Constitution, in about 1935, as the epoch of the decline of federalism and the end of judicial restriction of national power over economic affairs. He correctly describes the development of constitutional law and the Court's action. There is no question that what the Court said about the Constitution changed in a dramatic way during the New Deal period. A more profound question is whether or not the enactment of the New Deal and subsequent legislation was within the constitutional power of the national government.

The New Deal was a creation of Congress as well as of Franklin Delano Roosevelt. The underlying constitutional theme of the need for a properly structured and extensive republic was examined earlier (see Part I). This structure included as a paramount feature a legislature that was representative of a multiplicity of economic interests and religious sects. This multiplicity was the primary means of avoiding a legislative faction and of helping to ensure legislation that was consistent with individual rights and with the permanent and aggregate interests of the community. When a law has been passed by both houses of Congress and signed by the president, many of the safeguards depended on by the Constitution have been exhausted. Because of the impossibility of foreseeing exigencies such as the Great Depression, exceptions to the legislative power are few. The very system by which legislation is formulated was designed to provide optimal assurance that whatever legislation comes from this system is pursuant to the public interest.

Federalist No. 10 states: "The regulation of various and interfering" property interests is the "principal task of modern legislation." Madison also insists on the avoidance of class struggle as essential to a defensible republican government.[27] If one views the New Deal as an effort to achieve these two things, then it is not at all clear that American government since 1935 should be viewed as government under our third Constitution.[28] Leaving aside the question of the wisdom of the New Deal, the measures it embodied seem consistent with the Constitution's grants of power to the national government and the constitutional assumption of the necessity of regulating property interests. Kurland should examine the body of constitutional theory as a unified whole before assuming that a new line of judicial decisions departs from such theory and embodies a third Constitution.[29]

Kurland seems to believe that the U.S. Constitution demands limited government, but his view of the Constitution as "whatever the Justices of the Supreme Court want it to mean . . . subject to the acquiescence of the American people" belies even this minimal principled content of "limited government." What if the people acquiesce in judicial allowance of a violation of that principle? He explains the development of judicial decisions during different epochs of American constitutional history, but he essentially ignores the existence of the Constitution as a formative body of theory that attempted to mold the regime toward the ends to which its theory and principles point. Insofar as he fails to develop constitutional intent or theory, he has no standard by which to analyze the epochs he treats; he must simply describe the Court's activity. Kurland's principle of limited government requires further examination.

Separation of Powers

A subordinate element of Kurland's thesis is that the separation of powers was a major factor in limiting central authority. Kurland refers to the powers of the national government as "a limited delegation of powers" of the government that those in 1787 thought proper "to be tolerated." The Constitution "provided for dividing the relatively few powers that the central government was given among three branches and then added to this separation of powers a series of checks and balances of one branch on the other."[30]

Kurland characterizes the separation of powers as a "system of restraints on government" and quotes Professor Andrew McLaughlin with approval: "If it be asked why people were so unwise—and the question is often asked— as to hamper government by division of authority and by checks and balances, the answer is simple: such was the kind of government the leaders and probably men in general wanted."[31] Kurland understands the original underlying purpose of the separation of powers as one of limiting or restraining governmental activity, a purpose he sees implicit in the Constitution as a whole.[32] There is no question that one purpose underlying the separation of powers is the prevention of governmental tyranny over the governed.[33] There were, however, other purposes underlying the doctrine that Kurland does not recognize. A second purpose is to prevent a foolish or tyrannical majority from effecting its will into public law, at least in the short run. This purpose underlies the separation of powers as a whole, but it is most vividly illustrated in the institution of the Senate, where the six-year terms give that "sober and respectable body" an opportunity to check measures the people may call for, but later lament.[34] Thus, there is a more subtle purpose of the separation of powers that extends to the actions of the people themselves.

There is yet another aspect of separation of powers theory insofar as it makes possible the union of stability and energy in a government with a republican form.[35] These qualities are necessary to overcome the perennial republican proclivities toward instability and the violence of faction.[36] They help ensure that the republican government is competent. Bicameralism, a sub-species of the separation of powers, provides the possibility for the Senate, which is characterized by stability. The smaller number, the staggered elections, the greater continuity, and the six-year terms all work toward this end. These factors were designed to shape the character of the Senate, which is given more constitutional responsibilities than the House in important areas such as foreign affairs, where stability is critical.

The executive branch of government was designed to supply the principle of energy to the new Constitution, a principle best supplied by unified power in the president. In order to represent a diverse constituency adequately, to provide for responsiveness to changes in public opinion, and to promote deliberation, a numerous legislative body holding office for a short term is required. Such a body, the House, was anticipated to lack both stability and energy. In order to supply the energy, power, and force desired to remedy the defect of the legislature, the executive was separated from it and given a basis of power that was, in some respects, independent of the legislature.[37] This energy in the executive is crucial to our constitutional system—"a leading character in the definition of good government."[38]

The presidency manifests the balance struck by the framers between the protection of liberty and the exercise of governmental power. It is clear from the text of *The Federalist* that an energetic, powerful executive is essential to the competent functioning of the new government.[39] The constitutional provisions supporting the executive power help ensure that this energy is actualized. I do not wish to argue that *The Federalist* intended no restraints on the executive, for an executive with unlimited authority would run counter to the fundamental notion of republican liberty, a concern implicit in the Constitution. Indeed, the impeachment provision of the Constitution is proof enough of this. The separation of powers provides a means of checking the legislative branch of government as well as increasing the energy or power of the government as a whole. A strong and energetic executive is necessary to both these tasks.[40] Kurland's assumptions regarding the purposes of separation of powers neglect the doctrine's constitutional aims; consequently, he fails to convey the importance of energetic, stable, and competent government.

The view of the framers stands in contrast to that depicted by Kurland in his post-Watergate analysis of presidential power in *Watergate and the Constitution*. He characterizes the work of the Constitutional Convention in this way:

> This debate revealed some of the multitude of currents and contending forces at work in the Convention. . . . None of the individuals at the Convention, here or later, represented the attitudes of the Convention as a whole, which was more than the sum of its parts. The achievement of the Convention was its capacity for compromise on the major issues. And the

evolving principle of separation of powers as modified by a system of checks and balances was one of these compromises. If there was a dominant theme at the Convention, it related to no particular issue but rather to a consensus that whatever government was created, it must be one of limited powers. Concentration of power led to tyranny, whether the power was in the national government as a whole or in the legislative or executive branches of it.[41]

With the exception of its near consensus on limited government, Kurland believes that the only discernible agreement within the Convention was compromise on major issues. This view is problematic.[42] It ignores the fact that those called the Federalists prevailed and obscures the intended principles of the Constitution. If one begins with the view that the Constitution is simply a bundle of compromises, then one has little reason to pursue its underlying theory.

Kurland likewise debunks the authority of *The Federalist* in his description of the work Thomas Jefferson characterized as "the best commentary on the principles of government which ever was written."[43] Kurland describes *The Federalist* as "the polemics of its authors" and refers to Madison's essays in this work as "sophistical rather than forthright."[44] The Constitution described by *The Federalist*, with its assumption of the necessity for a strong executive power, was the Constitution adopted by the American people. Kurland cannot dispute this even though he discounts the importance of the theory of *The Federalist*. Whether we simply accept this theory, supplement it, or reject it, each of these alternatives requires that we "understand what they said, why they said it, and what they meant by it."[45] Kurland's treatment of the founding theory ignores much of the theory that is relevant to understanding the necessity for a strong executive power.[46]

Kurland is concerned by the fact that the Constitution has become imbalanced in favor of the executive power. He states: "But we need reform—before '1984.' "[47] Yet the actions, Kurland sees as leading to "1984" and an imbalanced executive meet his test of the Constitution. The Supreme Court has upheld these actions, and the American people have acquiesced. Within the context of Kurland's own definitions and understanding, he cannot object, in constitutional terms, to the course that the adjudication and public acquiescence have taken. For him, these elements are the Constitution.

A view that the purpose of separation of powers is simply to limit government is inadequate. An understanding of the subtlety of separation of powers theory is necessary to illuminate the operation of this government. Absent such an understanding, proposals for change in our governing institutions may result in frustration of that theory and bring on more serious diseases than those they are designed to cure.

Federalism

Kurland sees federalism as the other important element of the U.S. Constitution that limits central authority.[48] He regards federalism as directed toward the same ends as the separation of powers: "Both new concepts were directed to limiting the power of government to avoid such concentration as might lead to tyranny."[49] He summarizes his idea of the original constitutional view of federalism: "[T]he Constitution provided for a limited delegation of powers to the central government, thus dividing such government as was to be tolerated between the states on the one hand and the nation on the other. A new kind of federalism was thus created."[50] Kurland believes that the American conception of federalism is embodied in the definition of K. C. Wheare: "What is necessary for the federal principle is not merely that the general government, like the regional governments, should operate directly upon the people, but further, that each government should be limited to its own sphere, and within its sphere, should be independent of the other."[51]

Partly because of the role of federalism in limiting centralized government, but perhaps also because of the expansive role of the judiciary in modifying the balance, Kurland is disturbed by what he calls the death of American federalism.[52] His fears of excessive centralization are best conveyed by quoting from two of the many authors he cites with approval in his work. Kurland quotes Tocqueville: " 'It is generally believed in America that the existence and permanence of the republican form of government in the New World depend upon the existence and duration of the federal system.' "[53] He also quotes Lord Acton: "Of all the checks on democracy, federalism has been the most efficacious and congenial. . . . The Federal system limits and restrains sovereign power by dividing it, and by assigning to Government only certain defined rights."[54] In discussing these authors and his own view that "Federalism has become moribund in the United States," Kurland states: "The danger of the end of the republican form of government suggested by Tocqueville and the danger of the loss of individual freedom to rampant democracy predicted by Acton are not imminent but they are immanent in contemporary American society."[55]

In important areas of desegregation, criminal procedure, and reapportionment, the powers once exercised by the states have been assumed by the Court.[56] Kurland characterizes the justices who have taken such a large role in the death of federalism as "full of the devil."[57] Although he accords importance to other factors in the "ultimate demise" of federalism, he emphasizes the Court's role. He cites the prescience of Jefferson, who stated: "The judiciary of the United States is the subtle corps of sappers and miners constantly working underground to undermine the foundations of our Confederated fabric."[58] It is this undermining of the confederated fabric and the contribution of poorly reasoned Warren Court opinions to it that Kurland finds so objectionable.

Kurland is clearly disturbed by the condition of federalism, at least as it existed at the time he wrote *Politics, the Constitution and the Warren Court*. He is a perceptive analyst of case law that has shifted power from the states to the nation, especially to the national judiciary. It is not sufficient, however, to describe this shift and simply quote authors who have recognized federalism's salutary protection of republican liberty. In order to understand the role of "federalism" in our constitutional system and thereby to treat critically the view presented by Kurland, it is necessary to summarize the constitutional view of federalism and the ends it serves.[59]

Kurland cites K. C. Wheare with approval: "the Constitution of the United States establishes an association of states so organized that powers are divided between a general government which in certain matters . . . is independent of the governments of the associated states, and on the other hand, state governments which in certain matters are in their turn, independent of the general government."[60] Kurland adopts Wheare's view as an accurate depiction of the original constitutional understanding, that is, that federalism consists simply of a division of power between the general government and the state governments.[61]

In assessing this view, *The Federalist* is valuable, since it responds to the charge made by opponents of ratification that the Constitution "ought . . . to have preserved the *federal* form, which regards the Union as a Confederacy of sovereign states; instead of which, they have framed a national government, which regards the Union as a consolidation of the States."[62] From the framers' viewpoint, there were other elements besides the division of governmental powers that determined the federal character of the new Constitution,[63] resulting in Madison's statement: "The proposed Constitution, therefore, is, in strictness, neither a national nor a federal Constitution, but a composition of both."[64]

Kurland misunderstands what the term "federal" meant at the time of the founding. As Martin Diamond has clearly demonstrated, "federal" and "confederal" were interchangeable. Both terms meant "a relationship of independent, equal bodies politic that join together for limited purposes"; this form of government carries out its purposes by "the obligation of good faith" rather than by coercive governmental authority.[65]

The Federalist properly describes the Constitution as a composition of both national and federal elements. Kurland's definition describes the Constitution as simply federal and limits the application of his definition to the powers that are reserved to the states. His definition requires one to conceive of the entire machinery of the central government as *national* and thereby limits our vision to only one element of the Constitution's federal features.[66]

Because of his limited definition, Kurland, after reviewing the inroads made on reserved state power, pronounces federalism dead.[67] From the view of the framers, however, important elements of federalism remain in the composite foundation, structure, and function of the central government.[68] The Senate and the executive, under the electoral college system, continue as composite institutions; the amending process perseveres as a composite of federal and national elements; the very existence and authority of the states are provided by constitutional necessity. Exemplary of the vitality of the federal element in the amending process is the fact that the politics of states such as Illinois was dominated by debate over the proposed Equal Rights Amendment. Because of action by Illinois (and other states qua states), this amendment was not appended to the Constitution. Kurland's definition and analysis exclude this federal element in the amending process.

We saw in the 1980s a movement to return to the states certain powers that had been assumed by the national government and for government to retreat from some of its regulatory activities. One assumes that Kurland would generally applaud this movement as a step toward resuscitation of federalism as he defines it. What is significant according to the view set forth in *The Federalist* is that the structure and function of the central government that is taking these steps are laced with federal, constitutional features that have a resiliency that comes from being "constitutionalized" in our governmental structure and function. These structural and procedural manifestations of our compound system have never been moribund. They are important elements of the governmental system that is currently addressing the contemporary problem of division of governmental power between states and nation.

Kurland's concentration on division of governing powers as the definitive characteristic of federalism obscures the framers' decision to create a powerful and energetic central government. It also leads him to ignore the fact that matters other than this division ought to concern those who value the decentralizing characteristics of our compound system of government.[69] Presumably this is the case with Kurland, who predicts that the "Electoral College is about to disappear through constitutional amendment," but he fails to tell us why that is of consequence.[70] In fact, the federal effect of the electoral college, reinforced by almost all the states through the rule that the winner takes all, exerts a powerful decentralizing force on our political system. Both the primary elections and the national party conventions are decentralized as a consequence of the electoral college's utilizing states qua states.[71] Instead of understanding the electoral college's contribution to the decentralization he desires, Kurland dismisses it as a "dilution of democracy."[72]

Kurland's acceptance of the modern doctrine of federalism leads to a further problem. It assumes that republican liberty is to be achieved simply by limiting those powers that are given to the national government. He describes the founding principle as one of delegating to the nation relatively few of those powers given to government, thus leaving most to the states. This interpretation is consistent with the limited central authority that he assumes is one of the two fundamental constitutional concepts. In an article in which he laments the attrition of state powers that has resulted from judicial decisions, Kurland specifies the powers that should necessarily rest at the national level "in terms of the constitutional plan." These are powers "of war and peace, of foreign relation, of international commerce."[73]

It is certainly true that the powers delegated to the United States are relatively few, although not so few as Kurland implies in the above quotation. But contrast Kurland's view with that of *Federalist* No. 23, that these powers should be exercised with "an unconfined authority."[74] Ironically, and opposed to the view Kurland holds, the national element in the Constitution must be strong in order to protect republican liberty. That is, the scheme of multiplicity of economic interests and religious sects on which the Constitution is based is dependent on a large republic in which important governmental powers are transferred from the states to the nation. Only with the requisite powers vested in the national government, especially over economic matters, can this principle be effective. Representation makes possible an enlarged sphere of government in which no single interest or faction can effect its naked self-interest into law. Because of the greater number of interests in the United States as opposed to each individual state, *The Federalist* argues for a strong national government: "In the extended republic of the United States and among the great variety of interests, parties, and sects which it embraces, a coalition of a majority of the whole society could seldom take place on any other principles than those of justice and the general good."[75] A large republic is not only consistent with republican liberty but also necessary to it.[76] Quite opposed to Kurland's view, federalism is not simply the bulwark of liberty. As *The Federalist* understands the matter, the national elements of the Constitution must extend to more than just war and peace, foreign relations, and international commerce.

Kurland's definition of federalism emphasizes the restriction of national authority in order to protect liberty *against* government. This view of federalism, an incorrect reading of Tocqueville and the framers—improperly depicts the purpose of federalism as protecting liberty in a negative way, by impeding positive governmental action at the national level. Tocqueville, in fact, expects much more from federalism.[77] Although Kurland's work refers to Tocqueville numerous times, he does not explicate Tocqueville's subtle teachings regarding the ends or functions that the federal elements of our Constitution serve.[78] Appreciation of these virtues of federalism or decentralization strengthens the argument for judicial restraint in nationalizing elements of our political life that might best be left to states and localities.

The effects of the federal or decentralizing elements of our Constitution are much more subtle than merely protecting liberty against government. Tocqueville's protection of republican liberty focuses on the development of desirable republican qualities within the citizen body. His work emphasizes the importance of all those federal or decentralizing elements in the Constitution, not just the division of power, as significant to preserving republican liberty. Tocqueville gives persuasive reasons for concern over the centralization of power over so many aspects of American life.[79]

At one point in Kurland's account of the Court's mischief in contributing to the attrition of state power and the destruction of federalism as he defines it, he asks that "the Court understand not only the immediate but the ultimate effects of the judgements it renders."[80] His plea for reform may be appropriate in light of the theory of *The Federalist* and Tocqueville. But Kurland's understanding of federalism does not offer the Court insight into the "ultimate effects" about which he is concerned. His view leads one to an improper understanding of the constitutional plan for federalism's protection of republican liberty in any ultimate sense. A proper understanding of federalism is necessary if one is to make intelligent judgments and arguments about the very practical matters of reforming the allocation of governmental powers and institutions.

In summary, Kurland's definition of federalism and his view of its effects are inadequate. His definition obscures the composite nature of the regime and the fact that the national elements of the regime must be strong if republican liberty is to be secure. By failing to recognize the manner in which the national elements of the Constitution are necessary to liberty, we may in fact undermine liberty in our attempts to promote federalism. Certain powers were vested in the national government in order to preserve liberty. One example of this is the power over commerce (not just international commerce), a power that must rest at the national level to protect against the violence of faction over economic matters.[81] Such faction was characteristic of government under the Articles of Confederation and in the "petty republics of Greece and Italy."[82]

By neglecting federal elements that lie at the central level, Kurland forfeits the opportunity to defend thoughtfully those federal institutions such as the Senate and the operation of the electoral college. The electoral college has, of course, been under attack as a nonegalitarian feature of American government. The decentralizing effects, effects Tocqueville would regard as salutary, have largely been neglected in this debate. Those who seek more democratic control and protection of liberty by direct popular election of the president need the theoretical insight of Tocqueville, who argues that the consequent loss of decentralization will undermine those qualities necessary to liberty.

The inevitable consequence of Kurland's constitutional theory is that he is reduced to making simplistic observations about federalism and the project for reform. The fundamental reform he calls for is a return of powers to state governments: "In the revival of responsible state government lies a hope for the reconstruction of 'the only breakwater against the ever pounding surf which [has] threatened to submerge the individual and destroy the only kind of society in which personality could survive.'" As my previous argument made clear, this understanding is inadequate. It is also misleading insofar as it pits individual liberty against a strong national government. One need only reflect on the contributions of a strong national government toward advancing civil rights for racial minorities to appreciate the fact that a strong national government sometimes advances liberty. Some of his observations and suggestions for reform may be sound. One such example is his conclusion that states must "reassume their part in the maintenance of that balance of power which the Constitution seems to have contemplated."[83] But Kurland does not explore fully what the framers understood federalism to be or how the relationship between states and nation was designed to be productive of liberty. Thus, we are stopped short in our attempt to discover in his work just what it is they contemplated. Kurland characterizes the Constitutional Convention as compromise and *The Federalist* as polemic; he fails to probe the subtlety of Tocqueville's analysis and neglects to present a sufficient theory of his own.

The Role of the Court

Much of Kurland's view of the proper role of the Court may be drawn from his description and criticism of the Warren Court. He sees that Court as suffering from three basic failings. "First, it was unable or unwilling to adhere to step-by-step process that has long characterized the common-law and constitutional forms of adjudication." More specifically, this Court "preferred to write codes of conduct rather than resolve particular controversies" and "seemed to feel that every proposition had to be taken to its logical extreme." Exemplary of this latter tendency is the extension of the "one man–one vote formula with a mathematical precision that ignored the complexities of political life." His second criticism is that "the Court has failed to recognize the incapacities that inhere in its structure." This is particularly objectionable, since it "lacks the machinery to gather the data necessary for broad rule-making as distinguished from the resolution of particular litigation." Kurland's third criticism is that the Warren "Court's opinions have tended toward fiat rather than reason." He is concerned that too many of the Court's opinions are simply based on authority and lack sufficient reason to convince the public: "From now on, it [the Court] must seek to persuade rather than coerce." Such persuasion is necessary to the "restoration of public confidence," which he sees as "vital both to the continuance of the Court's power and to the maintenance of the rule of law in this country."[84]

Kurland provides a succinct statement of his view that the Court has become excessively political or nonjudicial:

> By politicization I mean only that the Court's function is no longer primarily the judicial one of resolving legal controversies between contesting parties, but the legislative one of making general governmental policies for the nation, and the executive one of enforcing the policies that it so declares. The meaning of the constitutional or statutory language or of judicial precedents no longer provides the principal guides to decision. Rather, each decision seems to represent a personal choice by the Justices preferring what they think is good over what they think is less good, or less bad over bad.[85]

He also enumerates other ways in which the Court has moved further than its predecessors "toward the legislative mode and away from the judicial mode of carrying on its business."[86]

Kurland regards the difference between their respective constituencies as one important distinction between the Court and the legislature: "The legislature represents that combination of groups and individuals that makes a majority on that issue; the Court has peculiar obligations to discrete minorities." The only instance in which the Court should thwart the majority will is when the "legislature imposes on individuals or minorities in so fundamental a fashion as to necessitate invoking the safeguards of the Constitution." Another legislative element in judicial behavior is the Court's tendency to be unfettered by judgments of other branches of government and by the states. An important distinction Kurland draws between the two functions is that a court resolves a particular case in a process that formally binds only the parties to the litigation; legislative acts are "directed to the entire population within the domain, or such portion of it as falls within the ken of the statute." Other practices of the Warren Court with a legislative character include giving certain decisions only prospective effect, the extensive use of amicus curiae briefs as a kind of lobbying practice, the "multiplying occasions on which the Justices have taken to the hustings in defense of their opinions or in anticipation of those that they have not yet written," and the tendency of both the legislature and the Court to "put off decision of their most important problems until adjournment is in the offing."[87]

A final characteristic of the Warren Court is that its "lawmaking is not justified by well-reasoned opinions."[88] Kurland's view is illustrated by a quotation from Professors Bickel and Wellington with which he concurs: "The Court's product has shown an increasing incidence of the sweeping dogmatic statement, of the formulation of results accompanied by little or no effort to support them in reason, in sum, of opinions that do not opine and of per curiam orders that quite frankly fail to build the bridge between the authorities they cite and the results they decree."[89] As a consequence of such opinions, the justices are freer to insert their personal policy preferences into the Constitution. Constitutional law can then become "no more than the current reflection of the predilections of the sitting justices."[90] Such poorly reasoned opinions also result in the substitution of sentimentality or emotion for reason in the decision-making process,[91] a substitution to which Kurland strongly objects.

Kurland believes that "the Court should abandon its activist role."[92] He presents a number of reasons to support his view. The Court is "restricted to the judicial form" and consequently cannot initiate appropriate policy. The Court is also limited by its necessary reliance on "evidence and materials brought before it by the litigants" or by similar prepublished data gathered by its small staff. A wide range of materials and opinions that should inform the decision of a major policy maker are unavailable to the Court because of the nature of the judicial process. The judiciary also lacks the means of properly enforcing and supervising the decrees it hands down. This problem is exacerbated when the Court issues controversial judgments in which the public does not acquiesce and that therefore, do not produce the results the Court desires (except for the particular litigants involved).[93] At the time he wrote *Politics, the Constitution and the Warren Court*, Kurland was concerned that the Court had lost much of the support of the public: "The Warren Court accepted with a vengeance the task of protector of the individual against government and of minorities against the tyranny of majorities. But it has failed abysmally to persuade the people that its judgements have been made for sound reasons."[94] For the reasons specified above, and others as well, Kurland counsels the Court to abandon its activism.[95]

In one article, he specifies additional reasons for rejecting both this activism and certain of its implications. His first reason is that judicial activism "replaces a representative legislature with a group which is neither representative nor responsible to anyone but itself." Such activism "is undemocratic." Second, judicial activism "undermines the public faith in the objectivity and detachment of the Court." At the root of this objection is Kurland's fear that the proper function of the Court will be undermined by a loss of public confidence—a loss that is the consequence of judicial activism. Finally, "the exercise of such naked power invites a reply in kind from those on whose domain the Court is poaching." In a contest of power, "Congress is endowed with the stronger weapons: the jurisdiction and membership of the Court are at its mercy." The defense against the occurrence of this contest is judicial objectivity.[96]

In criticizing the activism of the Warren Court, Kurland constructs his own view of the Court's role:

> [T]he Court is not a democratic institution, either in makeup or in function. . . . It is politically irresponsible and must remain so, if it would perform its primary function in today's harried society. That function, evolving at least since the days of Charles Evans Hughes, is to protect the individual against the Leviathan of government and to protect minorities against oppression by majorities.
>
> Essentially because its most important function is anti-majoritarian, it ought not to intervene to frustrate the will of the majority except where it is essential to its function as guardian of interests that would otherwise be unrepresented in the government of the country.[97]

Kurland concludes the volume on the Warren Court with a challenge to the Court "[t]o match the Warren Court attainments in the protection of individuals and minorities that today justifies the Court's existence; to restore the confidence of the American public in the rule of law. One or the other is not enough."[98]

Kurland's suggested retreat from judicial activism is a goal that I believe is generally consistent with the theory of the Constitution. His call for a restoration of public confidence is a sensible objective of any healthy political system. He presents these reforms in the context of subtly distinguishing the judicial power from the legislative power. Students of the U.S. Constitution benefit from his insights into these matters. Kurland pleads for a restrained Court, for a restoration of public confidence in the rule of law, and for a continuation of the "Warren Court attainments in the protection of individuals and minorities."[99] This contrasts sharply with the subtlety of his analysis regarding the roles of judge and legislator.

Assigning the Court to be the peculiar protector of civil liberties invites it to abandon the restraint Kurland counsels. The manner in which he presents to the Court the task of pursuing the greater good of civil liberty leads to judicial assumption of the very role to which Kurland objects: that of a Council of Platonic Guardians.[100] In fact, the end of civil liberty is so fundamental that the entire constitutional scheme of separation of powers and multiplicity of interests is designed, in part, to further this end. Kurland's formulation overlooks the various mechanisms other than the judiciary that, when allowed to function as intended, protect the liberty of minorities and individuals.

One example of this protection is the mechanism of multiplicity of interests, the purpose of which is to protect minorities and individuals from factious majorities while allowing just majorities the necessary power to govern. If the Court assumes the legislative task, the deliberative function lodged in

Congress is sacrificed to judicial supremacy. The constitutional design of balancing the competing interests of strong and responsible government and civil liberty through a properly constructed legislature is foreclosed. Depending on the Court as the peculiar guardian of civil liberty pits republican government against individual liberty in the context of a lawsuit—a lawsuit attended with all those disadvantages deplored by Kurland. If, as Kurland says, courts tend to take principles to their extremes, then assigning the Court the role of guardian of civil liberty may result in the problem warned about in *Federalist* No. 63: "[T]hat liberty may be endangered by the abuses of liberty as well as by the abuses of power; that there are numerous instances of the former as well as of the latter; and that the former, rather than the latter, are apparently most to be apprehended by the United States."[101]

Congress is designed to be a much more effective register of the competing goals with which government is perpetually confronted than is the Court. This realization, one that Kurland himself articulates, requires moderation in the role assigned to the Court.[102] It counsels against asking the Court to judge what groups are properly represented in government and come to their aid, as Kurland does when he speaks of the Court's "peculiar obligations to discrete minorities" or the need for subsequent Courts to match the Warren Court in the protection of individuals and minorities. The Court is justified in protecting minorities and individuals only when the Constitution has made exceptions to the legislative authority over such individuals and groups.

Other aspects of Kurland's role for the Court must be examined in the context of his criticism of judicial activism. As we have seen, he objects to this activism on a number of different grounds, some relative to the judiciary's mode of operation and others relative to its undemocratic character. These are valid criticisms, but they fail to recognize certain compelling objections to this activism, objections inherent in the Constitution's underlying theory. Insofar as an activist Court makes broad pronouncements of public policy, it thwarts much of the Constitution's protective scheme. This scheme nurtures the elements of stability, energy, and multiplicity of interests in government. Insofar as the judiciary assumes legislative or executive power, *The Federalist* recognizes an obvious problem relative to separation of powers theory: "Were the power of judging joined with the legislative, the life and liberty of the subject would be exposed to arbitrary control, for *the judge* would then be *the legislator.* Were it joined to the executive power, *the judge* might behave with all the violence of *an oppressor.*"[103] Broad judicial policy making may both violate separation of powers and deny a democratic check on policy-making.[104] When the Court assumes legislative powers, it bypasses that process of coalition among the multiplicity of interests in the legislative branch. This process is essential to both democratic consent and to the moderating and elevating effects of the multiplicity of interests discussed earlier (see Part I).

Although Kurland properly objects to taking power from the democratic legislature, he obscures the necessary contribution the legislative process makes to republican liberty. Insofar as the Court exerts executive powers, a similar argument holds true. Besides violating the separation of powers in an obvious sense, such an incursion may interfere with the executive energy that is essential to government. Exclusion of these considerations from his analysis follows from the fact that he depreciates "specialized functions" as an aspect of separated powers. He does not properly relate the role of the Court to functions assigned to other branches by the theorists of the Constitution.[105] This rich body of constitutional theory underlying the separation of powers and the scheme of multiplicity of interests is designed to produce a government with sufficient power to act with responsibility and wisdom and yet preserve republican liberty. Such theory is necessary to a thoughtful attack on judicial activism.

It is difficult to justify judicial review in a principled manner and at the same time counsel judicial restraint unless one acknowledges that the Constitution has a meaningful theoretical content and ascertainable principles that can inform the judgment of the Court as it hears cases. Inherent in this body of theory and principles are limitations on the judicial power. There are principles and guidance to be *discovered* in the Constitution. Insofar as a Court simply "creates" rather than "discovers," it is augmenting its power and its potential for many of the practices Kurland laments. Yet he encourages these practices in some respects by characterizing judicial lawmaking "as a conscious process of creation not discovery."[106]

Kurland urges that the quality of reason in the Court's opinions be improved in order to restore the people's confidence in the Court and the rule of law. This is a valid objective, but it too must be examined in light of his understanding of the Constitution and the judicial process. Kurland's standards for the internal logic of judicial opinions are high. His analysis is most instructive when it focuses on this internal consistency of judicial opinion and points to judges' deficiencies in reasoning or their failure to adhere to principle set forth in precedent. His standard is a reasoned judgment that can be applied to subsequent cases in a principled manner. In this regard, Kurland's work is valuable to analysts of case law. It is clear that important cases decided during the last twenty-five years deserve the criticism he levels at them.

Adherence to precedent and sound judicial reasoning may be necessary elements in restoring public confidence in the Court and in law, but they are not sufficient. Even the most tightly reasoned syllogisms can lead to the judicial activism to which Kurland objects if the Court's premises differ from his. Well-reasoned opinions will not restore the confidence of the public unless they are properly anchored in the Constitution. The confidence of careful constitutional analysts will not be restored if judicial opinions rest on an incomplete or incorrect understanding of the Constitution. The Constitution is the fountainhead of the law the Court adjudicates; it is the source and justification for the Court's exercise of legitimate power. The failure of the Court is not only, as Kurland states, "to persuade the people that its judgements have been made for sound reasons."[107] The Court must also persuade the people that its judgments have been made for constitutional reasons.

Contrary to Kurland's view that the Court ought to frustrate the will of the majority when "it is essential to its functions as guardian of interests that would otherwise be unrepresented in the government of the country,"[108] the Court ought to frustrate the will of the majority only when that majority is acting unconstitutionally. Kurland's charge to the Court "to match the Warren Court attainments in the protection of individuals and minorities that today justifies the Court's existence" and to "restore the confidence of the American public in the rule of law" should be reformulated. Judicial protection of individuals and minorities should be within the framework of the *Constitution's* exceptions to the legislative power. Only with this addendum is it likely that the American public's confidence in the rule of law will be restored.

The restoration of confidence in the rule of law, however lofty an end, is not a sufficient end for those who take the Constitution and its underlying theory as an expression of political wisdom. The Court must adhere to this constitutional wisdom. On this point, Kurland is perplexing. How can the Court apply this wisdom if, as Kurland states, "the words of the Constitution have remained the same, but their meaning has totally changed?" Or, to use another of his formulations, today's justices are "of a different era, working under a different constitution" from that of their distinguished predecessors.[109]

Another element of Kurland's analysis shares certain deficiencies with his treatment of the need for reasoned opinions. There is certainly an important element of truth in his observation that the Court should proceed step-by-step and formulate opinions applicable to the particular litigants before it rather than writing "codes of conduct."[110] In another context, he refers to the related problem of giving appropriate deference to the "institutional obligations to continuity" by reconciling "the need for change with the need for stability in constitutional construction." Kurland sees the means to this reconciliation as "reason derived from experience."[111] He also tells us that "experience and not textual analysis has given meaning to the Constitution."[112] We are thereby led away from textual analysis and the underlying theory of the Constitution to rely on "experience." This is an objectionable direction for legal analysis because it leads us away from the constitutional concepts that were designed to shape our political experience in a way that would fulfill the constitutional plan for competent government and republican liberty. Although there is no question that experience and reason should be important elements in applying the Constitution to contemporary circumstances, they must be used to fulfill the ends of the Constitution in a way that is consistent with the charter's integrity and principles. There is a great deal more subtlety and wisdom in those principles as originally conceived than Kurland's work acknowledges.

The fundamental defect in Kurland's understanding of the Constitution is that although he asks for a restrained Court, he sets forth a view of the Constitution that invites justices to insert their own values into it. By defining the Constitution as meaning whatever the justices of the Supreme Court want it to mean, subject only to the acquiescence of the American people, Kurland seems to say that the Constitution means whatever the Court can get away with saying that it means. Judicial opinions then become efforts on the part of the justices to rationalize their judgments in a way that will be acceptable to the American people.[113] This fundamental definition of the U.S. Constitution leads us to a contemporary situation in which the Court has used its power in a way to which Kurland objects. It seems—at least at this writing—that in spite of public expressions of discontent, the people are acquiescing in what the Court has done.[114] Thus, Kurland's understanding of the Constitution seems to belie his own criticisms of contemporary judicial activism. His understanding would be enriched by a careful examination of the Constitution's theoretical foundations, which give the document its fundamental integrity. As a result of this inadequate theory, Kurland does not avail himself of a source of wisdom that would illumine his analysis and aid his critique of judicial activism.

Constitutional Evolution and Institutional Considerations: Laurence Tribe

Laurence H. Tribe published the first edition of his treatise on constitutional law in 1978. Within the next ten years, his *American Constitutional Law* was cited in published opinions 24 times by the U.S. Supreme Court, 518 times by other federal courts, and 321 times by state courts.[115] One leading casebook in constitutional law lists 60 references to the treatise;[116] a search of the Lexis database ALLREV indicated more than 500 citations of the work in 40 leading law reviews.[117] The frequency of citation or comment, noted by Tribe himself in the preface to his second edition,[118] indicates that the treatise has been an important intellectual and practical force in American constitutional law. Commentators on Tribe's treatise refer to it in the same context as the great nineteenth-century commentaries by Joseph Story and Thomas Cooley.[119]

Given the success of the first edition, it is not surprising that Tribe updated his treatise in a second edition of almost 1,800 pages published in 1988. He describes his treatise as arising out of a commitment to constitutional analysis and not "reflective of any specific philosophy beyond this."[120] In fact, he indicates that since writing the first edition he has gained "a deeper appreciation of the very great difference between *reading* the Constitution we have and *writing* the Constitution some of us might wish to have."[121] The criterion this distinction points toward seems a fair one to use in reviewing the second edition of his treatise, since it is a standard he imposes on himself. This analysis necessarily concentrates on just a few examples that illustrate Tribe's jurisprudence.

Although the second edition disavows the preface to the first edition as "now a source of some embarrassment" because of "its rather grand tone,"[122] Tribe includes the earlier substantive preface in the second edition. The basic organization of the treatise has not changed. The preface to the second edition provides more than one clue to the underlying premises and purpose of the treatise. It opens with the purpose of the work: to provide "a unified analysis of constitutional law."[123] Such an ambitious undertaking takes on even greater dimensions when juxtaposed to Tribe's characterization of the Constitution as lacking such unity, as "an intentionally incomplete, often deliberately indeterminate structure for the participatory evolution of political ideals and governmental practices,"[124] as "an historically discontinuous composition; it is the product, over time, of a series of not altogether coherent compromises; it mirrors no single vision or philosophy but reflects instead a set of sometimes reinforcing and sometimes conflicting ideals and notions."[125] Thus, it appears that Tribe sees his own unified analysis of the Constitution as a necessary corrective of that document's original shortcomings. He believes that his analysis "can provide a coherent foundation for an active, continuing, and openly avowed effort to construct a more just constitutional order"[126] as a part of the "living development of constitutional justice" and in forming " 'a more perfect Union' between right and rights within that charter's necessarily evolutionary design." Although Tribe concedes to the courts "a less exclusive role as constitutional oracles," he cedes to the courts a "greater authority— and duty—to advance that justice overtly" (viii). One suspects that the crucial principle is the advancement of constitutional justice as Tribe defines it, irrespective of the particular institution that does the advancing. Institutional considerations assume subordinate importance in Tribe's work insofar as he rejects outright the assumptions of those such as Justice Frankfurter and Professor Bickel who, in Tribe's words, regard "the highest mission of the Supreme Court" as conserving "judicial credibility" (viii). Indeed, given Tribe's view that "judicial restraint is but another form of judicial activism," one must question on what basis one could distinguish an activist from a restrained judiciary or, for that matter, make any sensible analysis of a proper judicial function within his framework of analysis. This is ironic given the fact that the separation of powers is the leading institutional feature of the U.S. Constitution.

Models of Constitutional Evolution

This prolegomenon lays the foundation for understanding the central organizing feature of Tribe's work—the use of seven models that Tribe sees as marking the evolution of constitutional doctrine over time and that he uses to "expose otherwise concealed doctrinal connections and to reveal possibilities of freedom, equality, and fraternity latent in doctrinal alternatives," as well as to provide "a system of thought about constitutional law" (ix–x). These models roughly correspond, in Tribe's view, to various historical epochs and begin with Model I, which characterizes the earliest years of government under the Constitution.

In laying the foundation for Model I—the model of separated and divided powers—Tribe begins with the "oldest and most central tenet of American constitutionalism," that "all lawful power derives from the people and must be held in check to preserve their freedom." He sees the decentralization of power (vertically among federal, state, and local authority and horizontally along the axis of legislative, executive, and judicial power) as the essential constitutional principle designed to serve these ends and, more specifically, to preserve liberty. This model played its most pervasive role from the founding to the Civil War (2–3). Model II, that of implied limitations on government and the model most clearly identified with the rise and fall of contractual liberty, characterized the period from the Civil War through roughly the first quarter of the twentieth century (5–7). Models III and IV describe a set of "restraints on governmental power [that] both antedated and informed the Lochner era and survived that era's eclipse, retaining a measure of vitality even today." Model III, that of settled expectations—uncompensated takings and contract impairments—deals with "the norm of *repose* . . . the idea that government must respect 'vested rights' in property and contract—that certain settled expectations of a focused and crystalized sort should be secure against governmental disruption, at least without appropriate compensation" (587). Model IV, that of governmental regularity—ex post facto laws, bills of attainder, and procedural due process, is distinguished by Tribe from Model III, even though they frequently overlap in constitutional history and decisional law (629–30). He characterizes Model V, that of preferred rights, as liberty beyond contract. It is identified as the basic issue of post-1937 constitutional law and involves freedom of expression and association, rights of political participation, religious autonomy, and privacy and personhood. This model has not attempted "to define inherent limits on the power of all governmental institutions but has aimed more modestly to exclude governmental power from specific substantive spheres, by identifying and protecting certain 'preferred rights' from all but the most compellingly justified instances of governmental intrusion'' (770–71). Model VI–the model of equal protection–is particularly identified with the decades following the collapse of *Lochner* and of Model II (1436). Tribe's Model VII–toward a model of structural justice?–is described as ''a final if perhaps subsidiary model of constitutional argument.'' Its ''elements are drawn from themes and doctrines present in the first six models, but one that nonetheless seems distinctive in its potential reconnection of individual rights with institutional design'' (1673). The distinction arises, at least in part, from Tribe's view that '' 'neutral' principles of structure are worth embracing as constitutional precepts only to the extent that the substantive human realities they bring about help fulfill the constitutional design and that each prior model proved empty exactly to the degree that it sought to deny this truth'' (1673). Tribe does not spell out this final model, but one senses that he believes it is the end toward which the Constitution should have been aiming all along. Indeed, he refers to a time in which this model might reach its maturity and, he seems to assume, the Constitution will be perfected (1676–77).

Tribe's reasons for organizing the treatise around the seven models are not entirely clear, an observation made by Professor Telford Taylor, a reviewer of the first edition. These reasons are no more compelling in the second edition. Taylor raises the question whether any useful purpose is served by the models other than ''verbal shorthand, by (for example) rechristening 'equal protection' as 'Model VI.' ''[127] One may go beyond Taylor's characterization in observing that the shorthand of Model I for the separation of powers and federalism actually obscures the differing purposes served by these two leading institutional features of the U.S. Constitution—features that deserve subtle analysis and that should be centerpieces of any systematic work on the Constitution. Tribe indicates that he does not regard ''the rulings of the Supreme Court as synonymous with constitutional truth.''[128] Yet, insofar as some of the models are designed to serve as even imprecise labels for various historical epochs of the Constitution's development, they lead to a view that Tribe seems in one context to reject: that the Constitution is simply what the Court says it is during any particular historical era—a doctrine that rejects the view that the Constitution has a theory and meaning independent of the interpretation the Court attaches to it during a particular era. Tribe apparently views critically the judicial interpretation of the Constitution, not because of the independent existence of a coherent body of constitutional theory and principles within it, but because the ''living development of constitutional justice'' may proceed with more dispatch if other bodies are involved in the constitutional progress toward the goals Tribe posits.[129]

The Fundamental Model

Model I of Tribe's scheme, the model of separated and divided powers, provides an opportunity to examine his models and the most fundamental aspects of his constitutional theory. He relates this model to the principle that "all lawful power derives from the people" and to the thought prevalent at the founding that rights were "best preserved by inaction and indirection—shielded behind the play of deliberately fragmented centers of countervailing power." He believes that the separation of powers at the national level and the division of powers among federal, state, and local authority were designed to serve these ends.[130]

There are a number of difficulties with this characterization of the separation of powers and federalism and his combining them under the rubric of Model I. The ends of "inaction and indirection" are not the theoretical ends of the framers, and to so characterize them leads to a dismissal of their theory as outmoded and inadequate to meet the demands of contemporary government. Where the separation of powers is concerned, there is no question that Tribe is correct insofar as one purpose of the institution is to prevent governmental tyranny over the governed.[131] There are, however, other important purposes underlying the doctrine. A second purpose is to prevent a foolish or tyrannical majority from effecting its will into public law, at least in the short run. This purpose underlies the separation of powers as a whole, but it is most vividly illustrated in the institution of the Senate. *Federalist* No. 63 discusses the Senate's contribution to this end:

> [T]here are particular moments in public affairs when the people, stimulated by some irregular passion, or some illicit advantage, or misled by the artful misrepresentations of interested men, may call for measures which they themselves will afterwards be the most ready to lament and condemn. In these critical moments, how salutary will be the interference of some temperate and respectable body of citizens, in order to check the misguided career, and to suspend the blow meditated by the people against themselves, until reason, justice and truth can regain their authority over the public mind?[132]

Thus, there is a more subtle purpose of the separation of powers that extends to the scheme of representation in a democracy and to the actions of the people themselves.

There is yet another aspect of the separation of powers insofar as it makes possible the union of stability and energy in a government with a republican form.[133] These qualities are necessary to overcome the perennial republican proclivities toward instability and the violence of faction.[134] They help ensure that the republican government is competent. The separation of powers also provides an institutional home for qualities of government that are historically lacking in republics. Bicameralism, a subspecies of the separation of powers, provides the possibility for the Senate, the leading characteristic of which is stability. The smaller number of members, the staggered elections, the greater continuity, and the six-year terms all work toward this end. These factors were designed to shape the character of the Senate, which is given more constitutional responsibilities than the House in important areas such as foreign affairs, where stability is critical.

The executive branch of government was designed to provide energy to the government, a principle best supplied by unified power in the president. In order to represent a diverse constituency adequately, provide for responsiveness to changes in public opinion, and promote deliberation, a numerous legislative body holding office for a short term is required. But the framers thought that such a body, the House, would lack both stability and energy. In order to supply the energy, power, and force desired to remedy the defect of the legislature, the executive was separated from it and given a basis of power that was, in certain decisive respects, independent of the legislature. This energy in the executive, crucial to our constitutional system, "is a leading character in the definition of good government."[135]

Federalism and separation of powers as enunciated by *The Federalist* rest on the premise of the necessity of a strong national element in the Constitution in order to protect republican liberty. The scheme of multiplicity of economic interests, designed to secure economic liberty, and the scheme of multiplicity of religious sects, designed to secure religious liberty, are both dependent on transferring important elements of power from the states to the nation so that the diversity essential to republican liberty is present in the legislative body of the nation. Only with the requisite powers vested in the national government, especially over economic matters, can this principle of multiplicity be effective. Representation makes possible an enlarged sphere of government in which no single interest or faction is likely to effect its naked self-interest into law. Because of the greater number of interests in the United States as opposed to each individual state, *The Federalist* argues for a strong national government.[136] A strong government is not only consistent with republican liberty but is also necessary to it.[137] Thus, to understand separation of powers as a means of merely dispersing or fragmenting power or of providing a system of "inaction and indirection" is Madison is the matter simply in *Federalist* No. 10: "The regulation of these various and interfering [property] interests forms the principal task of modern legislation."[138] To understand the purpose of separation of powers and federalism as deadlocking the system of government is not consistent with the theory of the founding.

Federalism, properly understood, provides more than a mere limiting of national power. Its contribution to free government is subtle and goes beyond that hinted at by Tribe.[139] Tocqueville gives persuasive reasons to be concerned about the centralization of power over so many aspects of American life. His analysis of individual rights is particularly applicable to Tribe's work. According to Tocqueville, because all classes exercise these rights, "they refrain from attacking the rights of others in order that their own may not be violated."[140] Through the self-interested exercise of decentralized power, citizens gain a greater appreciation for their own rights and a greater sensitivity to the rights of others. Federalism or decentralization is necessary to the activities that nurture these rights.[141] What seems clear, according to Tocqueville's teaching, is that democratic participation, particularly at the local level, is important to the process of implanting in citizens' hearts and minds those qualities that are essential to a liberal democracy, including an appreciation for the rights of others. Herein lies an important foundation for civil liberty: respect for the rights of others on the part of the ruling majority.

The institutional feature of separated powers is important to the American system of government in another decisive respect, that of providing the structure and process through which representation takes place. A dependence on the people through a carefully structured system of representation is the primary safeguard the framers relied on to protect individual rights. However, in order to moderate excesses in majority rule and to help ensure both competent government and individual rights, this system of representation was coupled with auxiliary safeguards.[142] The framers designed a system of representation that required a large commercial republic that would allow for the possibility of refining and enlarging the public view rather than simply reflecting it.[143]

Separation of powers and federalism contain some common elements. Just as democracy at the local and state levels requires citizens to form majorities in order to choose state and local policy, the national system also requires that majorities form in diverse ways and within different geographic areas, depending on the constituency being represented. Majority rule is fundamental to the American scheme, and it is gathered in diverse ways as public opinion is elevated and refined into public law. The Constitution takes majority rule to be its root principle and establishes an intricate system for making that majority its best self as its will is transformed into public law. Although the Constitution answers some questions, particularly ones relating to the extent and proper structure of the Union, and although particular provisions put limits on government, many issues are left to be resolved by the subtle system of representation through the political branches of government—through the representatives of the people as they elevate and refine the opinion of their constituents in ordinary acts of legislation and in executive action.

Given the Constitution's emphasis on majority rule and its provision for institutions through which representation takes place, it is surprising that Tribe refers to arguments about the legitimacy of the judicial power in constitutional interpretation under the heading "The Limited Relevance of Institutional Questions." If one takes the democratic character of the Constitution seriously, the appropriate power of a judiciary that is appointed for life or good behavior is a fundamental constitutional and political question. Tribe seems to regard this question as one of limited relevance because of his own view that "it seems in truth a close question, in the long pull of time, whether the Constitution's implicit vision of a just society, or indeed any decent vision of justice couched in terms of our Constitution's partly indeterminate categories and phrases, would be more or less advanced by a greater or lesser role for the federal judiciary." Thus, he gives "but two and one half cheers for a mild form of judicial supremacy." Presumably, he leaves the other half cheer for that governmental body which, on some occasions, may more closely approximate his own view of a just society. The framework of his analysis throughout the treatise is one of addressing "the *substance* of constitutional issues without always reducing them to their institutional components."[144]

The Ends of the Constitution According to Tribe

Tribe's jurisprudence, centering on the living development of constitutional justice, raises the question of the ends toward which this justice should move. Among those ends are "human freedom rightly understood,"[145] "personal dignity and self-respect," "personal dignity and autonomy," "minimization of subservience and helplessness,"[146] "deeper concerns of personhood,"[147] "possibilities of freedom, equality and fraternity,"[148] and the "human need for closeness, trust, and love."[149]

One difficulty with the ends of constitutional justice toward which Tribe would have us aim is their ambiguity or imprecision, which leaves us adrift in terms of informing our constitutional understanding. Indeed, one suspects that their utility lies chiefly in being sufficiently vague that they allow one to define constitutional law in terms that are fundamentally subjective and consistent with the policy preferences of those espousing them. Although everyone presumably favors human dignity, the term is so broad as to embrace both the goals of Marxism and those of liberal democracy. One wonders what is to be gained by interpreting the provisions of the Bill of Rights and subsequent amendments or the grants of governmental powers in light of the even more general terms Tribe utilizes. Even if one accepts Tribe's characterization of the Constitution as a "shared social vision"[150] (as opposed to a document embodying consent of the governed and the fundamental theory and principles on which its institutions are based), one must still determine who defines that vision; the question remains, human dignity as defined by whom. The American answer to this question is unequivocal: the people. The justification for the Constitution, rooted in the principles of the Declaration, is that it was formed with the consent of the governed. One might even say that the American answer to providing for human dignity (or, more precisely, equality and liberty) is limited, representative government. The Constitution provides for a government that is representative in form and in which the people are sovereign. The system is designed to elevate and refine public opinion as this opinion becomes public law and to make public opinion its best self. But in the end, the system is democratic in form.

Alexander Hamilton, in *Federalist* No. 84, addresses a related problem in the context of the debate over whether the Constitution ought to have a bill of rights. One need not agree with his conclusion to benefit from his insight. He raises the question of whether the power to tax might be used to curtail the liberty of the press. The extent of taxation of newspapers that is reasonable and does not amount to a prohibition of the freedom of the press, Hamilton concludes, "must depend on legislative discretion, regulated by public opinion."[151] In some respects, this insight reminds one of Tribe's view that the judicial branch of government does not inevitably have a corner on wisdom as it relates to individual rights or constitutional protections. He would have organs of both the national and state governments act with an eye toward constitutional principles because of his doctrine of indeterminate constitutional law, a doctrine that "recognizes, within limits, the equal legitimacy of differing interpretations" of the Constitution.[152]

Applications of Tribe's Jurisprudence

Given his concern for other actors in the political system and his professed allegiance to some form of federalism, it is instructive to look toward Tribe's resolution of some of the issues that embody differing views of what the Constitution requires where the legislative bodies of the states are concerned. It happens that these examples fall within the rubric of the Fourteenth Amendment or the Bill of Rights, and one involves a case that Tribe argued before the Supreme Court of the United States. The examples involving issues of federalism are particularly interesting in light of Tribe's statements supporting a constitutional principle of federalism and characterizing the benefits of federalism as enhancing the opportunities for representative participation at the state level. He quotes with approval statements that a court "is without power to invent entirely new rights" and that the creating of "states' rights out of whole cloth in order to redress a perceived shift in power to central government is an arrogation of authority as illegitimate as conjuring rights of privacy or minimum income out of thin air."[153]

Tribe's adherence to federalism, as well as his theory of indeterminate constitutional law and representative government, is illustrated by his treatment of a crucial reapportionment decision, *Lucas v. Forty-Fourth General Assembly*.[154] Given Tribe's seeming concern with the virtues of federalism, and particularly his concern with enhancing the opportunities for representation at the state level, it is curious that in a helpful summary of reapportionment cases, he passes over *Lucas* with almost no analysis or criticism and simply assumes its legitimacy (in spite of his articulated objections to the Court's being the sole touchstone of constitutionality).[155]

One who is truly concerned with issues of representative government and federalism should at least recognize powerful arguments that run counter to the Court's ruling in *Lucas*. Tribe's failure to articulate these arguments is even more puzzling, since this case does not involve what he calls "*substantive* constraints" but seemingly consists of the same "fundamental threats to state sovereignty" that he finds objectionable because they "*restructure* the basic institutional design of the system a state's people choose for governing themselves."[156] If a majority of the people of a state can establish a state supreme court to protect their rights, there is little ground for arguing that a majority of the people of Colorado cannot apportion one house of their state legislature on a basis other than population, with a view toward the same end of protecting minority rights and interests. The same argument applies with even greater force to the legitimacy of the U.S. Supreme Court. In *Lucas,* the Court quashed the action of a contemporary popular majority of a state on the basis of a principle that will not sustain the legitimacy of its own action. Tribe's view of federalism, particularly the integrity of the basic institutional design of the system a state's people choose, would be much more plausible if it included a critical treatment of *Lucas* instead of merely accepting the decision as a constitutional given.

In his discussion of federalism, Tribe refers to the objectionable practice of "conjuring rights of privacy or minimum income out of thin air" and then in a footnote refers to his chapter 15 "[f]or proper approaches to rights of privacy and autonomy."[157] Chapter 15 is entitled "Rights of Privacy and Personhood."[158] He regards these rights as existing "against . . . even an overwhelming majority," and they must ultimately be defined and defended "against government in terms independent of consensus or majority will."[159] One suspects that Tribe will not allow rights such as those of privacy and personhood, in which he believes so strongly, to be subjected to the authority of the state legislatures (which he had earlier touted within the context of federalism) unless the state legislatures agree with Tribe's views on these rights. Our suspicions are confirmed by his treatment of such issues as abortion and homosexuality.

Where abortion is concerned, he characterizes deferral to legislative judgment as unsatisfactory because different states would arrive at different resolutions of this issue. He quotes Abraham Lincoln's warning, in the context of what Tribe calls "a different issue of fundamental liberty," that the Union could not long endure " 'half slave and half free.' "[160] But the "fatal flaw of this 'legislative solution' argument is that it presumes that fundamental rights can properly be reduced to political interests"; these fundamental rights, according to him, should not be submitted to vote, for "it is often when public sentiment is most sharply divided that the independent judiciary plays its most vital national role in expounding and protecting constitutional rights."[161] He then reinforces his position by quoting Chief Justice Warren in *Brown v. Board of Education:* " '[t]he vitality of . . . constitutional principles cannot be allowed to yield simply because of disagreement with them.' "[162] Tribe's equating of abortion with racial equality is not persuasive. The right of racial equality is rooted in the Declaration of Independence and is at the very heart of the Fourteenth Amendment and the Civil War that preceded that amendment. The right of abortion is not self-evident and should not be treated in a context that employs Lincoln's poetic language or the great self-evident truth of racial equality articulated in the Fourteenth Amendment.

The Georgia legislature's determination relating to sodomy also leads Tribe to sacrifice his doctrine of federalism to what he seems to regard as a higher principle. Tribe argued this case, *Bowers v. Hardwick,* before the U.S. Supreme Court, but his arguments for Michael Hardwick did not prevail. A majority of the Court did not support his view that "two adult homosexuals engaging in consensual sex in the privacy of their home are carrying on an intimate association entitled to constitutional protection."[163] It is instructive that Tribe pays almost no homage to particular constitutional provisions on which the case might rest. Instead, his analysis is devoted almost entirely to entwining the various privacy cases the Court has decided and constructing them in a manner that support's Hardwick's alleged right.[164] One would expect at least some attention to the Court's statement in the case that its judgment is not one of whether laws against sodomy between consenting adults are "wise or desirable" and the Court's conclusion that its judgments are "most vulnerable" and "nearest to illegitimacy when it deals with judge-made constitutional law having little or no cognizable roots in the language or design of the Constitution."[165] Tribe's disregard of this institutional consideration and the invocation of the attenuated constitutional theory necessary to support Hardwick's claim constitute at least three cheers for judicial supremacy, in spite of what he said earlier in the treatise.[166] *Hardwick* is also illustrative of the rights that Tribe seems to believe are so important that they supplant institutional considerations relating to representative government and the doctrine of federalism.

Conclusion

In constructing his own theory of privacy and personhood, seemingly to correct the Constitution's own deficiencies in this regard, he engages in characteristic Tribean analysis. He draws a thread from one case and a thread from another case and then forms these threads into a theory that reaches toward the doctrine of privacy and personhood as he understands it. There is little effort to return to the touchstone of constitutionality, the Constitution itself. In fact, such pivotal cases as *Stanley v. Georgia* are not subject to any extended analysis to determine whether they are constitutionally sound. The doctrine of these cases is simply used in a lawyerlike way to make a case for extending the rights to privacy and personhood. This is particularly puzzling, since Tribe's treatise proceeds from the premises that it is "a constitution, and not merely its judicial management, that we are expounding,"[167] and that the rulings of the Supreme Court are not "synonymous with constitutional truth."[168]

It seems more accurate to say that Tribe is expounding a theory that he imposes on the Constitution rather than expounding the Constitution itself, and in this process, he treats the rulings of the Court as synonymous with constitutional truth when they square with his theory. There is little evidence in the text of his being true to his own admonition that there is a "great difference between reading the Constitution we have and writing the Constitution some of us might wish to have."[169]

Tribe pays lip service to representative government and the doctrine that all lawful power derives from the people,[170] to federalism, and to the indeterminate nature of certain matters of constitutional law. But in the end, when these principles collide with Tribe's view of a just result, he characteristically favors imposing an authoritative judicial pronouncement that advances the social vision he sees as the perfection or correction of the Constitution. It seems to matter little to him that he might disagree with the will of the people or their representatives. He subscribes to a view of judicial supremacy when that supremacy advances the doctrine he favors. This is a vast departure from the characterization of the judicial role by Hamilton in *The Federalist* as "the steady, upright, and impartial administration of the laws."[171] Tribe's constitutional theory and the role he prescribes for the Court leave little room for the fundamental safeguard of the Constitution, a reliance on the people.

Chapter Eight
Rejection of the Constitution and Liberal Theory

Both Mark Tushnet's account of critical legal studies (CLS) and Catharine MacKinnon's explication of "feminism unmodified" rest on the premise that the Constitution and government are subordinate to more fundamental social forces that perpetuate inequality and injustice. Tushnet and MacKinnon reject the Constitution and the liberal theory on which it rests.

Critical legal studies challenges the premises and operation of the American political and legal system. Proponents of CLS attack existing legal structures, the Constitution, and the constitutional theory that attempts to justify and make the charter of government coherent. The conclude that each is indefensible. CLS theorists want to trash the Constitution and the legal system in the name of a higher vision of justice, but they do not propose any alternatives to replace what is trashed.

The CLS theorist who focuses most clearly and prolifically on the Constitution is Professor Mark Tushnet of Georgetown University.[1] He is clearly representative of the CLS movement, a movement which is, by its nature, not unified in its vision of justice but only in its condemnation of the existing legal system.[2] The common ground Tushnet finds for CLS scholars is "that critical legal studies is a political location for a group of people on the Left who share the project of supporting and extending the domain of the Left in the legal academy."[3] Another unifying element is the assertion that law is indeterminate; that is, standard legal theory does not constrain legal theorists from reaching sharply divergent results. Tushnet attributes these divergent results to the moral or political goals sought by the scholar or practitioner in question. For example, in the case of judges appointed by President Reagan, Tushnet argues that "we know what results they'll reach no matter what their theory [of interpretation] is."[4] Although more sophisticated deconstructionist techniques have evolved, adherents of CLS seem to hold to the perception that legal discourse is simply a smoke screen for extending ordinary, private moral and political discourse and agendas.[5]

Tushnet's work builds on a number of these common CLS elements. It is especially attractive as a vehicle for understanding the CLS critique of the Constitution and constitutional theory because, unlike many other CLS theorists, he systematically treats the Constitution and constitutional interpretation. Through Tushnet's work, we can examine the question of whether we should respond to the call of the CLS movement to trash the Constitution in service to this "higher" vision of justice.

Tushnet's critique of various traditional and contemporary constitutional theories concludes: "Critique is all there is."[6] Tushnet observes that "much of what I have written about constitutional law falls in the genre of 'deconstruction' or 'trashing.'" In response to criticisms that "trashing" provides little satisfaction and that a constitutional theorist should tell judges what to do about controversial constitutional issues, Tushnet answers by telling how he would proceed if he were a judge: "First, I would choose a currently fashionable theory. Second, I would use that theory to advance the cause of socialism."[7] Tushnet believes that the conflict between individual and society, which he sees as lying at the heart of liberalism, cannot be resolved by any constitutional theories derived from liberalism. He attempts to establish that any theory derived from the premises of liberal democracy is subject to the fatal inconsistency that he believes he has shown in his critique of each of the theories examined.[8]

Catharine MacKinnon is an outspoken and visible proponent of feminist jurisprudence. MacKinnon reveals her "unmodified feminism" in arguing that the Constitution, American law, and society embody a system of male domination in a hierarchy that subordinates women. Her project for reform uses the standard of "subordination of women" in analyzing the areas of law she regards as most important. Through her lens of "subordination," she trumps other constitutional considerations, such as First Amendment and due process principles, and recommends dramatic incursions into the private realm. Her emphasis on gender and subordination leads her to deny that there are objective standards or abstract principles and reduces her understanding to one based on women's own terms and on women's concrete experience. She denies the objectivity or neutrality of law and engages in special pleading for law to embody women's point of view. She justifies this on the grounds that existing law is special pleading for men. In spite of her disavowal of abstract principles and truth in favor of a gender orientation and subjective experience, her entire enterprise rests on an assumption that there is such a thing as justice or equality. This sense of injustice pervades her work.

Critical Legal Studies: Mark Tushnet

Mark Tushnet's seminal work in constitutional law is entitled *Red, White, and Blue: A Critical Analysis of Constitutional Law.*[9] His many articles and *Red, White and Blue* present what the book's subtitle, and the school of critical legal studies, promises: a critique of contending theories of constitutional law and theory. Tushnet observes that works on constitutional theory ordinarily present an alternative to their critique of competing theories, but his "book cannot end like that."[10] His critique of other theories and his skeletal suggestions for a new social order that is more productive of the common good, as he sees it, provide insight into his view of the Constitution and the role of the Court.[11] He believes the conflict between individual and society, which he sees as lying at the heart of liberalism, cannot be resolved by any constitutional theories derived from liberalism. He argues that any theory derived from the premises of liberal democracy is subject to a fatal inconsistency.[12]

What Is the Constitution?

Tushnet's view of the Constitution rests on his discussion of "The Revival of Grand Theory in Constitutional Law." He characterizes this theory as assuming that "at the core of the system things are basically all right," but it attempts to resolve problems that are merely derivative from the system itself. Grand theory has been particularly concerned with justifying the tension between the exercise of judicial review and a democratic form of government. Tushnet finds such theory wanting, for he does not regard "the system" as delivering the goods.[13]

Tushnet believes the Constitution was framed amidst two theories of citizenship that contended on roughly equal terms. This accounts for the tension implicit in the Constitution. The liberal tradition "emphasized the individualism of people acting in society and examined how social institutions rest on and constrain individual preferences"; the civic republican tradition "emphasized the essential social nature of individual being and examined how individual preferences rest on and constrain social institutions" (4–5). He further explains his view of the two traditions:

> The liberal tradition stresses the self-interested motivations of individuals and treats the collective good as the aggregation of what individuals choose; the republican tradition has an ill-defined notion that the whole is greater than the sum of its parts. Although it acknowledges the role of public institutions in providing the framework for individual development, the liberal tradition insists that such institutions be neutral toward competing conceptions of the good and tends to emphasize the risks of governmental overreaching. The republican tradition, seeing public institutions as important means by which private character is shaped, is less suspicious of government. (6)

The liberal tradition has become so dominant in contemporary life that Tushnet regards it as obscuring the merits of the civic republican tradition (6).

He believes that the unifying civic republican tradition's emphasis on civic-mindedness might produce judges who would discern the true interests of the nation. But this solution to current problems of constitutional law and interpretation is not available to us (11–17). He sees the most fundamental problem as the dilemma between legislative and judicial overreaching: "Judicial review is often defended as the only way to escape the potential tyranny of the majority, but it simultaneously creates the potential for the tyranny of the judges" (16). The task Tushnet sets for himself is to examine and critique the grand theories of constitutional interpretation that attempt to square judicial review with democracy.

Tushnet seems to believe that in an epoch in which civic republicanism thrives, judicial review is not a problem—that is, it will not be a vehicle for judicial tyranny. In a society characterized by civic republicanism, "the judges would share the general assumptions about public policy and the processes by which it is made."[14] Thus, according to his argument, civic republicanism is concomitant with shared general assumptions about policy issues. Judicial tyranny will be avoided because judges will share the same general assumptions of the democracy and its representatives in the other branches of government.

Under the conditions Tushnet describes, there would be little need for judicial review, since agreement would be so widespread. He equates civic republicanism with shared agreement on policy. But in the founding era, which he describes as being composed of important elements of civic republicanism, there was serious disagreement about the nature of the regime to be founded and other issues. The influence of civic republicanism did not produce unanimity on the question of national versus confederal government or on the issue of slavery. In fact, there were elements of compromise on both these issues, and both issues found their way to the judiciary amidst divided public opinion. Ultimately, it was a theoretical understanding of the means and ends of the Constitution (and the Declaration) that helped resolve the issues raised by *Marbury v. Madison*,[15] *McCulloch v. Maryland*,[16] and the *Dred Scott*[17] decision. Clearly these issues were not resolved by a shared vision of civic republicanism, but rather by a judiciary opining about the proper theory and principles of the Constitution.

An alternative view to Tushnet's invocation of "the shared vision" of civic republicanism as justifying judicial review is the classic defense of judicial review, a defense that he rejects. This defense justifies judicial review as a means of restraining temporary majorities by resorting to provisions and principles of a Constitution that was put into place by majorities who were not focused on temporary policy but rather on a more permanent and principled statement of restraints on temporary majorities. We now turn to Tushnet's examination and critique of this and other defenses of judicial review.

Tushnet's Critique of Grand Theory

THE JURISPRUDENCE OF HISTORY. Tushnet includes within the rubric of jurisprudence of history both the doctrine of originalism and the doctrine of neutral principles. His far-reaching critique of these theories can be summarized simply: Originalism is plagued with historical ambiguity and inference from limited evidence, and it also requires judges "to trace historical continuities between the institutions that the framers knew and those that contemporary judges know."[18] The doctrine of neutral principles requires judges to "rely on a shared conception of the proper role of judicial reasoning" (57). Tushnet believes that neither history nor legal principle provides the continuity necessary to guide and constrain judges (57). To understand original intent requires a "creative re-creation of the past" (57). As a result of the "gulf that separates the framers' world from ours," the past can be re-created in many different ways. Such re-creation destroys the possibility of originalism being an effective restraint on judges (44).[19] Neutral principles point toward judicial decisions that are consistent with precedent, but the theory of neutral principles fails to constrain judges and prevent judicial tyranny. Precedent can easily be manipulated; the choice among proper principles of adjudication is hotly contested.[20]

Tushnet further argues that within our liberal community, "radical indeterminacy of meaning" is inevitable.[21] The "atomistic premises of liberalism treat each of us as autonomous individuals whose choices and values are independent of those made and held by others," so we seem destined to indeterminate meaning as we struggle to construct constraints or principles to guide judicial action.[22] Insofar as the system of separated powers and the judicial process are constrained from such radical indeterminacy, he attributes this to the fact that the system within which judges operate is "deeply entrenched and resistant to change."[23]

Tushnet fundamentally disagrees with this system. One suspects that much of his critique of originalism and neutral principles is driven by his fundamental disagreement with the system rather than by the radical indeterminacy of meaning, which he claims makes principled adjudication impossible. Tushnet rejects both the entire system within which the Court operates and the Court's definition of this system as it decides individual cases. His rejection is based on his own vision of a just political and social order, one that would depart dramatically from the status quo and from the theory of the American political order. He believes justice requires socialism and radical equality.[24] Because he fundamentally opposes the "illegitimate" system, he rejects the Constitution and its judicial interpretation as radically indeterminate.

Tushnet purports to base much of his critique of liberalism on what he sees as the premise of liberalism: there is no public good or true interest, only individual conceptions of self-interest. Parts of his work communicate a longing for the community he identifies with the civic republican tradition, a community that goes beyond mere private interests to a public or true interest. Tushnet dismisses the view that the public good is difficult to discern because it is based on individual conceptions of the public good that are almost inevitably tainted with self-interest. As Madison observes in *Federalist* No. 10: "As long as the reason of man continues fallible, and he is at liberty to exercise it, different opinions will be formed. As long as the connection subsists between his reason and his self-love, his opinions and his passions will have a reciprocal influence on each other; and the former will be objects to which the latter will attach themselves."[25]

If our reason and opinions are influenced by our self-interest, how do we arrive at laws approximating the public good? *The Federalist* wisely rejects "giving to every citizen the same opinions, the same passions, and the same interests."[26] It also rejects the view that statecraft should be depended on to promote the public good: "It is in vain to say that enlightened statesmen will be able to adjust these clashing interests, and render them all subservient to the public good. Enlightened statesmen will not always be at the helm."[27] The Constitution's answer to this difficulty is to structure the institutions of government and representation so that the majority finally determines what is in the public interest. The majority also serves as a check on statecraft and acts as the final judge of the public good. Thus, *The Federalist* seems explicitly to reject the unifying view of civic republicanism as well as the imposition of the public good by presidents, members of Congress, or the judiciary. In contrast to this teaching, Tushnet asserts that if he were a judge, he would choose a fashionable constitutional theory and then use that theory to advance the cause of socialism.[28] For one who argues that "critique is all there is,"[29] it requires extraordinary confidence in one's own theory of socialism to suggest using the bench as a means to advance one's own view of justice, irrespective of the will of the majority, the theory of the Constitution, or the rule of law. But Tushnet would likely respond that if conditions evolved to the extent that a judge with his views were appointed to the bench, social conditions would allow the imposition of his views.[30]

Putting aside either the possibility or the desirability of such a consensus, as well as its inconsistency with the Constitution's theory, the question we must raise is this: If a majority of the people of the United States wants changes in the economic structure and enacts these changes, is any modern Court going to stand in the way of their implementation? The New Deal presumably answered this question, at least in the context of legislation effecting the welfare state, which the Court was ultimately unable or unwilling to stop. Tushnet's real objection is not the Constitution's theory but the resulting democracy that has not adopted his view of a just political order. If he imposed his views on the Constitution, the result would be a tyranny of his own opinions, not a tyranny of the legislature or the judiciary. Of course, he would not define it that way. To him, it is simply the implementation of his own vision of justice. The Constitution does not rest on the premise of uniform opinion for which Tushnet longs and with which he identifies the tradition of civic republicanism.

THE JURISPRUDENCE OF DEMOCRACY. Tushnet frames his treatment of the jurisprudence of democracy around John Hart Ely's theory of "representation reinforcing review."[31] The cornerstone of Ely's theory is judicial protection of political rights that are essential to the representative process. As Tushnet recognizes, Ely's theory focuses on rule by a true majority rather than on fundamental or basic rights not directly related to the political process.[32] Judicial intervention is justified in Ely's theory either to correct failures in the operation of the political market or "to mimic the results that would have occurred had the political market been operating properly."[33] The strength Tushnet sees in Ely's theory is that it limits the discretion of judges, but it also provides little limitation on the legislature and opens the way for legislative tyranny. Exemplary of the potential for legislative tyranny that Tushnet sees in this theory is the Education for All Handicapped Children Act of 1975, which imposes financial and organizational burdens on public schools without providing federal funding. He describes this act as an example of the failure of formal representation and a congressional exercise of tyranny over the states. If the Court were to enter the murky area of informal aspects of representation, taking into account what Tushnet calls "political reality," then judicial discretion would be nearly unbridled, with the potential for judicial tyranny (82–83). Similar problems occur when the Court attempts to distinguish between "discrete and insular minorities" and other minorities who simply lose to a majority in the representative process (94). As is characteristic of Tushnet's analysis of contending theories, he concludes that the theory of representation reinforcement is inadequate. Because of the complexity of the political process, a realistic, informal view of politics allows judges too much latitude and opens the way for judicial tyranny; if the reality of the process is discarded, he sees us left with a purely formal analysis that gives too much latitude to legislators (106). As is characteristic of his analysis generally, Tushnet's critique results in no resolution of the contradictions he sees within liberal theory and manifested in "representation-reinforcing review." Tushnet agrees with the egalitarianism that is both the strength and weakness of Ely's work and which is inconsistent with the Constitution's attempt to elevate and refine majority rule. Nonetheless, Tushnet is unwilling to use his critique to conclude that there is a strong commitment to majoritarianism and representation in the

Constitution; he chooses instead to stop his inquiry with his conclusion of internal contradiction.

THE JURISPRUDENCE OF PHILOSOPHY. Early in his treatment of moral philosophy, Tushnet raises the question of whether it is good for judges to assess a statute's constitutionality by invoking morality. As is characteristic of his analysis generally, he begins with a question, the answer to which may seem self-evident at one level (particularly if the alternative is to use immorality as the basis for adjudication), and then proceeds to show the defects in asking judges to invoke morality as they decide cases. As Tushnet puts it, "[t]he positive case for relying on moral philosophy thus turns on the ability of judges to distinguish between fundamental and other rights and then to decide what moral philosophy requires, all within the framework of the liberal tradition's concern that judges be appropriately constrained" (108–11). His other criticism of judicial reliance on moral philosophy is that there is no reason to presume that judges are better than legislators at discerning rules of right moral action. This is true whether one is viewing the problem from the perspective of systematic moral philosophy, from that of more pragmatic theory, or from that of the "best values in American society" (133).[34] He is also skeptical of asking judges to perform the task of identifying fundamental values that need judicial protection, since "judges are drawn from a narrow stratum of our society and what they consider to be common values may instead be the reflection of their personal experience."[35] Thus, he believes we should not expect judges to be much different from legislators.[36] Tushnet's observations raise compelling questions relative to democracy and the judiciary, whether or not one shares the orientation of the CLS movement that he represents. Given his acknowledgment of the perplexing nature of discerning right moral action, Tushnet's analysis seems to lead to a recommendation for a thoughtfully restrained judiciary; however, he is unwilling to depart from the critical nature of his analysis in order to reach such a conclusion.

ANTIFORMALISM, INTUITIONISM, AND LITTLE THEORY. Tushnet believes that antiformalism attempts to displace concern over the countermajoritarian character of judicial review.[37] This displacement is accomplished through antiformalist theory, which denies the necessity or possibility of controlling the legislative power through judicial review and controlling the judicial power through a limiting theory.[38] Variations on the theme of antiformalism reject formal or grand theory for different reasons. Anarchist antiformalists argue against the need to constrain coercive power, no matter where it is lodged. Anarchist antiformalists characterize judicial interpretation either as a continuation of a public dialogue about law, with the Constitution being used as a rhetorical device, or as simply opinion with no coercive power beyond the individual espousing that opinion. In rejecting the idea that there is one "law" as determined by the majority of the Supreme Court, anarchist antiformalists claim that no one is in the formal position to exercise coercive power (249–56).

Other antiformalists reject liberal constraints because of their view that individuals are able to give their lives meaning only by participating in a community guided by public values that transcend the aggregation of individual preferences. Some antiformalists advocate a balancing based on intuition or "little theories" of morality, a cognitive process of convincing any combination of the Court, Congress, and the public to arrive at certain judgments based on intuition. Indeed, there seems no reasonable way to use intuition to judge between those with disparate intuitions (158–60). Others believe in constitutional theory based on public values. These public values are determined through practical reason, a moral-intellectual ability to view the whole from a removed and passive perspective (160–68). Tushnet believes antiformalism necessarily draws on the civic republican tradition and is in that sense sympathetic to it. In his view, however, this tradition has been lost. In order to regain the civic republican foundations necessary for antiformalism, "we must transform society" (148). In Tushnet's words: "The task of constitutional theory ought no longer be to rationalize the real in one way or another. It should be to contribute to a political movement that may begin to bring about a society in which civic virtue may flourish" (187).

Tushnet believes the framers failed to understand that courts are inevitably part of a society's governing coalition. The dynamics of private property have transformed the society, including the judiciary and the other elements of the governing coalition, from that republican theory Tushnet regards as important in early American history (186). In his view, a constitutional theory that does not undertake the transformation of society is much too timid. He is fundamentally dissatisfied with the social fabric of the United States; thus, tampering with constitutional theory will not remedy the defects he sees. Tushnet sees in antiformalism some encouraging signs because it requires a radical decentralization of law and seeks a social transformation necessary to the republicanism he desires. It is one version of contemporary legal utopianism.[39] Such radical decentralization is inconsistent both with the Constitution's republican theory, which rests on centralization properly understood and with Tushnet's own desire for the Court to play a central role in the social reform he supports.[40]

Tushnet applauds the antiliberal attempt of antiformalism to shift the desired social policy away from concerns of the individual and to focus instead on the social good. He also likes the active role of law in our everyday dialogue, not just when we talk with those in governing positions.[41] "Law is what we do"; therefore, it necessarily involves community. Nonetheless, he finds grounds for criticizing antiformalism and thereby showing the pervasiveness of the CLS critique. Tushnet believes the civic republican tradition is no longer available to us and is not taken seriously by contemporary opinion which dismisses "appeals to the public interest as political rhetoric designed to mask a self-interested effort to advance a narrow goal."[42] He fails to acknowledge that the Constitution's republicanism is dependent on the centralization of important governmental powers, as was made clear in Chapter 2 of this volume.

The Constitution of Society

THE CONSTITUTION OF GOVERNMENT. Accepting all the usual criticisms of constitutional theory discussed previously, Tushnet analyzes the intellectual predecessor of CLS, legal realism, and its immediate heir, structural review. Legal realism attempts to use empirical methods of political science to illumine constitutional theory.[43] Legal realism insists that various legal doctrines do not dispose of particular problems: "The materials of legal doctrine are almost measureless, and the acceptable techniques of legal reasoning—distinguishing on basis of facts, analogizing to other areas of law where cognate problems arise, and the like—are so flexible that they allow us to assemble diverse precedents into whatever pattern we choose."[44] In legal realism's description of how rules of law work—that is, their independence on judges' value choices—the doctrine challenged not only the rule of law but also the liberal tradition itself. Tushnet describes the nerve of the realist argument: that "judges no less than legislators were political actors, motivated primarily by their own interests and values."[45] In legal realism's emphasis on sociology and political science and in its attempt to expose the "reality" of the law as simply dependent on value choices, we see a link between legal realism and structural review.[46]

Although he rejects legal realism as incomplete in its explanation of constitutional law, Tushnet recognizes that as its tenets became established, lawyers turned to political scientists to advance the descriptive process in constitutional law.[47] Tushnet uses Robert Dahl to illustrate this and to grapple with the question of democracy versus a nonelective Court that uses the Constitution as a means to advance its members' own personal values. Dahl concluded that "in the medium-to-long run, judicial review doesn't matter very much."[48] The primary constraint limiting judges' discretion is not constitutional theory but political reality. Indeed, Tushnet believes that "no internally coherent theory of politics will adequately account for both the individualist and social elements of human life"; thus, liberal theory cannot resolve the tension between individual and society.[49] Nor is Tushnet optimistic about going outside the bounds of liberal theory to resolve these problems. Yet he leaves those who wish to do so to continue conventional legal scholarship, "because it makes no less sense than anything else in the world."[50] Unlike the framers of the Constitution who relied on republican mechanisms to achieve the primary task of government—that of securing the public good and private rights—Tushnet seems to regard the task as simply impossible, or at least as preventing the social goals he embraces.

Tushnet sees a link between the conclusion implicit in realism—that judicial review does not matter much—and a more recent development in constitutional law, that of structural review. Structural review shifts emphasis from the normative decision to who makes the policy decision in question and how it is made. Thus, questions of executive, judicial, legislative, and administrative authority (and process) are central to structural review.[51] He criticizes decisions utilizing structural review because they do not impose substantive limits on the actions of government and because of the difficulty of knowing the proper agency of government to make the policy in question. Furthermore, structural review rests on a presumption of a policy process characterized by rational deliberation and puts judges in a position of choosing between two different imaginary processes that ignore the underlying political realities. Tushnet believes that because of the advantage incumbents have in the electoral process, elected officials are insulated from political accountability, much as bureaucrats are. He thinks that structural review of which body is to make policy is not very important because the representative character of the legislature and the bureaucracy does not differ significantly (203–8).

Tushnet sees no guidelines to constrain judges in determining which body is the proper one to make policy. For example, how does the Court determine how much attention an issue must get in the legislature if the requirements of structural review and congressional policy making are to be satisfied? The theory of structural review fails to limit the Court's discretion in determining which body should make policy decisions and thereby fails to meet the requirement of the liberal tradition (208).

The second element of structural review concerns the propriety of the processes that the agency uses in formulating policy. Tushnet sees two possible avenues for evaluating the process in question. One criterion would be to require a clear articulation of the reasons underlying the statute in question. But he objects that this approach would destroy the legislative process as it currently operates. Much state and local legislation is enacted with only rudimentary records of its history; furthermore, much legislation is in response to majoritarian constituent opinion or political interests or is the result of compromise and therefore lacks a reasoned basis. He suggests an alternative approach where important cases involving suspect or quasi-suspect classifications are concerned: the judiciary would allow virtually any legislative enactment to stand as long as the judiciary "is sure that is what the legislature really wants'' (210). The effect of this approach would be to allow unchecked legislative discretion in sensitive areas in which many are skeptical of its ability to act fairly. Tushnet responds to his own suggestions by concluding: "Structural review appears to avoid the problem of judicial tyranny by avoiding decision on what actions government may take'' (210–11). In other words, under the theory of structural review, the legislature is effectively unrestrained by constitutional prohibitions, and judges are given insufficient standards to guide their judgments. Tushnet seems to adopt the modern understanding of judicial review, which accepts judicial supremacy and denies the strictly republican nature of the Constitution as it was understood by the framers. Insofar as structural review rests on the desirability of preserving republicanism and avoiding judicial supremacy, it deserves more thorough analysis.

Structural review fails to meet the standards Tushnet sets for a constitutional theory. Although he rejects structural review as a theory, he draws on its presumption of a judicialized legislature that openly articulates and fairly balances competing interests against one another to frame his analysis of constitutional law in terms of a technocratic vision of society (213). This vision informs his descriptive treatment of religion and the market.

THE CONSTITUTION OF RELIGION. Tushnet echoes a general dissatisfaction with the constitutional law of religion, which has held that "[s]tates may subsidize the purchase of books by students at religious schools, but they may not subsidize the purchase of globes'' (247). He traces this muddled state of affairs to the liberal tradition's inability to accommodate itself to the deep passions that are intrinsic to the genuinely religious, an understanding that the republican tradition readily grasps. He identifies two principles that he sees underlying contemporary Supreme Court decisions. The first is the reduction of religious belief to ordinary free speech protections, with no additional consideration of its particular religious character. The second is the marginality principle, under which religion is protected as long as such protection has no social consequences. Tushnet undertakes to reconstitute the law of religion in a way that will support religious belief and yet fit, albeit uncomfortably, within the liberal tradition (248–49).[52] He extols the characteristics of solidarity and mutual action he sees arising within religious groups as akin to the republican tradition's dedication to the public interest. Religious groups, not having the coercive character of civil society, teach valuable lessons of accommodating private interests to the public interest. Tushnet sees the individualistic root of liberalism as alien to genuine religion in a way that the premises of the republican tradition are not.

His solution to the problem of school prayer draws on his understanding of civic republicanism. Stated simply, he asks for "mutual forbearance'' from litigants rather than their bringing the constitutional challenges they might, strictly speaking, be entitled to.[53] For example, in *Engel v. Vitale*,[54] those authorizing the school prayer might, out of respect for the totality of the community, have foregone the use of the prayer; likewise, those who found the prayer offensive "might have exercised a wise discretion to for[e]go the constitutional challenge they were in a strict sense entitled to bring. . . . [Citizens] might conclude that civic actions that generate intense hostility are unlikely to advance the public good and forbear from taking them."[55] At the practical level, one difficulty with his solution of mutual forbearance and civic republicanism is that only a single recalcitrant party is required to convert mutual forbearance to litigation. If brought to the Court, it seems unlikely that even the most clever Court can dodge such decisions without, finally, taking the arguments to the level of constitutional principle and resolving them.

At bottom, Tushnet seems to long for a community very different from the secular state we now live in. If he achieved his aim of such a community where religious issues are concerned, it is clear that he would also advocate the expansion of the community into a utopian socialist community in which diverse interests and views would emerge into his common vision of the public good. It is not surprising that his vision of a community, rather than a principled analysis of the religion clauses, guides his resolution of church and state issues.

THE CONSTITUTION OF THE MARKET. Tushnet sees contemporary constitutional law in the areas of regulation of campaign finance, commercial speech, and pornography as resting on a judicial preference for "instrumental rationality." He defines instrumental rationality as the means members of a pluralist society use to accomplish their private goals. In other words, people arrive at their goals privately, then determine (through instrumental rationality) how best to achieve their goals.[56]

Tushnet begins with the premise that regulation of campaign finance, commercial speech, and pornography promotes republican values through the creation of a more informed and rational electorate than would result from no regulation. He believes this view is doomed to failure because the liberal tradition—more specifically, the attachment to the marketplace of ideas—has eroded republicanism. But at a more fundamental level, he believes the republican tradition's theory of instrumental rationality, and the view that social institutions must be arranged to encourage its development, is simply flawed. He attempts to prove this through his examination of the above-mentioned areas of regulation and the constitutional doctrine that justifies it.[57]

Tushnet's treatment of thirty-second political commercials exemplifies his argument. Regulation of political expenditures is justified on the grounds that such expenditures lead to a type of advertising that distracts the voters from the merits of political issues through appeal to an emotional response rather than a rational one. Restriction of such expenditures would make it more likely that electoral responses would focus on the merits of political issues rather than on superficial emotional responses. He questions this argument based on his understanding of the nature of politics. Politics has traditionally used nonrational methods to advance rational goals.[58] But his fundamental critique of "instrumental rationality" as a defense of such regulation is that such "reforms are the products of the system that we are attempting to reform, and . . . this gives the reforms a deep orientation toward protecting incumbents and other aspects of the status quo."[59]

Tushnet undertakes an extensive analysis of rationality and the regulation of pornography, concentrating on the feminist arguments supporting such regulation, and concludes that regulation cannot be justified. The harms identified in these arguments include those associated with the women who participate in pornographic productions, the harm that comes from violence against women, and the subordination of women in society that results from pornography. Pornography is asserted to have a causal relationship to each of these harms. Tushnet believes such a connection should be susceptible to social scientific proofs that rely on instrumental rationality. Another strand of the feminist argument eschews causation and views pornography, by definition, as the subordination of women.[60] This strand of the argument rests on noncognitive or nonrational deliberative capacities rather than instrumental rationality and posits the view "that pornography persuades men to subordinate women." Tushnet argues that this objectification and subordination of women is an imagery that appeals to noncognitive or nonrational capacities. In this respect, "pornography is itself an argument."[61]

This poses a dilemma for feminist arguments, for in his judgment, "the feminist arguments begin by understanding the importance of nonrational capacities and by challenging the priority our culture gives to what it defines as rationality, but they end by relying on that priority."[62] Although constitutional argument elevates instrumental rationality as a preferred method of discourse, "the feminist antipornography argument rests on the view that instrumental rationality is not a favored mode of discourse," a position supporting Tushnet's own view that "the law of free expression favors one of many possible ways of coming to understand the world." In fact, he believes:

> The feminist argument against pornography seems to create a strong prima facie case *against* the constitutionality of regulating it. That argument is that pornography is itself an argument, appealing to noncognitive capacities, for a particular arrangement of power in society. Because politics involves the distribution of power, it looks like pornography is a political argument. . . . Political arguments are usually thought of as the kind of

thing that deserves the highest degree of protection under the first amendment.[63]

Issues such as pornography and campaign finance reveal problems that Tushnet sees as extraordinarily important to an analysis of instrumental rationality, the cognitive process, and constitutional law. He goes to particular lengths to reveal the shortcomings of instrumental rationality in the area of regulation of pornography, and he believes that it falls short as a justification for regulation. But at a more fundamental level, he expresses skepticism about the possibility of reform through regulation, since "efforts to regulate each type of speech are designed to reform the very system of rationality that produced both the speech and the regulatory urges."[64] His analysis of regulation of campaign finance and pornography is cut from the same cloth as his overall critique of constitutional theories. He believes that the theory of instrumental rationality and the First Amendment doctrines derived from it do not sufficiently limit the judiciary.[65]

In the case of pornography, as in much of his analysis, Tushnet strives to disprove too much. He criticizes the attempt to regulate pornography in the context of the feminist critique of pornography, not within a broader context of civil or decent social relations. Insofar as he considers the civic republicanism rationale for regulation, he rejects it as inconsistent with the feminist argument that pornography appeals to noncognitive or irrational deliberation in its "noncognitive argument" that women are subordinate members of the political order.

One might imagine that, according to Tushnet's analysis, the only way to combat the "argument" made by pornography would be to produce pornography that makes a counter "argument" that women are not subordinate. But an important justification for regulation of pornography remains: it is beyond constitutional protection because it appeals to the prurient interest; is patently offensive to contemporary community standards; lacks serious literary, artistic, or scientific value; and is not rational discourse.[66] The rather carefully formulated constitutional standards, which limit the range of materials that can be regulated, put tolerably precise constraints on judges and at the same time limit what state and national legislatures can regulate.

Although Tushnet longs for civic republicanism, he does not acknowledge the argument that the very things that make us a people are the principles expounded in the Declaration of Independence and given reality in the Constitution. It remains to be seen whether a Constitution that protects the type of "noncognitive argument" Tushnet sees exhibited in pornography is consistent with even the minimal standards of community Tushnet longs for—in this case, the self-evident truth of equality. At a more fundamental level, he is unwilling to acknowledge the role law plays in the elevation and civilization of human beings. One could understand this more easily if he were simply willing to dismiss community or civilization as indefensible according to his own standards of judgment. He is unwilling to make judgments about better and worse, about the role of law in civil society, or about what constitutes civilization. Yet he desires civic republicanism, or a revisionist civic republicanism, as the basis for the new social order he envisions. Tushnet is unwilling to acknowledge principles in the Declaration, in the Constitution, or in constitutional adjudication; his premise that "critique is all there is" debunks any acknowledged theory.[67]

Tushnet's only defense of this new social order is his own noncognitive or intuitive preference, perhaps the result of his own "noncognitive deliberation," whatever this term means. One is led to the conclusion that noncognitive deliberation is simply a smoke screen to describe irrational impulses or passions. It is unclear why we should take Tushnet's noncognitive deliberation with any seriousness; he asks us to substitute this noncognitive deliberation for a Constitution that has endured for two centuries and for the theory of republican government underlying it. He, and the school of critical legal studies he represents, asks us to substitute for rational deliberation his own subjective noncognitive deliberation, all in the context of a premise that "critique is all there is." The question we must raise is why take his critique based on noncognitive deliberation with any seriousness. Such impulses remind us of Hobbes's state of nature, where the human condition is the war of all against all.[68] It is through reason and civil society that we escape this undesirable condition. Tushnet dismisses the enterprise of using reason to rise above the defects of the state of nature through his radical critique of reason.

One may properly question the concept of "instrumental rationality" as resting on a premise of Hobbes or Locke that denies our capacity to reason about the objects of our desires, as opposed to how best to realize these desires. But this is not Tushnet's objection. He goes one step further than Hobbes or Locke and would substitute noncognitive deliberation for the reason they see as the means to avoid violent death and achieve self-preservation. This is the political philosophy of Hobbes and Locke with a vengeance. Whereas they saw reason as a means to achieve the elemental objects of human nature, Tushnet denies even this role for reason. In so doing, he destroys the justification for civil society as derived from the law of nature and the Declaration.

In discussing instrumental rationality, Tushnet describes it as a means individuals use to achieve their private goals through the political process, a process that consists of social institutions that aggregate the preferences of individuals. That is, people participate in politics to accomplish their private goals.[69] Tushnet longs for a "society as commonwealth, inhabited by citizens who seek to promote the common good rather than individual interests."[70]

The formulation in *The Federalist* is much more sensible. Rather than juxtaposing public and private interests as simply irreconcilable, it explicates a system consistent with our nature that recognizes private interest, passions, and faction and achieves a tolerable approximation of the common good through a system that often rests on private interests. *The Federalist* explains the accommodation of passions, impulses, and noncognitive deliberation through a Constitution that takes these factors into account and results in an approximation of reason and justice through its institutions and structure. Tushnet, however, wants to elevate noncognitive deliberation to the level of rational discourse. Does anyone seriously believe that noncognitive deliberation such as that described in Tushnet's discussion of pornography deserves the same support or protection as a serious discourse on politics or a debate between presidential candidates or the arguments made in political writings such as *The Federalist?*

Tushnet's observation that pornography and some campaign activities appeal to impulse and passion rather than to our rational faculties is not a novel one. He seems, however, to elevate impulse and passion to the level of reason in terms of the enjoyment of constitutional protections and thereby demonstrates that, once again, any constitutional theory that attempts to distinguish impulse or passion (or, to use his euphemism, "imagery") from reason is destined to failure. Contrast this with the political theory of *The Federalist,* which recognizes the problem of impulse and passion as having to be subordinated and controlled through government: "As long as the reason of man continues fallible, and he is at liberty to exercise it, different opinions will be formed. As long as the connection subsists between his reason and his self-love, his opinions and his passions will have a reciprocal influence on each other; and the former will be objects to which the latter will attach themselves."[71] Or, at another point: "Why has government been instituted at all? Because the passions of men will not conform to the dictates of reason and justice, without constraint."[72] Finally: "But it is the reason, alone, of the public, that ought to control and regulate the government. The passions ought to be controlled and regulated by the government."[73]

Tushnet offers no solution to the regulation of pornography; nor does he offer any alternative constitutional theory to replace those he "trashes." In his words: "Critique is all there is."[74] In the revisionist civic republicanism he halfheartedly supports, he suggests a fundamental revision of society: "a revitalized federalism demands expansion of 'new property' entitlements, development of the idea that the government must be the employer of last resort, creation of tenure in 'private' employment, and the like."[75] Such changes would, through decentralization, open the way for "consensus/unanimity in decision making." He sets forth a vision of a political life built on "warmth, love, and connectedness" as the true nerve of civic republicanism that holds promise for a new politics, one in which conflict resolution through noncognitive deliberation plays an important role. Instead of a constitution, we might have a document that "would not be a set of legal rules that were said to determine anything. It would contain a bunch of rules of thumb that experience had proven to be useful. Their utility in any new circumstances would be open to challenge, and nothing about the fact that they were written down would affect decisions to follow them under new circumstances."[76]

In the end, Tushnet believes his vision will not be realized. Neither the civic republican tradition, which emphasizes "love and connectedness," nor the liberal tradition, which emphasizes "threat, anger and autonomy," can accommodate to the other. But is there not a deeper reason that Tushnet's vision will not be realized? This vision is based not on reason but on his own subjective or "noncognitive" preference. Thus, he is right in believing that this vision will not be widely shared by the democracy that must implement it. Tushnet envisions even more than majority implementation of his vision. He longs for consensus, a consensus that he suggests is impeded by "the predominant role that instrumental rationality has come to play in constituting our society." He prefers conflict resolution through "noncognitive deliberative capacities."[77] *The Federalist* precisely summarizes Tushnet's vision: "Theoretic politicians . . . have erroneously supposed that by reducing mankind to a perfect equality in their political rights, they would, at the same time, be perfectly equalized and assimilated in their possessions, their opinions, and their passions."[78]

Conclusion

Tushnet dismisses *The Federalist* and its critique of his vision: "Thus, the interpretive project of *The Federalist,* and with it *The Federalist*'s defense of judicial review, cannot be sustained."[79] He sees the vision of *The Federalist* as "ultimately flawed" and any reliance on its theory of constitutional interpretation as "futile at best."[80] His dismissal of *The Federalist,* an authoritative commentary on the Constitution, is archetypal of his dismissal of constitutional theory generally.

The root of his critique of *The Federalist* is the same as that of his critique of reason generally. There is no real or "plain meaning" of the Constitution: "every meaning available to people who speak the language *is* a plain meaning."[81] But even more importantly, Tushnet believes that the system of constitutional adjudication consists of "misguided efforts to translate matters of legal importance into the unsuitable framework of language"; although these legal matters are beyond our capacity to understand through reason and language, perhaps these things "can be apprehended in other ways, by an esthetic understanding of rhetorical or visual form, for example."[82] In discrediting the view that there is a real or "plain meaning" of the Constitution, Tushnet dismisses the argument that even the mathematical provisions of the Constitution have a plain meaning as being true only because "as a matter of contingent historical fact, people have chosen not to raise disputes over language meaning" where these issues are concerned.[83] That is, we have not yet reached a point in history where society's questions of meaning related to religion, government, and language have reached the realm of mathematics. It seems inevitable that we will reach such a point if the premises of the CLS movement become widespread, however. Thus, even the clearest mathematical provisions of the Constitution will be without any sensible meaning.

The Federalist recognizes the difficulty of achieving government based on reason:

> The reason of man, like man himself, is timid and cautious when left alone, and acquires firmness and confidence in proportion to the number with which it is associated. When the examples which fortify opinion are *ancient* as well as *numerous,* they are known to have a double effect. In a nation of philosophers, this consideration ought to be disregarded. A reverence for the laws would be sufficiently inculcated by the voice of an enlightened reason. But a nation of philosophers is as little to be expected as the philosophical race of kings wished for by Plato. And in every other nation, the most rational government will not find it a superfluous advantage to have the prejudices of the community on its side. The danger of disturbing the public tranquillity by interesting too strongly the public passions, is a still more serious objection against a frequent reference of constitutional questions to the decision of the whole society. Notwithstanding the success which has attended the revisions of our established forms of government, and which does so much honor to the virtue and intelligence of the people of America, it must be confessed that the experiments are of too ticklish a nature to be unnecessarily multiplied.[84]

One answer to the problem raised in this passage, and to the questions raised by Tushnet, is simply to throw up one's hands in despair over who is to say what is just, what individual rights are, how we should govern ourselves, and how we should construct our laws. This seems to be Tushnet's response; as a consequence, he states, "[c]ritical legal studies does not have a positive program."[85] *The Federalist* recognizes the difficulty of these questions, but it structures a government that harnesses passions and interests in a complex system aimed toward reason and justice: "Justice is the end of government. It is the end of civil society. It ever has been and ever will be pursued until it be obtained, or until liberty be lost in the pursuit."[86] Questions of justice, government, and law simply will not go away, despite Tushnet's conclusion that "critique is all there is."[87] Nor is there evidence that they can be resolved by relying on impulse, feeling, or passion (what Tushnet calls "noncognitive deliberation"); by reducing the Constitution to "a bunch of legal rules of thumb";[88] or by asserting that constitutional adjudication consists of "misguided efforts to translate matters of legal importance into the unsuitable framework of language."[89] Tushnet attempts to relate his vision of American politics to the tradition of civic republicanism. But his efforts are not persuasive to those who have any clear understanding of the Anti-Federalists. The Anti-Federalists were not opposed to individual rights in the name of social good. They simply had a different conception than did the victorious Federalists of how best to secure liberty. Although one would have great difficulty fitting the Anti-Federalists into Tushnet's view of language, the Constitution as rules of thumb, or noncognitive deliberation, Tushnet's desire for a consensus in political decision making may have some roots in Anti-Federalist thought:

> The framers of the Articles of Confederation, misled by the vigor and good sense displayed by the people during the war, made the "amiable mistake" of thinking that the Americans needed no government, "that the people of America only required to know what ought to be done to do it." The Americans are, however, like other men, which is to say that they cannot be relied on to govern themselves voluntarily. The Anti-Federalists' fondness for the small republic and their concern with the inculcation of civic virtue amounted to an attempt to push aside this harsh truth.[90]

Tushnet relegates the founding theory, *The Federalist,* and the Constitution to relics of a bygone era that we cannot comprehend. There are great differences between his own views and those of the civic republicanism he relies on—a reliance stemming, perhaps, from rhetorical motives. Tushnet turns civic virtue—originally based on small republican government, individual rights, and the holding of property—into his vision of socialism. His transmogrified version of civic republicanism bears little likeness to the historical source from which he purports to derive it. His sketchy vision may be traced to some aspects of Anti-Federalist thought insofar as he seems to desire a government more like that of the Articles of Confederation than the one constituted in 1787. But these arguments were disposed of during the Constitutional Convention and ratification process, and the resulting large commercial republic was established. Thus, in certain respects, Tushnet's yearning is for a form of government (or lack thereof) that the American people decided against two hundred years ago.

Tushnet's fundamental complaint is that the structures of legal formalism and constitutionalism are obstacles to the vision he has for American society. He seems to believe that without the constraints of a strong national government, a Constitution, and the mechanisms that make up our governing theory, the American people will do the right thing—that is, what Tushnet envisions as justice. Ironically, the very questions he addresses in his writing and, more importantly, the questions at the center of contemporary politics are those derived from the Declaration and the Constitution: questions of equality, rights, consent of the governed, and limited government. Questions of racial injustice, rights of the accused, the death penalty, rights to welfare benefits, and privacy are important objects of constitutional adjudication. Each of these contended rights can be traced to the Declaration and is adjudicated through the Constitution and laws. One could say that our political life is a continuing discourse on the actualization of the principles of the Declaration and the law of the Constitution. Much progress in American political life in these and other areas is the result of the actualization of the Declaration's principles and application of the law of the Constitution to contemporary circumstances. Although the Constitution is not a "pharmacopoeia"[91] that sets forth clear grounds for decisions the Court must make in adjudicating cases, it structures the government and political power and sets aside some liberties in its body, the Bill of Rights, and subsequent amendments.

Tushnet's real objection seems to be with the way in which the Constitution and American politics frame the issues about which he is concerned. He has more faith in a goodness welling up from the people outside the framework of the Constitution than he has in the Constitution and its theory framing and informing issues as the political order attempts to approximate justice. We may respond to Tushnet's conclusion by saying that "politics is the art of the best possible," and limited government emanating from the principles of the Declaration and the law of the Constitution may be the best a democracy can do. The utopianism of Tushnet and other CLS scholars and their ultimate conclusion that "critique is all there is" stand in sharp contrast to the Constitution's sober understanding of human limitations and its mechanisms for lawful change and improvement through properly constituted majority rule.

Feminism Unmodified as a Theory of the State: Catharine MacKinnon

Catharine MacKinnon is an outspoken and visible proponent of feminist jurisprudence. She represents feminist jurisprudence at its foundations, and, therefore, my analysis of her is justified not only by the fact that she is well-known but also by the fact that she presents feminist jurisprudence unmodified. MacKinnon reveals her feminism unmodified in her argument that the Constitution, American law, and society embody a system of male domination in a hierarchy that subordinates women. Her project for reform uses the standard of "subordination of women" in analyzing the areas of law she regards as most important. I focus on her proposed reforms in the areas of pornography and rape which are central to her work. Through her lens of "subordination," she trumps other constitutional considerations, such as First Amendment and due process principles, and recommends dramatic incursions into the private realm. Her emphasis on gender and subordination leads her to deny that there are objective standards or abstract principles and reduces her understanding to one based on women's own terms and on women's concrete experience. She denies the objectivity or neutrality of law and engages in special pleading for law to embody women's point of view. She justifies this on the ground that existing law is special pleading for men.

In spite of her disavowal of abstract principles and truth, her entire enterprise rests on an assumption that there is such a thing as justice or equality. A sense of injustice pervades her work. But her objections to gender subordination are legitimate only insofar as subordination is intrinsically wrong. The problem or the injustice is not gender, it is subordination. In her work, however, truth is gender-relative and is based on the concrete experience of women. Although her work cries injustice, her own premises deny any objective ground for determining what justice is and what part equality plays in it. She dismisses abstractions and rights, including the right to equality, as male constructs and thereby undermines her own arguments, which must ultimately rest on equality and justice. This is a basic epistemological difficulty that characterizes her entire work. Her treatment of pornography, rape, the judiciary, and the Constitution reduces all these matters to gender and rejects considerations of objectivity, neutrality, or nature.

MacKinnon's "subordination" rationale rests on a view of politics as power and denies the existence of abstractions or neutral principles. Her subordination rationale for that regulation of pornography in some respects reaches a defensible result, but she rejects important justifications for such regulation that are sounder and would not result in the sweeping potential for undermining First Amendment principles of free speech and free press. Her proposed reforms of rape law would seriously erode due process considerations that apply to all criminal proceedings. But most fundamentally, by disavowing neutral principles such as equality and rights, she undermines her legitimacy in arguing for reforms to correct gender inequality. Her rejection of moral claims and neutral principles in favor of "special pleading" reduces politics to power. Comprehensive claims of principle—in this case, equality—are sacrificed to individual and group claims to power. This view reduces politics to a contest over power and ultimately to a war of all against all, without guidance of the abstract principles of justice, equality, or rights—principles that apply to all individuals and that justify government.

The Constitution as a Reflection of the Social Subordination of Women

MacKinnon focuses on social theory in explaining the pervasive subordination of women that is central to her work. Because of her conviction that law and the Constitution are primarily effects rather than causes, she directs her analysis at the underlying social conditions she sees as determinative rather than at the legal structures and the Constitution, which she sees as derivative. She clarifies her argument in her treatment of force, legitimacy, and law:

> In liberal regimes, law is a particularly potent source and badge of legitimacy, and site and cloak of force. The force underpins the legitimacy as the legitimacy conceals the force. When life becomes law in such a system, the transformation is both formal and substantive. It reenters life marked by power.
>
> In male supremacist societies, the male standpoint dominates civil society in the form of the objective standard—that standpoint which, because it dominates in the world, does not appear to function as a standpoint at all. Under its aegis, men dominate women and children, three-quarters of the world. Family and kinship rules and sexual mores guarantee reproductive ownership and sexual access and control to men as a group. Hierarchies among men are ordered on the basis of race and class, stratifying women as well. The state incorporates these facts of social power in and as law. Two things happen: law becomes legitimate, and social dominance becomes invisible. Liberal legalism is thus a medium for making male dominance both invisible and legitimate by adopting the male point of view in law at the same time as it enforces that view on society.[92]

MacKinnon sees the Constitution as a force for legitimizing a hierarchy that subordinates women. The Constitution and law are formed from the male standpoint and shroud the subordination of women under the cloak of objectivity, that is, legalism and constitutionalism. Through this legitimacy and the institutionalizing of dominance through Constitution and law, the social dominance of women becomes invisible. The law and the Constitution are created by men from their own viewpoint. *"Power to create the world from one's point of view is power in its male form."*[93] Sexism is "not merely legal error—a few mistakes made at the margins of doctrine—but [is] an integral part of an entire social system geared for the advantage of one sex at the expense of the other."[94] Through law, this male dominance is disguised as a feature of the Constitution, of law, and of life rather than being shown as what it is, "a one-sided construct imposed by force for the advantage of a dominant group."[95] She argues that the Constitution and law legitimize a male-dominant view of life, which becomes the status quo, assumes the legitimacy of subordination of women, and, through doctrines of liberal democracy, leaves a male-dominated private sphere free from government interference. The result is the perpetuation of male-dominated society and the legitimation of this domination in the private sphere.

MacKinnon's "dominance" approach to feminist legal theory is based on the social subordination of women. Her position departs from the "difference" approach associated with the proposed Equal Rights Amendment, which argues for women's competition on equal terms with men in the public arena and strives for women's legal entitlement to compete equally with men, for example, for jobs. MacKinnon's substitute for the proposed Equal Rights Amendment reads: "the subordination of women to men is hereby abolished."[96] Her proposal would eliminate the need to establish state action in order to challenge actions of subordination. The goal of the "difference" approach is to eliminate second-class citizenship for women. MacKinnon would, among other things, extend her remedies to the private realm by allowing government action designed to eliminate subordination whether or not there is state action involved in the domination she is trying to eliminate.[97] In spite of a diversity of feminist perspectives, MacKinnon speaks of her view as "the feminist view"[98] and ignores other feminist views with which she disagrees.

For MacKinnon, the fundamental problem of gender inequality is not that of "arbitrary or irrational differentiation" but the subordination of women in society. This subordination results not from different treatment of those similarly situated but from men's dominance of women, primarily through sexual practices. Pornography, rape, and prostitution are visible examples of the widespread subordination of women. The centerpiece of MacKinnon's theory is her emphasis on sexuality and sexual practices as the cause of gender inequality:[99] "I think the fatal error of the legal arm of feminism has been its failure to understand that the mainspring of sex inequality is misogyny and the mainspring of misogyny is sexual sadism. The misogyny of liberal legalism included."[100]

Sexuality occupies the same place in MacKinnon's analysis as work does in Marx's: "that which is most one's own" is that which is "most taken away." MacKinnon's feminism shares with Marxism the view that its premise and theory explain the totality of social relations. Sexuality is, therefore, not a "natural essence" but is "*created* by [hierarchical] social relations."[101] MacKinnon sees current sexual practices as instruments of male domination and sees women as being defined by "what turns men on."[102] One has difficulty attributing any substantial meaning to sexuality in MacKinnon's work, since she defines it in terms of what it does, not what it is. She defines sexuality as "a social process that eroticizes dominance and submission and that creates men and women as the social creatures as we know them."[103] The male viewpoint constructs both social life and knowledge about it.[104] MacKinnon points to additional difficulties, which raise fundamental problems for her theory. Male domination is "metaphysically nearly perfect,"[105] and the resulting alienation of women is unknown because it is so pervasive and profound. Male power exists in duality, "as total on one side and a delusion on the other." Women "freely" choose women's roles because they have little choice. Because women "freely" choose women's roles, "the reality of women's oppression is, finally, neither demonstrable nor refutable empirically."[106] Women's condition, MacKinnon argues, raises the problem of "how the object can know herself as such" or "how the alienated can know its own alienation." This, in turn, poses the problem of feminism's account of women's consciousness. How can women, as created, "thingified in the head," complicit in the body, see their condition as such?[107]

MacKinnon regards the subordination of women as beyond the reach of objective or empirical observation and inquiry. According to her premise, the liberal device of laws to correct injustice or further the equality of women is bogus because such laws result from the very system that male dominance created. In the face of an objective determination that women have made gains in employment opportunities prompted in part by law, she would respond that this success is measured by a male standard in which women attempt to fit into a male world. Yet if a woman chooses to devote her time and energy to rearing a family and forming the character of children, as opposed to being a real estate salesperson, MacKinnon argues that this choice is dictated by the male social structure and is not really a free choice among competing views of what is valuable and fulfilling. According to her own unidimensional premise, the "free choice" she refers to is not a free choice at all. She makes this clear in her assertion that because of the pervasiveness of male domination, women are not able to see it. This raises the question of how MacKinnon can see this male domination if, as she claims, it is completely pervasive. She argues that women cannot know what sexual equality would be because they have not experienced it. Yet she argues that through their concrete reality, women "know inequality because they have lived it, so they know what removing barriers to equality would be."[108] MacKinnon has apparently escaped the pervasiveness of male domination and knows domination when she sees it—an approach feminists ridicule as a determinative test or definition of pornography.[109] Such a subjective test perplexes those who see law as expressing standards that can be shared by other jurists and communicated to others. Without such standards or objective tests, even those judges most sympathetic to feminist claims in areas such as pornography may come to very different conclusions because of the subjectivity of their judgments and the rejection of overarching principles.

If equality is simply an abstraction, a bogus male abstraction, one has difficulty understanding the basis of MacKinnon's subjective complaint of male domination. Absent this abstraction of equality, what ground is there for arguing domination as an objectionable feature of social and political life? MacKinnon defines equality "on women's own terms and in terms of women's concrete experience,"[110] a definition that presumably rescues it from the defects of the bogus male abstraction by substituting a concrete, experiential meaning. But if one accepts equality as a necessary cornerstone to her argument, then the doctrine of rights, including a right to equality, and limited government follow. This right applies to all human beings. MacKinnon argues that her definition of equality is legitimate. She grants that it is not neutral because it embodies "women's point of view," but she responds that current law is from "the male point of view."[111] Absent an abstract right to equality, the law becomes a vehicle for a struggle of one gender against the other in which perspective and interest define justice. MacKinnon's theory leads to naked self-interest as the beginning and end of public law and policy. Human qualities and standards are subordinated to gender standards, and there is no objective truth according to her theory. Thus, there is nothing in her theory to prevent any group from following her lead in legitimizing its claims to justice and equal treatment. Her theory reduces to a war of all against all, based simply on perspective and interest. Because she disavows truth, power replaces both the dialogue over justice and the place of equality in justice. The foundations of her argument—experience and feeling—are ones that liberal democracy accommodates through equality and majority rule and elevates and refines through a constitutional system of separated powers and resolution of competing interests and views.[112]

MacKinnon disavows abstract principles and natural essences and argues for a nearly absolute subjectivity. But her proposed reforms create a system that would result in a kind of subjective totalitarianism that rejects liberal democracy and its principles of separation of powers, consent of the governed, constitutional limitations, and the private realm. She argues that these principles are simply a result of the male-dominated system that has formed both society and our knowledge of this system. Her system rejects any theory of knowledge and substitutes for it her own subjective feeling and experience, which she would elevate to the ruling premise of government and society. She shares with Marx and Freud an attempt to explain the complexity and resolution of competing goods with a reductionism that constructs a complete social theory from one part of reality.

A more persuasive rationale for assessing equality claims relative to law and public policy arises from the idea or abstraction of equality, which has served as a guidepost of American life since Jefferson's Declaration borrowed this idea from John Locke. Despite her protestations to the contrary, MacKinnon's critique of male dominance gains its legitimacy from the fact that the abstraction of equality is an important element of justice. Much of her argument's appeal results not only from equality's claim being rooted in justice but also from the centrality of equality in our political and social history. The abstraction of equality is not simply a male construct or the result of male domination, as MacKinnon argues. Equality forms the very fountainhead of her argument. This abstract principle is difficult to actualize, and much of our political life has been committed to realizing it. But the demand for equality arises out of this abstract principle, the same principle that informs our attempts to actualize it in the name of justice. This abstract principle informs much of our political discourse, including that of MacKinnon. One may condemn subordination and yet maintain respect for the abstract principle that allows us to critique practice on the basis of theory and to strive for a more equal and just political order. In fact, acceptance of the abstract principle of equality is necessary to justify the condemnation. Equality is both an abstraction and a fundamental principle, and it was most persuasively articulated in the theory of Locke and in Jefferson's Declaration. Equality derives its truth not from the fact that it was articulated in these works by men but because it is just. As an abstract concept that includes but is not limited to gender, it remains the most powerful foundation of the claim men and women have to equality, including the feminist claim on behalf of women.

The Court as a Reflection of Male Domination

MacKinnon argues that the Constitution reflects the pervasive social problem of male domination and social hierarchy. Unlike many constitutional commentators, she does not pin her hopes for reform on a strong judiciary. She is critical of the judiciary:

> From a feminist perspective, male supremacist jurisprudence erects qualities valued from the male point of view as standards for the proper and actual relation between life and law. Examples include standards for scope of judicial review, norms of judicial restraint, reliance on precedent, separation of powers, and the division between public and private law. Substantive doctrines like standing, justiciability, and state action adopt the same stance. Those with power in civil society, not women, design its norms and institutions, which become the status quo. Those with power, not usually women, write constitutions, which become law's highest standards. Those with power in political systems that women did not design and from which women have been excluded write legislation which sets ruling values. Then, jurisprudentially, judicial review is said to go beyond its proper scope—to delegitimate courts and the rule of law itself—when legal questions are not confined to assessing the formal correspondence between legislation and the constitution, or legislation and social reality, but

scrutinize the underlying substance. . . . Doctrines of standing suggest that because women's deepest injuries are shared in some way by most or all women, no individual woman is differentially injured enough to be able to sue for women's deepest injuries.[113]

Viewed from MacKinnon's perspective, the characteristics of judicial power (the scope of judicial review, norms of restraint, precedent, separation of powers, the division between public and private law, and the doctrines of standing, justiciability, and state action) result from a male supremacist jurisprudence and prevent the judiciary from eliminating male domination. This is a peculiar interpretation of the character of the judicial power. The characteristics she speaks of result from an attempt to accommodate the uneasy tension between judicial review, constitutional interpretation, and democracy and are necessary to maintain a democratic political order and prevent judicial domination. The alternative explanation for these traditional characteristics of the judicial power is the recognition by judges and others that an unrestrained judicial power is dangerous to democracy. These devices are designed to sustain democracy and to maintain a system of separated powers with the knowledge that in this political order, the final social power rests with majorities. It is unclear that even an unrestrained judiciary would embrace and effect MacKinnon's agenda.

Because MacKinnon regards the judiciary as hopelessly captured by characteristics of male hierarchy, she does not rely on it as the vehicle for her reforms. If she could transform the judiciary, she would have it embody her own view of justice and impose that view on the political order. She would have the judiciary abandon those characteristics that distinguish it from the legislative power, disregard the rule of law, erode the separation of powers and its role for the judiciary, and use its power to abandon the distinction between private and public actions. She rejects the constitutional role of the judiciary in deference to her agenda. But if the judiciary adopted her agenda and abandoned the restraints on judicial power, she would readily embrace it as the best alternative available. In this regard, she is like those commentators who criticize the old Courts that protected slavery and stood in the way of the New Deal but who embrace the Court when it advances civil liberties as these commentators understand them. MacKinnon shares with them the defect of basing their judgment of a proper judicial role on whether they agree with the substance of the judiciary's rulings rather than on a thoughtful analysis of the proper role of the judiciary in democracy. The judiciary MacKinnon desires would destroy the democratic character of government. The judicial role she rejects retains some of the characteristics that maintain democratic rule and the separation of powers.

MacKinnon seems to have no alternative but to rely on social rather than judicial reform. But if she were to succeed in her social reform, would she not want the judiciary to utilize the traditional axioms of judicial restraint in determining whether these reforms were constitutional? Her project for social reform is itself problematic since it rests on concrete experience, is designed to end an alienation that is unknowable because of its pervasiveness, and is therefore not widely shared even among women. It is difficult to see success for her project, dependent as it is on a nonabstract and substantive view that is difficult to communicate to a majority, even a majority of women.[114] An abstract theory of equality, including human beings of both genders, is a much more likely vehicle for forming majorities and communicating in a manner that is not based simply on subjective, abstract experience.

MacKinnon regards the procedural and precedential characteristics of the judiciary and constitutional law as obstacles to her reforms. This view is undoubtedly informed by the fact that the judiciary declared unconstitutional the civil rights ordinance that she and Andrea Dworkin framed, an ordinance that would have outlawed pornography as a violation of women's civil right to equality.[115] Since MacKinnon believes that the Constitution expresses both abstract principles and male hierarchy, she does not regard it as a reliable means for achieving her ends. The judiciary might uphold stricter pornography regulation, recognize sexual harassment as male domination and sex discrimination, and require funding of abortion, all of which she would applaud. But many of her proposals for reform of the private sphere seem to require executive or legislative action,[116] not to mention the overhauling of the public conception of equality as a conception shared by men and women and not reducible to the point of view of one gender or the other.

Pornography

MacKinnon sees pornography as the cornerstone of the social construction of women as objects for male pleasure: "I draw on pornography for its form and content, for the gaze that eroticizes the despised, the demeaned, the accessible, the there-to-be-used, the servile, the child-like, the passive, and the animal. *That* is the content of the sexuality that defines gender female in this culture, and the visual thingification is its method."[117] She argues that heterosexuality is simply a social construct that "institutionalizes male sexual dominance and female sexual submission."[118] By characterizing heterosexuality as "male supremacy's paradigm of sex,"[119] she divorces heterosexuality from procreation and nature and relegates heterosexuality to a social construct that is part of the overarching scheme of male dominance. Homosexuality and other nontraditional sexual unions assume a preferred position in her theory because they are not part of the pervasive social fabric of male domination, which uses heterosexual and procreative sex as an instrument of male dominance. Her theory of sexuality denies that heterosexuality has any natural roots. Her view that heterosexuality is a social construct derived from male subordination of women cannot dispose of the fundamental fact that reproduction and perpetuation of the species are heterosexual.

MacKinnon's treatment of pornography offers a specific example of her critique of abstract principles. She proceeds from the concrete facts of women's experience. Thus, her treatment of pornography is a paradigm of her general arguments about the Constitution and law. She also sees pornography as illustrating the male dominance of law and the protection of this dominance through a doctrine of privacy. She believes the presumption that this privacy is a neutral principle is mistaken because the judicial creation of a zone of privacy simply protects the domination of women by men from any governmental interference:

> [P]ornography is an industry that mass produces sexual intrusion on, access to, possession and use of women by and for men for profit. It exploits women's sexual and economic inequality for gain. It sells women to men as and for sex. It is a technologically sophisticated traffic in women. . . .
>
> When pornography and the law of pornography are investigated together, it becomes clear that pornography is to women's status, hence its critique is to feminism, as its preservation is to male supremacy in its liberal legal guise. (195)

The state, according to MacKinnon, approaches the pornography problem through the guise of regulating expression under the First Amendment. This approach is grounded in obscenity as a moral idea, one concerned with "good and evil, virtue and vice" (196). In contrast to this view, feminism is concerned "with power and powerlessness," concerns that are fundamentally political, not moral: "Obscenity conveys moral condemnation as a predicate to legal condemnation. Pornography identifies a political practice that is predicated on power and powerlessness—a practice that is, in fact, legally protected. The two concepts represent two entirely different things" (196). MacKinnon's framing of pornography regulation as an eminently practical concern rooted in consciousness of power relationships is characteristic of her view of legal and social issues generally. It explains her focus not only on pornography but also on "practical" issues of sexual harassment, abortion, and rape. Her treatment of these issues begins with the practical and, to a large degree, leaves it to the reader to construct a constitutional theory and a theory of adjudication. MacKinnon explains the reliance on the practical in her work as a response to the empty, universal abstractness of liberal theory: "Not to be emptily universal, to leave your concreteness showing, is a sin among men" (197). As a result of this abstraction in obscenity law—an abstraction based on morality from the male standpoint—"the law of obscenity reproduces the porno-graphic point of view of women on the level of constitutional jurisprudence" (197). The male view proceeds from a moral standard of male dominance "robed in gender-neutral good and evil"; the feminist view proceeds from the standard of men subordinating women (197–99). She believes that the discourse about good and evil disguises the power relationship and subordination of women, which in actuality is furthered by that discourse (200).

MacKinnon sees a fundamental conflict between the liberal view that "speech must never be sacrificed for other social goals" and her conclusion that "women do not simply have freedom of speech on a social level" (205). She acknowledges the difficulty in demonstrating that pornography silences women: "That pornography chills women's expression is difficult to demon-strate empirically because silence is not eloquent."[120] She uses Linda Mar-chiano (whose stage name is Linda Lovelace, star of the movie *Deep Throat*) as an example to support her position and asks how Marchiano, who was co-erced into making the film, could possibly remedy her situation through the exercise of speech.[121] MacKinnon's argument seems to be that pornography humiliates and frightens women into silence and makes men unable to under-stand what women say.[122] MacKinnon does not explain why Marchiano could not have reported her coercion to state and federal authorities, who were eager to prosecute obscenity cases. Nor does she explain her conclusion that all women (and men?) who perform in pornographic films do so unwillingly.[123]

MacKinnon argues that free speech is unavailable to women, allows gov-ernment to stay out of the regulation of speech, and serves the interest of males who dominate at the social level. Pornography law is simply a male-dominated law of the Constitution that protects the inequality of the status quo under the guise of liberalism, a liberalism that does not apply to the situa-tion of women. Although she admits that the constitutional definition of ob-scenity "looks neutral," this is only because the male viewpoint and social in-equality are mirrored by the state.[124] She regards pornography as the ruling ideology: "Pornography can invent women because it has the power to make its vision into reality, which then passes, objectively, for truth."[125] MacKin-non therefore devotes much of her analysis to the problem of pornography, a problem she sees as one of power relationships rather than of morality, and in which "pornography dispossesses women of the same power of which it pos-sesses men: the power of sexual, hence gender, definition."[126]

MacKinnon believes that the status of women is at stake in the pornogra-phy issue.[127] She thinks that pornography constructs who women are and most importantly, defines women as those over whom men hold power.[128] Her central concern is that women are rendered powerless, both by being overtly or covertly coerced into making pornography and by their subordina-tion in works of pornography that are viewed and accepted by others. Pornography constructs the social reality of women's subordination and determines who women can be in society—a group without power.[129] She regards moral objections to pornography as mistaken liberal concerns that divert our attention from the real issues of power and male domination.[130]

Some of MacKinnon's objections to pornography have substance. She properly recognizes that pornography is "more actlike than thoughtlike," and "[t]he fact that pornography, in a feminist view, furthers the idea of the sexual inferiority of women, a political idea, does not make the pornography itself a political idea."[131] MacKinnon disputes the idea of a distinction between being a victim of a crime and performing in pornography by arguing that in pornography, women are raped so that they can be filmed; they are not "raped by the idea" of rape.[132] She quotes with approval the admission by nude dancers that "*they* were not expressing anything" as they performed.[133] Pornography works through appeal to the genital organs rather than "through its ideas as such, at least not in the way thoughts and ideas are protected."[134] Ironically, viewing pornography through MacKinnon's equality lens gives credence to those who argue that it is political speech rather than speech without ideational content. Indeed, this is precisely the argument of Judge Easterbrook for the court of appeals in the *Hudnut* case, in which the Indianapolis pornography ordinance drafted by Andrea Dworkin and Catharine MacKinnon was declared unconstitutional. Easterbrook argued that the ordinance outlawed pictures or words on the basis of their "viewpoint," notwithstanding their literary, artistic, political, or scientific value.[135]

Some of what MacKinnon says about pornography is persuasive. Pornography is not central to the great purposes of the First Amendment, and it is difficult to see why it should enjoy the scope of protection that it has by being equated with other types of speech.[136] Although she argues that pornography "sets de facto community standards,"[137] she rejects the view that pornography should be regulated because it dehumanizes human beings.[138] By rejecting the argument that pornography dehumanizes both the audience and those performing it, and by viewing pornography regulation as an equality issue, she leaves herself open to the criticism Judge Easterbrook made in the *Hudnut* case, that materials depicting men and women as equals are legal, no matter how graphic they are. In other words, if pornography depicts male and female domination equally, it is protected by MacKinnon's equality standard, a standard she regards as being based on politics or power rather than on moral considerations.

There are difficulties with her rejection of a moral standard and her use of an "equality" standard for deciding First Amendment cases. Her standard of equality rejects unequal power and male domination. The principle of equality in the exercise of power does not reach deeply enough to rest on its own bottom. Equal power is justified only on the basis of a principle that reaches to the essential quality of human beings, an inalienable right and abstract truth that apply to both men and women. MacKinnon rejects such abstract principles. But it is precisely these inalienable rights and abstract truths that define us as human beings and that justify prohibitions on pornography because it is dehumanizing and without serious value. Pornography objectifies human beings and treats them as a sum total of their bodily parts. One need not deny the despicable character of pornography that portrays rape or other actions to argue that the essence of pornography is demeaning or dehumanizing to both men and women. This is the essence of the "dehumanizing" argument that MacKinnon rejects. In rejecting this argument, and arguing that the term " 'human being' is a social concept with many possible meanings,"[139] she undermines the ground of her own "equality" argument. Ironically, at another point in her work, she argues that pornography depicts "women as less than human."[140] Nonetheless, she rejects the "dehumanizing" rationale for pornography regulation and thereby reduces her equality argument to her own conception of what a human being is, a conception that, according to her own understanding, may not be shared by others. This raises the question of why we should take her conception any more seriously than anyone else's conception, including those who argue that there is nothing wrong with pornographic descriptions of domination because it is just another point of view.

Another difficulty with MacKinnon's "equality" argument for speech and press cases is its far-reaching, prohibitive character. Although the Indianapolis ordinance focuses on pornography, at other places in her writing she argues for regulating other forms of speech that she believes foster inequality. At one point she draws a distinction between obscenity (nudity, explicitness, and prurience) and pornography (forced sex) and remarks that "[o]bscenity as such probably does little harm."[141] At another point, she includes *Playboy's* objectification of women in her definition of pornography.[142] At yet another place, she suggests that those who oppose certain types of classroom materials should be able to suppress these materials: those who oppose materials questioning the biological equality of men and women, who oppose arguments that reports of rape are frequently fabricated, or who oppose the view that African Americans should be eliminated from some parts of the United States "should not be legally precluded from trying [to suppress such materials] on the grounds that the ideas contained in them cannot be assumed false."[143] This sweeping view would legally prohibit works such as those of Augustus Washington (an African American who advocated geographic racial segregation), Abraham Lincoln, and Stephen Douglas, as well as materials that show a concern for traditional canons of due process in rape trials and argue that a woman's allegation of rape should not be taken as dispositive. Her view might result in gutting college courses in history or American political thought and excluding *Dred Scott v. Sandford*[144] and other cases from courses in constitutional law.

Yet another difficulty with MacKinnon's work is her presumption of the pervasiveness and influence of pornography. Ronald Dworkin properly questions whether pornography is as pervasive an influence on the social view of equality as are soap operas, popular fiction, and ordinary advertising.[145] Her work frequently refers to snuff movies (movies in which a performer is murdered) to support her view of the feminist "equality" conception of free speech. One would be hard-pressed to find a defender of snuff movies (or one who has viewed such a movie), and murder remains a crime that is not dependent on MacKinnon's condemnation of it as a violation of her "equality" conception of speech and press. One may condemn much of the pornography MacKinnon properly finds objectionable without resorting to her far-reaching incursions on First Amendment freedoms.

At the heart of MacKinnon's critique of pornography and other speech that does not advance equality is her premise: "The law of equality and the law of freedom of speech are on a collision course in this country."[146] One can oppose hard-core pornography as outside First Amendment protection without resorting to the sweeping restrictions on First Amendment freedoms that MacKinnon proposes under her "equality" test. Although it may not be troublesome that her First Amendment theory would justify banning John Cleland's *Memoirs of a Woman of Pleasure,* her test might also extend to outlaw such performances as *The Merchant of Venice,* films portraying the neglect of children by professional women, or nightclub routines that parody homosexuality.[147]

Even more problematic is the collision MacKinnon posits between First Amendment freedoms and equality. Free speech and a free press rest on the proposition that everyone will have an opportunity to influence government, notwithstanding the fact that not everyone's opinion will prevail in the electoral process. As Ronald Dworkin recognizes, in the short run, African Americans and women would benefit if those citizens who have persistently expressed sexist or racist views (or views in disagreement with MacKinnon) were denied the vote or denied the freedom to voice their views. That, of course, would be unconstitutional and violate the principle of equality in a fundamental manner, as well as being foolish in the long run.[148] First Amendment freedoms both rest upon and serve the same principle of equality with which MacKinnon believes they collide. By proposing suppression of views that perpetuate inequality as she understands it, she is undermining the equality that rests at the foundation of First Amendment and other constitutional freedoms. Ironically, most gains in racial and gender equality have been furthered by the First Amendment freedoms MacKinnon would modify.

Rape

MacKinnon's treatment of rape is characterized by the same far-reaching and imprecise definitions that we saw in her proposals for regulating pornography and related materials. She objects to the standard of a woman's consent for determining whether rape has been committed. She also objects that "[l]ike heterosexuality, the crime of rape centers on penetration."[149] MacKinnon believes it is "difficult to avoid the conclusion that penetration itself is known to be a violation and that women's sexuality, our gender definition, is itself stigmatic."[150] She argues that the defect of defining rape as "violence" rather than as sex is to "affirm sex (heterosexuality) while rejecting violence (rape)."[151] Her reforms would nearly obliterate the distinction between ordinary sexual relations and rape, as evidenced by her statement that it is difficult to distinguish rape from sexual intercourse because of the "conditions of male dominance."[152] Her definition of rape is ambiguous and, as a result, far-reaching: "Women are raped by guns, age, white supremacy, the state—only derivatively by the penis."[153] Her position seems to be that any domination or unfairness in society is the equivalent of rape. One feminist reviewer observes that "[t]his would be interesting news to rape victims."[154]

MacKinnon's critique of rape law emphasizes the inadequacy of the consent defense in determining whether rape has been committed. She argues that the crime of rape is defined from the male viewpoint:

> Rape, like many crimes and torts, requires that the accused possess a criminal mind (mens rea) for his acts to be criminal. The man's mental state refers to what he actually understood at the time or to what a reasonable man should have understood under the circumstances. The problem is this: the injury of rape lies in the meaning of the act to its victims, but the standard for its criminality lies in the meaning of the same act to the assailants. Rape is only an injury from women's point of view. It is only a crime from the male point of view, explicitly including that of the accused.[155]

MacKinnon believes that whether or not a woman has been violated is legally and wrongfully determined by the man's perception of the woman's desires. Furthermore, she questions the possibility of objectively determining what actually happened in the context of the alleged rape because, in her view, the reality of what happened is "split by divergent meanings, such as those inequality produces."[156] She rejects the assumption underlying rape law "that a single, objective state of affairs existed, one which merely needs to be determined by evidence,"[157] and argues that the outcome to this question is gender-determined. Thus, under her premise of sexual inequality, "whether a contested interaction is rape comes down to whose [men's or women's] meaning wins." Her suggested alternative is to view rape from the perspective of "the *meaning* of the act from women's point of view." From MacKinnon's perspective, "consent is a communication under conditions of inequality," and it does not communicate "what the woman actually wanted."[158]

In summary, MacKinnon believes that rape law purports to be objective, but through its abstractions, it obscures the fact that it reflects the male hierarchy of the social system. This is reflected in the centrality of consent in rape law, the use of prior social interaction as an indicator of consent, and the minimization of the victim's perspective and maximization of the perpetrator's perspective.[159]

MacKinnon's primary objection to current rape law is its feigned objectivity and abstraction, which she believes mask the male domination at the foundation of this law. Ironically, at one level, the similarities she sees between ordinary sexual relations and rape weaken her case by pointing to the difficulties of making a legal determination of when rape has actually occurred.

MacKinnon's remedy is to base rape law on the woman's perspective and thereby make possible more rape convictions. MacKinnon, of course, did not discover the fact that discerning the truth in rape cases is very difficult. Most often it is a matter of weighing a woman's word against a man's word as to what transpired. The problem of women falsely charging men with rape does not present an obstacle to MacKinnon's views. In fact, she suggests restricting the freedom to teach from materials that assert "that reports of rape are routinely fabricated."[160] Evidence indicates that rape reports are not *routinely* fabricated, but to prevent such views from being taught and considered in the context of resolving the difficulties presented by rape charges is an unacceptable limitation on free speech. Women have suffered discrimination. Rape victims clearly suffer violence and injury of a profound nature. But the fact remains that both men and women are susceptible to self-deception, one of the factors that makes discerning the truth in rape cases so difficult. A history of discrimination does not free one from ordinary human limitations, even though the victim may have suffered from general social and political injustice. Judgments regarding who is a victim require recourse to standards of neutrality, objectivity, and justice.

MacKinnon argues that if a woman feels it is rape, it is rape. Her solution seems to presume that the legal maxims of guilt beyond a reasonable doubt and innocent until proven guilty are designed to make rape convictions more difficult. In fact, these practices are justified out of an abhorrence for wrongly convicting innocent individuals. Even more troubling is her view that objectivity in finding innocence or guilt in rape proceedings is impossible and that consent does not necessarily communicate "what the woman actually wanted."[161] We are left with the conclusion that, according to MacKinnon, a woman often does not know her own will, a view that hardly elevates the status of women and that many women find objectionable.

Contrary to MacKinnon's view, there are such things as neutral principles of law. These principles include defining crimes with tolerable specificity; safeguards for those charged with any type of crime, including rape; and a First Amendment right to disagree with MacKinnon's view of whether rape charges are fabricated. One advantage of these principles is that they are designed to rise above various divisions within society, including the gender division.

Conclusion

MacKinnon's insistence that rape, like pornography, is about power and her dismissal of neutral principles of justice reduce her own arguments to ones of simple power—arguments not grounded in principles of justice. Although her work is "special pleading for a particular group [women]," she denies that this makes it illegitimate, for in her view, "existing law is already special pleading for a particular group [men]."[162] But what justification is there for special treatment in the realm of politics understood as merely power—a view MacKinnon embraces? Why should anyone be moved by her arguments if they are simply special pleading for one group over another? If there is no abstract or objective standard beyond self-interest and power, then MacKinnon cannot condemn male domination except to say that she disapproves of it. As one female reviewer of her work comments, "she [MacKinnon] seems entirely uninterested in what women should do with power, should they ever get any."[163] MacKinnon spends little effort in pursuing the problematic questions of justice and equality in her work. This both weakens her critique of existing law and policy and leaves that the reader uncertain as to what her program would lead to once women have power. If there is no standard of politics beyond advancing our own power, then political life is reduced to a war of all against all in which each of us simply attempts to advance our own self-interest and power. For one who believes objectivity or neutrality must give way to gender-split realities and subjective experience, it becomes impossible to rise above a gender perspective. Her premise makes it impossible both for men to know women's perspective and for women, including MacKinnon, to know men's perspective. Her premise also imposes a uniformity on both men's and women's views, a uniformity that is not exhibited in the various perspectives of feminists who disagree with one another on fundamental issues. MacKinnon dismisses feminist lawyers who disagree with her as tools of the male hierarchy: "I also really want you on our side. But, failing that, I want you to stop claiming that your liberalism, with its elitism, and your Freudianism, with its sexualized misogyny, has anything in common with feminism."[164] As one female reviewer commented, MacKinnon seems to assert that women possess both "an unshakeable knowledge of reality" and "an infinite capacity to be duped."[165]

Given her own premise of gender-split reality, it is remarkable that Mac-Kinnon claims to understand what goes on in men's minds. This would not be a problem for her if she adopted neutral standards that apply to all citizens, such as those lying at the foundation of the "dehumanizing" critique of pornography. *Only Words* leads the reader to believe that men have an insatiable appetite for pornography that leads to the "snuffing" or murdering of women.[166] The stereotyping of men (and, I would add, stereotyping combined with her view of politics as power) led one reviewer to suggest that her work invites "a kind of Hobbesian vision of a perpetual gender war, with no way to pursue or to secure an equal and non-coercive peace."[167]

MacKinnon not only works from a gender-split view of reality but further splinters the feminist agenda by her reliance on concrete, subjective experience. In spite of her rejection of alternative feminist views, it is inconsistent with her premise of concrete experience and subjectivity to disavow the views of other feminists. By elevating personal experience and distrusting objective, overarching principles, which she associates with dominating reason, it is extraordinarily difficult to move from subjective experience to a unified program for reform. Such a program is necessary if MacKinnon hopes to reform society and politics.[168]

Fortunately for us, our political tradition, including the Constitution, rests on the view that there are principles of justice that surpass self-interest, that justice is not merely the interest of the stronger, and that politics encompasses more than simply power. This view, unlike MacKinnon's, provides a standard for addressing and resolving questions of equality based on a principle that goes beyond power politics and special pleading. But this works both ways. Just as equality provides a basis for criticizing current political practices, it also provides a standard for proposed solutions—one that rises above specific groups of race or gender—and insists on standards that include all. Constitutional safeguards should not be disregarded simply because they are obstacles to one's cause. First Amendment freedoms and standards of due process may be obstacles to those who are impatient to achieve their political agendas, but much of the value of constitutional principles arises from the fact that they are designed to endure for the ages and to supersede immediate political agendas.

MacKinnon believes her goal justifies radical modifications in the role of the judiciary, in the Constitution's First Amendment guarantees, in criminal process, and in the ability to invade matters that current law leaves to the private realm in order to preserve individual freedom. She justifies her reforms on the basis of her own concrete experience and her views as a woman, not as a human being. This is precisely why Hobbes, Locke, and the Constitution require a sovereign—to avoid reliance on such private judgments. The Constitution is one of principle, it requires the rule of law resulting from many different interests and views to be elevated and refined through the constitutional system. The Constitution gains its legitimacy from the abstraction and principles on which it is based, and which MacKinnon disavows. These principles provide a basis for critique and reform through a complex system of government that does not legitimize special pleading but does provide for equal protection of the laws and for democratic changes in the law to better realize the principles of equality and justice.

EPILOGUE

This book began with an inquiry into the proper judicial role under a written constitution that provides for majority rule and representative government but contains exceptions to the power of majorities and the government. The problem arises in determining how these limitations are to be enforced, for whichever body has this power to make penultimate determinations of constitutionality (the ultimate power rests with the people, who have the authority to change even the Constitution) assumes a supremacy that may upset the intricate system of separated powers and the Constitution's root principle of republican government. This problem arises within the context of a proper concern that majorities and government act in ways consistent with both the public good and private rights.

It is reassuring to believe that our rights will be protected no matter what exigencies arise and what claims emerge on behalf of the public good as a result of these exigencies. In spite of dramatic differences among the ten commentators examined, many of them depend on the judiciary for this reassurance that our rights will be protected. This dependency on the judiciary rests on the presumption that judges are wiser than the elective branches of government in determining how to balance the claims of the public good and private rights. This presumption is difficult to support from historical evidence and is inconsistent with the republican theory of the Constitution which relies primarily on rule by majority and moderation of that rule through constitutional structures that, at their foundation, are republican in nature.

Ronald Dworkin and Michael Perry start their analysis with the Constitution but allow it to exert almost no constraint on their policy preferences. Dworkin believes the judiciary has the responsibility to define rights according to the strongest moral argument.[1] Perry asks the Court to act as prophet in a process of moral evolution that advances human rights.[2] Richard Epstein tries to put the judiciary under constitutional constraints, but in the end, he uses the Constitution to advance his own policy of law and economics and to advocate overturning much twentieth-century legislation.[3]

Philip Kurland, in spite of his reputation as a judicial conservative and his concern with preserving public confidence in the judiciary, sets forth a theory of the Constitution that invites justices to supplant the Constitution with their own values. He argues that the Constitution means whatever Supreme

Court justices want it to mean, subject to the people's acquiescence.[4] Archibald Cox shares Kurland's concern with preserving judicial credibility. But Cox asks the Court to assume a role as the ''voice of natural law''[5] and thereby opens the way to a system of judicial supremacy in which judges are the penultimate voice in deciding what governmental actions are consistent with ''the Laws of Nature and Nature's God.''[6] Given the features of our constitutional system, the penultimate judge in many respects becomes the final judge, unless amendment or other extraordinary action is undertaken. Laurence Tribe makes little effort to reveal his purpose, which is to provide a unified analysis of the Constitution. This unified analysis is designed to correct the Constitution's original shortcomings and to guide the judiciary in shaping its evolution in the direction Tribe prescribes.[7]

John Hart Ely properly emphasizes the Constitution's democratic foundations, its representative structures, and its crucial concern with process. But he transmogrifies the Constitution by interpreting all its provisions, even the substantive provisions of the Bill of Rights, according to a view of equality that departs sharply from that of the Constitution.[8] Although Robert Bork argues for a form of judicial supremacy, the role he prescribes for the judiciary differs in important ways from that of the other commentators. Bork properly insists that the Constitution is law and that it ought to control judges. When judges treat the Constitution as a malleable text that they may rewrite so that particular groups or political causes prevail, they usurp the legislative power and undermine democracy. He believes his doctrine of original understanding avoids these defects.[9]

Mark Tushnet and Catharine MacKinnon are the most extreme insofar as they simply reject the Constitution and liberalism in favor of their respective theories of justice. Tushnet would use the judicial power ''to advance the cause of socialism.''[10] Catharine MacKinnon regards the Constitution as embodying the male hierarchy and would transform the Constitution in order to redress the gender subordination she sees in its theory.[11] With the exception of Robert Bork, all the modern commentators examined ask the Court to pursue constitutional and political reform through a judicial power that relies heavily on the doctrine of unenumerated rights.

As the analysis of contemporary commentators has revealed, these modern theorists generally begin with their own strongly held views of justice and then construct a theory of constitutional interpretation that advances policies consistent with this view and, in many cases, runs counter to the republican character of the Constitution.[12] The Constitution, in contrast, regards its republican nature as a fundamental element of justice. The Constitution creates a representative regime with sufficient power to meet future exigencies and to secure individual rights, but it does not incline the political system in one policy direction. The Constitution avoids the extremes of unrestrained democracy on the one hand and the absolutizing of individual rights on the other. Unrestrained democracy results in mob rule. Absolutizing individual rights takes us back to the state of nature that Hobbes, Locke, Montesquieu, and any sensible theorist counsel us to escape. Avoidance of these extremes is a central theme of the various theorists and the historical materials surveyed. It is instructive that these theorists and historical materials provide no support for the sort of judicial supremacy implicit in the views of many of the contemporary commentators examined.

Hobbes paints the most vivid picture of the horrors of the state of nature, where rights are at once absolute and utterly insecure. Proceeding from this premise, he advocates the creation of a commonwealth whose power is nearly absolute and that protects us from one another. The commonwealth is the judge of what rights are to be actualized, and private judgment is given up to its authority. He argues that judges are not to determine "what is commodious, or incommodious to the commonwealth."[13] Hobbes's theory provides no support for a judicial power to obstruct the nearly absolute sovereign.

Locke begins his inquiry into the relationship between natural rights and government by rejecting absolute monarchy. Although Locke is sometimes regarded as a proponent of the view that there is a catalog of natural rights that justify judicial intervention to obstruct the legislative power, I have argued that this is a misinterpretation of his theory. Locke is nearly as cautious as Hobbes in refraining from setting forth a body of substantive rights that are beyond the power of the legislature. Far from justifying a role for the Court to void government action on the basis of a theory of unenumerated substantive rights advocated by many modern commentators, Locke depends on consent of the governed and procedural mechanisms to protect individual rights (see Chapter 1).

Montesquieu is commonly cited as authority for the separation of powers and an independent judiciary, both of which are important features of the U.S. Constitution and essential to its protection of liberty. Although he separates the judicial power from the legislative and executive powers, he does not advocate the doctrine that a catalog of natural rights justifies the judiciary's voiding governmental action that is inconsistent with these rights. Institutions are essential to Montesquieu's protection of liberty through laws that reserve a wide latitude for legislative discretion and cannot be limited by absolute rules. This reliance on institutions is a central feature of the U.S. Constitution. Although it is essential to Montesquieu's theory that the judiciary be sufficiently independent to be protected from the other branches of government, the judicial power does not rival that of the legislature or executive. Thus, even Montesquieu, the oracle of separation of powers, does not set forth a theory anywhere approaching the judicial supremacy that characterizes so many modern commentators (see Part I).

The Declaration of Independence, which depends so heavily on Locke's theory, follows the same pattern as that of the political philosophers examined. The Declaration teaches that there are standards beyond the positive law by which governments are judged, but its broad principles and statements of the ends of American government do not stipulate that the judiciary is to be the enforcer of the "unalienable rights" to which it refers. The Declaration rests firmly on the view that majority consent to the form of government will best achieve the rights it articulates, but it does not specify the form of government to which this consent will be given. In fact, the Declaration does not even require the existence of an independent judiciary with the power of judicial review, much less a judiciary empowered to define and enforce the inalienable rights that legitimize the government to which a majority of the people consent (see Chapter 1).

The constitutional limitations around which our inquiry revolves are rooted in the Declaration's conception of "the Laws of Nature and of Nature's God," but they are embodied in the Constitution as legal protections of traditional civil rights. This status as legal protections of traditional civil rights—a status narrower than the sweeping and fundamental conceptions of the Declaration—is one foundation of the proper judicial role. But these protections must be understood within the context of the entire Constitution and its underlying theory, which depends on procedural mechanisms to secure the public good and private rights. These mechanisms rest on the sound premise that governing is a difficult business and that rights are best protected by a strong government, which, among other things, protects us from one another. This premise is clearly expressed in *Federalist* No. 51: "In framing a government which is to be administered by men over men, the great difficulty lies in this: you must first enable the government to control the governed; and in the next place oblige it to control itself."[14]

Recognizing the unforeseen exigencies that government inevitably faces and the difficulty in balancing considerations of the public good with private rights, the Constitution created a strong government in which the scheme of representation, other constitutional structures, and dependence on the people are the primary securities of the public good and private rights. Hamilton states the matter clearly when he addresses the lack of a bill of rights in the Constitution: " 'WE, THE PEOPLE of the United States, to secure the blessings of liberty to ourselves and our posterity, do *ordain* and *establish* this Constitution for the United States of America.' Here is a better recognition of popular rights, than volumes of those aphorisms which make the principal figure in several of our State bills of rights, and which would sound much better in a treatise of ethics than in a constitution of government."[15]

Each of the theorists, the Declaration, the Constitution, and the commentary of *The Federalist* wrestle with the problem of republican government, the public good, and private rights. What is remarkable about these sources is that none of them anticipates that judges will be the primary protectors of individual rights, and not one of them prescribes a system of judicial supremacy. The Constitution and *The Federalist* depend on a strictly republican form of government in which moderate majority rule is to be achieved through properly structured institutions designed to secure the public good and private rights. The Constitution's theory rests on a sober view of human nature, avoids utopian solutions to problems of government, and settles for moderation as the best that we can hope for in politics.

Leaving the determination of unenumerated rights to the legislative body and the republican processes of the Constitution has a number of advantages. It preserves the democratic nature of the Constitution and assumes an ultimate trust in the sovereign power under our Constitution. It also underscores the status of the Constitution as law, rather than as a grant of power to the judiciary to define unenumerated rights according to its view of what these rights ought to be. Confining the limitations on the popular branches of government to the particular prohibitions on their powers, rather than giving nearly unlimited discretion to the judiciary to define these powers, has the additional advantage of leaving majorities free to define rights within the circumstances that arise from unforeseen exigencies and to adjust or redefine these rights as experience helps determine the wisdom of the scope of these rights. Such flexibility is difficult when such rights are pronounced as constitutional rights by the judiciary. When the judiciary, which is only a "remote choice of the people,"[16] makes such pronouncements, the method to change unwise decisions is either to modify or overrule the previous decision or to undertake the cumbersome process of constitutional amendment. If the sovereign people become persuaded that the Constitution is nothing more than what the judges say that it is, a danger warned against in *Federalist* No. 49 arises: that the Constitution and the government will be deprived of "that veneration which time bestows on every thing, and without which perhaps the wisest and freest governments would not possess the requisite stability." Publius continues: "In a nation of philosophers . . . reverence for the laws would be sufficiently inculcated by the voice of an enlightened reason. But a nation of philosophers is as little to be expected as the philosophical race of kings wished for by Plato. And in every other nation, the most rational government will not find it a superfluous advantage to have the prejudices of the community on its side."[17] A Constitution that changes with the composition of the Court and is interpreted according to the strongest moral argument of the justices, with little or no guidance from the Constitution's provisions, is not likely to sustain the reverence *The Federalist* regards as necessary to the republic.

Much of the task of government under the Constitution consists of reconciling the public good with private rights. The practical effect of a doctrine of unenumerated rights and judicial supremacy is to transfer the authority for this reconciliation from the people's elected representatives and the written Constitution's provisions to a nearly unbridled judiciary empowered to determine how we ought to be governed. There is little evidence that the judiciary is better equipped to make these judgments than are the elected branches of government that are responsible to the people. The theory of the Constitution rests firmly on the principle of majority rule, moderated through constitutional mechanisms that elevate and refine majority opinion and are constrained by the exceptions to the legislative power found in the provisions of the Constitution.

Many of the modern commentators examined in Part II of this book are impatient with the results of policy produced under this system; consequently, they would empower the judiciary to rule in ways that the commentators believe would be more consistent with the commentators' own views of justice. These commentators seem to believe that the judiciary and other intellectual elites know the interests and rights of the citizen body better than the citizens themselves know them and that the judiciary should enforce its view of interests and rights through a doctrine of unenumerated rights.

This doctrine both contradicts the principle of republican government and undermines the written Constitution, often in the name of individual rights that are not found in the Constitution. Such a view of government and the role of the judiciary rests on a utopian view of human nature and government in which rights may be endlessly expanded at the discretion of the judiciary. It discards the wisdom of the political philosophers who laid the foundations for the Constitution and rejects the Constitution's reliance on properly structured majority rule as the security for the public good and private rights. The reconciliation of the public good and private rights is a fundamental question of political philosophy that Hobbes, Locke, Montesquieu, and the U.S. Constitution sought to resolve. Neither these theorists nor the framers of the Constitution believed it wise to establish a government on the premise that individual rights could be perennially expanded without consideration of the unforeseen exigencies that inevitably face government and that require defining such rights in relationship to requirements of the public good. The difficulty of this task is one reason that the Constitution did not establish a judiciary empowered to govern in the name of unenumerated rights, but instead constructed an intricate system of government in which the government as a whole, not the judiciary, makes such judgments. The judiciary is to a large degree insulated from public opinion. Its institutional place was designed to "secure a steady, upright, and impartial administration of the laws."[18] There was no presumption, however, that judges are necessarily wiser or superior in their capacity to reconcile the public good and private rights or that judges should depart from the law, including the law of a written constitution. If the judiciary assumes the authority to make such judgments beyond those specified by law, it sacrifices the genius of a written constitution and assumes a supremacy inconsistent with the republican theory and the complex structures upon which the Constitution is based.

NOTES

Introduction

1. Alexander Hamilton, John Jay, and James Madison, *The Federalist: A Commentary on the Constitution of the United States,* ed. Henry Cabot Lodge, with an introduction by Edward Mead Earle (New York: Modern Library, 1941), No. 78, p. 503.

2. Ibid., No. 39, p. 245.

3. Ibid., No. 10, p. 57.

1. Constitutional Antecedents: The Doctrines of Natural Right, Natural Law, and Separation of Powers

1. Hobbes argues that rights arising from "the security of a man's person, in his life, and in the means of so preserving life" are not alienable. Therefore, one has a right to resist those who "assault him by force, to take away his life. . . . The same may be said of wounds, and chains, and imprisonment." Thomas Hobbes, *Leviathan,* ed. Michael Oakeshott, with an introduction by Richard S. Peters (London: Collier-Macmillan, 1962), 105.

2. Ibid., 100.

3. Ibid., 103. Hobbes observes: "But this Right of all men to all things, is in effect no better than if no man had a Right to anything, for there is little use and benefit of the Right a man hath, when another as strong, or stronger than himself, hath Right to the same." Thomas Hobbes, original manuscript of the *Elements of Law,* n.d., p. 94, Devonshire Mss., Hobbes Group, Chatsworth, Bakewell, Derbyshire.

4. Hobbes, *Leviathan,* 103–4. Hobbes characterizes the prepolitical state as follows: "irresistible Might, in the state of nature, is Right." Hobbes, *Elements of Law,* 96.

5. Hobbes, *Leviathan,* 102–4. "One precept of the law of nature therefore is this, that every man divest himself of the Right he hath to all things by nature." Hobbes, *Elements of Law,* 99.

6. Hobbes, *Leviathan,* 113. It is instructive to note that Hobbes characterizes justice as one of the "other laws of nature," presumably because it arises only from the covenant formed in pursuit of the first and second laws of nature.

7. Laurence Berns, "Hobbes," in *History of Political Philosophy,* ed. Leo Strauss and Joseph Cropsey (Chicago: Rand McNally, 1963), 369.

8. Harvey C. Mansfield, Jr., "Hobbes and the Science of Indirect Government," *American Political Science Review* 65 (1971): 102.

9. Hobbes, *Leviathan,* 132.

10. Ibid., 172.

11. Joseph Cropsey, "Hobbes and the Transition to Modernity," in *Ancients and Moderns: Essays on the Tradition of Political Philosophy in Honor of Leo Strauss,* ed. Joseph Cropsey (New York: Basic Books, 1964), 216, 225.

12. Hobbes, *Leviathan,* 124. Hobbes also presents other laws of nature, examination of which is not necessary to discuss the fundamental law of nature. Examples of these other laws of nature are gratitude, modesty, equity, and mercy. Ibid.

13. Leo Strauss, "On the Basis of Hobbes's Political Philosophy," in *What Is Political Philosophy? And Other Studies* (New York: Free Press, 1959), 192.

14. Hobbes, *Leviathan,* 123.

15. For an instructive analysis of this and related issues in Hobbes, see Matthew J. Franck, "Statesmanship, the Law of Nature, and Judicial Usurpation" (Ph.D. diss., Northern Illinois University, 1992), 207–22. I drew some of these references from this source.

16. Hobbes, *Leviathan,* 124.

17. John Locke, *Second Treatise of Government,* ed. C. B. Macpherson (Indianapolis: Hackett, 1980), sec. 4.

18. Robert A. Goldwin, "John Locke," in *History of Political Philosophy,* ed. Leo Strauss and Joseph Cropsey (Chicago: Rand McNally, 1963), 442.

19. Ibid., 440.

20. Locke, *Second Treatise,* sec. 135.

21. *Federalist* No. 43, p. 287.

22. Locke, *Second Treatise,* sec. 90.

23. Goldwin, "John Locke," 460–61.

24. Ibid.

25. Locke, *Second Treatise,* sec. 136.

26. Richard G. Stevens, *Frankfurter and Due Process* (New York: University Press of America, 1987), xxviii–xxix. I am deeply indebted to Professor Stevens for his teaching and insights into Locke, the Constitution and *The Federalist.*

27. Locke, *Second Treatise,* sec. 138.

28. Stevens, *Frankfurter,* xxix.

29. Locke, *Second Treatise,* sec. 143.

30. Ibid., sec. 144. Locke follows this with a discussion of the federative power, "the power of war and peace, leagues and alliances, and all the transactions, with all persons and communities without the common-wealth." The federative power should not be placed in different hands from the executive power. Ibid., secs. 146–48.

31. Ibid., sec. 159.

32. Ibid., sec. 87, quoted in Walter Berns, *In Defense of Liberal Democracy* (Chicago: Gateway Editions, 1984), 43.

33. Montesquieu is cited or quoted in *The Federalist* at Nos. 9, 43, 47, and 78, where this quotation appears (p. 504).

34. Montesquieu, *The Spirit of the Laws,* 2 vols., trans. Thomas Nugent (New York: Hafner, 1949), 1:4–5.

35. Ibid., 3.

36. Thomas L. Pangle, *Montesquieu's Philosophy of Liberalism: A Commentary on "The Spirit of the Laws"* (Chicago: University of Chicago Press, 1973), 33, 41. For a view of Montesquieu's *The Spirit of the Laws* that distinguishes Locke and Hobbes from

Montesquieu and focuses on Montesquieu's concern with "spirit and character, rather than law and principle," see Anne M. Cohler, *Montesquieu's Comparative Politics and the Spirit of American Constitutionalism* (Lawrence: University Press of Kansas, 1988), 10.

37. Pangle, *Montesquieu's Philosophy*, 49.

38. Montesquieu, *Spirit of the Laws*, 1:150.

39. Pangle, *Montesquieu's Philosophy*, 108.

40. Montesquieu, *Spirit of the Laws*, 1:6.

41. Leo Strauss, *Natural Right and History* (Chicago: University of Chicago Press, 1953), 164.

42. Montesquieu, *Spirit of the Laws*, 1:150.

43. Ibid.

44. Pangle, *Montesquieu's Philosophy*, 111–12.

45. In describing the institutionalization of liberty, Montesquieu focuses on those institutional features that ensure that the law will produce liberty. He defines political liberty as "a tranquillity of mind arising from the opinion each person has of his safety," and a prerequisite of this liberty is that "government be so constitued as one man need not be afraid of another." Both the realization of liberty and the security that liberty will prevail within the constitution are important to Montesquieu. In limiting the end of politics to liberty, Montesquieu departs from the classical view of the end of politics, that of forming the character of citizens. Montesquieu, *Spirit of the Laws*, 1:151.

46. Ibid., 155.

47. Ibid., 154.

48. Pangle, *Montesquieu's Philosophy*, 127–28.

49. Montesquieu, *Spirit of the Laws*, 1:151–52.

50. Pangle, *Montesquieu's Philosophy*, 128–29.

51. Montesquieu, *Spirit of the Laws*, 1:159.

52. Ibid., 157.

53. Ibid., 159.

54. Montesquieu addresses the objection that his separation of powers in the legislative and executive will result in government inaction: "But as there is a necessity for movement in the course of human affairs, they are forced to move, but still in concert." Nonetheless, the system of dividing the legislative power and separating the executive or monarch does help preserve an arena of freedom for citizens in which commerce and other activity may be pursued without undue governmental interference. Ibid., 160.

55. Ibid., 151–56.

56. Pangle, *Montesquieu's Philosophy*, 132.

57. Montesquieu, *Spirit of the Laws*, 1:153.

58. Pangle, *Montesquieu's Philosophy*, 133. Montesquieu also provides for the nobles in the legislature to "moderate the law in favor of the law itself, by mitigating the sentence." We might regard this as a kind of modification of the law by a part of the legislative body. Montesquieu, *Spirit of the Laws*, 1:159.

59. Montesquieu, *Spirit of the Laws*, 1:183–85.

60. Ibid., 193.

61. Ibid., 199.

62. Pangle, *Montesquieu's Philosophy,* 268–69.

63. Ibid., 269–70. This appears to be Pangle's translation of Montesquieu.

64. Cohler, *Montesquieu's Comparative Politics,* 112.

65. The Declaration of Independence, par. 2 (U.S. 1776). As Eva Brann recognizes, the people referred to in the Declaration exercise their right to institute a new government by seceding, not by absolutely abolishing the old government. Eva Brann, "Concerning the 'Declaration of Independence,' " *The College,* Bicentennial Issue (July 1976): 4.

66. Richard G. Stevens, "The Constitution and What It Meant to Corwin," *Political Science Reviewer* 10 (1980): 44. Walter Berns makes a similar point in refuting Garry Wills's view that "there is not even an 'echo' of the [Second] Treatise in any of Jefferson's writings. In fact, of course, there is much more than an 'echo' of the one in the other. The Declaration speaks of 'a long train of abuses,' for example a phrase taken word for word from section 225 of the Treatise, and of 'mankind [being] more disposed to suffer' which in section 230 of the Treatise reads, 'the people, who are more disposed to suffer.' Rather than serving to disconnect Jefferson from Locke's Treatise, even a cursory comparison of their texts tends to connect them." Walter Berns, *Taking the Constitution Seriously* (New York: Simon & Schuster, 1987), 247–48, refuting Garry Wills, *Inventing America: Jefferson's Declaration of Independence* (Garden City, N.Y.: Doubleday, 1978).

67. Harvey C. Mansfield, Jr., "Thomas Jefferson," in *American Political Thought: The Philosophic Dimension of American Statesmanship,* 2d ed., ed. Morton J. Frisch and Richard G. Stevens (Itasca, Ill.: F. E. Peacock, 1983), 24.

68. "And man is not either beast or god. Whether the God whom the Signers assume to exist can be proved to exist is not necessary to the argument of the Declaration. What can be proved is that a divine nature is of a certain sort. Such a nature would carry to absolute perfection those partially existing perfections perceivable in man (such as reason, justice, mercy), without the corresponding imperfections (above all, the passionate self-love that corrupts the perfections). Men form the idea of such a perfect being, as much to understand the limits of their own humanity, as to decide objectively of that superior being's existence." Harry V. Jaffa, "What Is Equality? The Declaration of Independence Revisited," in *Readings in American Democracy,* ed. Paul Peterson (Dubuque, Iowa: Kendall/Hunt, 1979), 33.

69. Brann, "Concerning the Declaration," 7.

70. Carl Becker gives a different and, I believe, improper account of the Declaration. He regards the truth of the Declaration as "essentially a meaningless question" and views the Declaration as primarily a rationalization for action. Carl Becker, *The Declaration of Independence: A Study in the History of Political Ideas* (New York: Alfred A. Knopf, 1942), 277–78. His interpretation raises a difficulty insofar as he refers in this context to men being "impelled to withdraw their allegiance to the established law," and he refers to the "humane and engaging faith" of the Declaration, one that "preached toleration in place of persecution, goodwill in place of hate, peace in place of war." These references seem more consistent with the interpretation presented in the text rather than that of the Declaration as rationalization.

71. George Anastaplo, "The Declaration of Independence," *St. Louis University Law Journal* 9, no. 3 (Spring 1965): 400.

72. Ibid., 400–401.

73. It may be instructive that the Declaration refers to "the right of Representation in the Legislature" as "a right inestimable" rather than an inalienable right. Ibid., 403.

74. Jaffa, "What Is Equality?" 38.

75. Richard G. Stevens, ed., *The Declaration of Independence and the Constitution of the United States of America,* with an introduction by Richard G. Stevens (Washington, D.C.: Georgetown University Press, 1984), iii.

76. Declaration, par. 2, quoted in Jaffa, "What Is Equality?" 38. For a differing view, see Becker, *Declaration,* 234, where he seems to interpret consent of the governed as applying to both the institution of government and the operation of the government that is instituted.

77. Anastaplo, "The Declaration," 401. The Declaration condemns King George III not because he is king but because of his "history of repeated injuries and usurpations, all having in direct object the establishment of an absolute Tyranny over these States" (par. 2). These injuries and usurpations are enumerated in the Declaration following par. 2.

78. Jaffa, "What Is Equality?" 38–39. Jaffa makes the interesting point that "the God of the Declaration appears in three roles (besides Creator): first, as . . . legislator; second, that of 'Supreme Judge of the World'; and finally, that of 'Divine Providence,' or that executive power, upon whom the Signers place a 'firm reliance' for their protection. It is an absolutely necessary condition of the rule of law that these three powers of government never be united in the same *human* hands." Citing Anastaplo, "The Declaration," 390.

79. Brann, "Concerning the 'Declaration,'" 8.

80. Locke, *Second Treatise,* sec. 8.

81. Martin Diamond, "The Declaration and the Constitution: Liberty, Democracy, and the Founders," in *As Far as Republican Principles Will Admit: Essays by Martin Diamond,* ed. William A. Schambra (Washington, D.C.: American Enterprise Institute Press, 1992), 233–34.

82. Quoted in ibid., 234.

83. *Federalist* No. 85, p. 574.

84. The vitality of the Declaration's principles is demonstrated by the fact that one would be hard-pressed to peruse the front page of a major newspaper without finding reference to equality or rights, both in the United States and abroad.

2. *The Constitution,* The Federalist, *and Constitutional Principles*

1. Alexander Hamilton, John Jay, and James Madison, *The Federalist: A Commentary on the Constitution of the United States,* ed. Henry Cabot Lodge, with an introduction by Edward Mead Earle (New York: Modern Library, 1941), No. 81, p. 524.

2. Other examples of such provisions that depend on a unified theoretical understanding of the Constitution are the commerce clause, explicated in such cases as *Gibbons v. Ogden,* 9 Wheat. (22 U. S.) 1 (1824), and the "necessary and proper" clause, explicated in *McCulloch v. Maryland,* 4 Wheat. (17 U. S.) 316 (1819).

3. *Federalist* No. 2, p. 8.

4. Ibid., No. 84, p. 558.

5. Irving Brant, *The Bill of Rights: Its Origin and Meaning* (New York: New American Library, 1965), 19.

6. *Federalist* No. 1, p. 6.

7. Ibid., No. 39, pp. 242–43.

8. Noah Webster, *A Compendious Dictionary of the English Language: A Facsimile of the First (1806) Edition* (New Haven, Conn.: Increase Cooke & Co., 1806), 129.

9. *Federalist* No. 51, p. 337.

10. Irving Brant identifies "twenty-four elements of a Bill of Rights" in the original Constitution, including seven relating to the structure of government, such as separation of powers and the power of the people to elect their representatives. We would characterize most of these as procedural protections. Brant, *Bill of Rights,* 20.

11. U.S. Constitution, art. III, sec. 2; art. I, sec. 9. Other prohibitions on state governments are found in art. I, sec. 10.

12. *Federalist* No. 84, p. 559.

13. Ibid., 558.

14. Ibid.

15. Ibid., 560.

16. This appears in an asterisked footnote in ibid.

17. Herbert J. Storing, "The Constitution and the Bill of Rights," in *Taking the Constitution Seriously: Essays on the Constitution and Constitutional Law,* ed. Gary L. McDowell (Dubuque, Iowa: Kendall/Hunt, 1981), 267.

18. *Barron v. The Mayor and City Council of Baltimore,* 7 Pet. (32 U.S.) 243 (1833).

19. *Federalist* No. 51, p. 337.

20. Ibid., No. 23, p. 141.

21. Ibid., 142, 144.

22. Herbert J. Storing, *What the Anti-Federalists Were For: The Political Thought of the Opponents of the Constitution* (Chicago: University of Chicago Press, 1981), 69. This passage is particularly applicable to the Ninth Amendment, which some commentators would use to enlarge judicial power. For an analysis of the Ninth Amendment, see Chapter 6.

23. Jonathan Elliot, ed., *The Debates in the Several State Conventions on the Adoption of the Federal Constitution, as Recommended by the General Convention at Philadelphia in 1787,* 2d ed. (Philadelphia: J. B. Lippincott, 1836), 2:87–88, cited and quoted in part in Storing, *What the Anti-federalists Were For,* 98, n. 31.

24. Elliot, *Debates,* 2:87.

25. Ibid., 3:191. Randolph's discussion is clearly heated and in response to Patrick Henry. Randolph clearly values the republicanism of the Constitution as the primary safeguard of liberty. His discussion of bills of rights may relate to whether bills of rights are part of a constitution and have the same authority as constitutions themselves and whether they are prior or subsequent to the constitution in question. Reference to this fulsome debate and its context is recommended to the reader.

26. Robert Allen Rutland, *The Birth of the Bill of Rights* (Chapel Hill: University of North Carolina Press, 1955), 198, citing John C. Fitzpatrick, ed., *The Writings of*

Washington from the Original Manuscripts Sources, 1745–1799 (Washington, D.C.: U.S. Government Printing Office, 1931–44), 30:295.

27. See Richard G. Stevens, *Frankfurter and Due Process* (New York: University Press of America, 1987), xxviii–xxxvii.

28. Storing, "The Constitution," 276.

29. Ibid., 273.

30. Elliot, *Debates,* 3:448, quoted in Storing, "The Constitution," 274.

31. Max Farrand, ed., *The Records of the Federal Convention of 1787,* 3d ed. (New Haven, Conn.: Yale University Press, 1966), 3:290. This is taken from Martin's "Reply to the Landholder."

32. Joseph Gales Sr., ed., *The Debates and Proceedings in the Congress of the United States* (Washington, D.C.: Gales & Seaton, 1834), 1:758–59.

33. Storing, "The Constitution," 275.

34. *Federalist* No. 10, p. 57.

35. These are terms used by Patrick Henry and Edmund Randolph. Storing, "The Constitution," 277.

36. Elliot, *Debates,* 3:190.

37. Storing, "The Constitution," 277.

38. Gales, *Debates and Proceedings,* 1:804–5.

39. Elliot, *Debates,* 3:561.

40. Gales, *Debates and Proceedings,* 1: 441.

41. Ibid., 444.

42. Ibid., 447. Mr. Jackson spoke along similar lines: "If we actually find the constitution bad upon experience, or the rights and privileges of the people in danger, I here pledge myself to step forward among the first friends of liberty to prevent the evil; and if nothing else will avail, I will draw my sword in the defence of freedom, and cheerfully immolate at that shrine my property and my life. But how are we now proceeding? Why, on nothing more than theoretical speculation, pursuing a mere *ignis fatuus,* which may lead us into serious embarrassments." Ibid., 461.

43. Ibid., 442.

44. Ibid., 450.

45. Madison considered this "the most valuable amendment in the whole list." Ibid., 784. The proposals Madison made in the First Congress are found in ibid., 451–52.

46. Ibid., 734.

47. Storing, "The Constitution," 277.

48. *Federalist* No. 49, p. 329.

49. Storing, "The Constitution," 277.

50. Elliot, *Debates,* 2:438.

51. Ibid., 3:445.

52. Ibid., 2:79.

53. *Federalist* No. 54, pp. 353–54.

54. Martin Diamond, "*The Federalist:* 1787–1788," in *As Far as Republican Principles Will Admit: Essays by Martin Diamond,* ed. William A. Schambra (Washington, D.C.: American Enterprise Institute Press, 1992), 40. I am profoundly indebted to Martin Diamond for both his teaching and his scholarship on *The Federalist.*

55. *Federalist* No. 1, p. 6.

56. Ibid., No. 78, p. 503.

57. Ibid., No. 10, pp. 53, 58, 59.

58. Diamond, "*The Federalist,*" 52.

59. *Federalist* No. 10, p. 54.

60. Ibid., 57–58. Madison adds that moral and religious motives are not adequate controls on individuals and "lose their efficacy in proportion to the number combined together, that is, in proportion as their efficacy becomes needful." Ibid., 58.

61. Ibid., No. 51, p. 339.

62. Alexis de Tocqueville, *Democracy in America,* trans. Henry Reeve, rev. Francis Bowen, corr. and ed. Phillips Bradley (New York: Vintage Books, 1945), 1:270.

63. *Federalist* No. 10, p. 58.

64. Ibid., No. 9, p. 49.

65. Ibid., No. 10, pp. 60–61.

66. Martin Diamond, "Democracy and *The Federalist:* A Reconsideration of the Framers' Intent," in *As Far as Republican Principles Will Admit: Essays by Martin Diamond,* ed. William A. Schambra (Washington, D.C.: American Enterprise Institute Press, 1992), 33–34.

67. *Federalist* No. 10, p. 56. Morton J. Frisch develops this theme of Franklin Roosevelt as preserver of the American political order in "Franklin D. Roosevelt," in *American Political Thought: The Philosophic Dimension of American Statesmanship,* 2d ed., ed. Morton J. Frisch and Richard G. Stevens (Itasca, Ill.: F. E. Peacock, 1983), 319.

68. *Federalist* No. 10, pp. 57–61.

69. Ibid., No. 63, p. 413.

70. Tocqueville, *Democracy,* 2:131.

71. *Federalist* No. 10, p. 59.

72. Ibid., No. 63, pp. 409–10.

73. Ibid, No. 42, p. 274.

74. Hanna Fenichel Pitkin, *The Concept of Representation* (Berkeley: University of California Press, 1967), 196. Although I differ with Pitkin on this point, her thoughtful treatment of representation is highly recommended.

75. James MacGregor Burns, *Deadlock of Democracy: Four-Party Politics in America* (Englewood Cliffs, N.J.: Prentice-Hall, 1963).

76. Cornelius, "Essay by Cornelius," *Hampshire Chronicle,* 18 December 1787, quoted in Herbert J. Storing, ed., *The Complete Anti-Federalist* (Chicago: University of Chicago Press, 1981), 4:141.

77. Gales, *Debates and Proceedings,* 1:761.

78. Ibid., 761–66.

79. Ibid., 768.

80. Ibid., 775–76.

81. *Federalist* No. 56, pp. 365–66.

82. Philip B. Kurland and Ralph Lerner, eds., *The Founders' Constitution* (Chicago: University of Chicago Press, 1987), 1:384, quoting the *Essex Massachusetts Result,* 29 April 1778.

83. *Federalist* No. 57, pp. 370–71.

84. Ibid., No. 10, p. 59.

85. Ibid., No. 57, p. 371.

86. Ralph A. Rossum, "Representation and Republican Government: Contemporary Court Variations on the Founders' Theme," in *Taking the Constitution Seriously: Essays on the Constitution and Constitutional Law,* ed. Gary L. McDowell (Dubuque, Iowa: Kendall/Hunt, 1981), 427.

87. Farrand, *Records,* 1:50.

88. *Federalist* No. 63, p. 413.

89. Ibid., No. 28, p. 173.

90. Ibid., No. 51, p. 339.

91. Ibid., No. 10, p. 62.

92. Diamond, *"The Federalist,"* 52.

93. Federalist No. 10, p. 58; Diamond, *"The Federalist,"* 52.

94. Diamond, "The Federalist," 53.

95. Tocqueville, *Democracy,* 1:270.

96. *Federalist* No. 10, pp. 61–62.

97. Ibid., No. 47, p. 313.

98. John Locke, *Second Treatise of Government,* ed. C. B. Macpherson (Indianapolis: Hackett, 1980), sec. 159.

99. Montesquieu, *The Spirit of the Laws,* trans. Thomas Nugent (New York: Hafner, 1949), 1:153.

100. Martin Diamond, *The Founding of the Democratic Republic* (Itasca, Ill.: F. E. Peacock, 1981), 87–89.

101. This account is found in Louis B. Boudin, *Government by Judiciary* (New York: Russell & Russell, 1968), 1:120–21.

102. *Federalist* No. 51, p. 337.

103. Ibid., No. 72, p. 470.

104. Diamond, *Founding of the Democratic Republic,* 92–94.

105. *Federalist* No. 51, p. 337.

106. Quoted in Harry V. Jaffa, "Abraham Lincoln," in *American Political Thought: The Philosophic Dimension of American Statesmanship,* 2d ed., ed. Morton J. Frisch and Richard G. Stevens (Itasca, Ill.: F. E. Peacock, 1983), 206.

107. *Federalist* No. 37, pp. 226–27.

108. Ibid., No. 62, p. 403.

109. Ibid., No. 37, pp. 227–28.

110. Ibid., No. 70, p. 454.

111. Ibid., No. 55, p. 364.

112. Publius does refer at an earlier point to the judges as "a remote choice, of the people themselves." Ibid., No. 39, pp. 244–45.

113. The distinction between the necessity for the national government to have full powers over distributive justice, the focus of *Federalist* No. 10, and leaving of retributive justice to the states was suggested to me by Professor Richard G. Stevens. The concern for retributive justice is reflected in the Bill of Rights' treatment of the criminal process, a concern that resulted in the limitations on the national government embodied in the Bill of Rights. The problematic application of these limitations to the states is the topic of another book and is beyond the scope of the present endeavor. It has been treated in a competent manner by others, including Raoul Berger, *Government*

by Judiciary: The Transformation of the Fourteenth Amendment (Cambridge: Harvard University Press, 1977).

114. *Federalist* No. 23, pp. 142–44.

115. Ibid., No. 14, p. 82.

116. Ibid., No. 44, p. 292.

117. Elliot, *Debates,* 3:553.

118. *Federalist* No. 27, p. 169. In No. 39, p. 249, Madison refers to the national government as extending "to certain enumerated objects only," and he says that it "leaves to the several States a residuary and inviolable sovereignty over all other objects."

119. The understanding of *federal* as opposed to *national* is clearly indicated by Gerry's comments in the First Congress, where he observes that the very terms Federalist and Anti-Federalist turn the argument on its head: "Those who were called anti-federalists at that time complained that they had injustice done them by the title, because they were in favor of a Federal Government, and the others [Federalists] were in favor of a national one. . . . Their names then ought not to have been distinguished by federalists and antifederalists, but rats [ratificationists] and antirats [antiratificationists]." Gales, *Debates and Proceedings,* 1:759. Martin Diamond argues persuasively that at the time of the Constitutional Convention, "Federalism meant then exactly what we mean now by confederalism." Diamond's argument is thoughtful, subtle, and, to this author, dispositive on this issue. Martin Diamond, "What the Framers Meant by Federalism," in *As Far as Republican Principles Will Admit: Essays by Martin Diamond,* ed. William A. Schambra (Washington, D.C.: American Enterprise Institute Press, 1992), 96.

120. *Federalist* No. 9, p. 52.

121. Ibid., No. 39, p. 250.

122. I believe this term is suggested by Professor Richard G. Stevens.

123. *Federalist* No. 39, pp. 246–47.

124. Ibid., 247–50.

125. Henry J. Abraham specifies fewer than seventy instances in which the Supreme Court has held federal statutes unconstitutional from 1937 to 1972. Of this number, "all but ten did so because they infringed on certain personal rights and liberties safeguarded under the Constitution." Henry J. Abraham, *The Judicial Process: An Introductory Analysis of the Courts of the United States, England, and France,* 6th ed. (New York: Oxford University Press, 1993), 272; a useful table enumerating these instances is found at 273–80.

126. *Federalist* No. 39, p. 249.

127. Martin Diamond's probing explication of Tocqueville is, in the author's judgment, the best treatment of the salutary, decentralizing effects of what we call the federal features of our system of government. This section of the text draws extensively from that treatment. Martin Diamond, "The Ends of Federalism," in *As Far as Republican Principles Will Admit: Essays by Martin Diamond,* ed. William A. Schambra (Washington, D.C.: American Enterprise Institute Press, 1992), 157–66.

128. Alexis de Tocqueville, *Democracy in America,* ed. J. P. Mayer and Max Lerner, trans. George Lawrence (New York: Harper & Row, 1966), 482.

129. Ibid., 481.

130. Ibid., 481–82.
131. *Federalist* No. 17, p. 101.
132. Tocqueville, *Democracy,* ed. Mayer and Lerner, 482–83.
133. Ibid., 219.
134. Ibid., 219–20.
135. Ibid., 220.
136. Martin Diamond recognizes other effects that Tocqueville sees arising from the "decentralist federalism" of the Constitution. These include the fostering of a kind of patriotism that is dependent on putting the part of policy making that most immediately affects the citizenry within their reach. Another effect is that of nurturing activity and energy through local political activity, again made possible by "decentralist federalism." Diamond, "Ends of Federalism," 161–66.

3. The Role of the Judiciary

1. Alexander Hamilton, John Jay, and James Madison, *The Federalist: A Commentary on the Constitution of the United States,* ed. Henry Cabot Lodge, with an introduction by Edward Mead Earle (New York: Modern Library, 1941), No. 81, pp. 523–24. Publius (Hamilton) is stating the criticism of Brutus's Anti-Federalist objection to the judicial power.
2. Alexander Bickel is among the legal analysts who have questioned the textual defense for judicial review. The defense begins with the supremacy clause's requirement that state judges are bound to adhere to the Constitution as supreme over the laws of their respective states. It follows that these state judges must refuse to enforce state statutes that conflict with the Constitution. Determining the consistency of state statutes with the Constitution imposed the duty on these judges to exercise judicial review over state statutes. Since the Constitution grants federal courts jurisdiction over all cases "arising under" the Constitution and provides for the Supreme Court to have appellate jurisdiction over such cases, the Constitution appears to provide for appeal of state cases involving the Constitution to the Supreme Court. When the Supreme Court reviews such cases, this review must include the constitutional issues decided by the state court. Thus, Supreme Court review of state court judgments on the constitutionality of state actions seems required, or at least necessary, to fulfill the relevant constitutional provisions. Supreme Court review certainly fulfills the important purpose of uniform construction and application of the Constitution to state laws throughout the country. Alexander M. Bickel, *The Least Dangerous Branch: The Supreme Court at the Bar of Politics* (Indianapolis: Bobbs-Merrill, 1962), 8–13. Bickel's point of departure in this discussion is *Marbury v. Madison,* 1 Cranch (5 U.S.) 137 (1803).

Textual support for federal courts' exercise of judicial review of congressional statutes is both more tentative and less necessary to preserve either uniformity or union. The argument begins with the supremacy clause, which requires state courts to adhere both to the Constitution and to "laws of the United States which shall be made in pursuance thereof." State courts do not appear to be bound by federal laws that are not "in pursuance" of the Constitution. The phrase "in pursuance thereof" may be read, however, to require only that the laws in question be "duly" passed according to constitutional processes, without consideration of whether such laws are within Congress's constitutional powers. State judges might simply assume the constitutionality of a federal statute from the authority of Congress and the president who enacted the statute. Bickel, *Least Dangerous Branch,* 9–10. If state courts are empowered to decide whether state laws are within the constitutional powers of the states, it is arguable that they should make the same determination of federal laws as well. If state courts are granted the power to judge the constitutionality of federal statutes, the Supreme Court should also have this power when such cases are appealed to it; thus, the Supreme Court must exercise the final power of judicial review over federal laws when it exercises its appeal power. Such review, it must be noted, can be interpreted to apply only to the determination that federal laws have been enacted through the prescribed constitutional processes—that is, measures in which both houses concur and that are signed by the president—without going to the question of whether Congress has surpassed its constitutional powers or acted in ways that are constitutionally prohibited. Ibid. As Bickel recognizes, this subtle and complex textual justification for judicial review not only is subject to differing conceptions of the reviewing power but also assumes a definition of the judicial power that includes the very power of judicial review it sets out to prove. This tenuous defense of federal judicial review of acts of co-ordinate branches of government also lacks the support of any of the important figures who contested the judicial power during the founding era. Martin Diamond, Winston Mills Fisk, and Herbert Garfinkel, *The Democratic Republic: An Introduction to American National Government,* 2d ed. (Chicago: Rand McNally, 1970), 302.

I am grateful to Professor Richard G. Stevens for another persuasive interpretation of the phrase "in pursuance thereof," which he suggests may have been designed to give constitutional blessing to statutes made following the adoption of the Constitution. Read this way, the supremacy clause of Article VI and its counterpart in Article III give even less support for a general power of judicial review by the Supreme Court of acts of Congress. Part II of this book examines some of this contemporary commentary.

3. *Federalist* No. 1, p. 6.

4. Ibid., No. 22, p. 138.

5. Publius takes up this issue again in No. 80, p. 516.

6. Ibid., No. 78, pp. 502–3.

7. Ibid., No. 57, p. 373.

8. Ibid., No. 70, p. 454.

9. U.S. Constitution, art. III, sec. 2.

10. *Federalist* No. 78, p. 504. In an asterisked note, Publius quotes Montesquieu: " 'Of the three powers above mentioned, the judiciary is next to nothing.' " Montesquieu, *The Spirit of the Laws,* trans. Thomas Nugent (New York: Hafner, 1949), 1:186.

11. *Federalist* No. 78, p. 504.

12. Montesquieu, *Spirit of the Laws,* 1:152–53.

13. *Federalist* No. 78, p. 504.

14. Ibid., 504–5.

15. The prohibitions on bills of attainder and ex post facto laws are found in the U.S. *Constitution,* art. I, sec. 9, among limitations on the national government; they are also included in the prohibitions on the states enumerated in art. I, sec. 10.

16. *Federalist* No. 78, pp. 505–6.

17. *Federalist* No. 79 addresses some of the means necessary to achieve judicial independence. It explains the necessity for fixed judicial salaries so that the threat of a salary reduction may not deter judges from their duty. The paper supports the impeachment power as consistent with judicial independence and argues that this removal power does not apply to "inability." It argues against a fixed retirement age for judges because, in Publius's view, the "deliberating and comparing faculties" generally remain vital beyond the usual retirement age. Ibid., 512–15.

18. Ibid., 515–16. Publius specifically mentions the prohibition in art. I, sec. 10, on states' imposing duties on imported articles and the emission of paper money as examples.

19. Ibid., 516.

20. Ibid., No. 80, p. 520. Publius discusses other constitutional powers of the judiciary in No. 80, pp. 516–22.

21. Ibid., No. 81, pp. 523–24.

22. Ibid., 526.

23. Boudin draws from this passage a striking parallel between the British Parliament and the U.S. Constitution. He asks, "Did he [Hamilton] mean that, for instance, after the decision of the United States Supreme Court in *Pollock* v. *Farmers Loan & Trust Co.*, the Congress of the United States could proceed to enact and enforce another income tax law, although it could not reverse the judgment in the particular case of *Pollock* v. *Farmers Loan & Trust Co.?*

"It may sound startling to those who get their notions on the subject from our regular historians, *but that is exactly what Hamilton seems to have meant.*" Louis B. Boudin, *Goverment by Judiciary* (New York: Russell & Russell, 1968), 1:112–13. Although Boudin glosses over important distinctions between the sovereignty of the British Parliament and the sovereignty of the people in the United States with its written Constitution, his argument deserves serious consideration, particularly where questions of division or separation of political powers are concerned. As Boudin himself acknowledges, a different case may be presented when there are specific constitutional prohibitions that limit Congress. Ibid., 114–16. Robert Clinton emphasizes the distinction between a determination in a particular case and a new rule for future cases and defines other aspects of the judicial power and develops these distinctions in a thoughtful manner. Robert Lowry Clinton, Marbury v. Madison *and Judicial Review* (Lawrence: University Press of Kansas, 1989), 70–77.

24. Abraham Lincoln, "First Inaugural Address on March 4, 1861," in *The Collected Works of Abraham Lincoln,* ed. Roy P. Basler (New Brunswick, N.J.: Rutgers University Press, 1953), 4:268.

25. *Federalist* No. 81, pp. 526–27. For a well-supported argument that Congress has evaded its constitutional duty to oversee the federal courts through regulating their structure and procedure, see Gary L. McDowell, *Curbing the Courts: The Constitution and the Limits of Judicial Power* (Baton Rouge: Louisiansa State University Press, 1988).

26. *Federalist* No. 81, pp. 530–33.

27. Ibid., No. 83, p. 554.

28. In a thoughtful article on Brutus and the substance of his constitutional objections, Anne Stuart Diamond presents good evidence that this is the pseudonym of

Robert Yates, as is generally thought to be the case. But the question of authorship of the Anti-Federalist essays by Brutus is not decisively answered. "The Anti-Federalist Brutus," *Political Science Reviewer* 6 (Fall 1976): 249–53.

29. Leonard W. Levy, ed., *Judicial Review and the Supreme Court: Selected Essays* (New York: Harper & Row, 1967), 6.

30. *Federalist* No. 78, p. 505.

31. Levy, *Judicial Review*, 6.

32. *Federalist* No. 33, p. 200.

33. Ibid., 198–201.

34. Ibid., No. 44, p. 295.

35. James Wilson refers to the judicial power's relationship to the laws as one that "give[s] them effect." Max Farrand, ed., *The Records of the Federal Convention of 1787*, 3d ed. (New Haven, Conn.: Yale University Press, 1966), 2:74.

36. This plan "was not formally before the Convention in any way," although several delegates made copies. Farrand, *Records*, 1:282–93, 3:617–19. A plan that was not submitted to the Convention contains no reference to judicial review. Ibid., 3:619–30.

37. Levy, *Judicial Review*, 7. Charles Beard, Edward S. Corwin, Andrew C. McLaughlin, Charles Warren, and Charles Grove Haines are among the historians who argue that judicial review was so well established that the framers took it for granted. Leonard Levy properly characterizes the evidence on which these historians rely as "sparing." Of the seven state precedents Haines specifies between 1776 and 1787, Levy persuasively argues that only two legitimately support a power of judicial review. Levy concludes, following the analysis of Louis B. Boudin and W. W. Crosskey, that the precedents tended to arise when legislatures interfered with either the normal jurisdiction of courts or their trial procedures. *Bayard v. Singleton*, one of the legitimate examples of a declaration of unconstitutionality, involved the North Carolina court's taking jurisdiction of a case although a statute directed dismissal. "The legislature then summoned the judges to explain their audacious disregard of its supreme authority . . . but took no disciplinary action. The court [in *Trevett v. Weeden*, 1 N. C. (Mart.) 42 (1787)] in unmistakable terms then held the disputed statute unconstitutional." Levy, *Judicial Review*, 7–11.

38. Robert Lowry Clinton attributes the origin of the term "judicial review" to Edward S. Corwin in an article Corwin published in 1910. Clinton, *Marbury v. Madison*, 138.

39. Farrand, *Records*, 2:430.

40. In this case, a state court took jurisdiction even though a statute directed dismissal, clearly an action of a judiciary nature. Levy, *Judicial Review,*, 10.

41. Farrand, *Records*, 2:440.

42. Gerry further observed that some state judges had actually "set aside laws as being agst. the Constitution. This was done too with general approbation." Ibid., 1:97–98. King's notes report a comment on this date, apparently Dickinson's: "the Judges must interpret the Laws they ought not to be legislators." Ibid., 108.

43. Farrand, *Records*, 1:98.

44. Thomas Hobbes, *Leviathan*, ed. Michael Oakeshott, with an introduction by Richard S. Peters (London: Collier-Macmillan, 1962), 218, 219, 231.

45. Farrand, *Records*, 2:430.

46. Ibid., 440.

47. Jonathan Elliot, ed., *The Debates in the Several State Conventions on the Adoption of the Federal Constitution, as Recommended by the General Convention at Philadephia in 1787,* 2d ed. (Philadelphia: J. B. Lippincott, 1836), 2:469.

48. Ibid., 489.

49. Elliot, *Debates,* 3:532.

50. Ibid., 553.

51. Ibid., 559.

52. Joseph Gales, Sr., ed., *The Debates and Proceedings in the Congress of the United States* (Washington, D.C.: Gales & Seaton, 1834), 1:457.

53. Madison also observes: "It is therefore a fair question, whether this great point may not as well be decided, at least by the whole Legislature as by a part, by us as well as by the Executive or Judiciary." Ibid., 520. In this same context, Gerry asks "if the judges are not ex officio judges of the law; and whether they would not be bound to declare the law a nullity, if this clause is contained in it, and is inconsistent with the constitution? There is a clause in this system of government that makes it their duty. I allude to that which authorized the President to obtain the opinions of the heads of departments in writing; so the President and Senate may require the opinion of the judges respecting this power, if they have any doubts concerning it." Ibid., 524. The Court refused President Washington's request, through his secretary of state, to issue an advisory opinion regarding a proposed treaty on the grounds that such an opinion was beyond its competency. C. Herman Pritchett, *Constitutional Law of the Federal System* (Englewood Cliffs, N.J.: Prentice-Hall, 1984), 157. Sherman, in apparent response to Gerry's suggestion, observed in a manner reminiscent of the Convention's debate over the Council of Revision: "It has been said, that the Legislature may give their opinion on the constitution. I agree with gentlemen if they mean that, as an individual, we may give our single opinion; but I never can admit it to be right in our legislative capacity to influence the judges, and throw our weight into either scale to warp their decision. I think it highly criminal to attempt to bias their judgment in any way." Gales, *Debates and Proceedings,* 1:530. White, former delegate to the Virginia Ratifying Convention, said: "I imagine the Legislature may construe the constitution with respect to the powers annexed to their department, but subject to the decision of the judges. The same with regard to the executive: the President and Senate may construe the power in question, and as they determine respecting the mode of removal, so they may act, but liable also to the decision of the Judiciary." Ibid., 539. Sylvester defended the House's power to make judgments on the constitutionality of laws it considers but said: "It is certain that the Judiciary will be better able to decide the question of constitutionality in this way than any other. If we are wrong, they can correct our error; if we are right, the question will be decided at a time when no ill can result from factious or contentious parties; all is now still, and a favorable disposition to listen to reason prevails." Ibid., 585.

Later in a debate on the same issue, Gerry took exception to Sylvester and others: "Sir, we are not the expositors of the constitution; but if we were the expositors, we ought to give our exposition by a declaratory act, and not foist it in where no one would ever look for it. But if it were done by a declaratory act, I conceive it would be impossible to draw the line at which declaratory acts should stop. Hence we should alter the constitutional mode of amending the system of Government. Another difficulty would also arise: the judges are the expositors of the constitution and the acts of Congress. Our exposition, therefore, would be subject to their revisal. In this way the constitutional balance would be destroyed; the Legislature, with the Judiciary, might remove the head of the Executive branch. But a further reason why we are not the expositors is, that the Judiciary may disagree with us, and undo what all our efforts have labored to accomplish. A law is a nullity, unless it can be carried into execution; in this case, our law will be suspended." Ibid., 596.

54. This term—to lay down a rule of conduct—is used by Boudin in a different context; *Government by Judiciary,* 1:99.

55. As for other delegates to the Constitutional Convention who made statements that can be interpreted as supporting some theory of judicial review, these statements "imply neither a general power to expound the Constitution nor an obligation on the part of the other branches to regard a judicial decision on the constitutionality of their actions as binding." Ralph A. Rossum, "The Courts and the Judicial Power," in *The Framing and Ratification of the Constitution,* ed. Leonard W. Levy and Dennis M. Mahoney (New York: Macmillan, 1987), 233. After reviewing evidence from a number of sources, including the Convention debates, Leonard Levy concludes that "decisive evidence cannot be marshalled to prove what the framers had in mind." Levy, *Judicial Review,* 2.

To assist the reader in interpreting various statements made in the Constitutional Convention, the following excerpts may be more helpful than merely quoting a phrase or sentence here and there.

On 29 May, resolutions known as the Virginia Plan were introduced. These resolutions included a power of the national legislature "to negative all laws passed by the several States, contravening in the opinion of the National Legislature the articles of Union." The subsequent resolution read "that the Executive and a convenient number of the National Judiciary, ought to compose a council of revision with authority to examine every act of the National Legislature before it shall operate, & every act of a particular Legislature before a Negative thereon shall be final; and that the dissent of the said Council shall amount to a rejection, unless the Act of the National Legislature be again passed, or that a particular Legislature be again negatived by [number left blank] of the members of each branch." Farrand, *Records,* 1:21. The national legislature clearly retained final authority over constitutionality of acts of Congress and the states under this resolution. Elbridge Gerry spoke against the Council of Revision on 4 June: "Mr. Gerry doubts whether the Judiciary ought to form a part of it, as they will have a sufficient check agst. encroachments on their own department by their exposition of the law, which involved a power of deciding on their constitutionality. In some states the Judges had (actually) set aside laws as being agst. the Constitution. This was done too with general approbation. It was quite foreign from the nature of ye. office to make them judges of the policy of public measures." Ibid., 97–98. Rufus King spoke after Gerry and observed "that the Judges ought to be able to expound the law as it should come before them free from the bias of having participated in its formation." Ibid., 98.

William Pierce's notes in Farrand read: "Mr. King was of opinion that the Judicial ought not to join in the negative of a Law, because the Judges will have the expounding of those Laws when they come before them; and they will no doubt stop the operation of such as shall appear repugnant to the constitution." Ibid.,109. According to Pierce's notes, Madison responded to Franklin's concern over a veto solely by the executive that no man should have the power to negate laws passed by the legislature: "Mr. Maddison [*sic*] was of opinion that no Man would be so daring as to place a veto on a Law that had passed with the assent of the Legislature." Ibid. Pierce's notes continue: "Mr. Dickinson could not agree with Gentlemen in blending the national Judicial with the Executive, because the one is the expounder, and the other the Executor of the Laws." Ibid., 110. King's notes report a comment on this date, apparently Dickinson's: "the judges must interpret the Laws they ought not to be legislators." Ibid., 108.

Returning to Madison's account of the debates on 4 June: "Mr. Bedford was opposed to every check on the Legislative, even the Council of Revision first proposed. He thought it would be sufficient to mark out in the Constitution the Boundaries to the Legislative Authority, which would give all the requisite security to the rights of the other departments. The Representatives of the People were the best judges of what was for their interest, and ought to be under no external controul whatever. The two branches would produces [*sic*] a sufficient controul within [the Legislature itself]." Ibid., 100–101.

On 21 July, James Wilson argued that the "Natl Judiciary should be associated with the Executive in the Revisionary power." He observed: "The Judiciary ought to have an opportunity of remonstrating agst. projected encroachments on the people as well as on themselves. It had been said that the Judges, as expositors of the Laws, would have an opportunity of defending their constitutional rights. There was weight in this observation; but this power of the Judges did not go far enough. Laws may be unjust, may be unwise, may be dangerous, may be destructive; and yet not be so unconstitutional as to justify the Judges in refusing to give them effect. Let them have a share in the Revisionary power, and they will have an opportunity of taking notice of these characters of a law, and of counteracting, by the weight of their opinions the improper views of the Legislature." Ibid., 2:73.

Nathaniel Gorham responded that he "did not see the advantage of employing the Judges in this way. As Judges they are not to be presumed to possess any peculiar knowledge of the mere policy of public measures." Ibid. Mr. Gerry argued that the Council of Revision was a "combining & mixing together the Legislative & the other departments. It was establishing an improper coalition between the Executive & Judiciary. It was making Statesmen of the Judges; and setting them up as guardians of the Rights of the people. He relied for his part on the Representatives of the people as the guardians of their Rights & interests." Ibid., 74–75. "Mr. Strong thought with Mr. Gerry that the power of making ought to be kept distinct from that of expounding, the laws. No maxim was better established. The Judges in exercising the function of expositors might be influenced by the part they had taken, in framing the laws." Ibid., 75.

Continuing the debate of 21 July, Luther Martin "considered the association of the Judges with the Executive as a dangerous innovation; as well as one which, could not produce the particular advantage expected from it. A knowledge of mankind, and of Legislative affairs cannot be presumed to belong in a higher deger [sic] degree to the Judges than to the Legislature. And as to the Constitutionality of laws, that point will come before the Judges in their proper official character. In this character they have a negative on the laws." Ibid., 76.

George Mason responded: "[I]t had been said (by Mr. L. Martin) that if the Judges were joined in this check on the laws, they would have a double negative, since in their expository capacity of Judges they would have one negative. He would reply that in this capacity they could impede in one case only, the operation of laws. They could declare an unconstitutional law void. But with regard to every law however unjust oppressive or pernicious, which did not come plainly under this description, they would be under the necessity as Judges to give it a free course. He wished the further use to be made of the Judges, of giving aid in preventing every improper law. Their aid will be the more valuable as they are in the habit and practice of considering laws in their true principles, and in all their consequences." Ibid., 78.

Nathaniel Gorhan argued: "All agree that a check on the Legislature is necessary. But there are two objections agst. admitting the Judges to share in it which no observations on the other side seem to obviate. the lst. is that the Judges ought to carry into the exposition of the laws no prepossessions with regard to them. 2d. that as the Judges will outnumber the Executive, the revisionary check would be thrown entirely out of the Executive hands, and instead of enabling him to defend himself, would enable the Judges to sacrifice him." Ibid., 79. John Rutledge "thought the Judges of all men the most unfit to be concerned in the revisionary Council. The Judges ought never to give their opinion on a law till it comes before them." Ibid., 80.

On 15 August, Madison introduced a motion clarifying the veto of the Executive and Supreme Judiciary Departments. If either of these departments objects to acts before they become laws, it would take two-thirds of each house to give the act the effect of law; if both branches object to the legislative act, it would require three-fourths of each to "overrule the objections and give to the acts the force of law." Ibid., 298. This scheme retains legislative supremacy over the objections of the executive and supreme judiciary. "Mr. Pinckney opposed the interference of the Judges in the Legislative business: it will involve them in parties, and give a previous tincture to their opinions." Ibid. "Mr. Mercer heartily approved the motion. It as [*sic*] an axiom that the Judiciary ought to be separate from the Legislative: but equally so that it ought to be independent of that department. The true policy of the axiom is that legislative usurpation and oppression may be obviated. He disapproved of the Doctrine that the Judges as expositors of the Constitution should have authority to declare a law void. He thought laws ought to be well and cautiously made, and then to be uncontroulable." Ibid. John Dickinson "was strongly impressed with the remark of Mr. Mercer as to the power of the Judges to set aside the law. He thought no such power ought to exist. He was at the same time at a loss what expedient to substitute. The Justiciary of Aragon he observed became by degrees the law-giver." Ibid., 299. Gouverneur Morris argued for an absolute negative in the executive. "He could not agree that the Judiciary which was part of the Executive, should be bound to say that a direct violation of the Constitution was law. A controul over the legislature might have its inconveniences. But view the danger on the other side. The most virtuous citizens will often as members of a legislative body concur in measures which afterwards in their private capacity they will be ashamed of. Encroachments of the popular branch of the Government ought to be guarded agst." Ibid. Mr. Sherman observed that "He disapproved of Judges meddling in politics and parties." Ibid., 300.

On 22 August, in the context of discussing whether or not prohibitions on bills of attainder and ex post facto laws should be made part of the Constitution, Hugh Williamson argued for inclusion: "Such a prohibitory clause is in the Constitution of N. Carolina, and tho it has been violated, it has done good there & may do good here, because the Judges can take hold of it." Ibid., 376.

On 27 August, in the context of debating the jurisdiction of the Supreme Court, "Mr. Madison doubted whether it was not going too far to extend the jurisdiction of the Court generally to cases arising Under the Constitution, & whether it ought not to be limited to cases of a Judiciary Nature. The right of expounding the Constitution in cases not of this nature ought not to be given to that Department." Ibid., 430. The motion was agreed to, "it being generally supposed that the jurisdiction given was constructively limited to cases of a Judiciary nature." Ibid. On 28 August, Madison spoke in response to a proposal to prohibit states from retrospective interference in private contracts: "Is not that already done by the prohibition of ex post facto laws, which will oblige the Judges to declare such interferences null & void." Ibid., 440.

56. Judicial review in "cases of a judiciary nature" is consistent with the theory of Federalist No. 51 insofar as Publius refers to the necessity for each branch of government to possess the "necessary constitutional means . . . to resist encroachments of the others" p. 337.

57. 358 U.S. 1 (1958).

58. 1 Cranch (5 U.S.) 137 (1803).

59. 358 U.S. 1, 18 (1958).

60. Charles Grove Haines, *The American Doctrine of Judicial Supremacy* (Berkeley: University of California Press, 1932; reprint, New York: Da Capo Press, 1973), 193–94 (page references are to the reprint edition).

61. 1 Cranch (5 U.S.) 137, 154–56, 173–76 (1803).

62. Marshall also observes that in declaring "what shall be the supreme law of the land," the oath refers not to "the laws of the United States generally, but those only which shall be made in pursuance of the constitution, have that rank." Ibid., 180.

63. Ibid., 180.

64. Boudin, *Government by Judiciary,* 1:230.

65. 6 Wheat. (19 U.S.) 264, 400 (1821). Marshall observes: "It is a maxim not to be disregarded, that general expressions, in every opinion, are to be taken in connection with the case in which those expressions are used. If they go beyond the case, they may be respected, but ought not to control the judgment in a subsequent suit when the very point is presented for decision. The reason for the maxim is obvious. The question actually before the court is investigated with care and considered in its full extent. Other principles which may serve to illustrate it, are considered in their relation to the case decided, but their possible bearing on all other cases is seldom completely investigated." Ibid., 399–400. Later, in *Cohens,* Marshall characterizes the *Marbury* opinion as "much broader than the decision, and not only much broader than the reasoning with which that decision is supported, but in some instances contradictory to

its principle." Ibid., 401. Marshall is referring in these quoted passages from *Cohens* to the question of the Court's original versus its appellate jurisdiction as prescribed in Article III of the Constitution. Gerald Gunther refers to *Cohens* as containing "a rare admission of error" on Marshall's part. I am grateful to Gunther for drawing Marshall's statements in *Cohens* to my attention. Gerald Gunther, *Constitutional Law*, 12th ed. (Westbury, N.Y.: Foundation Press, 1991), 12.

66. 358 U.S. 1, 18 (1958).

67. Clinton, *Marbury v. Madison*, 98–99.

68. Ibid., 99.

69. 1 Cranch (5 U.S.) 137, 180 (1803).

70. Boudin, *Government by Judiciary*, 1:230 (emphasis in original).

71. Ibid., 231–32 (emphasis in original).

72. Ibid., 233.

73. Bickel, *Least Dangerous Branch*, 6–7.

74. Ibid., 7.

75. Ibid., 8. Bickel makes it clear that although the interpretation he gives here is "textually permissible," he does not "advocate it or . . . vouch for its workability." Ibid., 7.

76. Boudin, *Government by Judiciary*, 1:99.

77. *Federalist* No. 78, p. 504.

78. 1 Cranch (5 U.S.) 137, 179 (1803).

79. Haines, *American Doctrine of Judicial Supremacy*, 200.

80. Clinton, *Marbury v. Madison*, 99. Boudin also supports this position in *Government by Judiciary*, 1:231–32.

81. 1 Cranch (5 U.S.) 137, 176 (1803).

82. Ibid., 178. Raoul Berger presents a formidable refutation of this view. He argues that much of the historical evidence will not support a theory of judicial review restricted to judicial "self-defense" and that this narrow interpretation of the reviewing power presents the anomaly of "two classes of Congressional 'usurpation,' both of which are 'unconstitutonal and void' (for the 'unconstitutional and void' statements were *never* confined to invasions of judicial prerogatives), but only invasion of judicial prerogatives may be *declared* void by the courts." Berger's analysis does not, in my view, take sufficient account of the fact that many statements in the Constitutional Convention were made in the context of the proposed Council of Revision, the decisions of which were not to have been binding, since they would have been subject to legislative override. Raoul Berger, *Congress v. the Supreme Court* (Cambridge: Harvard University Press, 1969), 154–55, 156–65.

83. 1 Cranch (5 U.S.) 137, 177 (1803).

84. Ronald Dworkin, *Taking Rights Seriously* (Cambridge: Harvard University Press, 1977), 180.

85. Richard A. Epstein, *Takings: Private Property and the Power of Eminent Domain* (Cambridge: Harvard University Press, 1985), 3, 19, 283, 306.

86. Michael J. Perry, *The Constitution, the Courts, and Human Rights: An Inquiry into the Legitimacy of Constitutional Policymaking by the Judiciary* (New Haven, Conn.: Yale University Press, 1982), 99.

87. Laurence H. Tribe, *American Constitutional Law,* 2d ed. (Mineola, N.Y.: Foundation Press, 1988), 761.

Part II. Contemporary Constitutional Commentary

1. Joseph Story, *Commentaries on the Constitution of the United States,* 3 vols., with an introduction by Arthur E. Sutherland (Boston: Hilliard, Gray, 1833; reprint, New York: Da Capo Press, 1970), 1:vi (page references are to the reprint edition).
2. Thomas Hobbes, *Leviathan,* ed. Michael Oakeshott, with an introduction by Richard S. Peters (London: Collier-Macmillan, 1962), 205–9.
3. Alexander Hamilton, John Jay, and James Madison, *The Federalist: A Commentary on the Constitution of the United States,* ed. Henry Cabot Lodge, with an introduction by Edward Mead Earle (New York: Modern Library, 1941), No. 81, p. 524.

4. The Concept of Rights and Natural Law as Fundamental Constitutional Principles

1. Ronald Dworkin, *Life's Dominion: An Argument About Abortion, Euthanasia, and Individual Freedom* (New York: Alfred A. Knopf, 1993), 146. A large portion of this book is an engaging and informative examination of historical and theological issues surrounding abortion and the place of abortion in contemporary feminist theory and in the policy of other nations.
2. In addition to his extensive work as a commentator on the Constitution and the role of the Court, Archibald Cox has held a number of important positions of public service, such as solicitor general of the United States. He also directed the Office of the Watergate Special Prosecution Force. There is an obvious link between Cox's academic analysis of the Court's role, which emphasizes legitimacy and the rule of law, and his undertaking duties with the Special Prosecution Force in order to restore confidence in government.
3. Archibald Cox, *The Role of the Supreme Court in American Government* (London: Oxford University Press, 1976), 32. In a later book, he seems to change his emphasis from the Court as "the voice of natural law" to the necessity for legitimacy in constitutional rulings. One important source of such legitimacy is the link between constitutional rulings and natural law. Archibald Cox, *The Court and the Constitution* (Boston: Houghton Mifflin, 1987), 374.
4. Cox, *Supreme Court in American Government,* 103. Cox argues, for example, that it was "[o]nly public support for the Court's decision" that forced President Nixon to obey the judicial subpoena for the Watergate tapes. Archibald Cox, "The Role of the Supreme Court: Judicial Activism or Self-Restraint?" *Maryland Law Review* 47 (1987): 122.
5. Cox, *Supreme Court in American Government,* 146.
6. Joseph Story, *A Familiar Exposition of the Constitution of the United States: Containing a Brief Commentary on Every Clause, Explaining the True Nature, Reasons, and Objects Thereof* (Boston: Marsh, Capen, Lyon, & Webb, 1840), 36–37.

7. Ronald Dworkin, *Taking Rights Seriously* (Cambridge: Harvard University Press, 1977).

8. Thomas Pangle, "Rediscovering Rights," *The Public Interest,* no. 50 (Winter 1978): 158.

9. Dworkin, *Taking Rights Seriously,* 180.

10. Pangle, "Rediscovering Rights," 160.

11. Ibid.

12. Dworkin, *Taking Rights Seriously,* 277.

13. Ibid., 277–78.

14. Pangle, "Rediscovering Rights," 159.

15. Alexander Hamilton, John Jay, and James Madison, *The Federalist: A Commentary on the Constitution of the United States,* ed. Henry Cabot Lodge, with an introduction by Edward Mead Earle (New York: Modern Library, 1941), No. 10, p. 56.

16. Dworkin, *Taking Rights Seriously,* 87–89, 106.

17. Dworkin, *Life's Dominion,* 146. Dworkin treats his concept of "integrity" at some length, for example, in its application to the legislature, in Ronald Dworkin, *Law's Empire* (Cambridge: Harvard University Press, 1986), 221–24.

18. Dworkin, *Taking Rights Seriously,* 88–89, 106.

19. Ibid., 106.

20. Ibid., 107.

21. In *Taking Rights Seriously* and Dworkin's other work, there is little reference to either *The Federalist* or the *Records of the Federal Convention.* In one rare reference to *The Federalist,* Dworkin dismisses the text by arguing: "There is no convention either tying various passages in the Federalist Papers to the Constitution itself or denying that connection, for example." Ronald Dworkin, "The Forum of Principle," in *A Matter of Principle* (Cambridge: Harvard University Press, 1985), 42.

22. Dworkin, *Taking Rights Seriously,* 106.

23. Ibid., 106–7.

24. I am particularly indebted to constitutional scholar Peter M. Schotten for his suggestions regarding this part of my book. Professor Schotten also made helpful comments on the manuscript as a whole.

25. Dworkin, *Taking Rights Seriously,* 135–36.

26. Ibid., 136.

27. The Constitution assumes the death penalty not only in these clauses but also in the Fifth Amendment's provision for grand jury indictment and its prohibition of double jeopardy. Article I, sec. 2, gives the president power to grant reprieves.

28. *Federalist* No. 10, p. 54.

29. Pangle, "Rediscovering Rights," 159.

30. *Federalist* No. 10, p. 56.

31. Ibid., 55.

32. Pangle, "Rediscovering Rights," 159.

33. Publius addresses this issue in *Federalist* No. 63, p. 410. He discusses the role of the Senate when the people are misled in their judgment by "irregular passion, or some illicit advantage, or misled by artful misrepresentations of interested men [and] call for measures which they themselves will afterwards be the most ready to lament and condemn. In these critical moments, how salutary will be the interference of some

temperate and respectable body of citizens, in order to check the misguided career, and to suspend the blow meditated by the people against themselves, until reason, justice, and truth can regain their authority over the public mind?''

34. Dworkin, *Taking Rights Seriously*, 274.

35. Ronald Dworkin, "Liberalism," in *A Matter of Principle* (Cambridge: Harvard University Press, 1985), 191.

36. Ronald Dworkin, "Do We Have a Right to Pornography?" in *A Matter of Principle* (Cambridge: Harvard University Press, 1985), 354. Dworkin qualifies this statement by characterizing this supposition as "only academic speculation, because there is no reason to suppose a sufficiently direct connection between crime and either *Sex Kittens* or *Hamlet* to provide a ground for banning either one as private entertainment." Ibid., 355.

37. Regulation of pornography requires a sustained argument to support it. See Lane V. Sunderland, *Obscenity: The Court, the Congress and the President's Commission* (Washington, D.C.: American Enterprise Institute for Public Policy Research, 1974).

38. Dworkin, "Do We Have a Right to Pornography?" 355.

39. Stanley Brubaker, "Taking Dworkin Seriously," *Review of Politics* 47, no. 1 (1985): 58–59. I draw from Professor Brubaker's insightful analysis on this point as well as others in this section of my work.

40. Ronald Dworkin, "Liberty and Pornogrpahy," *New York Review of Books* 38, no. 14 (15 August 1991): 15.

41. Ronald Dworkin, "Pornography: An Exchange," *New York Review of Books* 41, no. 5 (3 March 1994): 48–49. Dworkin is responding to Catharine A. MacKinnon in this exchange.

42. *Miller v. California*, 413 U.S. 15 (1973).

43. Dworkin, "Do We Have a Right to Pornography?" 358.

44. Robert George makes related arguments about equal dignity and respect: "But where demeaning, degrading, or destructive self-regarding conduct is involved, there certainly need be nothing inegalitarian in legislative action aimed at preventing it. Such legislative action certainly (but not arbitrarily) prefers some types of *conduct* over others; but it just as certainly need reflect no preference of one person (or class of persons) over another. It condemns some conduct as unworthy of persons; but it need condemn no human being as less worthy than any other. The paternalism involved in a decision to intervene in persons' lives to prevent them from demeaning, degrading, or destroying themselves by their own wrongful choices might well, as Finnis suggests, be motivated precisely by an appreciation of their equal worth and dignity." Robert P. George, *Making Men Moral: Civil Liberties and Public Morality* (Oxford: Clarendon Press, 1993), 100, 96–97.

45. Ibid.

46. Sunderland, *Obscenity*, 79–84.

47. Dworkin, "Do We Have a Right to Pornography?" 358.

48. Brubaker, "Taking Dworkin Seriously," 58–59.

49. *Federalist* No. 10, p. 54.

50. Brubaker, "Taking Dworkin Seriously," 60.

51. Dworkin, *Life's Dominion*, 101.

52. 381 U.S. 479 (1965).

53. Dworkin, *Life's Dominion,* 106.

54. Justice Scalia's concurring opinion in *Cruzan v. Director, Missouri Department of Health,* 497 U.S. 261 (1990), casts doubt on Dworkin's Herculean model of justices. In this "right to die" case, Scalia observed: "The point at which life becomes 'worthless,' and the point at which the means necessary to preserve it become 'extraordinary' or 'inappropriate,' are neither set forth in the Constitution nor known to the nine Justices of this Court any better than they are known to nine people picked at random from the Kansas City telephone directory."

55. Dworkin, *Life's Dominion,* 124.

56. Ibid., 146.

57. Thomas Hobbes, *Leviathan,* ed. Michael Oakeshott, with an introduction by Richard S. Peters (London: Collier-Macmillan, 1962), 205–6.

58. John Locke, *Second Treatise of Government,* ed. C. B. Macpherson (Indianapolis: Hackett, 1980), sec. 134.

59. Ibid., sec. 137.

60. Montesquieu, *The Spirit of the Laws,* trans. Thomas Nugent (New York: Hafner, 1949), 1:150.

61. Dworkin, *Life's Dominion,* 146.

62. Dworkin, *Taking Rights Seriously,* 134–35.

63. Stanley Brubaker, "Reconsidering Dworkin's Case for Judicial Activism," *Journal of Politics* 46, no. 2 (1984): 513.

64. Dworkin, *Taking Rights Seriously,* 123–26. Dworkin distinguishes a judge's reliance on "the naked fact" he holds as a belief or preference from beliefs held on the basis of their truth or soundness. He believes it is proper for Hercules to rely on the latter, but not the former. Ibid., 124.

65. *Federalist* No. 1, p. 4.

66. Ibid., No. 78, p. 505.

67. Dworkin, *Life's Dominion,* 146.

68. *Federalist* No. 51, p. 337.

69. Ibid., No. 54, pp. 353–54.

70. Ibid., No. 10, pp. 57–58.

71. Max Farrand, ed., *The Records of the Federal Convention of 1787,* 3d ed. (New Haven, Conn.: Yale University Press, 1966), 2:73.

72. Ibid., 78, 430. In the First Congress, Madison refutes the idea that the judiciary has an exclusive prerogative to lay down an absolute constitutional rule for other branches of government when he argues that no department "draws from the constitution greater powers than another, in marking out the limits of the powers of the several departments." Joseph Gales, Sr., *The Debates and Proceedings in the Congress of the United States* (Washington, D.C.: Gales & Seaton, 1834), 1:520.

73. Dworkin, *Life's Dominion,* 146.

74. *Federalist* No. 1, p. 6.

75. Herbert J. Storing, "The Constitution and the Bill of Rights," in *Taking the Constitution Seriously: Essays on the Constitution and Constitutional Law,* ed. Gary L. McDowell (Dubuque, Iowa: Kendall/Hunt, 1981), 276.

76. Cox, *Supreme Court in American Government,* 32.

77. Ibid.

78. Archibald Cox, *Freedom of Expression* (Cambridge: Harvard University Press, 1980), 89.

79. Cox, *Supreme Court in American Government*, 7. See also Archibald Cox, *The Warren Court: Constitutional Decisions as an Instrument for Reform* (Cambridge: Harvard University Press, 1968), 113.

80. Archibald Cox, "The Role of the Supreme Court in American Society," *Marquette Law Review* 50 (1967): 575.

81. Cox, *Supreme Court in American Government*, 30.

82. Cox, *Warren Court*, 21.

83. Cox, "Supreme Court in American Society," 575.

84. Cox, *Warren Court*, 21, 89, 116; Cox, *Freedom*, 89.

85. Archibald Cox, *Understanding the Supreme Court* (Pittsburgh: University of Pittsburgh School of Law, 1962), 9–13.

86. Learned Hand, "Mr. Justice Cardozo," quoted in Cox, *Understanding the Supreme Court*, 13.

87. Cox, *Supreme Court in American Government*, 16.

88. Cox, "Supreme Court in American Society," 579.

89. Archibald Cox, "Federalism and Individual Rights Under the Burger Court," *Northwestern University Law Review* 73, no. 1 (March/April 1978): 9–10.

90. 426 U.S. 833 (1976), treated in Cox, "Federalism," 19. This case ruled that federal wage and hour requirements for state and municipal employees, which were enacted by Congress in 1974, were unconstitutional.

91. Ibid., 22.

92. Ibid., 25.

93. Archibald Cox, "Congress v. the Supreme Court," *Mercer Law Review* 33 (1982): 717.

94. Cox, *Supreme Court in American Government*, 32.

95. Ibid., 103.

96. Ibid., 103–4.

97. Ibid., 105–6. Cox borrows the phrase "dull and traditional habit of mankind" from Walter Bagehot's *The English Constitution*.

98. Cox, *Supreme Court in American Government*, 107.

99. Ibid., 109.

100. Ibid., 110–11.

101. "It is at this point that the legitimating influence of the idea of natural law becomes important. We should use different words [for natural law] today: 'impersonal and durable principles,' 'enduring values,' 'fundamental aspirations,' 'vital lessons of liberty and equal opportunity,' 'human rights' and so on; but the very persistence of such evocative, rather than sharply definitive, phrases attests the strength of our natural law inheritance *as authority for legal change*. . . . Natural law in this sense legitimizes change, if indeed it does not impel it; and it legitimizes for the public and perhaps even for the judge himself a measure of constitutional adjudication as an instrument of reform." Ibid., 111–12.

102. Ibid., 112–13.

103. Ibid., 113.

104. Ibid. Perhaps because of the public controversy over the abortion decisions,

which undermines their legitimacy, Cox approaches these decisions in a later work in a more neutral manner, emphasizing the need to strike a balance between self-government and the judicial protection of human rights. Cox, *Court and Constitution,* 322, 328.

105. Cox, *Supreme Court in American Government,* 114.

106. Cox, *Court and Constitution,* 355.

107. "For myself it would be most irksome to be ruled by a bevy of Platonic Guardians, even if I knew how to choose them, which I assuredly do not. If I were in charge, I should miss the stimulus of living in a society where I have, at least theoretically, some part in the direction of public affairs." Learned Hand, *The Bill of Rights: The Oliver Wendell Holmes Lectures* (Cambridge: Harvard University Press,1958), 73–74, quoted in Cox, *Supreme Court in American Government,* 116.

108. Ibid.

109. James Bradley Thayer and others, *John Marshall* (Chicago: University of Chicago Press, 1967), 106–7, quoted in Cox, *Supreme Court in American Government,* 116–17.

110. Cox, *Court and Constitution,* 377.

111. Cox also tells us that the Court is the "voice of the spirit." Cox, "Supreme Court in American Society," 590.

112. Cox, "Congress," 720–21.

113. Cox, *Freedom,* 89.

114. Ibid.

115. Cox suggests that the Court has a closer relationship with the intellectual community than does Congress. Cox, *Warren Court,* 12.

116. 16 Wall. (83 U.S.) 36 (1873). In interpreting the Fourteenth Amendment's privileges and immunites clause, the Court narrowly confined the civil rights that are attributes of United States citizenship.

117. 19 How. 393 (1857). In the case of *Dred Scott v. Sandford,* the Court's main holdings were that "no Negro slave could be a citizen with power to sue in the federal courts" and, more fundamentally, that "all persons of African descent, whether slaves or not, were barred from access to the federal courts . . . and from the enjoyment of any rights or protections under the Constitution." C. Herman Pritchett, *The American Constitution* (New York: McGraw-Hill,1977), 291.

118. 163 U.S. 537 (1896). The Supreme Court in the case of *Plessy v. Ferguson* found segregation to be compatible with equality, in regard to Negroes. Despite Justice Harlan's dissent that "our Constitution is color-blind, and neither knows nor tolerates classes among citizens," the majority used the "separate but equal" formula to reconcile the protection of the Fourteenth Amendment with state-enforced segregation. Pritchett, *American Constitution,* 490.

119. 274 U.S. 200 (1927). The case of *Buck v. Bell* upheld a Virginia statute under which "persons affected with hereditary insanity, idiocy, imbecility, feeblemindedness, or epilepsy could be subjected to compulsory sexual sterilization." Justice Holmes's justification for supporting the statute held that "[i]t is better for all the world, if instead of waiting to execute degenerate offspring for crime, or to let them starve for their imbecility, society can prevent those who are manifestly unfit from continuing their kind. The principle that sustains compulsory vaccination is broad enough to cover cut-

ting the Fallopian tubes. . . . Three generations of imbeciles are enough." Ibid., 207. These judicial decisions reveal instances in which the people did acquiesce, at least for a time, in the decisions. Pritchett, *American Constitution*, 537–38.

120. Levy discusses other remarkable cases that illustrate his point, including *U.S. v. Cruikshank*, 92 U.S. 542 (1876); *U.S. v. Reece*, 92 U.S. 214 (1876); and *Civil Rights Cases*, 109 U.S. 3 (1883). For other examples, see Leonard Levy, ed., *Judicial Review and the Supreme Court* (New York: Harper & Row, 1967), 33–36.

121. *Federalist* Nos. 9 and 10.

122. Ibid., No. 1, p. 6. This argument is set forth in Chapter 2.

123. Ibid., Nos. 9 and 10.

124. Cox, *Supreme Court in American Government*, 32.

125. *Federalist* No. 10, p. 54.

126. Cox, *Supreme Court in American Government*, 32.

127. Kurland enumerates a number of these disadvantages. Phillip B. Kurland, *Politics, the Constitution and the Warren Court* (Chicago: University of Chicago Press, 1970), 196–99. Robert H. Jackson also treats in an instructive manner the disadvantages of the lawsuit's format for formulating broad policy: "Litigation procedures are clumsy and narrow, at best, technical and tricky at their worst. . . . Since it [the Court] could act or speak only through deciding lawsuits, it was certainly never expected to play much part in deciding the policy of government." Robert H. Jackson, *The Struggle for Judicial Supremacy: A Study of a Crisis in American Power Politics* (New York: Alfred A. Knopf, 1941), 288.

128. *Federalist* No. 63, p. 413.

129. Cox, *Supreme Court in American Government*, 69.

130. Montesquieu, *Spirit of the Laws*, quoted in *Federalist* No. 47, p. 315.

131. Cox, "Congress," 717.

132. *Federalist* No. 51, p. 337.

133. Hand, *Bill of Rights*, 73, quoted in Cox, *Supreme Court in American Government*, 63.

134. "Thus we prefer to choose our own lawyers and physicians, rather than have the assignment of all such in the hands of self-appointed boards of physicians and lawyers. . . . The idea of representation, as it applies to the business of government, as distinct from the establishment of government, involves the same idea of competence or wisdom, on the part of the representatives, combined with the idea of attachment to the interest of those they represent." Harry V. Jaffa, "What Is Equality? The Declaration of Independence Revisited," in *Readings in American Democracy*, ed. Paul Peterson (Dubuque, Iowa: Kendall/Hunt, 1979), 39.

135. *Federalist* No. 78, p. 505.

136. Ibid.

137. Ibid., No. 81, p. 524.

138. Cox, *Court and Constitution*, 377.

139. "Enlightened statesmen will not always be at the helm." *Federalist* No. 10, p. 57.

140. "Truly ambitious men do not readily yield to momentary popular clamor because thus yielding produces little *lasting* fame or power. Ambitious presidents and judges know that the dignity and privileges of their offices will be diminished in the long run if they make

themselves mere puppets of the legislature and popular opinion. They will not want these offices made foolish or servile. The constitutional belief is that presidents and judges will stand firm for reasons of self-interest. They will gamble that their own power and prestige will be greater than ever when the majority comes to its senses. In this way, separation seeks to supply democracy with officers who, because they hold important and powerful offices and because they can satisfy their ambitions in those offices, will tend to oppose momentary follies and self-destructive errors on the part of the democracy." Martin Diamond, Winston Mills Fisk, and Herbert Garfinkel, *The Democratic Republic: An Introduction to American National Government,* 2d ed. (Chicago: Rand McNally, 1970), 110.

141. "The most important quality of law in a free society is the power to command acceptance and support from the community." Cox, *Supreme Court in American Government,* 103.

142. Ibid., 105.

143. Thus, Cox asserts that the claim of the reapportionment cases to be law rests on the Court's ability "to command a national consensus." Cox, *Warren Court,* 119.

144. Cox, *Supreme Court in American Government,* 105.

145. Ibid., 109, 112.

146. John Locke, *Second Treatise,* secs. 119–22.

147. The Declaration of Independence, par. 2 (U.S. 1776).

148. Cox, *Supreme Court in American Government,* 32.

149. Ibid.

150. Ibid.

151. Ibid., 32, 113.

152. Storing, "Constitution and Bill of Rights," 277.

153. Ibid., 273, 279–80.

154. John Hart Ely might well respond by pointing to open-ended provisions of the Ninth Amendment or the privileges and immunites clause and asking how they are to be interpreted. The theory of the Constitution seems to demand that such provisions be interpreted with fidelity to the intent of those who consented to them. The Court must also interpret such protections with the knowledge that judicial departures from such intent is inconsistent with the basic principle of the consent of the governed; therefore, judicial activism or judicial creativity should be minimized. Ely is treated in Chapter 6.

155. A few examples of cases in which the Court has obstructed federal legislative action in a way unfriendly to Cox's thesis include the legislative assertion of federal authority to regulate or prohibit the extension of slavery into U.S. territory, the Civil Rights Act of 1875, the first child-labor law, minimum wage legislation, and, of course, early New Deal legislation. For a useful catalog of cases that blocked legislative attempts to enlarge the liberties of individuals and to effect the principle of equality, see John Agresto, *The Supreme Court and Constitutional Democracy* (Ithaca, N.Y.: Cornell University Press, 1984), 27–29.

5. Property Rights and Human Rights

1. Richard A. Epstein, *Takings: Private Property and the Power of Eminent Domain* (Cambridge: Harvard University Press, 1985).

2. Epstein, *Takings,* 3.

3. Michael J. Perry, *The Constitution, the Courts, and Human Rights: An Inquiry into the Legitimacy of Constitutional Policymaking by the Judiciary* (New Haven, Conn.: Yale University Press, 1982), hereafter cited as *Human Rights*.

4. Epstein's core arguments are set forth in *Takings*. He applies this form of analysis in a thoughtful and controversial manner to employment discrimination in a later book that proceeds from his interpretation of Locke and his conviction that Locke's scheme of self-ownership is generally advantageous to everyone. Richard A. Epstein, *Forbidden Grounds: The Case Against Employment Discrimination* (Cambridge: Harvard University Press, 1992), 23.

5. Epstein, *Takings*, 3.

6. Ibid., 19, 283, 306. In commenting on his book, Epstein states, "*Takings* is an effort to find in a single clause of the Constitution the distillation of a comprehensive political theory. If the book is correct, then it is possible to find guidance in a single provision to the fundamental problems of political obligation. The same analysis that applies to the acquisition of original property rights carries over to the largest questions of social organization." Richard A. Epstein, "An Outline of Takings," *University of Miami Law Review* 41, no. 1 (1986): 19.

7. Epstein, *Takings*, 281.

8. 170 U.S. 283, 288 (1898), quoted in Epstein, *Takings*, 304.

9. Epstein, *Takings*, 304–5.

10. Richard A. Epstein, "Establish Justice," in "We the People: Thoughts on Liberty in the Preamble's Light," *Reason* 20 (May 1988): 33, 37.

11. Epstein, *Takings*, 30–31. But at another point, he states, "One only has to read the opinions of the Supreme Court on economic liberties and property rights to realize that these opinions are intellectually incoherent and that some movement in the direction of judicial activism is clearly indicated." Richard A. Epstein, "Economic Liberties and the Judiciary: On the Merits of the Frying Pan/the Active Virtues," *Regulation* 9, no. 1 (January/February 1985): 18.

12. Epstein, *Takings*, 327.

13. Ibid., 328. In the context of analyzing the contract clause, he makes some observations relevant both to this clause and to the First Amendment. He characterizes the general view of the contract clause as being that the clause cannot be given a literal meaning because such interpretation would deprive the states of an "essential attribute of sovereignty—the power to pass legislation that is in the public interest." Epstein counters that this argument is not made with regard to other arguably absolute provisions of the Constitution, for example, the First Amendment speech provisions. Although the First Amendment is not interpreted literally, the clause does provide broad protections, reaching even state common-law actions for defamation—an area where the framers might not have thought it applicable. He advocates a similar approach to the contract clause, "a middle ground between an absolute interpretation of the contract clause and the near total disregard that it receives today." Richard A. Epstein, "Toward a Revitalization of the Contract Clause," *University of Chicago Law Review* 51, no. 3 (Summer 1984): 717. Epstein's view of the standard of judicial deference appropriate to economic regulation is that of intermediate scrutiny of the type currently applied in gender cases involving the equal protection clause. Epstein, *Takings*, 144–45.

14. Ibid., 328–29.

15. Herman Schwartz, "Property Rights and the Constitution," *The American University Law Review* 37, no. 1 (1987): 13–14, citing Epstein, *Takings,* 344–46.

16. Epstein, *Takings,* 329.

17. John Locke, *Second Treatise of Government,* ed. E. B. Macpherson (Indianapolis: Hackett, 1980), chap. 12.

18. Ibid., chap. 11, sec. 134.

19. Ibid., secs. 136–38 (emphasis added).

20. Ibid., sec. 139.

21. Ibid., sec. 142. I am grateful to Professor Richard Stevens for his treatment of Locke's limitations on the legislative power. Richard G. Stevens, "Politics, Economics and Religion in the Constitution," special issue, *Symposium on the Constitution and the Founding,* ed. Lane V. Sunderland, *Teaching Political Science* 14 (1986): 11–16.

22. Madison defines faction as "a number of citizens, whether amounting to a majority or minority of the whole, who are united and actuated by some common impulse of passion, or of interest, adverse to the rights of other citizens, or to the permanent and aggregate interests of the community." Alexander Hamilton, John Jay, and James Madison, *The Federalist: A Commentary on the Constitution of the United States,* ed. Henry Cabot Lodge, with an introduction by Edward Mead Earle (New York: Modern Library, 1941), No. 10, p. 54.

23. Ibid., No. 51, p. 338.

24. Ibid., No. 78, p. 505.

25. Martin Diamond, "Convervatives, Liberals, and the Constitution," in *As Far as Republican Principles Will Admit: Essays by Martin Diamond,* ed. William A. Schambra (Washington, D.C.: American Enterprise Institute Press, 1992), 74.

26. *Federalist* No. 31, p. 190.

27. Ibid., No. 23, p. 144.

28. Perry, *Human Rights,* ix. The core of Perry's work is more difficult to discern in his later books. His later work seems to indicate that, upon further reflection, he has reservations about the judicial role set forth in *Human Rights.* The role of judges as "moral prophets" does not emerge in his later book, *Morality, Politics, and Law,* where he writes of the Court as imposing the American aspirations to justice on the democracy. Michael J. Perry, *Morality, Politics, and Law* (New York: Oxford University Press, 1988). In this latest book, however, Perry is much more concened with the consistency of the judicial power and democracy and with the dialogue among the three branches of government in determining the proper application of the Constitution to contemporary circumstances. Michael J. Perry, *The Constitution in the Courts: Law or Politics?* (New York: Oxford University Press, 1994). Thus, Perry's later work indicates a modification of his position that judges should be prophets and gives more emphasis to the legislative and executive roles. Nonetheless, treatment of his original position is justified in order to show the implications of a theory of constitutional interpretation that is a significant part of contemporary constitutional discourse, that is, a competing theory of constitutional interpretation. In my judgment, Perry's later position is sounder than his earlier one. I indicate in notes when Perry's latest work seems to depart in important ways from the position he sets forth in *Human Rights.*

29. Perry, *Human Rights,* ix.

30. Although Perry leaves open the theoretical possibility of judicial invalidation of an act of Congress involving issues of federalism, he states that "[i]t is exceedingly difficult to imagine enactment of congressional legislation so far afield that it could be invalidated on federalism grounds in the exercise of interpretive review." Ibid., 46.

31. Perry illustrates his position using judicial opinions of both Justice Jackson and Justice Powell.

32. Perry, *Human Rights,* 59.

33. Ibid., 60.

34. 1 Cranch (5 U.S.) 137 (1803).

35. 17 U.S. 316 (1819).

36. 343 U.S. 579 (1952).

37. Perry, *Human Rights,* 7.

38. But compare this statement with Perry's argument in his latest book that courts should look both backward to determine constitutional principles and forward to determine the world in which the principles are to function. Perry, *Constitution in the Courts,* 204.

39. Perry, *Human Rights,* 123–24.

40. Perry raises the following question in the epilogue to his book: "Would the judiciary press its institutional capacity, even its legitimate authority, to and perhaps past the breaking point were it to undertake to resolve complex issues of social and economic welfare and, hence, to reallocate scarce and perhaps diminishing fiscal resources?" Ibid., 164.

41. Ibid., ix.

42. Ibid., 111.

43. Perry believes that he rejects an "imperial judicial role" and uses the abortion issue to illustrate his disagreement with the Court's handling of *Roe v. Wade,* 410 U.S. 113 (1973). It turns out that the major ground of his objection to the Court's role is that he thinks it would have been better policy to be more protective of the fetus in a way that would have allowed state legislatures to follow the Court's lead, but with the understanding that the Court should be the final judge of abortion policy for the nation. Perry, *Morality, Politics, and Law,* 172–78. In another book, Perry writes that the objection to legislation outlawing abortion based on its violation of the establishment clause is "quite opaque." He believes that such legislation rests just as much on a secular purpose as "legislation outlawing the slaughter of Alaskan wolves." Michael J. Perry, *Love and Power: The Role of Religion and Morality in American Politics* (New York: Oxford University Press, 1991), 116–17.

44. Perry, *Morality, Politics, and Law,* 172–78.

45. But there are other arguments that support a form of originalism. Ibid., 128, 161. In his latest book, Perry states: "In the absence of an argument for nonoriginalism that is persuasive, or even plausible, in the context of American political-legal culture, the serious question, in my view, is not whether the originalist approach should inform the pracice of judicial review (it should) but what follows from that fact—and what does not follow from it." The originalism Perry endorses accepts the constitutional directives established by the framers but not the framers' views of how those directives apply in particular contexts. Perry, *The Constitution in the Courts,* 49, 53.

46. Perry, *Morality, Politics, and Law,* 161–62.

47. Ibid., 167–68. Perry believes that the weight given to the community's majority and to that of the Supreme Court is a choice that is ultimately an inconclusive enterprise: "One's decision to accept or reject, one's argument for or against, any conception of judicial role, including the originalist conception, is always contingent, speculative, and provisional and therefore revisable. The decision is contingent because it is rooted partly in one's sense or vision of justice—in one's view of the proper interpretation of the tradition, of the correct mediation of the past of the tradition with its present." Ibid., 169. Perry's view comes very close to one that favors a powerful judiciary when one agrees with its decisions but not when one disagrees with its decisions. See Part I of this volume for an argument against this view.

48. Perry observes: "If the issue is one about which other officials—including not merely other judges, but also legislative and executive officials—have truly deliberated, and if, after deliberation, they have concluded that the policy choice is not ruled out by the relevant aspiration, the judge must face the possibility that they are right. To the degree that possibility seems to her a realistic one, to that degree she should hesitate to invalidate the policy choice." Ibid., 170.

49. Ibid., 171–72.

50. For an interpretation of Perry that sees his view of judicial self-restraint as more potent and that emphasizes the dialogic nature of judicial action with the other branches of government and with the states in Perry's work, see Ronald Kahn, *The Supreme Court and Constitutional Theory, 1953–1993* (Lawrence: University Press of Kansas, 1994), 224–49. This interpretation is certainly accurate when derived from Perry's latest book, *Constitution in the Courts.*

51. *Federalist* No. 51, p. 337.

52. Herbert J. Storing, "The Constitution and the Bill of Rights," in *Taking the Constitution Seriously: Essays on the Constitution and Constitutional Law,* ed. Gary L. McDowell (Dubuque, Iowa: Kendall/Hunt, 1981), 277–80. See Chapter 2 for a discussion of the character of the Bill of Rights.

53. 19 How. (60 U.S.) 393 (1857). Among other things, this case barred persons of African descent from access to federal courts and from enjoyment of rights or protections under the Constitution.

54. 161 U.S. 537 (1896). The Court in Plessy found state-enforced racial segregation compatible with the Fourteenth Amendment's equal protection clause.

55. 274 U.S. 200 (1927). This case upheld a Virginia statute that subjected persons affected with hereditary insanity, idiocy, imbecility, feeblemindedness, or epilepsy to compulsory sterilization. It argued: "Three generations of imbeciles are enough."

56. Perry, *Human Rights,* 111. But in his latest book, Perry argues: "At its best, constitutional adjudication looks in two directions: backward, toward the past, for the constitutional principles—the directives—to which fidelity is to be maintained, and forward, toward the future, for the likely shape of the world in which the principles are to function and for which, therefore, they must be specified (if they are indeterminate, as some of them are). Because, and to the extent, it looks backward, constitutional adjudication is "authoritarian" (though I do not use the term in the pejorative sense Frank Michelman and others have used it); but because, and to the extent it looks forward, constitutional adjudication is "pragmatic." To conceive of constitutional adjudication as *either* authoritarian *or* pragmatic is to misconceive it." Perry, *The Constitution in the Courts,* 204.

57. *Federalist* No. 51, p. 337.

58. Learned Hand, *The Bill of Rights: The Oliver Wendell Holmes Lectures* (Cambridge: Harvard University Press, 1958), 73–74.

59. James Bradley Thayer and others, *John Marshall* (Chicago: University of Chicago Press, 1967), 106–7.

60. "Thus we prefer to choose our own lawyers and physicians, rather than have the assignment of all such in the hands of self-appointed boards of physicians and lawyers. . . . The idea of representation, as it applies to the business of government, as distinct from the establishment of government, involves the same idea of competence or wisdom, on the part of representatives, combined with the idea of attachment to the interest of those they represent." Harry V. Jaffa, "What Is Equality? The Declaration of Independence Revisited," in *Readings in American Democracy,* ed. Paul Peterson (Dubuque, Iowa: Kendall/Hunt, 1979), 29, 38–39.

61. *Federalist* No. 78, p. 505.

62. Ibid.

63. Ibid., No. 81, p. 524.

64. "Enlightened statesmen will not always be at the helm." Ibid., No. 10, p. 57.

65. Ibid., No. 51, p. 337. "Truly ambitious men do not readily yield to *momentary* popular clamor because thus yielding produces little *lasting* fame or power. Ambitious presidents and judges know that the dignity and privileges of their offices will be diminished in the long run if they make themselves mere puppets of the legislature and popular opinion. They will not want these offices made foolish or servile. The constituitonal belief is that presidents and judges will stand firm for reasons of self-interest. They will gamble that their own power and prestige will be greater than ever when the majority comes to its senses. In this way, separation of powers seeks to supply democracy with officers who, because they hold important and powerful offices and because they can satisfy their ambitions in those offices, will tend to oppose momentary follies and self-destructive errors on the part of the democracy." Martin Diamond, Winston Mills Fisk, and Herbert Garfinkel, *The Democratic Republic: An Introduction to American National Government,* 2d ed. (Chicago: Rand McNally, 1970), 110.

66. Perry has apparently reconsidered the adequacy of the jurisdiction-limiting power as a check on the judiciary. In his latest book, he suggests appointing judges, especially Supreme Court justices, not for life but for a term of years. He also suggests that the United States consider, as a resolution of the problem of rights and the courts, a congressional override of the Supreme Court, modeled after the Canadian scheme. Perry believes that such a scheme might enrich the political deliberations regarding "constitutional morality." Perry also expresses in this book the hope that deliberation about constitutional commitments will often take place through democratic channels rather than through the Court. Perry, *Constitution in the Courts,* 196–98, 201. These observations are radical departures from the tenor of his argument in *Human Rights.*

6. Representation and Democratic Theory in the Constitution

1. John Hart Ely, *Democracy and Distrust: A Theory of Judicial Review* (Cambridge: Harvard University Press, 1980), 87.

2. Bork believes the American people are also subject to this temptation. Robert H. Bork, *The Tempting of America: The Political Seduction of the Law* (New York: Simon & Schuster, 1990), 1–2.

3. Ibid., 2.

4. Bork believes that what matters is the public understanding, not the subjective understanding of any of the framers. He relies on Madison's understanding that "what mattered was the intention of the ratifying conventions." Ibid., 144.

5. Ely, *Democracy and Distrust,* 87.

6. Ibid., 82 (quoting Professor Dworkin; citation omitted).

7. For example: "[T]he Seventeenth extends to all of us the right to vote for our Senators directly, the Twenty-fourth abolishes the poll tax as a condition of voting in federal elections, the Nineteenth extends the vote to women, the Twenty-Sixth to eighteen-year-olds. Extension of the franchise to groups previously excluded has therefore been the dominant theme of our constitutional development since the Fourteenth Amendment, and it pursues both of the broad constitutional themes we have observed from the beginning: the achievement of a political process open to all on an equal basis and a consequent enforcement of the representative's duty of equal concern and respect to minorities and majorities alike." Ibid., 99.

8. Harry V. Jaffa, "What Is Equality? The Declaration of Independence Revisited," in *Readings in American Democracy,* ed. Paul Peterson (Dubuque, Iowa: Kendall/Hunt, 1979), 29, 38.

9. As Jaffa states, "we can see why they [the people] would think it safer to keep the government close to themselves. Certainly they may now require special majorities of three-fourths or four-fifths for certain purposes; although such requirement always rest at bottom, upon the underlying majority." Ibid., 38–39.

10. Ibid., 38.

11. Martin Diamond, "The Declaration and the Constitution: Liberty, Democracy, and the Founders," in *As Far as Republican Principles Will Admit: Essays by Martin Diamond,* ed. William A. Schambra (Washington, D.C.: American Enterprise Institute Press, 1992), 234.

12. Herbert J. Storing, "The Constitution and the Bill of Rights," in *Taking the Constitution Seriously: Essays on the Constitution and Constitutional Law,* ed. Gary L. McDowell (Dubuque, Iowa: Kendall/Hunt, 1981), 266, 278.

13. Ely, *Democracy and Distrust,* 49.

14. Kurland enumerates a number of these disadvantages, such as the Court's lack of machinery for gathering a wide range of facts and opinions and the absence of means for supervising and enforcing the decrees that the Court promulgates. Philip B. Kurland, *Politics, the Constitution and the Warren Court* (Chicago: University of Chicago Press, 1970), 196–99. Robert Jackson also treats in an instructive manner the disadvantages of the lawsuit's format for formulating broad policy: "Litigation procedures are clumsy and narrow, at best; technical and tricky at their worst. . . . Since it [the Court] could act or speak only though deciding lawsuits, it was certainly never expected to play much part in deciding the policy of government." Robert H. Jackson, *The Struggle for Judicial Supremacy : A Study of a Crisis in American Power Politics* (New York: Alfred A. Knopf, 1941), 288.

15. Alexander Hamilton, John Jay, and James Madison, *The Federalist: A Commen-*

tary on the Constitution of the United States, ed. Henry Cabot Lodge, with an introduction by Edward Mead Earle (New York: Modern Library, 1941), No. 63, p. 413.

16. Ibid, No. 47, p. 315, citing Montesquieu (emphasis in original).

17. Ely, *Democracy and Distrust,* 100–101.

18. 377 U.S. 713 (1964).

19. Ibid., 738.

20. Ibid., 717.

21. Ely, *Democracy and Distrust,* 239, n. 60.

22. Ibid., 89–90.

23. Ibid., 117.

24. *Federalist* No. 51.

25. Ibid., No. 10.

26. "Thus, the Founders sought to provide for both reflective and refining representation—for enough popular influence for republican safety and enough refinement and competence for good administration." Ralph A. Rossum, "Representation and Republican Government: Contemporary Court Variations on the Founders' Theme," in *Taking the Constitution Seriously: Essays on the Constitution and Constitutional Law,* ed. Gary L. McDowell (Dubuque, Iowa: Kendall/Hunt, 1981), 417, 427.

27. Ely, *Democracy and Distrust,* 125.

28. Ibid., 126–27.

29. Ibid., 11–12.

30. Rossum, "Representation and Republican Government," citing Alexander M. Bickel, *The Supreme Court and the Idea of Progress* (New York: Harper & Row, 1970), 111–12.

31. Ely, *Democracy and Distrust,* 89–90.

32. Ibid., 159. If legislators really thought that the punishments were to be imposed on "us," it is not clear that any just punishments would be prescribed by law. That is, such a personalization of the criminal law shifts the analysis from one of the punishment appropriate to the crime to one of punishments appropriate to "us." Such a theory is not consistent with the hard edge to the law that is necessary to civil society or with the various functions, such as deterrence, that the criminal law must fulfill.

33. *Louisiana ex rel. Francis v. Resweber,* 329 U.S. 459 (1947).

34. *Trop v. Dulles,* 356 U.S. 86 (1958).

35. *Weems v. United States,* 217 U.S. 349 (1910).

36. *Wilkerson v. Utah,* 99 U.S. 130, 133 (1878).

37. *O'Neil v. Vermont,* 144 U.S. 323, 339–40 (1892) (Field, J., dissenting).

38. The case of *Delaware v. Prouse,* 440 U.S. 648 (1979), in which the Court declared unconstitutional the warrantless stopping of motorists for random license and vehicle registration checks, provides a test of Ely's characterization of the Fourth Amendment "as another harbinger of the equal protection clause." Ely, *Democracy and Distrust,* 97. This case seems to belie a case of discrimination by the legislature—of "us" discriminating against "them." From the legislators' perspective, this case presents a classic "us-us" situation, given the random character of a statute authorizing such checks. The practice of randomly checking registrations applies equally to majority and minority, to legislator and ordinary citizen. Ely's test seems to require up-

holding the Delaware practice. When the problem of prescribed freedom from unreasonable searches and seizures is viewed as a personal constitutional right, the Court's decision in *Prouse* is much more defensible. The Fourth Amendment specifically refers to its protections as rights and specifies that the right to be secure from unreasonable searches and seizures applies to one's person, houses, papers, and effects. A fundamental rights analysis relates much more directly to the words of the amendment than does Ely's "us and them" analysis. Traditional tests arising from a fundamental rights analysis provide a reasonable framework within which to debate issues such as that raised by *Prouse*. Even legislation authorizing warrantless searches seems to stand under Ely's equality principle, insofar as such warrantless searches may be made in the case of both innocent and guilty persons. Of course, this would violate an explicit constitutional principle, the warrant requirement. Mark Tushnet, "Darkness on the Edge of Town: The Contributions of John Hart Ely to Constitutional Theory," *Yale Law Journal* 89, no. 6 (May 1980): 1037, 1046.

As in the case of the Eight Amendment, the Fourth Amendment embodies a principle of justice that was thought by its framers to be sufficiently important to include in the Bill of Rights. The provisions of the amendments require substantial judgment in their application to specific cases, yet they do not simply leave judges free to insert their own values into the Constitution. It is not at all clear how Ely's theory aids judges in their difficult task. In fact, his theory's emphasis on avoiding inequities in treatment seems to make more complex and attenuated the application of the Fourth Amendment's principles to specific factual contexts and in some instances even contradicts those principles.

39. Ely, *Democracy and Distrust*, 172.

40. *University Bd. of Regents v. Bakke*, 438 U.S. 265 (1978).

41. Ely, *Democracy and Distrust*, 15.

42. *Lucas v. Colorado Gen. Assembly*, 377 U.S. 713 (1964).

43. Ely, *Democracy and Distrust*, 48–54, 72.

44. Storing, "Constitution and Bill of Rights," 277.

45. Ely might well respond by pointing to open-ended provisions of the Ninth Amendment or the privileges and immunites clause and asking how they are to be interpreted. The theory of the Constitution seems to demand that such provisions be interpreted with fidelity to the intent of those who consented to them. The Court must also interpret such protections with the knowledge that judicial departures from such intent are inconsistent with the basic principle of the consent of the governed; therefore, judicial activism or judicial creativity should be minimized.

46. *U.S. Constitution*, preamble.

47. Declaration of Independence, par. 1.

48. Bork, *Tempting*, 10. In some respects, the charge that Bork was out of the mainstream was directed at his opposition to an unenumerated right to privacy and the contentious issue of abortion. Ibid., 290–91.

49. Bork believes that the American people are also subject to this temptation. Ibid., 1–2.

50. Ibid., 2.

51. Bork believes that what matters is the public understanding, not the subjective

understanding of any of the framers. He relies on Madison's understanding that "what mattered was the intention of the ratifying conventions." Ibid., 144.

52. Ibid., 5, 143.

53. Ibid., 139.

54. Ibid., 162–63.

55. Ibid.,10. Although Bork refers to original understanding as a philosophy, he states that *The Tempting of America* is not "ultimately about legal theory." Ibid., 11.

56. Ibid., 139.

57. Ibid.

58. Ibid., 140.

59. For a discussion of this issue in the context of *Marbury* v. *Madison,* see Chapter 3.

60. Bork, *Tempting,* 147. Bork states the matter as follows: "The legal principle to be applied is never neutral in its content, of course, because it embodies a value that is to be applied to the exclusion of other contending values." Ibid., 78.

61. Ibid., 147.

62. Ibid., 148–50.

63. *Regents of the University of California v. Bakke,* 438 U. S. 265 (1978).

64. Bork, *Tempting,* 149–50. Bork thus supports the constitutional doctrine that gender and sexual orientation statutes are not to be analyzed under the standard of strict scrutiny.

65. 347 U. S. 483 (1954).

66. Bork, *Tempting,* 76.

67. Ibid., 75–76.

68. Ibid., 81–82. Bork also refers to the practical matter that "[t]he Supreme Court was faced with a situation in which the courts would have to go on forever entertaining litigation about primary schools, secondary schools, colleges, washrooms, golf courses, swimming pools, drinking fountains, and the endless variety of facilities that were segregated, or else the separate-but-equal doctrine would have to be abandoned." Ibid., 82.

69. 163 U.S. 537, 557 (1896). Bork, however, would rely on the equality principle rather than relying on personal freedom of citizens, as Harlan did in his dissent.

70. 347 U.S. 497 (1954).

71. Bork, *Tempting,* 83–84. Bork observes that the "Court-invented 'equal protection component of the due process clause' " has the practical effect of providing the primary basis for attacking federal legislation that compels "affirmative action or reverse discrimination." Ibid., 84.

72. 334 U.S. 1 (1948).

73. Bork, *Tempting,* 151–52, quoting 334 U.S. 19 (1948).

74. *Runyon v. McCrary,* 427 U.S. 160 (1976).

75. Bork, *Tempting,* 153.

76. Ibid.

77. Ibid., 154–55.

78. John Locke, *Second Treatise of Government,* ed. C. B. Macpherson (Indianapolis: Hackett, 1980), sec. 96.

79. Ibid., sec. 134.

80. *Federalist* No. 1, p. 6.

81. Bork, *Tempting,* 161–70.

82. 1 Cranch (5 U.S.) 137 (1803), cited in Bork, *Tempting,* 165.

83. Bork, *Tempting,* 165.

84. Abraham Lincoln, "First Inaugural Address on March 4, 1861," in *The Collected Works of Abraham Lincoln,* ed. Roy P. Basler (New Brunswick, N.J.: Rutgers University Press, 1953), 4:268.

85. Bork, *Tempting,* 177–78.

86. Ibid., 179.

87. Ely, *Democracy and Distrust;* quoted in Bork, *Tempting,* 180.

88. Bork, *Tempting,* 181.

89. Ibid., 166.

90. For a more detailed argument supporting this view, see Walter Berns, *In Defense of Liberal Democracy* (Chicago: Gateway Editions, 1984), 22–23.

91. Bork, *Tempting,* 183.

92. Ibid., 183–84.

93. Letter from James Madison to Thomas Jefferson, 17 October 1788, in *The Papers of James Madison,* ed. Robert A. Rutland and Charles F. Hobson (Charlottesville: University Press of Virginia, 1977), 11:298–99.

94. Joseph Gales, Sr., ed., *The Debates and Proceedings in the Congress of the United States* (Washington D. C.: Gales & Seaton, 1834), 1:457.

95. Ibid., 456–57. A part of Madison's argument was that a bill of rights would become part of the "national sentiment" and be a means of appealing to "the sense of the community" if government violated those rights. This issue is illustrated by the contemporary issue of gun control. The Second Amendment reads: "A well regulated Militia, being necessary to the security of a free State, the right of the people to keep and bear Arms, shall not be infringed." The Supreme Court has held that the Second Amendment does not simply guarantee the right to own and possess guns; in order for the right to enjoy constitutional protection, it has to be related to the maintenance of a militia. The Court has not used its power to prevent gun control legislation. In spite of the Court's allowance of gun control, the "right of the people to keep and bear Arms" maintains a powerful hold on the national sentiment and the sense of the community. Whether or not one agrees with those who oppose gun control, one must acknowledge that the right to bear arms is an important force in their arguments.

96. Letter from Madison to Jefferson, 11:299.

97. For treatment of these matters, see Part I.

98. *Federalist* No. 81, p. 524.

99. Bork, *Tempting,* 11. Bork properly rejects the sort of legal theory he describes, which supplants the theory of the Constitution: "The groves of legal academe are thick with young philosophers who propose various systems of morality that judges must use to create new constitutional rights." Robert H. Bork, "Styles in Constitutional Theory," *South Texas Law Journal* 26 (1985): 387.

100. Bork, *Tempting,* 173–74.

101. 19 How. 393 (1856).

102. This is the description of Harry V. Jaffa in "The Closing of the Conservative Mind: A Dissenting Opinion on Judge Robert H. Bork," in *Original Intent and the*

Framers of the Constitution: A Disputed Question, ed. Harry V. Jaffa, Bruce Ledewitz, Robert L. Stone, and George Anastaplo, with a foreword by Lewis E. Lehrman (Washington, D.C.: Regnery Gateway, 1994), 297.

103. Bork, *Tempting,* 28.

104. Ibid., 31.

105. Ibid.

106. *Dred Scott v. Sandford,* 19 How. 393, (60 U.S.) 407 (1856).

107. U.S. Constitution, amend. V (emphasis added).

108. Ibid., art. I, sec. 9 (emphasis added).

109. Ibid., sec. 2. These points are made by Harry V. Jaffa in a number of places, for example, in "Who Killed Cock Robin? A Retrospective on the Bork Nomination and a Reply to 'Jaffa Divides the House,' " in *Original Intent and the Framers of the Constitution: A Disputed Question,* ed. Harry V. Jaffa and others, with a foreword by Lewis E. Lehrman (Washington, D.C.: Regnery Gateway, 1994), 276–77.

110. Bork, *Tempting,* 184.

111. 317 U.S. 11 (1942).

112. Bork, *Tempting,* 56.

113. Gerald V. Bradley, "Slaying the Dragon of Politics with the Sword of Law: Bork's *Tempting of America,*" *University of Illinois Law Review* (1990): 267.

114. Walter Berns, "The Meaning of the Tenth Amendment," in *A Nation of States: Essays on the American Federal System,* 2d ed., ed. Robert Goldwin (Chicago: Rand McNally, 1974), 141.

115. For an argument that carefully examines the theoretical basis of the Tenth Amendment, see Harry V. Jaffa, "Partly Federal, Partly National: On the Political Theory of the Civil War," in *A Nation of States: Essays on the American Federal System,* ed. Robert Goldwin, 2d ed. (Chicago: Rand McNally, 1974), 109–37.

116. 312 U.S. 100, 124 (1941).

117. 4 Wheat. (17 U.S.) 316 (1819).

118. Bork, *Tempting,* 93. One, and by no means the only, theoretical problem with the so-called incorporation doctrine is that it makes the due process clause of the Fourteenth Amendment incorporate the due process clause of the Fifth Amendment. For an alternative explanation of due process, see Lane V. Sunderland, "The Exclusionary Rule: A Requirement of Constitutional Principle," *Journal of Criminal Law and Criminology* 69, no. 2 (1978): 141–59.

119. Bork, *Tempting,* 94.

120. 372 U.S. 368, 381 (1963), cited in Robert L. Stone, "Professor Harry V. Jaffa Divides the House: A Respectful Protest and a Defense Brief," in *Original Intent and the Framers of the Constitution: A Disputed Question,* ed. Harry V. Jaffa and others, with a foreword by Lewis E. Lehrman (Washington, D.C.: Regnery Gateway, 1994), 150.

121. 372 U.S. 368, 379 (1963).

122. 377 U.S. 713 (1964).

123. Bork, *Tempting,* 87.

124. Robert H. Bork, "Tradition and Morality in Constitutional Law," in *Views from the Bench: The Judiciary and Constitutional Politics,* ed. Mark W. Cannon and David M. O'Brien (Chatham, N.J.: Chatham House, 1985), 167.

125. Bork acknowledges these sources, such as the records of the Constitutional

Convention and the ratifying conventions, *The Federalist,* other writings during the founding period, and writings of those such as Joseph Story, who were steeped in the thought of this period. Bork, *Tempting,* 165.

126. Ibid., 144.

127. *Federalist* No. 1, p. 3.

128. 462 U.S. 919 (1983).

129. 1 Cranch 137 (5 U.S.) (1803).

130. Bork addressed the relationship of law and morality in a speech before the Thomas More Society of America: "The first thing to be observed is that, contrary to some impressions, for Thomas More, in a real sense, law *was* morality. It is equally true that for More morality was superior to law and was the standard by which law is judged. If that seems a paradox, I do not think it is a true one." In the context of civil disobedience, he asserts: "If disobedience is ever justified, it is only when the issue is of transcendent importance and when you are absolutely sure of the right and wrong of the matter." Robert H. Bork, "Law, Morality, and Thomas More," *Catholic Lawyer* 31, no. 1 (Winter 1987): 2, 6. In contrast, at another place he argues: "In our system there is no absolute set of truths, to which the term 'political truth' can refer." Robert H. Bork, "Neutral Principles and Some First Amendment Problems," *Indiana Law Journal* 47 (Fall 1971): 30.

131. Bork, *Tempting,* 6.

132. Ibid.

133. 19 How. (60 U.S.) 393 (1857).

134. 106 U.S. 629 (1883). This case and the following four cases are cited in John Agresto, *The Supreme Court and Constitutional Democracy* (Ithaca, N.Y.: Cornell University Press, 1984), 27–28.

135. 109 U.S. 3 (1883).

136. 208 U.S. 161 (1908).

137. 247 U.S. 251 (1918).

138. 261 U.S. 525 (1923).

139. *Federalist* No. 63, pp. 409–10.

140. Bradley, "Slaying the Dragon of Politics," 256.

141. Bork, *Tempting,* 139–40.

142. Bork also eschews absolutist protections of political speech, which he characterizes as "impossible." Bork, "Neutral Principles," 20–21.

143. Bork, *Tempting,* 159.

144. Ironically, Bork argues that the Madisonian problem of defining majority power and minority freedom is primarily the function of the Supreme Court. He argues that this creates a pressing need for constitutional theory. Yet Bork does not pursue the foundations of this theory in historical or philosophical materials. Robert Bork, "The Constitution, Original Intent, and Economic Rights," *San Diego Law Review* 23, no. 4 (1986): 825.

7. Separation of Powers, Federalism, and Other Institutional Considerations

1. Philip B. Kurland, "American Systems of Laws and Constitutions," in *American Civilizations: A Portrait from the Twentieth Century,* ed. Daniel J. Boorstin (New York: McGraw-Hill, 1972), 142.

2. Laurence H. Tribe, *American Constitutional Law,* 2d ed. (Mineola, N.Y.: Foundation Press, 1988), viii.

3. Kurland, "American Systems,"141.

4. Philip B. Kurland, "The Supreme Court and its Judicial Critics," *Utah Law Review,"* 6, no. 4 (Fall 1959): 465.

5. Kurland, "American Systems," 141.

6. Ibid. Ironically, in another place, Kurland refers to the "false equation of the Constitution with constitutional law," thereby supporting the view that the Constitution has a meaning separate from what the Court says it means. Philip B. Kurland, "Judicial Review Revisited: 'Original Intent' and 'The Common Will,' " *Cincinnati Law Review* 55 (1987): 738. He makes the same point in another article. Philip B. Kurland, "The Constitution: The Framers' Intent, the Present and the Future," *St. Louis University Law Journal* 32 (1987): 18–19.

7. Tribe, *American Constitutional Law,* vii.

8. Ibid., viii.

9. Ibid., 583.

10. Ibid., ix.

11. Ibid., 1418. This formulation is in the context of Tribe's treatment of "rights of privacy and personhood," in which he suggests that relationships that meet these human needs may be facilitated in ways that "may jar some conventional sensibilities but without which there can be no hope of solving the persistent problem of autonomy and community."

12. This comment is taken from a review that appeared in the *Villanova Law Review* (no further citation given) and is quoted on the back cover of Philip B. Kurland, *Watergate and the Constitution* (Chicago: University of Chicago Press, 1978).

13. Philip B. Kurland, *Politics, the Constitution and the Warren Court* (Chicago: University of Chicago Press, 1970).

14. Kurland, "American Systems," 142. It is not at all clear by what criterion Kurland disqualifies the Civil War as political chaos. It certainly does not qualify as peaceful change.

15. Walter Berns, "Does the Constitution 'Secure These Rights'?" in *How Democratic Is the Constitution?* ed. Robert A. Goldwin and William A. Schambra (Washington, D.C.: American Enterprise Institute for Public Policy Research, 1980), 78.

16. Alexander Hamilton, John Jay, and James Madison, *The Federalist: A Commentary on the Constitution of the United States,* ed. Henry Cabot Lodge, with an introduction by Edward Mead Earle (New York: Modern Library, 1941), No. 1, p. 6.

17. Ibid., No. 10, p. 54.

18. Ibid.

19. Ibid., 61.

20. Kurland, "American Systems," 141.

21. *Federalist* No. 51, p. 337

22. Ibid., No. 23, p. 145.

23. Ibid., 142.

24. Ibid., No. 51, p. 336.

25. Lester S. Jayson, ed., *Constitution of the United States of America: Analysis and Interpretation* (Washington, D.C.: U.S. Government Printing Office, 1973), 1597–1619.

26. Although it would be unduly repetitive and beyond the scope of this chapter to examine the periods of Kurland's second and third Constitutions in any detail, some remarks are appropriate. The neglect of the intent of and the theory underlying the Constitution has similar consequences in his treatment of these two epochs. It reduces his analysis to mere description.

27. *Federalist* No. 10, p. 56.

28. See Morton J. Frisch, "Franklin Delano Roosevelt," in *American Political Thought: The Philosophic Dimension of American Statesmanship,* 2d ed., ed. Morton J. Frisch and Richard G. Stevens (Itasca, Ill.: F. E. Peacock, 1983), 219–235, for a clear treatment of the constitutional aspects of the New Deal.

29. Regarding the specific prohibitions invoked to quash the New Deal legislation and its predecessors, very little can be said in this context. It is instructive to note how Kurland himself characterized the Fifth and Fourteenth Amendments in his comment on *Murray's Lessee v. Hoboken Land and Improvement Co.,* 18 How. (59 U.S.) 272 (1855): "[T]he due process clause was in fact concerned with procedure, a point that might seem apparent from the words but which the Court was shortly thereafter to abandon." Philip B. Kurland, "Magna Carta and Constitutionalism in the United States: 'The Noble Lie,' " in *The Great Charter: Four Essays on Magna Carta and the History of our Liberty,* ed. Samuel E. Thorne, William H. Dunham Jr., Philip B. Kurland, and Sir Ivor Jennings, with an introduction by Erwin N. Griswold (New York: Pantheon Books, 1965), 63. Thus, it seems that from Kurland's own point of view, the due process clauses of the Fifth and Fourteenth Amendments would not impede legislation such as that embodied in the New Deal. Given this fact, it is difficult to understand Kurland's characterization of this epoch as a departure from the Constitution that requires the label the "third constitution."

30. Kurland, "American Systems," 141.

31. Ibid., 144.

32. Kurland, *Watergate,* 155. See Kurland, *Politics,* 10, for a related statement emphasizing the creation of a system in which each branch could check the other.

33. *Federalist* No. 47, p. 313.

34. Ibid., No. 63, pp. 409–10.

35. Ibid., No. 37, pp. 226–27.

36. Ibid., No. 9, p. 47; No. 10, pp. 53–54.

37. The mode of election, fixed term of office, and veto power are important examples of this executive independence.

38. *Federalist* No. 70, pp. 454–55.

39. Paul Peterson, "The Constitution and Separation of Powers," in *Taking the Constitution Seriously: Essays on the Constitution and Constitutional Law,* ed. Gary L. McDowell (Dubuque, Iowa: Kendall/Hunt, 1981), 194.

40. Ibid., 199–200.

41. Kurland, *Watergate,* 158–59.

42. In discussing one provision of the Constitution in another context, Kurland refers to the framers' intent as "an amorphous concept at best." Philip B. Kurland, " '*Brown v. Board of Education* Was the Beginning': The School Desegregation Cases in the United States Supreme Court: 1954–1979," *Washington University Law Quarterly,* no. 2 (Spring 1979): 315.

43. Thomas Jefferson, "Letters to James Madison, November 18, 1788," in *The Works of Thomas Jefferson*, ed. Paul L. Ford (New York: G. P. Putnam's Sons, 1904), 5:434. Ironically, Kurland refers to *The Federalist* as a "usually helpful source" in *Watergate*, 78.

44. Kurland, *Watergate*, 159, 161.

45. Martin Diamond, "Democracy and *The Federalist*: A Reconsideration of the Framers' Intent," in *As Far As Republican Principles Will Admit: Essays by Martin Diamond*, ed. William A. Schambra (Washington, D.C.: American Enterprise Institute Press, 1992), 17–18.

46. At another place in his writing, he refers to another discernible principle of the Constitution as that of the rule of law. Kurland, "American Systems," 141.

47. Kurland, *Watergate*, 179.

48. Kurland, "American Systems," 141.

49. Kurland, *Watergate*, 155.

50. Kurland, "American Systems," 141.

51. Ibid., 142–43.

52. Ibid., 143.

53. Ibid., 143; Kurland, *Politics*, 52.

54. Kurland, "American Systems," 143; Kurland, *Politics*, 52.

55. Kurland, "American Systems," 143.

56. Kurland, *Politics*, 51–97.

57. Ibid., 97.

58. Kurland, "American Systems," 143.

59. I am indebted to Martin Diamond for much of the theoretical content of this section, particularly his treatment of the framers' view of federalism and the ends it serves in American democracy.

60. Kurland, *Watergate*, 156.

61. Ibid.

62. *Federalist* No. 39, p. 245.

63. Martin Diamond, "*The Federalist* on Federalism: 'Neither a National nor a Federal Constitution, but a Composition of Both,'" in *Taking the Constitution Seriously: Essays on the Constitution and Constitutional Law*, ed. Gary L. McDowell (Dubuque, Iowa: Kendall/Hunt, 1981), 157.

64. *Federalist* No. 39, p. 250.

65. Diamond, "Democracy and *The Federalist*," 154–57.

66. Ibid., 156.

67. At another point in his analysis, Kurland speaks of vestiges of federalism in the constitutional provisions for the Senate and the electoral college, but these institutions do not fit within his definition. Kurland, "American Systems," 143.

68. Diamond, "Democracy and *The Federalist*," 159.

69. Ibid.

70. Kurland, "American Systems," 143.

71. Diamond, "Democracy and *The Federalist*," 161.

72. Kurland, *Watergate*, 164.

73. Philip B. Kurland, "The Supreme Court and the Attrition of State Power," *Stanford Law Review* 10 (March 1958): 282.

74. *Federalist* No. 23, p. 145.

75. Ibid., No. 51, pp. 340–41.

76. Martin Diamond, Winston Mills Fisk, and Herbert Garfinkel, *The Democratic Republic: An Introduction to American National Government,* 2d ed. (Chicago: Rand McNally, 1970), 145–46.

77. Martin Diamond, "The Ends of Federalism," in *As Far as Republican Principles Will Admit: Essays by Martin Diamond,* ed. William A. Schambra (Washington, D.C.: American Enterprise Institute Press, 1982), 159.

78. See Chapter 2 for a treatment of Tocqueville in the context of enumerated powers.

79. Diamond, "Ends of Federalism," 159–64.

80. Kurland, "Supreme Court and Attrition," 296.

81. Ibid., 282.

82. *Federalist* No. 9, p. 47.

83. Kurland, "Supreme Court and Attrition," 283.

84. Kurland, *Politics,* xx–xxiii.

85. Philip B. Kurland, review of *The Brethren: Inside the Supreme Court,* by Bob Woodward and Scott Armstrong, *University of Chicago Law Review* 47 (1979): 195.

86. Kurland, *Politics,* 172.

87. Ibid., 174, 182, 184, 188, 191, 192, 194.

88. Ibid., 182.

89. Ibid., 183.

90. Philip B. Kurland, "The Irrelevance of the Constitution: The Religion Clauses of the First Amendment and the Supreme Court," *Villanova Law Review* 24 (1978–79): 24.

91. Kurland, " '*Brown v. Board of Education* Was the Beginning,' " 398.

92. Kurland, "Supreme Court and Judicial Critics," 465.

93. Kurland, *Politics,* 194.

94. Ibid., 204–5.

95. Kurland, "Supreme Court and Judicial Critics," 465.

96. Ibid., 465–6.

97. Kurland, *Politics,* 204.

98. Ibid., 206.

99. Ibid.

100. Ibid., 302–4.

101. *Federalist* No. 63, p. 413.

102. Kurland, *Politics,* 174.

103. *Federalist* No. 47, p. 315. *The Federalist* is quoting Montesquieu (no citation given).

104. Kurland, of course, recognizes the nondemocratic nature of judicial activism. Kurland, *Politics,* 204.

105. Kurland, "American Systems," 144.

106. Kurland, *Politics,* 173.

107. Ibid., 205.

108. Ibid., 204.

109. Philip B. Kurland, "Government by Judiciary," *Modern Age: A Quarterly Review* (Fall 1976): 362.

110. Kurland, *Politics,* xx.

111. Philip B. Kurland, "1970 Term: Notes on the Emergence of the Burger Court," *Supreme Court Review* (1971): 266–67.

112. Kurland, "American Systems," 141.

113. Ibid.

114. Ibid.

115. Ira C. Lupu, "Risky Business," review of *American Constitutional Law,* by Laurence H. Tribe, *Harvard Law Review* 101 (1988): 1303–4.

116. Ibid., 1304, citing William Lockhart, Yale Kamisar, Jesse Choper, and Steven Shiffrin, *Constitutional Law: Cases, Comments, Questions,* 6th ed. (St. Paul, Minn.: West, 1986).

117. Lupu, "Risky Business," 1304, n. 8.

118. Tribe, *American Constitutional Law,* iii.

119. For example, D. Grier Stephenson, review of *American Constitutional Law,* by Laurence H. Tribe, *New York Law School Law Review* 25 (1979): 187–88.

120. Tribe, *American Constitutional Law,* iii.

121. Ibid. (emphasis Tribe's).

122. Ibid., iv.

123. Tribe addresses the unity of the Constitution in another work where he considers the propriety of the Court's power to "invalidate amendments because of poor fit" with the "unified although not . . . wholly coherent document." Tribe argues that the Constitution provides "suggestive" guidance "for assessing the appropriateness of proposed amendments." He concludes, however, that the judiciary should not invalidate constitutional amendments because this "would unequivocally subordinate the amendment process to the legal system it is intended to override and would thus gravely threaten the integrity of the entire structure. Such criteria must therefore be applied by Congress (or by a constitutional convention) when it considers whether to propose an amendment, and by state legislatures (or state conventions) when they vote on ratification. The merit of a suggested constitutional amendment is thus a true 'political question'—a matter that the Constitution addresses, but that it nevertheless commits to judicially unreviewable resolution by the political branches of government." Laurence H. Tribe, *Constitutional Choices* (Cambridge: Harvard University Press, 1985), 25–27.

124. Tribe, *American Constitutional Law,* vii.

125. Ibid., 1. In a later book, Tribe and Dorf make the following observation: "When all of the Constitution's supposed unities are exposed to scrutiny, criticisms of its inconsistency with various readers' sweeping visions of what it ought to be become considerably less impressive. Not all need be reducible to a single theme. Inconsistency—even inconsistency with democracy—is hardly earth-shattering." Laurence H. Tribe and Michael C. Dorf, *On Reading the Constitution* (Cambridge: Harvard University Press, 1991), 30.

126. Tribe, *American Constitutional Law,* vii.

127. Telford Taylor, review of *American Constitutional Law,* by Laurence H. Tribe, *Columbia Law Review* 79, no. 6 (1979): 1209.

128. Tribe, *American Constitutional Law,* vii.

129. Ibid., viii.

130. Ibid., 2–3.

131. *Federalist* No. 47, p. 313.

132. Ibid., No. 63, p. 410.

133. Ibid., No. 37, pp. 226–27.

134. Ibid., No. 9, p. 47; No. 10, pp. 53–54.

135. Ibid., No. 70, pp. 454–55.

136. Ibid., No. 51, pp. 340–41.

137. Diamond, Fisk, and Garfinkel, *The Democratic Republic,* 105–6.

138. *Federalist* No. 10, p. 56.

139. Tribe, *American Constitutional Law,* 398. See Chapter 2 for a treatment of Tocqueville in the context of enumerated powers.

140. Alexis de Tocqueville, *Democracy in America,* trans. Henry Reeve, rev. Francis Bowen, corr. and ed. Phillips Bradley (New York: Vintage Books, 1945), 1:254.

141. Diamond, "Ends of Federalism," 161–62.

142. *Federalist* No. 51, pp. 337–41.

143. Ibid., No. 10, p. 59.

144. Tribe, *American Constitutional Law,* 15–16. Tribe makes statements throughout his work that support a view of judicial supremacy, for example: "Constitutional value choices cannot be made, however, without recourse to a system of values that is at least partly external to the constitutional text, since neither the liberty to decide whether to carry a pregnancy to term not the liberty to work for less than four dollars per hour is explicitly mentioned in the Constitution." One answer to this, of course, is to let legislative majorities decide, a choice Tribe characteristically rejects. Tribe and Dorf, *On Reading the Constitution,* 66.

145. Tribe, *American Constitutional Law,* 583.

146. Ibid., 761. In another work, Tribe refers to the "fundamental constitutional values of privacy, individual autonomy, and equality." Tribe, *Constitutional Choices,* 25.

147. Tribe, *American Constitutional Law,* 890.

148. Ibid., ix.

149. Ibid., 1418. This formulation is in the context of Tribe's treatment of "rights of privacy and personhood," in which he suggests that relationships that meet these human needs may be facilitated in ways that "may jar some conventional sensibilities but without which there can be no hope of solving the persistent problem of autonomy and community."

150. Ibid., 451.

151. This appears in an asterisked footnote in *Federalist* No. 84, p. 560.

152. Tribe, *American Constitutional Law,* 38.

153. Ibid., 399.

154. In *Lucas,* the Court struck down an apportionment scheme in which only one house of the state legislature was to be apportioned strictly on the basis of population (relying on the federal analogy), a scheme that had been approved by voters in a statewide referendum. 337 U.S. 713, 717–18 (1964).

155. Tribe, *American Constitutional Law,* 1065–66, 1461.

156. Ibid., 397.

157. Ibid., 399; 399, n. 2.

158. Ibid., 1302.

159. Ibid., 1311.

160. Ibid., 1351, quoting Abraham Lincoln, "Speech at Springfield, Illinois on June 16, 1857," in *The Collected Works of Abraham Lincoln,* ed. Roy P. Basler (New Brunswick, N.J.: Rutgers University Press, 1953).

161. Tribe, *American Constitutional Law,* 1351.

162. Ibid., quoting Warren in *Brown v. Board of Education* (Brown II), 349 U. S. 249, 300 (1955).

163. Tribe, *American Constitutional Law,* 1422, citing *Bowers v. Hardwick,* 478 U.S. 186 (1986).

164. In the context of rejecting "process-based approaches" to constitutional interpretation and discussing the constitutional status of homosexual activities, Tribe argues that the true ground for recognizing nonenumerated rights is that laws outlawing homosexual activities amount to a denial of the individuals involved of "a meaningful opportunity to realize their humanity." Tribe, *Constitutional Choices,* 17.

165. 478 U.S. 186, 190, 194 (1986).

166. Tribe, *American Constitutional Law,* 15. Tribe suggests that James Madison may have held a view of natural rights that supported "a special case of a right to associate if you so incline with any person you can persuade" as an argument for the constitutional right at issue in *Hardwick.* Laurence H. Tribe, "Essay in Law: On Reading the Constitution," *Utah Law Review,* no. 4 (1988): 795.

167. Tribe, *American Constitutional Law,* 17.

168. Ibid., vii.

169. Ibid., iii. In a work written subsequent to the second edition of his treatise, Tribe characterizes his objection to a simply subjective reading of the Constitution: "Is reading the [Constitution's] text just a *pre*text for expressing the reader's vision in the august, almost holy terms of constitutional law? Is the Constitution simply a mirror in which one sees what one wants to see?" Tribe and Dorf, *On Reading the Constitution,* 7.

170. Tribe, *American Constitution Law,* 2.

171. *Federalist* No. 78, p. 503.

8. Rejection of the Constitution and Liberal Theory

1. Tushnet has been identified as probably the most prolific of the critical legal studies authors. Stephen B. Presser and Jamils Zainaldin, eds., *Law and Jurisprudence in American History: Cases and Materials* (St. Paul, Minn.: West, 1989), 970.

2. Mark Tushnet, "Perspectives on Critical Legal Studies," *George Washington Law Review* 52, no. 2 (January 1984): 239.

3. Mark Tushnet, "Critical Legal Studies: A Political History," *Yale Law Journal* 100 (1991): 1516.

4. Mark Tushnet, "The U.S. Constitution and the Intent of the Framers," *Buffalo Law Review* 36 (1987): 217, 225.

5. Tushnet, "Critical Legal Studies," 1524.

6. Mark Tushnet, *Red, White, and Blue: A Critical Analysis of Constitutional Law* (Cambridge: Harvard University Press, 1988), 318.

7. Mark Tushnet, "Does Constitutional Theory Matter? A Comment," *Texas Law Review* 65, no. 4 (March 1987): 777, 781–82. Later in this article, Tushnet makes the point that in order for him to become a judge, profound political and doctrinal changes would have to occur beforehand. These same changes would make it possible for him to use the bench to advance socialism. Ibid., 786.

8. As Tushnet puts it, in explaining the dependence of liberalism on formalism: "The critical legal studies approach, if its critiques of all versions of formalism succeed, will render unavailing the solutions liberal political theory offers for the Hobbesian problem of social order. Because the critical legal studies approach aims to critique all versions of formalism, however, its task can never be concluded. Some formalism can always be invented to survive the critiques mounted against the formalisms we have addressed so far. That is inescapable. But the critical legal studies approach has been successful often enough to provide a reasonably solid basis for an inductive generalization, or at least to place the burden on those who defend the rule of law to articulate a coherent version of it." Tushnet, "Perspectives," 239, 241–42.

9. Tushnet describes the book as an integration of his prior work, which makes his argument clearer to those who have read parts of it published in previous articles. A number of these articles are named in the preface. Tushnet, *Red, White, and Blue*, ix–x.

10. Ibid., ibid.

11. See, for example, ibid.

12. See note 8.

13. Tushnet, *Red, White, and Blue*, 3.

14. Mark Tushnet and Jennifer Jaff, "Why the Debate Over Congress' Power to Restrict the Jurisdiction of the Federal Courts is Unending," *Georgetown Law Review* 72 (April 1984): 1311, 1329.

15. 1 Cranch (5 U.S.) 137 (1803).

16. 1 Wheat. (14 U.S.) 316 (1819).

17. 19 How. (60 U.S.) 393 (1857).

18. Tushnet, *Red, White, and Blue*, 34, 57.

19. See Mark Tushnet, "Following the Rules Laid Down: A Critique of Interpretivism and Neutral Principles," *Harvard Law Review* 96, no. 4 (February 1983): 781, 793–804, for an extended discussion of the defects of interpretivism and its reliance on history. Tushnet also discusses the intent of the framers in another article and concludes that "original intention" just doesn't make any sense at all, and everyone who has thought about the question knows that. Tushnet, "Constitution and Intent," 217–18.

20. Tushnet, *Red, White, and Blue*, 46–51. Tushnet's work itself demonstrates the disputed nature of the proper principles of adjudication and judicial craftsmanship. Tushnet also recognizes the difficulty that the neutral principles approach imposes on a new judge's future decisions insofar as "the first time a judge decides a case, he or she is to some extent committed to particular decisions for the rest of his or her career." Tushnet, "Following the Rules Laid Down," 809.

21. Tushnet, *Red, White, and Blue*, 63.

22. Tushnet, "Following the Rules Laid Down," 781, 805.

23. Tushnet, *Red, White, and Blue*, 57.

24. Mark Tushnet, "Dia-Tribe," review of *American Constitutional Law,* by Laurence Tribe, *Michigan Law Review* 78, no. 2 (March 1980): 694, 696, 701.

25. Alexander Hamilton, John Jay, and James Madison, *The Federalist: A Commentary on the Constitution of the United States,* ed. Henry Cabot Lodge, with an introduction by Edward Mead Earle (New York: Modern Library, 1941), No. 10, p. 55.

26. Ibid.

27. Ibid., 57.

28. Tushnet, "Does Constitutional Theory Matter?" 786. Indeed, he asserts "that socialism is required by principles of justice."

29. Tushnet, *Red, White, and Blue,* 318.

30. Tushnet, "Does Constitutional Theory Matter?" 786.

31. John Hart Ely, *Democracy and Distrust: A Theory of Judicial Review* (Cambridge: Harvard University Press, 1980), quoted in Tushnet, *Red, White, and Blue,* 70–71.

32. As developed by Ely, however, these political rights are surprisingly comprehensive. Ely sees aspects of representation explicitly or implicitly in many of the amendments of the Constitution. See Lane V. Sunderland, "Constitutional Theory and the Role of the Court: An Analysis of Contemporary Constitutional Commentators," *Wake Forest Law Review* 21, no. 4 (1986): 855–900.

33. Tushnet, *Red, White, and Blue,* 71.

34. He makes the same point in a number of places, for example, Mark Tushnet, "Darkness on the Edge of Town: The Contributions of John Hart Ely to Constitutional Theory," *Yale Law Journal* 89, no. 6 (May 1980): 1037, 1042.

35. Tushnet, *Red, White, and Blue,* 134–35.

36. Mark Tushnet, "Anti-Formalism in Recent Constitutional Theory," *Michigan Law Review* 83, no. 6 (May 1985): 1502, 1527, 1534.

37. Tushnet, *Red, White, and Blue,* 147. See also Tushnet, "Anti-Formalism," 1502, 1506–8.

38. Tushnet, *Red, White, and Blue,* 147–48.

39. Tushnet, "Anti-Formalism," 1502, 1544. Tushnet's general approval of decentralization is reflected in his treatment of "The Constitution of the Bureaucratic State," in which he argues that bureaucracy should be repoliticized to allow communities to control bureaucracies and to allow clients to participate in bureaucratic decisions. Ironically, he also proposes that there be a comprehensive income maintenance scheme to eradicate large disparities of wealth between the rich and the poor. By suggesting that there is nothing standing in the way of the Court's adopting his proposals, Tushnet endorses a radical centralization of political power. Tushnet, *Red, White, and Blue,* 240–46.

40. Kahn observes that the decentralization Tushnet advocates would result in political decentralization, but with economic power so controlled that it "would make things even worse." Ronald Kahn, *The Supreme Court and Constitutional Theory: 1953–1993* (Lawrence: University Press of Kansas, 1994), 234.

41. Ibid., 156.

42. Tushnet, "Anti-Formalism," 1540. Tushnet finds other grounds for criticizing this antiformalist approach. In the case of Sunstein, Fiss, and Michelman, they are tentative about the content of the public values they invoke. Tushnet argues that Fiss's

intention that judges articulate and enforce public values is mistaken, both because of the nature of contemporary judges and because we do not have a sufficiently viable republican tradition or influence to support a "public life." This is clearly a sharp indictment of contemporary political life on Tushnet's part. Ibid., 1539–41.

43. Tushnet, *Red, White, and Blue*, 191.

44. Ibid., 192.

45. Tushnet, "Following the Rules Laid Down," 781, 784.

46. Tushnet, *Red, White, and Blue*, 196.

47. Tushnet persuasively concludes that the realists, in following the Progressive tradition, "tended to attribute outcomes in the legal system to the self-conscious and usually self-serving decisions of actors in the system. Although they understood that their analysis of legal rules led inevitably to an analysis of the operation of power, they reduced power to the self-interested actions of a few wilful men or to pure subjectivity. Debunking the pretensions of those who say they are motivated only by the public interest is frequently valuable, but it is almost always an incomplete account of the exercise of power." Mark Tushnet, "Legal Scholarship: Its Causes and Cure," *Yale Law Journal* 90, no. 5 (April 1981): 1205, 1222. As is often the case, Tushnet's insight is valuable, although the conclusion to which he points seems nearly indistinguishable from the raw exercise of power which lies at the foundation of the realist argument.

48. Tushnet, *Red, White, and Blue*, 197–98.

49. Tushnet, "Perspectives," 242.

50. For an analysis of the inconsistency of existentialism and American liberal democracy, see Werner J. Dannhauser, "Existentialism and Democracy," in *Confronting the Constitution: The Challenge to Locke, Montesquieu, Jefferson, and the Federalists from Utilitarianism, Marxism, Freudianism, Pragmatism, Existentialism . . .*, ed. Allan Bloom and Steven J. Kautz (Washington, D. C.: American Enterprise Institute Press, 1990), 402–10.

51. Tushnet, *Red, White, and Blue*, 200–202.

52. He argues in another place that the "framers' generation had not developed a conceptual scheme to express its understanding of the proper relation between religion and government." Whether or not this is true—and I would argue that it is not—this statement reveals Tushnet's position on the religion clauses as well as his understanding of original intent, history, and constitutional interpretation. Mark Tushnet, "The Origins of the Establishment Clause," *Georgetown Law Journal* 75, no. 4 (April 1987): 1509, 1513.

53. Tushnet, *Red, White, and Blue*, 272–76.

54. 370 U.S. 421 (1962).

55. Tushnet, *Red, White, and Blue*, 276.

56. Ibid., 277–78. Instrumental rationality, as defined by Tushnet, operates in the private sphere, but not necessarily in the private sphere. In other words, reason assumes the status Hobbes assigned it as simply a scout or spy that finds the way to the things desired and thereby subordinates reason to the passions.

57. Ibid., 279.

58. Ibid., 282–83. Tushnet outlines a number of other justifications for regulating campaign expenditures and refutes them. Ibid., 282–88.

59. Ibid., 288–89. Tushnet is skeptical of a sharp division between political and commercial speech, which would allow governmental regulation of the latter. He suggests that

the best that can be hoped for is an assessment and doctrine that rests on whether regulations of commercial speech serve republican values. Ibid., 289–92.

60. Ibid., 293–96.

61. Ibid., 299.

62. Ibid., 293.

63. Ibid., 305. Tushnet properly recognizes that this is not the Supreme Court's understanding of the matter. Ibid., 306.

64. Ibid., 312.

65. Ibid., 309.

66. *Miller v. California,* 413 U.S. 15 (1973).

67. Tushnet, *Red, White, and Blue,* 318.

68. Thomas Hobbes, *Leviathan,* ed. Michael Oakeshott, with an introduction by Richard S. Peters (London: Collier-Macmillan, 1962).

69. Tushnet, *Red, White, and Blue,* 277–78.

70. Ibid., 314.

71. *Federalist* No. 10, p. 55.

72. Ibid., No. 15, p. 92.

73. Ibid., No. 49, p. 331.

74. Tushnet, *Red, White, and Blue,* 318.

75. Ibid., 315.

76. Ibid., 317.

77. Ibid., 316.

78. *Federalist* No. 10, p. 58.

79. Mark Tushnet, "Constitutional Interpretation and Judicial Selection: A View from the *Federalist Papers,*" *Southern California Law Review* 61 (1988): 1669, 1699.

80. Ibid., 1693.

81. Ibid., 1695.

82. Ibid.

83. Ibid., 1697. Tushnet uses as an example of the indeterminancy of even these mathematical provisions the constitutional requirement that the president be at least thirty-five years old. He argues that we might replace these words with "fifty years" or "thirty years" and not impair "the integrity of the constitutional structure." He uses the example of a sixteen-year-old guru's eligibility for the presidency. According to the ordinary understanding, he would be ineligible for the office, but the guru's religion includes a belief in reincarnation. Because of his previous lives, the guru is well over thirty-five. Thus, we cannot make sense of even the mathematical provisions of the Constitution. Tushnet, *Red, White, and Blue,* 60–62.

84. *Federalist* No. 49, p. 329.

85. Tushnet, "Perspectives," 239, 241.

86. *Federalist* No. 51, p. 340.

87. Tushnet, *Red, White, and Blue,* 318.

88. Ibid., 316–17.

89. Tushnet, "Constitutional Interpretation," 1695.

90. Herbert J. Storing, *What the Antifederalists Were For: The Political Thought of the Opponents of the Constitution* (Chicago: University of Chicago Press, 1981), 71–72.

91. This term is borrowed from Justice Frankfurter.

92. Catharine A. MacKinnon, *Toward a Feminist Theory of the State* (Cambridge: Harvard University Press, 1989), 237.

93. Catharine A. MacKinnon, "Feminism, Marxism, Method, and the State: An Agenda for Theory," *Signs: Journal of Women in Culture and Society* 7, no. 3 (Spring 1982): 515, 537.

94. Raymond A. Belliotti, *Justifying Law: The Debate over Foundations, Goals, and Methods* (Philadelphia: Temple University Press, 1992), 191.

95. MacKinnon, *Feminist Theory of the State*, 238.

96. MacKinnon, *Feminism Unmodified: Discourses on Life and Law* (Cambridge: Harvard University Press, 1987), 28.

97. The "different voice" approach of feminist theory, articulated by Carol Gilligan, argues that the distinctly female approach to moral and legal problems has been undervalued or ignored in both law and legal scholarship. Gilligan's view emphasizes the value women place on relationships and connections rather than the emphasis in male analysis "on abstraction, rights, autonomy, separation, formality, and neutrality—an 'ethic of justice.'" The "different voice" strand of feminism argues that prevailing morality proceeds from a partial, male morality that supposes itself to be universal. Cass Sunstein, "Feminism and Legal Theory," *Harvard Law Review* 101, no. 4 (February 1988): 827–29.

98. MacKinnon, *Feminist Theory of the State*, 10, quoted in Jean Bethke Elshtain, "Feminism and the State," review of *Toward a Feminist Theory of the State*, by Catharine A. MacKinnon, *Review of Politics* 53, no. 4 (1991): 736. Elshtain recognizes other instances of MacKinnon's exclusive view of feminist theory in MacKinnon's use of terms such as "feminists charge," "feminists argue," "feminism sees," feminists believe," and "feminism's search." These references are from MacKinnon, *Feminist Theory of the State*, 5, 10, 38, cited in ibid., 736.

99. Elshtain, "Feminism and the State," 828–29, 834.

100. MacKinnon, *Feminism Unmodified*, 5.

101. Ibid., 48–49.

102. MacKinnon, "An Agenda for Theory," 515, 531.

103. MacKinnon, *Feminism Unmodified*, 6.

104. Ibid., 50.

105. Catharine A. MacKinnon, "Feminism, Marxism, Method, and the State: Toward Feminist Jurisprudence," *Signs: Journal of Women in Culture and Society* 8, no. 4 (Summer 1983): 638.

106. MacKinnon, "An Agenda for Theory," 542.

107. Ibid., 12.

108. MacKinnon, *Feminist Theory of the State*, 241.

109. Belliotti, *Justifying Law*, 200–201. As Belliotti recognizes, this formulation is taken from a concurring opinion of Justice Stewart in *Jacobellis v. Ohio*, 378 U.S. 184, 197 (1964), in which Stewart admitted the difficulty in defining hard-core pornography but insisted that he knew it when he saw it. MacKinnon doubts that what Stewart sees is the same thing she sees when viewing pornography, and that his statement is clearly made from the male standpoint and from his position of power. MacKinnon, *Feminism Unmodified*, 147–48, 163–64.

110. MacKinnon, *Feminist Theory of the State*, 244.

111. Ibid., 249.

112. Ronald Dworkin uses a premise similar to MacKinnon's to create a private moral universe that results in his reaching dramatically different conclusions in the area of pornography regulation from those reached by MacKinnon. Dworkin starts from much the same premise as MacKinnon does—that of a radical subjectivity about how human beings should live their lives. MacKinnon departs from Dworkin's view, however. She believes her subjective view should be the basis for changing the public law relating not only to pornography but to other areas of law as well. She also believes public law should invade the private sphere because privacy perpetuates male domination. She regards the doctrine of individual rights that supports the concept of privacy as a distinctly male doctrine. Ibid., 244.

113. Ibid., 238–39.

114. One reviewer believes that MacKinnon's insistence on the pervasiveness of male domination is so strong that it does not provide for the possibility of change in society. Ruth Colker, "Feminist Consciousness and the State: A Basis for Cautious Optimism," review of *Toward a Feminist Theory of the State*, by Catharine A. MacKinnon, *Columbia Law Review* 90 (1990): 1170.

115. Catharine A. MacKinnon, *Only Words* (Cambridge: Harvard University Press, 1993), 91–92. This pornography ordinance, drafted by MacKinnon and Andrea Dworkin, outlawed pornography as a practice that discriminates against women. The Seventh Circuit Court of Appeals ruled in 1985 that the ordinance violated the First Amendment (*American Booksellers Association v. Hudnut*, 771 F.2d 323).

116. Sunstein, "Feminism and Legal Theory," 538–39.

117. MacKinnon, *Feminism Unmodified*, 53–54.

118. MacKinnon, "An Agenda for Theory," 533.

119. MacKinnon, *Feminist Theory of the State*, 172.

120. MacKinnon, *Feminism Unmodified*, 156.

121. Ibid., 181.

122. Ronald Dworkin, "Women and Pornography," review of *Only Words*, by Catharine A. MacKinnon, *New York Review of Books* 40, no.17 (21 October 1993): 38.

123. Ibid.

124. MacKinnon, *Feminist Theory of the State*, 213.

125. Ibid., 205.

126. Ibid., 209.

127. Ibid., 214.

128. Ibid., 197.

129. MacKinnon, *Feminism Unmodified*, 166.

130. MacKinnon, *Feminist Theory of the State*, 196–97.

131. Mackinnon, *Feminism Unmodified*, 154.

132. MacKinnon, *Only Words*, 15.

133. Ibid., 31–32.

134. Ibid., 21. MacKinnon does not argue that pornography is conduct and not speech. Quite to the contrary, she argues that pornography says things and has meaning. Ibid., 29–30.

135. *American Booksellers Association v. Hudnut*, 771 F.2d 323 (7th Cir. 1985).

136. MacKinnon contrasts protections of pornography with protections of political speech in Communist Party cases and argues that the latter are about ideas and words. MacKinnon, *Only Words*, 39–40.

137. Ibid., 88.

138. MacKinnon, *Feminist Theory of the State*, 209; MacKinnon, *Feminism Unmodified*, 151, 158–61, 175.

139. MacKinnon, *Feminism Unmodified*, 158.

140. MacKinnon, *Only Words*, 62.

141. MacKinnon, *Feminist Theory of the State*, 196–97.

142. MacKinnon, *Only Words*, 22–23.

143. Ibid., 107–8.

144. 19 How. (60 U.S.) 393 (1857).

145. Dworkin, "Women and Pornography," 36.

146. MacKinnon, *Only Words*, 71.

147. Dworkin, "Women and Pornography," 36–40.

148. Ibid., 41.

149. MacKinnon, "Toward Feminist Jurisprudence," 647.

150. Ibid., 648.

151. Ibid., 646.

152. Ibid., 647.

153. MacKinnon, *Feminist Theory of the State*, 173.

154. Elshtain, "Feminism and the State," 737.

155. MacKinnon, "Toward Feminist Jurisprudence," 652.

156. Ibid.

157. Ibid., 654.

158. Ibid., 652.

159. Belliotti, *Justifying Law*, 192.

160. MacKinnon, *Only Words*, 107.

161. MacKinnon, "Toward Feminist Jurisprudence," 652.

162. MacKinnon, *Feminist Theory of the State*, 249.

163. Katharine T. Bartlett, "MacKinnon's Feminism: Power on Whose Terms," review of *Feminism Unmodified: Discourses on Life and Law*, by Catharine A. MacKinnon, *California Law Review* 75, no. 4 (July 1987): 1565.

164. MacKinnon, *Feminism Unmodified*, 205.

165. Katharine T. Bartlett, review of *Feminism Unmodified: Discourses on Life and Law*, by Catharine A. MacKinnon, *Signs: Journal of Women in Culture and Society*, 13, no. 4 (Summer 1988): 881.

166. Jonathan Yardley, "Sticks and Stones," review of *Only Words*, by Catharine A. MacKinnon, *Book World* 23 (19 September 1993): 3.

167. Neil MacCormick, "Law, State and Feminism: MacKinnon's Theses Considered," review of *Toward a Feminist Theory of the State*, by Catharine A. MacKinnon, *Law and Philosophy* 10 (1991): 450.

168. Daryl McGowan Tress, "Feminist Theory and Its Discontents," *Interpretation* 18, no. 2 (Winter 1990–91): 304.

Epilogue

1. Ronald Dworkin, *Life's Dominion: An Argument About Abortion, Euthanasia, and Individual Freedom* (New York: Alfred A. Knopf, 1993), 146.

2. Michael J. Perry, *The Constitution, the Courts, and Human Rights: An Inquiry into the Legitimacy of Constitutional Policymaking by the Judiciary* (New Haven, Conn.: Yale University Press, 1982), 99–101.

3. Richard A. Epstein, *Takings: Private Property and the Power of Eminent Domain* (Cambridge: Harvard University Press, 1985), 281.

4. Philip B. Kurland, "American Systems of Laws and Constitutions," in *American Civilization: A Portrait from the Twentieth Century,* ed. Daniel J. Boorstin (New York: McGraw-Hill, 1971), 141–42; Philip B. Kurland, "The Supreme Court and Its Judicial Critics," *Utah Law Review* 6, no. 4 (Fall 1959): 465.

5. Archibald Cox, *The Role of the Supreme Court in American Government* (London: Oxford University Press, 1976), 32.

6. The Declaration of Independence, par. 1.

7. Laurence H. Tribe, *American Constitutional Law,* 2d ed. (Mineola, N.Y.: Foundation Press, 1988), 1.

8. John Hart Ely, *Democracy and Distrust: A Theory of Judicial Review* (Cambridge: Harvard University Press, 1980), 87.

9. Robert H. Bork, *The Tempting of America: The Political Seduction of the Law* (New York, Simon & Schuster, 1990), 1–2, 144.

10. Mark Tushnet, "Does Constitutional Theory Matter? A Comment," *Texas Law Review* 65, no. 4 (1987): 777, 781–82.

11. Catharine A. MacKinnon, *Toward a Feminist Theory of the State* (Cambridge: Harvard University Press, 1989), 237; Catharine A. MacKinnon, "Feminism, Marxism, Method and the State: An Agenda for Theory," *Signs: Journal of Women in Culture and Society* 7, no. 3 (Spring 1982): 515, 537.

12. Although I believe that Robert Bork is mistaken in some of his analysis and prescription, he largely avoids this sort of partisanship that simply advances his own policy views.

13. Thomas Hobbes, *Leviathan,* ed. Michael Oakeshott, with an introduction by Richard S. Peters (London: Collier-Macmillan, 1962), 209. See Part I for a discussion of Hobbes.

14. Alexander Hamilton, John Jay, and James Madison, *The Federalist: A Commentary on the Constitution of the United States,* ed. Henry Cabot Lodge, with an introduction by Edward Mead Earle (New York: Modern Library, 1941), No. 51, p. 337.

15. Ibid., No. 84, pp. 558–59.

16. Ibid., No. 39, p. 245.

17. Ibid., No. 49, p. 329.

18. Ibid., No. 78, p. 503.

BIBLIOGRAPHY

Abraham, Henry J. *The Judicial Process: An Introductory Analysis of the Courts of the United States, England, and France.* 6th ed. New York: Oxford University Press, 1993.

Agresto, John. *The Supreme Court and Constitutional Democracy.* Ithaca, N.Y.: Cornell University Press, 1984.

Anastaplo, George. "The Declaration of Independence." *St. Louis University Law Journal* 9, no. 3 (Spring 1965): 390–415.

Bartlett, Katharine T. "MacKinnon's Feminism: Power on Whose Terms." Review of *Feminism Unmodified: Discourses on Life and Law,* by Catharine A. MacKinnon. *California Law Review* 75, no. 4 (July 1987): 1559–70.

_____. Review of *Feminism Unmodified: Discourses on Life and Law,* by Catharine A. MacKinnon, In *Signs: Journal of Women in Culture and Society* 13, no. 4 (Summer 1988): 879–85.

Becker, Carl. *The Declaration of Independence: A Study in the History of Political Ideas.* New York: Alfred A. Knopf, 1942.

Belliotti, Raymond A. *Justifying Law: The Debate over Foundations, Goals and Methods.* Philadelphia: Temple University Press, 1992.

Berger, Raoul. *Congress v. the Supreme Court.* Cambridge: Harvard University Press, 1969.

Berns, Laurence. "Hobbes." In *History of Political Philosophy,* ed. Leo Strauss and Joseph Cropsey, 354–78. Chicago: Rand McNally, 1963.

Berns, Walter. "Does the Constitution 'Secure These Rights'?" In *How Democratic Is the Constitution?* ed. Robert A. Goldwin and William A. Schambra, 59–78. Washington, D.C.: American Enterprise Institute for Public Policy Research, 1980.

_____. *In Defense of Liberal Democracy.* Chicago: Gateway Editions, 1984.

_____. "The Meaning of the Tenth Amendment." In *A Nation of States: Essays on the American Federal System,* 2d ed., ed. Robert Goldwin, 139–61. Chicago: Rand McNally, 1974.

_____. *Taking the Constitution Seriously.* New York: Simon & Schuster, 1987.

Bickel, Alexander M. *The Least Dangerous Branch: The Supreme Court and the Bar of Politics.* Indianapolis: Bobbs-Merrill, 1962.

_____. *The Supreme Court and the Idea of Progress.* New York: Harper & Row, 1970.

Bork, Robert H. "The Constitution, Original Intent, and Economic Rights." *San Diego Law Review* 23, no. 4 (1986): 823–32.

_____. "Law, Morality, and Thomas More." *Catholic Lawyer* 31, no. 1 (Winter 1987): 1–6.

———. "Neutral Principles and Some First Amendment Problems." *Indiana Law Journal* 47 (Fall 1971): 1–30.

———. "Styles in Constitutional Theory." *South Texas Law Journal* 26 (1985): 383–95.

———. *The Tempting of America: The Political Seduction of the Law.* New York: Simon & Schuster, 1990.

———. "Tradition and Morality in Constitutional Law." In *Views from the Bench: The Judiciary and Constitutional Politics,* ed. Mark W. Cannon and David M. O'Brien, 166–72. Chatham, N.J.: Chatham House, 1985.

Boudin, Louis B. *Government by Judiciary.* 2 vols. New York: Russell & Russell, 1968.

Bradley, Gerald V. "Slaying the Dragon of Politics with the Sword of Law: Bork's *Tempting of America.*" *University of Illinois Law Review* (1990): 243–87.

Brann, Eva. "Concerning the 'Declaration of Independence.' " *The College,* Bicentennial Issue (July 1976): 1–17.

Brant, Irving. *The Bill of Rights: Its Origin and Meaning.* New York: The New American Library, 1965.

Brubaker, Stanley. "Reconsidering Dworkin's Case for Judicial Activism." *The Journal of Politics* 46, no. 2 (1984): 503–19.

———. "Taking Dworkin Seriously." *Review of Politics* 47, no. 1 (1985): 45–65.

Burns, James MacGregor. *Deadlock of Democracy: Four-Party Politics in America.* Englewood Cliffs, N.J.: Prentice-Hall, 1963.

Clinton, Robert Lowry. Marbury v. Madison *and Judicial Review.* Lawrence: University Press of Kansas, 1989.

Cohler, Anne M. *Montesquieu's Comparative Politics and the Spirit of American Constitutionalism.* Lawrence: University Press of Kansas, 1988.

Colker, Ruth. "Feminist Consciousness and the State: A Basis for Cautious Optimism." Review of *Toward a Feminist Theory of the State,* by Catharine A. MacKinnon. *Columbia Law Review* 90 (1990): 1146–70.

Cox, Archibald. "Congress v. the Supreme Court." *Mercer Law Review* 33 (1982): 707–22.

———. *The Court and the Constitution.* Boston: Houghton Mifflin Co., 1987.

———. "Federalism and Individual Rights Under the Burger Court." *Northwestern University Law Review* 73, no. 1 (March/April 1978): 1–25.

———. *Freedom of Expression.* Cambridge: Harvard University Press, 1980.

———. "The Role of the Supreme Court: Judicial Activism or Self-Restraint?" *Maryland Law Review* 47 (1987): 118–38.

———. *The Role of the Supreme Court in American Government.* London: Oxford University Press, 1976.

———. "The Role of the Supreme Court in American Society." *Marquette Law Review* 50 (1967): 575–93.

———. *Understanding the Supreme Court.* Pittsburgh: University of Pittsburgh School of Law, 1962.

———. *The Warren Court: Constitutional Decision as an Instrument of Reform.* Cambridge: Harvard University Press, 1968.

Cropsey, Joseph. "Hobbes and the Transition to Modernity." In *Ancients and Moderns: Essays on the Tradition of Political Philosophy in Honor of Leo Strauss,* ed. Joseph Cropsey, 213–37. New York: Basic Books, Inc., 1964.

Dannhauser, Werner J. "Existentialism and Democracy." In *Confronting the Constitution: The Challenge to Locke, Montesquieu, Jefferson, and the Federalists from Utilitarianism, Marxism, Freudianism, Pragmatism, Existentialism . . .,* ed. Allan Bloom and Steven J. Kautz, 304–410. Washington, D.C.: American Enterprise Institute Press, 1990.

Diamond, Anne Stuart. "The Anti-Federalist Brutus." *The Political Science Reviewer* 6 (Fall 1976): 249–81.

Diamond, Martin. "Conservatives, Liberals, and the Constitution." In *As Far as Republican Principles Will Admit: Essays by Martin Diamond,* ed. William A. Schambra, 68–89. Washington, D.C.: American Enterprise Institute Press, 1992.

———. "The Declaration and the Constitution: Liberty, Democracy, and the Founders." In *As Far as Republican Principles Will Admit: Essays by Martin Diamond,* ed. William A. Schambra, 224–40. Washington, D.C.: American Enterprise Institute Press, 1992.

———. "Democracy and *The Federalist:* A Reconsideration of the Framers' Intent." In *As Far as Republican Principles Will Admit: Essays by Martin Diamond,* ed. William A. Schambra, 17–36. Washington, D.C.: American Enterprise Institute Press, 1992.

———. "The Ends of Federalism." In *As Far as Republican Principles Will Admit: Essays by Martin Diamond,* ed. William A. Schambra, 144–66. Washington, D.C.: American Enterprise Institute Press, 1992.

———. "*The Federalist 1787–1788.*" In *As Far as Republican Principles Will Admit: Essays by Martin Diamond,* ed. William A. Schambra, 37–57. Washington, D.C.: American Enterprise Institute Press, 1992.

———. "*The Federalist* on Federalism: 'Neither a National nor a Federal Constitution, but a Composition of Both.' " In *Taking the Constitution Seriously: Essays on the Constitution and Constitutional Law,* ed. Gary L. McDowell, 153–62. Dubuque, Iowa: Kendall/Hunt, 1981.

———. *The Founding of the Democratic Republic.* Itasca, Ill.: F. E. Peacock, 1981.

———. "What the Framers Meant by Federalism." In *As Far as Republican Principles Will Admit: Essays by Martin Diamond,* ed. William A. Schambra, 93–107. Washington, D.C.: American Enterprise Institute Press, 1992.

Diamond, Martin, Winston Mills Fisk, and Herbert Garfinkel. *The Democratic Republic: An Introduction to American National Government.* 2d ed. Chicago: Rand McNally, 1970.

Dworkin, Ronald. "Do We Have a Right to Pornography?" In *A Matter of Principle.* Cambridge: Harvard University Press, 1985.

———. "The Forum of Principle." In *A Matter of Principle.* Cambridge: Harvard University Press, 1985.

———. *Law's Empire.* Cambridge: Harvard University Press, 1986.

———. "Liberalism." In *A Matter of Principle.* Cambridge: Harvard University Press, 1985.

———. "Liberty and Pornography." *New York Review of Books* 38, no. 4 (15 August 1991): 12–15.

———. *Life's Dominion: An Argument About Abortion, Euthanasia, and Individual Freedom.* New York: Alfred A. Knopf, 1993.

————. "Pornography: An Exchange." *New York Review of Books* 41, no. 5 (3 March 1994): 47–49.

————. *Taking Rights Seriously.* Cambridge: Harvard University Press, 1977.

————. "Women and Pornography." Review of *Only Words,* by Catharine A. MacKinnon. *New York Review of Books* 40, no. 17 (21 October 1993): 36–42.

Elliott, Jonathan, ed. *The Debates in the Several State Conventions on the Adoption of the Federal Constitution, as Recommended by the General Convention at Philadelphia in 1787.* 2d ed. 5 vols. Philadelphia: J. B. Lippincott, 1836.

Elshtain, Jean Bethke. "Feminism and the State." Review of *Toward a Feminist Theory of the State,* by Catharine A. MacKinnon. *Review of Politics* 53, no. 4 (1991): 735–38.

Ely, John Hart. *Democracy and Distrust: A Theory of Judicial Review.* Cambridge: Harvard University Press, 1980.

Epstein, Richard A. "Economic Liberties and the Judiciary: On the Merits of the Frying Pan/the Active Virtues." *Regulation* 9, no. 1 (January/February 1985): 10–18.

————. "Establish Justice." In "We the People: Thoughts on Liberty in the Preamble's Light." *Reason* 20 (May 1988): 33–45.

————. *Forbidden Grounds: The Case Against Employment Discrimination Laws.* Cambridge: Harvard University Press, 1992.

————. "An Outline of *Takings.*" *University of Miami Law Review* 41, no. 1 (1986): 3–19.

————. *Takings: Private Property and the Power of Eminent Domain.* Cambridge: Harvard University Press, 1985.

————. "Toward a Revitalization of the Contract Clause." *University of Chicago Law Review* 51, no. 3 (Summer 1984): 703–51.

Farrand, Max, ed. *The Records of the Federal Convention of 1787.* 3d ed. 4 vols. New Haven, Conn.: Yale University Press, 1966.

Fitzpatrick, John C., ed. *The Writings of George Washington from the Original Manuscripts Sources, 1745–1799.* 31 vols. Washington, D.C.: U.S. Government Printing Office, 1931–44.

Franck, Matthew J. "Statesmanship, the Law of Nature, and Judicial Usurpation." Ph.D. diss., Northern Illinois University, 1992.

Frisch, Morton J. "Franklin D. Roosevelt." In *American Political Thought: The Philosophic Dimension of American Statesmanship,* 2d ed., ed. Morton J. Frisch and Richard G. Stevens, 319–35. Itasca, Ill.: F. E. Peacock, 1983.

Gales, Joseph, Sr., ed. *The Debates and Proceedings in the Congress of the United States.* 42 vols. Washington, D.C.: Gales & Seaton, 1834.

George, Robert P. *Making Men Moral: Civil Liberties and Public Morality.* Oxford: Clarendon Press, 1993.

Goldwin, Robert A. "John Locke." In *History of Political Philosophy,* ed. Leo Strauss and Joseph Cropsey, 433–68. Chicago: Rand McNally, 1963.

Gunther, Gerald. *Constitutional Law.* 12th ed. Westbury, N.Y.: Foundation Press, 1991.

Haines, Charles Grove. *The American Doctrine of Judicial Supremacy.* Berkeley: University of California Press, 1932. Reprint, New York: Da Capo Press, 1973.

Hamilton, Alexander, John Jay, and James Madison. *The Federalist: A Commentary on the Constitution of the United States.* Edited by Henry Cabot Lodge. With an introduction by Edward Mead Earle. New York: Modern Library, 1941.

Hand, Learned. *The Bill of Rights: The Oliver Wendell Holmes Lectures.* Cambridge: Harvard University Press, 1958.

Hobbes, Thomas. *Elements of Law.* Original manuscript, Devonshire Mss., Hobbes Group, Chatsworth, Bakewell, Derbyshire, n.d.

_____. *Leviathan.* Edited by Michael Oakeshott. With an introduction by Richard S. Peters. London: Collier-Macmillan, 1962.

Jackson, Robert H. *The Struggle for Judicial Supremacy: A Study of a Crisis in American Power Politics.* New York: Alfred A. Knopf, 1941.

Jaffa, Harry V. "Abraham Lincoln." In *American Political Thought: The Philosophic Dimension of American Statesmanship,* 2d ed., ed. Morton J. Frisch and Richard G. Stevens, 195–213. Itasca, Ill.: F. E. Peacock, 1983.

_____. "The Closing of the Conservative Mind: A Dissenting Opinion on Judge Robert H. Bork." In *Original Intent and the Framers of the Constitution: A Disputed Question,* ed. Harry V. Jaffa, Bruce Ledewitz, Robert L. Stone, and George Anastaplo, 291–302. With a foreword by Lewis E. Lehrman. Washington, D.C.: Regnery Gateway, 1994.

_____. "Partly Federal, Partly National: On the Political Theory of the Civil War." In *A Nation of States: Essays on the American Federal System,* 2d ed., ed. Robert Goldwin, 109–37. Chicago: Rand McNally College, 1974.

_____. "What Is Equality? The Declaration of Independence Revisited." In *Readings in American Democracy,* ed. Paul Peterson, 29–40. Dubuque, Iowa: Kendall/Hunt, 1979.

_____. " 'Who Killed Cock Robin?' A Retrospective on the Bork Nomination and a Reply to 'Jaffa Divides the House.' " In *Original Intent and the Framers of the Constitution: A Disputed Question,* ed. Harry V. Jaffa, Bruce Ledewitz, Robert L. Stone, and George Anastaplo, 269–90. With a foreword by Lewis E. Lehrman. Washington, D.C.: Regnery Gateway, 1994.

Jayson, Lester S., ed. *Constitution of the United States of America: Analysis and Interpretation.* Washington, D.C.: U.S. Government Printing Office, 1973.

Jefferson, Thomas. "Letters to James Madison, November 18, 1788." In *The Works of Thomas Jefferson,* ed. Paul L. Ford, 5:433–37. New York: G. P. Putnam's Sons, 1904.

Kahn, Ronald. *The Supreme Court and Constitutional Theory, 1953–1993.* Lawrence: University Press of Kansas, 1994.

Kurland, Philip B. "American Systems of Laws and Constitutions." In *American Civilization: A Portrait from the Twentieth Century,* ed. Daniel J. Boorstin, 141–48. New York: McGraw-Hill, 1972.

_____. " 'Brown v. Board of Education Was the Beginning': The School Desegregation Cases in the United States Supreme Court: 1954–1979." *Washington University Law Quarterly* 2 (Spring 1979): 309–405.

_____. "The Constitution: The Framers' Intent, the Present and the Future." *St. Louis University Law Journal* 32 (1987): 17–25.

———. "Government by Judiciary." *Modern Age: A Quarterly Review* (Fall 1976): 358–71.

———. "The Irrelevance of the Constitution: The Religion Clauses of the First Amendment and the Supreme Court." *Villanova Law Review* 24 (1978–79): 3–27.

———. "Judicial Review Revisited: 'Original Intent' and "the Common Will.' " *Cincinnati Law Review* 55 (1987): 733–43.

———. "Magna Carta and Constitutionalism in the United States: 'The Noble Lie.' " In *The Great Charter: Four Essays on Magna Carta and the History of Our Liberty,* ed. Samuel E. Thorne, William H. Dunham, Jr., Philip B. Kurland, and Sir Ivor Jennings, 48–74. With an introduction by Erwin N. Griswold. New York: Pantheon Books, 1965.

———. "1970 Term: Notes on the Emergence of the Burger Court." *Supreme Court Review* (1971): 265–322.

———. *Politics, the Constitution and the Warren Court.* Chicago: University of Chicago Press, 1970.

———. Review of *The Brethren: Inside the Supreme Court,* by Bob Woodward and Scott Armstrong. *University of Chicago Law Review* 47 (1979): 185–98.

———. "The Supreme Court and the Attrition of State Power." *Stanford Law Review* 10 (March 1958): 274–96.

———. "The Supreme Court and Its Judicial Critics." *Utah Law Review* 6, no. 4 (Fall 1959): 457–66.

———. *Watergate and the Constitution.* Chicago: University of Chicago Press, 1978.

Kurland, Philip B., and Ralph Lerner, eds. *The Founders' Constitution.* 5 vols. Chicago: University of Chicago Press, 1987.

Levy, Leonard W., ed. *Judicial Review and the Supreme Court: Selected Essays.* New York: Harper & Row, 1967.

Lincoln, Abraham. "First Inaugural Address on March 4, 1861." In *The Collected Works of Abraham Lincoln,* ed. Roy P. Basler, 4:262–71. New Brunswick, N.J.: Rutgers University Press, 1953.

———. "Speech at Springfield, Illinois, on June 16, 1857." In *The Collected Works of Abraham Lincoln,* ed. Roy P. Basler, 2:398–410. New Brunswick, N.J.: Rutgers University Press, 1953.

Locke, John. *Second Treatise of Government.* Edited by C. B. Macpherson. Indianapolis: Hackett, 1980.

Lockhart, William, Yale Kamisar, Jesse Choper, and Steven Shiffrin. *Constitutional Law: Cases, Comments, Questions.* 6th ed. St. Paul, Minn.: West, 1986.

Lupu, Ira C. "Risky Business." Review of *American Constitutional Law,* by Laurence H. Tribe. *Harvard Law Review* 101 (1988): 1303–22.

MacCormick, Neil. "Law, State and Feminism: MacKinnon's Theses Considered." Review of *Toward a Feminist Theory of the State,* by Catharine A. MacKinnon. *Law and Philosophy* 10 (1991): 447–52.

McDowell, Gary L. *Curbing the Courts: The Constitution and the Limits of Judicial Power.* Baton Rouge: Louisiana State University Press, 1988.

MacKinnon, Catharine A. "Feminism, Marxism, Method, and the State: An Agenda for Theory." *Signs: Journal of Women in Culture and Society* 7, no. 3 (Spring 1982): 515–44.

_____. "Feminism, Marxism, Method, and the State: Toward Feminist Jurisprudence." *Signs: Journal of Women in Culture and Society* 8, no. 4 (Summer 1983): 635–58.

_____. *Feminism Unmodified: Discourses on Life and Law.* Cambridge: Harvard University Press, 1987.

_____. *Only Words.* Cambridge: Harvard University Press, 1993.

_____. *Toward a Feminist Theory of the State.* Cambridge: Harvard University Press, 1989.

Madison, James, letter to Thomas Jefferson, 17 October 1788. In *The Papers of James Madison,* ed. Robert A. Rutland and Charles F. Hobson, 11:295–300. Charlottesville: University Press of Virginia, 1977.

Mansfield, Harvey C., Jr. "Hobbes and the Science of Indirect Government." *American Political Science Review* 65 (1971): 97–110.

_____. "Thomas Jefferson." In *American Political Thought: The Philosophic Dimension of American Statesmanship,* 2d ed., ed. Morton J. Frisch and Richard G. Stevens, 23–50. Itasca, Ill.: F. E. Peacock, 1983.

Montesquieu. *The Spirit of the Laws.* Translated by Thomas Nugent. 2 vols. New York: Hafner, 1949.

Pangle, Thomas L. *Montesquieu's Philosophy of Liberalism: A Commentary on "The Spirit of the Laws."* Chicago: University of Chicago Press, 1973.

_____. "Rediscovering Rights." *Public Interest* 50 (Winter 1978): 157–60.

Perry, Michael J. *The Constitution, the Courts, and Human Rights: An Inquiry into the Legitimacy of Constitutional Policymaking by the Judiciary.* New Haven, Conn.: Yale University Press, 1982.

_____. *The Constitution in the Courts: Law or Politics?* New York: Oxford University Press, 1994.

_____. *Love and Power: The Role of Religion and Morality in American Politics.* New York: Oxford University Press, 1991.

_____. *Morality, Politics, and Law.* New York: Oxford University Press, 1988.

Peterson, Paul. "The Constitution and Separation of Powers." In *Taking the Constitution Seriously: Essays on the Constitution and Constitutional Law,* ed. Gary L. McDowell, 193–208. Dubuque, Iowa: Kendall/Hunt, 1981.

Pitkin, Hanna Fenichel. *The Concept of Representation.* Berkeley: University of California Press, 1967.

Presser, Stephen B. and Jamils Zainaldin, eds. *Law and Jurisprudence in American History: Cases and Materials.* St. Paul, Minn.: West, 1989.

Pritchett, C. Herman. *The American Constitution.* New York: McGraw-Hill, 1977.

_____. *Constitutional Law of the Federal System.* Englewood Cliffs, N.J.: Prentice-Hall, Inc., 1984.

Rossum, Ralph A. "The Courts and the Judicial Power." In *The Framing and Ratification of the Constitution,* ed. Leonard W. Levy and Dennis M. Mahoney, 222–41. New York: Macmillan, 1987.

_____. "Representation and Republican Government: Contemporary Court Variations on the Founders' Theme." In *Taking the Constitution Seriously: Essays on the Constitution and Constitutional Law,* ed. Gary L. McDowell, 417–34. Dubuque, Iowa: Kendall/Hunt, 1981.

Rutland, Robert Allen. *The Birth of the Bill of Rights*. Chapel Hill: University of North Carolina Press, 1955.

Schwartz, Herman. "Property Rights and the Constitution." *The American University Law Review* 37, no. 1 (1987): 9–39.

Stephenson, D. Grier. Review of *American Constitutional Law*, by Laurence H. Tribe. *New York Law School Law Review* 25 (1979): 187–214.

Stevens, Richard G. "The Constitution and What It Meant to Corwin." *Political Science Reviewer* 10 (1980): 1–53.

_____, ed. *The Declaration of Independence and the Constitution of the United States of America*. With an introduction by Richard G. Stevens. Washington, D.C.: Georgetown University Press, 1984.

_____. *Frankfurter and Due Process*. New York: University Press of America, 1987.

_____. "Politics, Economics and Religion in the Constitution." Special issue, *Symposium on the Constitution and the Founding*, ed. Lane V. Sunderland, *Teaching Political Science* 14 (1986): 11–16.

Stone, Robert L. "Professor Harry V. Jaffa Divides the House: A Respectful Protest and a Defense Brief." In *Original Intent and the Framers of the Constitution: A Disputed Claim*, ed. Harry V. Jaffa, Bruce Ledewitz, Robert L. Stone, George Anastaplo, 133–65. With a foreword by Lewis E. Lehrman. Washington, D.C.: Regnery Gateway, 1994.

Storing, Herbert J., ed. *The Complete Anti-Federalist*. 7 vols. Chicago: University of Chicago Press, 1981.

_____. "The Constitution and the Bill of Rights." In *Taking the Constitution Seriously: Essays on the Constitution and Constitutional Law*, ed. Gary L. McDowell, 266–81. Dubuque, Iowa: Kendall/Hunt, 1981.

_____. *What the Antifederalists Were For: The Political Thought of the Opponents of the Constitution*. Chicago: University of Chicago Press, 1981.

Story, Joseph. *Commentaries on the Constitution of the United States*. Boston: Hilliard, Gray, and Co., 1833. Reprint, 3 vols., with and introduction by Arthur E. Sutherland, New York: Da Capo Press, 1970.

_____. *A Familiar Exposition of the Constitution of the United States: Containing a Brief Commentary on Every Clause, Explaining the True Nature, Reasons, and Objects Thereof*. Boston: Marsh, Capen, Lyon, & Webb, 1840.

Strauss, Leo. "On the Basis of Hobbes's Political Philosophy." In *What Is Political Philosophy? And Other Studies*. New York: Free Press, 1959.

_____. *Natural Right and History*. Chicago: University of Chicago Press, 1953.

Sunderland, Lane V. "Constitutional Theory and the Role of the Court: An Analysis of Contemporary Constitutional Commentators." *Wake Forest Law Review* 21, no. 4 (1986): 855–900.

_____. "The Exclusionary Rule: A Requirement of Constitutional Principle." *Journal of Criminal Law and Criminology* 69, no. 2 (1978): 141–59.

_____. *Obscenity: The Court, the Congress and the President's Commission*. Washington, D.C.: American Enterprise Institute for Public Policy Research, 1974.

Sunstein, Cass. "Feminism and Legal Theory." *Harvard Law Review* 101, no. 4 (February 1988): 826–48.

Taylor, Telford. Review of *American Constitutional Law,* by Laurence H. Tribe. *Columbia Law Review* 79, no. 6 (1979): 1209–25.

Thayer, James Bradley, and others. *John Marshall.* Chicago: University of Chicago Press, 1967.

Tocqueville, Alexis de. *Democracy in America.* Edited by J. P. Mayer and Max Lerner. Translated by George Lawrence. New York: Harper & Row, 1966.

———. *Democracy in America.* 2 vols. Translated by Henry Reeve. Revised by Francis Bowen. Corrected and edited by Phillips Bradley. New York: Vintage Books, 1945.

Tress, Daryl McGowan. "Feminist Theory and Its Discontents." *Interpretation* 18, no. 2 (Winter 1990–91): 293–311.

Tribe, Laurence H. *American Constitutional Law.* 2d ed. Mineola, N.Y.: Foundation Press, 1988.

———. *Constitutional Choices.* Cambridge: Harvard University Press, 1985.

———. "Essay in Law: On Reading the Constitution." *Utah Law Review* 4 (1988): 747–98.

Tribe, Laurence H., and Michael Dorf. *On Reading the Constitution.* Cambridge: Harvard University Press, 1991.

Tushnet, Mark. "Anti-Formalism in Recent Constitutional Theory." *Michigan Law Review* 83, no. 6 (May 1985): 1502–44.

———. "Constitutional Interpretation and Judicial Selection: A View from the *Federalist Papers.*" *Southern California Law Review* 61 (1988): 1669.

———. "Critical Legal Studies: A Political History." *Yale Law Journal* 100 (1991): 1515–44.

———. "Darkness on the Edge of Town: The Contributions of John Hart Ely to Constitutional Theory." *Yale Law Journal* 89, no. 6 (May 1980): 1037–62.

———. "Dia-Tribe." Review of *American Constitutional Law,* by Laurence Tribe. *Michigan Law Review* 78, no. 2 (March 1980): 694–710.

———. "Does Constitutional Theory Matter? A Comment." *Texas Law Review* 65, no. 4 (March 1987): 777–87.

———. "Following the Rules Laid Down: A Critique of Interpretivism and Neutral Principles." *Harvard Law Review* 96, no. 4 (February 1983): 781–827.

———. "Legal Scholarship: Its Causes and Cure." *Yale Law Journal* 90, no. 5 (April 1981): 1205–23.

———. "The Origins of the Establishment Clause." *Georgetown Law Journal* 75, no. 4 (April 1987): 1509–17.

———. "Perspectives on Critical Legal Studies." *George Washington Law Review* 52, no. 2 (January 1984): 239–79.

———. *Red, White, and Blue: A Critical Analysis of Constitutional Law.* Cambridge: Harvard University Press, 1988.

———. "The U.S. Constitution and the Intent of the Framers." *Buffalo Law Review* 36 (1987): 217–26.

Tushnet, Mark and Jennifer Jaff. "Why the Debate Over Congress' Power to Restrict the Jurisdiction of the Federal Courts is Unending." *Georgetown Law Journal* 72 (April 1984): 1311–31.

Webster, Noah. *A Compendious Dictionary of the English Language: A Facsimile of the First (1806) Edition.* New Haven, Conn.: Increase Cooke & Co., 1806.

Wills, Garry. *Explaining America: The Federalist.* New York: Penguin Books, Inc., 1981.

_____. *Inventing America: Jefferson's Declaration of Independence.* Garden City, N.Y.: Doubleday, 1978.

Yardley, Jonathan. "Sticks and Stones." Review of *Only Words,* by Catharine A. MacKinnon. *Book World* 23 (19 September 1993): 3.

INDEX